the Ukrainians
From Kyiv to the Kosmos

First published in Great Britain 2024
by Spenwood Books Ltd
2 College Street, Higham Ferrers, NN10 8DZ.

Copyright © Len Liggins & Peter Solowka 2024

The right of Len Liggins & Peter Solowka to be identified as author of this work has been asserted in accordance with Sections 77 & 78 of the Copyright, Design and Patents Act 1988.

A CIP record for this book is available from the British Library.

ISBN 978-1-915858-23-8

Printed and bound by Sound Performance Ltd, 3 Greenwich Quay, Clarence Road, Greenwich, London, SE8 3EY

Design by Bruce Graham, The Night Owl.

Front cover image: Marc McGarraghy
Rear cover images: The Ukrainians
All other image copyrights: As captioned.

spenwoodbooks.com

The Ukrainians
From Kyiv to the Kosmos

Len Liggins & Peter Solowka

Spenwood Books
Manchester, UK

While the empire seeks to destroy not only Ukraine, but also Ukrainian culture, we are doing our best to spread this culture. This is yet another form of our resistance – a cultural, value-based one. Through books and scholarly works, not just through the news, the world will learn how much Ukraine has given it and understand us better.

Olena Zelenska, First Lady of Ukraine

THE UKRAINIANS

FOREWORD

This story probably started in a small village generations ago. A mother tells her son that his culture is different from that of the Russians, Poles, and Germans that continually occupy it, and that he is Ukrainian and one day he will have his own country. That son was my dad, and as the story in this book is being written, that country is fully grown but fighting against the odds for its survival.

Our journey with Ukrainian culture has been closely entwined with the development of Ukraine itself. Our music changed perspectives in both east and west, as we changed while watching Ukraine grow.

I've learned so much about what we did from this book. Seeing our time through the eyes of others has led me to value our journey even more. I warmly invite you to share our story.

Peter Solowka

During my teenage years I developed two obsessive fascinations, one with music, and one with eastern Europe. When my school teachers were telling us to think about what we wanted to do with our lives, I never dreamt there could be something that involved the fusion of the two, let alone something I'd be willing to dedicate a large proportion of my life to.

Little did I know that there was another person, who lived up in Leeds, who was passionate about the same things. What were the chances of our paths crossing? And yet they did, and we soon discovered we shared a similar vision, and that vision set us on a trajectory that would lead to our music being played all over Europe, then across the world, and finally in space! This book exists to take you on that journey…

Len Liggins

CONTENTS

Beginnings 07

Ukrainski Vistupi 22

The Ukrainians 55

Vorony 87

Official Tour of Ukraine 109

Kultura 131

Respublika 198

Diaspora 232

A History Of Rock Music 254

Summer in Lviv 263

Together for Ukraine 285

Afterword 305

Gigography 307

Special Thanks 320

Acknowledgements 320

THE UKRAINIANS

BEGINNINGS

PETER SOLOWKA

History is a complicated subject, and there are many official histories of Ukraine. If you belong to a people though, you have your own story of who you are, a narrative that describes your similarities and differences to others. Here's just a small part of mine – enough, I hope, to help you with the story.

When I was a kid, I remember some of the more educated primary teachers would see my name and they'd say, 'Ah, your name is Solowka, that's a Russian name, isn't it?' I'd say, 'No, it's Ukrainian,' and they'd say 'pardon?' as though I'd said something wrong. And that's how it felt. I had no friends of my age who were Ukrainian. There was one other kid at my school who had a Ukrainian background. She was a girl who had nothing to do with me. Luckily for me, all the bullying and the anti-immigrant stuff that went on was aimed at her, and at the one black lad at school. Because whenever anyone said anything to her, she'd fight back. If someone said anything to me, I'd just slide into the background. I had my books. I was into dinosaurs and stars, so they went for the other people, not me. Racism isn't always deliberate. Sometimes the constant questioning of why you are different is genuine, trying to understand what's different about you. But it doesn't make you feel good, always having to justify your difference, especially as a kid. It's a horrible feeling. There was a time when I was a kid when just to say that you're Ukrainian was a political statement. I didn't realise it was political, but just saying you are here and you exist can be seen as that – like if you say you're Palestinian now.

My dad ended up in Britain after the Second World War. He was a kid growing up in what is now Ukraine but what then was Poland. Every single border of eastern Europe has changed since the Second World War. There's a line that goes Holland-Belgium-France-Italy in Europe, and those borders haven't changed. Every other country to the east of that has had its borders moved in some way.

My dad lived in a Ukrainian-speaking village and he learnt two languages, Ukrainian and Polish, in school. As a kid growing up in Poland, he was allowed to do a couple of hours of Ukrainian a day. Ukrainian was accepted as being there but it was the language of the peasants in the countryside, the people who were going nowhere. If you wanted to learn anything or do anything, you had to do it in Polish before the war and Russian after the war. Russian was considered the language of progress, the language that moves forward. Russian was the language where you could be something, the language of high culture, of the classical composers and the real novelists, not the language of little folk songs in the village.

The war started for my dad in 1939, because when war was declared against Poland by Germany, the Soviet Union came and took half of Poland. And that was the half my dad was in. So he grew up in Poland, spent two years under Stalin and then the Germans came in and they stayed until 1944, and so he lived for three and a bit years under the Nazis. He lived under Stalin and Hitler, and he didn't have a lot to say about either of them!

The Nazis had only been there six months when they took people as labourers, one from each family, to go and work in the fields and farms in Germany, because the German men were in the army.

It was January '42 when my dad went with a truckload of teenagers and was driven all the way through to Germany. He spent about three years working on farms and in factories until the war finished. He then had a chance to go back home, and my dad said 'there's nothing there – I'll spend the rest of my life looking after sheep.' He said that once you'd been to the West – and they regarded Germany even under the Nazis as the West – if you tried to go back to the Soviet system, you'd never get a job anyway because you're tainted with the idea of the West. So he stayed in Germany until about 1947.

And then Britain was looking for immigrants from eastern Europe to come over and work in the farms and factories, so he came over to Britain. They asked him 'what can you do?' and he said 'I can grow stuff' so initially he worked on a farm. Eventually, my dad found work in the cotton mills of the north – Middleton, Manchester became his home.

Ukrainian émigrés went to Britain, they went to Canada, they went to America. They set up Ukrainian clubs to try and keep Ukrainian culture alive in the West, taking their kids there on a Saturday morning, teaching them how to speak and how to dance, and showing them all the romantic images. My dad helped run the very, very small Ukrainian club in Middleton for four or five years. It was an old Co-operative Society building which had a little bar downstairs and a small room upstairs. It was probably big enough to have a modern wake in. My dad would be in the bar, getting the barrels in. He'd put his spare time into keeping it open at weekends. But it only ran for about four or five years. I remember those days of being in that club. When I was at the Ukrainian school at the age of seven, the kids were all different ages. They might be 14 or 15, or they might be three or four.

It was the only time I came across Ukrainian culture, at the Ukrainian school on Saturday mornings, where people tried to teach you with these terrible school books. They were doing their best but they weren't teachers. I'd call them shouters. They'd shout out a letter or a word and you'd have to shout it back. There was no conversation at home so I didn't learn a single thing about the Ukrainian language. I hated it as a kid.

But I remember there were music events there, at parties and at New Year. And as kids we were taught this Ukrainian dancing, all that leg-kicking stuff with the embroidered shirts. I remember that. I remember the dance tunes and just the general atmosphere of the Ukrainian club, with people sitting and being very serious. There'd be food there but you couldn't eat the meal because there was someone giving a speech about the future of Ukrainian independence. *In Ukrainian*. When you're seven, eight, nine and ten years old, you don't want to do that. There were only about ten kids in Ukrainian school and I was the only one of my age who went. I began to resent it. On a Saturday morning, I wanted to go to the swimming baths or go out and play football.

There were rows at home about it. My mum was German and I can remember my mum and dad rowing about it, screaming. And my mum won in the end. She said, 'Look, he's only young. He doesn't know the difference. He hates the Ukrainian school. What's going to happen if he hates all schools?' She was right. So then I didn't go. That must have been a real thing for my dad, because he was one of the people who ran the club. It must have been tough for him when I stopped going. I've got an older sister, Norah, and the same thing happened to her. She never learned the language but she did a lot more dancing. She went abroad a couple of times to events in Paris and Amsterdam with the Manchester dance group, Orlyk. But Ukrainian culture didn't really stick with her and the only thing that stuck with me was the music.

I don't know why. As a kid I wasn't particularly musical. My mum did try and get me to play an accordion. I had formal accordion lessons at a music school near Manchester Town Hall. But the accordion was just too big and heavy. It was the formality of the lessons. If your parents aren't musical, and my mum and dad weren't teachers, that drive for musical culture doesn't come across well. It was certainly an aspiration of my mum that the family should be musical. My sister Norah had ballet and piano lessons – I can remember the struggles of two pretty burly men helping my dad drag an old pub piano into our living room. In long summer holidays I would tease out some tunes by ear, but only very rarely. So I didn't learn to play music. It wasn't until I taught myself music as a teenage kid, when I got a guitar at the age of 12, that I started appreciating music. And in my early twenties I started playing some of these Ukrainian tunes that were still stuck in my head and began trying to reclaim some of my missing culture.

LEN LIGGINS

Neither my mum, Ellen, nor my dad, also called Len, played a musical instrument, but they both enjoyed singing when they were young. My mum used to tell me that as a child she would sing, in Irish and English, at concerts and plays performed at the crossroads in the small village of Emly, County Tipperary. Unfortunately, after coming to London in May 1947, at the age of 21, to see the bright lights, find work and dance the nights away in Hammersmith Palais, she never really sang again. I think she realised pretty quickly that spontaneously bursting into song 'wasn't done' in the stiff and reserved English metropolis. Not only that, I think her youthful idealism evaporated and her spirit was broken by the racist comments that Irish people attracted on a daily basis, and by the 'no dogs, no blacks, no Irish' notices in rental accommodation windows. My mum's father, Patrick O'Shea, played the fiddle though. It was given to him by the local canon and he'd play it at family gatherings, sitting in an armchair, pure white-haired, roll-up dangling from the corner of his mouth.

As for my dad, who was a pure East Ender, he would sing songs around the house at the drop of a hat. Not complete songs, just a verse or two and a chorus. Mostly they were songs by the famous tenors Enrico Caruso, Josef Locke and Mario Lanza, though you never knew when you might be treated to an old music hall number. The one I remember most is my dad's rendition of Billy Bennett's 'She Was Poor But She Was Honest':

It's the same the 'ole world over,
It's the poor what gets the blame.
It's the rich what gets the pleasure,
Isn't it a blinkin' shame

I still love music hall songs and comedy routines now, and have hundreds of recordings… Harry Champion, Marie Lloyd, Gus Elen, Florrie Forde, Vesta Tilley, Harry Tate… marvellous stuff. If you're the kind of person who doesn't feel an overwhelming urge to 'cancel' everything non-PC, then there's fascinating insight into the past to be had here. What made people mad and what made people laugh a hundred years ago? Harry, Marie, Gus and Florrie will tell you.

My world transformed from black and white to absolutely scintillating colour the day my mum and dad bought a radiogram from my Auntie Poppy. It was the early 1960s and I must have been about five or six years old. I remember it being carried into our front room at 92 Suttons Avenue in Hornchurch. I was transfixed. My mum opened up the top to reveal a record deck, and to the right of the deck was a radio with short, medium and long wave. I still remember the dusty smell of the valves warming up when you switched it on. And, as you turned the dial, you could tune in to prgrammes from exotic places I never imagined I would ever see: Warsaw, Budapest, Kyiv, Prague. I would try to listen as the signal faded in and out, barely audible through the thick layer of ethereal whistles and spacey bleeps.

At primary school I had recorder and violin lessons and joined the choir. At St Mary's we had a formidable violin teacher in Miss Cleave, who tried with varying levels of success to get her pupils to turn their disturbing scrapings into something resembling music. Not an easy task given that each pupil had a slot of just 15 minutes a week. Anyhow, credit to Miss Cleave, because by the time I was eleven I was leader of the school orchestra. To be honest, I fared better with the recorder. I played tenor as well as descant and got put into a quartet by our teacher, whose real name I forget. We knew him as 'Tobor' because we thought he behaved like a backward robot. He was a good taskmaster though, and soon myself and Brendan O'Connor, who was a better recorder player than me, found ourselves representing St Mary's in Essex schools' music competitions.

THE UKRAINIANS

Actually, thinking now about Miss Cleave, during a lesson one day she asked me a question out of the blue that really flummoxed me. She said, 'Leonard, do you have any oriental in you? You know, your eyes…' I had no idea what she meant. At that age, I didn't understand the meaning of the word 'oriental'. I was about nine years old. 'You know, from the east,' she pursued. I thought, what… you mean Canvey Island? That was about the furthest east I could imagine. But, looking through the Liggins' family photos now I can see what she meant. As you go back through the last four generations of the male line, the Liggins eyes look increasingly non-British, non-Western even.

I have fond memories of my secondary school. We had some really inspiring teachers at Hornchurch's St Edmund Campion. Our music teacher, Mr Hocking, was a tyrant, but without him I'd never have discovered the genius of classical composers Albinoni, Carl Orff and Benjamin Britten, who I still love. I would almost certainly never have got into languages without the influence of our enthusiastic French teacher Arthur Woods, the super-chilled moustachioed hippy Italian teacher Tony Bruton or the Nicolai Gogol-loving Russian teacher Paul Adams.

I had Polish friends at school, such as Eugene Czauderna, and I saw copies of the *Dziennik Polski* (Polish Daily) newspaper on the table at his house, which fascinated me. All those 'sz's and 'cz's. It was like an impenetrable code. I got invited round to tea regularly at his house, so I experienced the wonderful cakes, salads and pickles, and heard the language spoken by his parents. When, in my third form, the school introduced two new subjects, Russian and Ancient Greek, the thought of learning Russian really excited me, so I opted to take Russian O-level at school. During the summer holidays, my dad went into WH Smiths in London's Baker Street and bought me a pocket-sized Collins Russian-English dictionary. I was so chuffed when he brought it home. There was a guide to the pronunciation of the Cyrillic alphabet, so I made sure I'd become thoroughly familiar with that before term started. That was a wise move in retrospect, because I continued to stay a good few steps ahead of my classmates, which gave me confidence going forward.

When it came to my A-level choices, I opted for Mathematics, Physics and Chemistry. The deadline for any changes was approaching and at the last minute I changed them to Russian, French and English Literature. I never regretted it. I found sciences easy and I found languages challenging, but I got so much enjoyment and a sense of fulfilment from languages and literature.

I must admit, I was worried what my parents would say when I got home, especially my mum. She would have liked to have seen me become a doctor or a banker, or maybe even a priest – something which, with her Irish background, she would have seen as prestigious. As it happened, she completely supported me, as she always did with anything I wanted to do. My dad, having spent his childhood in poverty in London's East End, would have liked to have seen me do an apprenticeship in the building industry. 'You'll never be out of work if you've got a trade,' he used to say. He was easy-going though, so whatever I wanted to do was fine by him, as long as I wasn't going to go hungry.

My school had suggested that I stay on in the sixth form for a third year to do the Oxbridge exam. They told my mum and dad I was 'Oxford or Cambridge material' but I found that idea very daunting. I was from a very working-class background. My dad was a plumber and my Mum was a housewife who'd worked for a few years in an electronics factory. I was scared I'd be out of my depth, and I was too shy and self-deprecating to deal with it. So, at the last minute, I applied through clearing to Nottingham and Leeds. I found the Russian Department at Nottingham very staid and old-fashioned. The corridors were brown and drab and the lecturers wore old-fashioned suits. It was like stepping back to the 1930s. By contrast, when I walked into the Leeds Russian Department, it was bright and lively. There were colourful posters for their *Troika* magazine, there were events and films advertised, and the lecturers dressed casually and smiled. This was the place for me!

So I started my first term in September 1975 studying Russian and Czech, with Italian as a subsidiary subject. That also gave me some travel opportunities, a month in Leningrad (now St Petersburg), three months in Brno (then Czechoslovakia) and a month in Italy's beautiful Perugia.

PETER

After doing the sixth form at Middleton, I went to Liverpool University for three years. I wasn't really in bands in Liverpool, although I did one or two jamming things. But I used to go to a lot of gigs. You had the Cavern legacy, and you had Eric's on Mathew Street, where we used to go and watch all the post-punk bands. And then I went to do a teacher training course in Leeds. That's where David Gedge (who I'd been best mates at school with) was, so I could do music with him. I was in four different bands in Leeds at one time. Bands would fade in and fade out. I remember playing in a band with David and his girlfriend and then not playing with them. We were just playing stuff in a cellar.

I never went into full-time teaching. I did my teaching course and from 1982 to 1985, I did three-month jobs. Just enough to get enough money to travel around Europe with a backpack, or buy a new guitar. And when I got that money, I didn't want anything else except to sit down, do music, play music. I met Len in 1985 or '86. It was towards the end of the miners' strike. I was very active in that.

I remember when I was involved in picket lines and when I told my dad I was defending my class against the encroachment of capitalist society on working class communities by supporting the miners in the '80s. He said, 'That's not politics.' I said, 'It is, it's really important.' 'No,' he said. 'Politics is when you go to sleep at night and you don't know if someone's going to knock on your door at four in the morning and take you away.' It used to really anger me when he said that. But, compared to what he's been through, he's right. No matter how bad things got in Britain, people striking or protesting or whatever, no one's being taken away and shot in a forest somewhere for it.

LEN

At school I just did the exams but with no real idea of what to do when I grew up. I couldn't imagine myself in an office, in a suit, though I spent many years doing exactly that. A Russian degree wasn't a ticket to career success, it's got to be said, unless you go into teaching or something like GCHQ (Government Communications Headquarters) in Cheltenham, intercepting and translating internet messages and mobile calls, amongst other things. I applied twice for a course to teach Russian but I couldn't get a job unless I also taught French, and I felt less confident about that. Also, I'd hate the unruly nature of teenagers. To my mind they can be annoying, badly-behaved, ungrateful little bastards. As for working at GCHQ, I like people of all nationalities, so there was no way I was going to work for one government against another. You could argue that what they do is defensive – about the UK's national security – but the young hippy me wouldn't have seen it that way, and I'm not sure I'm 100 per cent convinced of it now.

I did a lot of different jobs, over twenty in the first few years after Uni. I was a bus conductor based at the Headingley depot in Leeds, following in the footsteps of my mum who had been a clippie in London in the late 1940s and early 1950s. They were the days before buses were 'one man operated' (even if you were a woman).

I also sold potatoes door-to-door in Leeds, Bradford and Huddersfield, getting paid on a commission basis. We'd be allocated about eight streets a day. I was their best salesman! One day I knocked on the door of artist David Hockney's mum. I knew in advance that she lived there, as I'd helped my girlfried, now wife, Rebecca get press cuttings about Hockney from the *Telegraph & Argus* archive when she was doing her Fine Art dissertation. Bradford's Hutton Terrace, the street where David Hockney grew up, was always mentioned in those early articles. I had a really nice chat with Mrs Hockney. I told her how Rebecca and myself had gone over to California to interview him, but when we got over there, he was back in Bradford visiting her! She thought that was hilarious! She was a lovely woman, clearly a very kind soul. She didn't buy any potatoes though.

Music-wise, I had begun to play in a band called The Sinister Cleaners, which would have been from about 1982 to 1987. Like fellow bands The Three Johns and The Sisters Of Mercy, we were two guitarists, a bass player and a drum machine.

After a few gigs we decided we needed a proper, human drummer. Fellow Cleaner John Parkes by this time had another band called The Chorus, which had Peter Solowka on bass and Simon Smith on drums. Simon was happy to play with us as well as The Chorus, so now the Cleaners were 'a proper band'. Three twelve-inch vinyls followed, the six-track mini-LP *Lemon Meringue Bedsit*, which sold out its 500 copies within just a few weeks, *Goodbye Ms Jones* and *Longing For Next Year*. John Peel played them all except for *Goodbye Ms Jones*, which was however picked up by BBC DJ Janice Long. The lead track was 'I'll Never Forget This' and she played it a good few times, even inviting us for tea with her at Broadcasting House. She arranged an appointment for us to see her brother Jeff Chegwin (twin brother of TV presenter Keith), and he offered us a publishing deal. We turned it down. I'm not suggesting there was any connection, but Janice Long never played us again.

By 1987, when we did three tours in Europe, things began to change. Fellow band member Andrew Middleton was getting itchy feet and wanted to do other things. So, we decided to call it a day. For me though, another door was about to open. On the grapevine, I heard that Pete Solowka had been trying to contact me…

The Sinister Cleaners were playing the 1 in 12 Club in Bradford, at the Royal Standard on Manningham Lane. Because we shared gear, The Chorus were due to pick up the amps and drums after we'd played. Sure enough, their van parked up outside the venue and me, John, Simon and Andrew started lugging the heavy gear up the steps to the van, which was parked outside. Sitting in the back of the van was Pete Solowka, flat cap neatly in place and tucking into a portion of chips.

'Er, Pete,' I said, 'are you going to help us lugging this gear?'

'I'm eating me chips,' he replied, not even looking up.

'Come on, Pete, many hands and all that. Get your arse into gear.'

There was a short silence, then he just repeated: 'I'm eating me chips.'

My second experience of Pete was when The Chorus came over to 13 Hartley Avenue to pick up some gear while The Sinister Cleaners were rehearsing in the basement. I was playing bass and working out a part for a new song. Pete stood right in front of me, watching what I was doing.

'What are you doing?' he said. 'What are the chords?'

I said, 'I don't know. I don't want to know what the chords are when I work out bass parts. Otherwise, you're too tempted to play root notes and stick in a few predictable connecting runs. I like to work out a part in my head that's melodic as well as punchy and once I've hit on it, I learn it.'

'You can't work out a bass part without knowing the chords,' said Pete.

'I *can*, Pete. Now go away.' Actually, I might have used slightly stronger language than that.

You would have thought from our first two meetings that a 35-year plus creative working relationship would have been impossible, but we shared a very similar vision when it came to The Ukrainians.

Pete and I were both very excited at the idea of forming a punk band that played Ukrainian music, and I was keen to start learning the language and writing lyrics. So we got together in his bedroom, Pete on accordion and me on fiddle and singing. There was no thought of whether this might or might not be a commercial thing. It was never discussed. We knew what we wanted to do and we set about it. Without wanting to demystify our process too much, Pete and I have very complementary abilities, and arguments only tended to occur when one would try to encroach on the other's 'area of expertise'. Pete's better at coming up with very authentic-sounding eastern European chord sequences and melodies. I'm better at attributing a subject matter to a melody and writing lyrics. Pete's better at arranging who should play where in a song. I'm better at working out vocal harmonies. Each of us is good at things the other is a bit weaker in, so it works.

At that stage in our lives the excitement and creative spark we generated overruled any desire to make money. Neither Pete nor myself are particularly money-orientated. We both had ambition but that was more to do with an outlet for our Ukrainian language songs and recordings rather than making a fortune. If we'd wanted to do that we'd have started a band like the Pet Shop Boys, U2, Erasure or Guns 'n' Roses, although I can't really see me and Pete in a glam metal band.

The thing is, too, that me and Pete may have our differences of opinion, like all people in bands, but we realise that we have to compromise, and neither of us is the kind of person to hold a grudge! After all these years, I think I can still say we're friends and enjoy each other's company. We can still make each other laugh, especially after downing a few post-gig horilkas.

I don't remember finding time to work on the Ukrainian project being an issue. I had a full-time job as a press officer for the environmental charity Groundwork at the time, so I was pretty busy and stressed out with that. I guess we just got together when we both had time. It helped that we lived around the corner from each other, me in Brudenell Mount and Pete in Brudenell Road.

PETER

After The Wedding Present had recorded *George Best*, our new drummer was Simon Smith, who lived in the same house as me in Leeds. He heard me in my lonely little Ukrainian bedsit world with my accordion and my guitar, playing these songs, and he said, 'Oh, you should meet my mate, Len. Because he does the same as you.' And I said 'really?' 'Yes, he's got his fiddle and he keeps playing Russian and Polish songs. He said you should meet. Do you want to meet?' I said 'yeah!'. Simon introduced us and we've been together musically since then.

Like me, Len didn't want to do a career, so he was doing lots of different jobs in Leeds. He just wanted to play music. He was in a couple of bands. He was doing his own stuff and he played in The Sinister Cleaners. Practically everybody I knew was in a band. Some people were in a couple of bands and everybody knew somebody who was in a band who was doing well. And everyone had talked to that band that weren't doing so well, that they weren't so keen on, but who were going to give it another go. There was a band culture. It's what you did in your spare time.

Len went to Leeds University to study Russian because it was one of the few places you could study Russian. He did a lot of travelling around eastern Europe as part of his course. I think he had friends from Poland at school. He said, 'I can do Russian. Ukrainian is different but part of the same family of languages.' He had to change quite a few vowel sounds. When we sang it together it sounded far too Russian, so he modified it.

Back then, we had to research how to stress things differently and change the word order around to make sure we got the correct meaning from the words. That was very hard then. Google Translate makes it a lot easier now. Len did a lot of it and he'd pass it on to other people he knew in Britain who were Ukrainian but had learned to speak English and people who were English but very fluent in Ukrainian. Because everyone's got a different opinion on the words and what they mean.

My language skills were rubbish. I taught myself to pronounce Ukrainian but not very well. If you give me a script I can almost sight read it and I can pronounce it properly but I might not stress everything in the right place. But if you were speaking Ukrainian to me, you'd have to speak as if you were speaking to a four or five-year-old child.

In the early days Len and I used to meet once a week. I was never a great reader of music, but because I was trying to find Ukrainian sources, when I went to these shops like The Russian Shop in London, there was also a small Ukrainian shop which had mainly things from Canada in it. It was located in the headquarters of the Association of Ukrainians in Great Britain, the head organisation of the charity which runs all the little clubs like the one my dad used to run. In the mid-80s, there were about 48 of them scattered around the country, mainly in the industrial north, because that's where most of the people went to work – Rochdale, Bolton, Bury, everywhere up there. Now there's only about 16 clubs left. A couple of generations have gone by since then, and people have stopped doing it.

But they had a little bookshop as part of their headquarters building. They were very paranoid because they were a Ukrainian language organisation, always worrying about the KGB. It's quite a posh Victorian three or four storey building with pillars at the front door and rooms either side of it. There was no door that you opened. You'd just press a buzzer and they'd go 'dobryy den' in Ukrainian and you'd say, in English, 'I'd like to visit the bookshop please.' And then a buzzer would go and you could go in.

And the bookshop was in this one room and there'd be a lady stood behind the counter staring at you and you'd be the only person in the bookshop. And there'd be a few records and cassettes from Canada. No CDs, and nothing from the Soviet Union. But they had loads of books of sheet music, because they assume that people can read music, which I never could. I realised that teaching myself to read music was one of the few ways that I was going to get into this. So, as well as doing a little bit of teaching myself to speak Ukrainian, remembering tunes in my head, I bought books of sheet music that had Ukrainian songs in them. So you'd have the melody line with no accompaniment and the lyrics underneath it, and I'd go and buy a few books every time I went there.

Len and I would get these books and we'd say 'let's learn *that* one' (or two, if we were feeling ambitious), and then he'd go away for a week and learn the lyrics and the tune and I'd get the tune and learn to play the guitar chords and the accompaniment. And we'd come back and we'd play them.

We just worked on folk music and got a grounding in how all these chords changed and all these different harmonies. We enjoyed just playing. We'd get a guitar and just sing the songs and work out harmonies. We grounded ourselves in Ukrainian folk music, and it wasn't the same as the Russian he'd learnt at all. And when Len said, 'Russians would say it like this', it was a vindication of what my dad had been saying - that Ukrainian and Russian are not the same.

When we started off, we quite happily included Russian lyrics and Russian melodies in our songs. And it was always 'this is the music of Ukraine'. In the 30 years since, the Ukrainian side of the culture has evolved to become dominant and the people with the Ukrainian identity feel that it's something that they've had to struggle to keep alive. The feeling amongst Ukrainians now is 'Ukrainian good, Russian bad'. So if we played the songs now that we were playing in 1989, that would be regarded as an horrendously bad thing to do. Whereas at the time, it was, 'Hey, this is interesting. You've got Ukrainian culture and Russian culture there.' Most people in Ukraine would happily have said 'this is our music', because most people grew up with this dual culture. Now they won't. The war has made people draw a line between the cultures, removing any crossovers.

There were Ukrainian records made by the Soviet Union. But they were little village songs with a classical piano behind them and not at all wild, meaningful and raucous. Any song that had anything to do with anything beautiful or aspirational or not to do with the Russian state was not done. That's the sort of culture that was kept alive in the West. That's what the diaspora Ukrainians grew up with, the passionate folk songs.

There was some music from Canada and with lots of effort you could get those records, but there was none of that in my house. My dad was not into culture from that point of view. He was somebody who spoke the language, went out and worked and brought some money back and looked after his kids. He was not an artist, not a poet, not a singer. I know some people from Ukrainian backgrounds whose parents were like that. But in our house, there were no records. Nothing.

So I started playing songs that I remembered. Sometimes I'd be playing the guitar, sometimes other instruments. I'd still got the accordion, and I've got a brilliant old violin which I got from a childless couple I used to help out as a teenager. They had this violin and they gave it to me. It's beautiful. I can't play more than three or four songs on it.

As the East started to disintegrate, and communism started to break down, you found that you could find some records. In the mid-Eighties, a shop opened up in London called The Russian Shop which had some records of Ukrainian folk music on this label called Melodiya, which just means melody. I went down to London a few times with The Wedding Present but I also went down on some political marches in '85, '86 and I picked up some records for the first time.

And as The Wedding Present became a little more popular, we went to Germany for the first time and we actually went to East Germany on a day trip and did a gig. There were a couple of record shops there. If I saw anything with the word 'Ukrainian' on it, or even the word 'cossack', I'd just buy carrier bags of the stuff. Because they cost peanuts compared with what you'd pay for a record here. And I'd just come back with them and listen to them all.

I always thought the Canadian interpretations were as lacking in soul as the stuff I got from the Soviet Union, because in Canada, the emigre communities were a couple of generations older than ours and they made all the music sound like 'country' music. People there have a very settled life and it's very, very easy for them. None of that sounded like real roots music to me, so whenever I was playing that music, it was more inspired by the punk ethos I'd picked up in the late '70s and early '80s. It had to be aggressive. It had to have energy behind it. It had to sound like The Wedding Present. It had to make you want to listen to it because it was different. Because there's loads of energy in those old songs. Songs don't survive for hundreds of years if there's nothing behind them.

Those Soviet recordings were very formalised. You didn't get four or five people in a pub with a microphone. That would have been more real. It would be a big choir with their version of the song, or someone singing almost operatically. When I was hearing those tunes, I was trying to put the energy back into them that should have been there. But the system that was there, in the Soviet Union, had stopped that happening. No doubt if you'd gone to the villages, you'd get seven old ladies and a couple of people with drums and they'd sound fantastic. And that's what I was trying to imagine they'd be like, and then pump it up.

That was the ethos behind it, the exploration of what I had in my head. I didn't sit there thinking 'one day I'm going to make a record'. Or 'one day I'm going to be in a band that plays this'.

There were folk artists and folk bands but in the back of your mind you were thinking 'who on earth are we going to play this to? Who's going to even bother to listen to it?' We didn't imagine that this was an art form that was worth doing. People in the Ukrainian clubs would play Ukrainian music to each other at weddings and other events, and we did start to go to one or two Ukrainian clubs, but even there it was very,

very formal and light. Music's a powerful thing. It changes feelings and emotions and moods but everything I ever heard in Ukrainian clubs in the West was lifeless, energy-less and lethargic. It was like cabaret waltz music. I hated it even more.

These were 200, 300-year-old songs about really important, life-changing things. The traditional image of the classic Ukrainian song is about loss in war and fighting. It's a bloke reluctantly sat on the back of his horse, saying goodbye to his girlfriend or wife. The girlfriend's crying, or his wife is crying and his kids are crying, because he's going off because he has to fight. That's why it's very relevant today.

And when I listened to the way that people in the Ukrainian community in Britain, Russia or Canada played these songs there was no passion. Somebody was going off to fight and they're probably going to die – because Ukraine has never won – and I was thinking 'where's the passion in this?'. It frustrated me no end. I just thought it wasn't being done right.

I still didn't think there was ever a place where we could play the music. Because if you couldn't play it in the Ukrainian clubs and you couldn't play it in the Soviet Union and you couldn't go to Canada and play it, what are you going to do? It was just me and Len in a room. And we didn't play it with really fast electric guitars. We played it with acoustic guitars. It had an edge to it, but we didn't have a full drum kit.

For about six months, all we used to do was learn Ukrainian folk songs from these books and a few versions we heard on records. So we'd reconstitute Ukrainian folk music in a live way in my bedsit in Leeds 6, just the two of us.

LEN

The lyrics and pronunciation were something I worked on at home myself really. It was a lot of work and a lot of learning, but I enjoyed it. A lot of people used to think that Ukrainian was a dialect of Russian, but it is a language in its own right. Sure, it's related to Russian but it's also related to all the other Slavic languages in the same way that Spanish is to Italian.

Vowel sounds are really important to get right when learning Ukrainian, especially if you've learned another language like Russian first. It took me a while, and of course I will always sing Ukrainian with a bit of an English accent. How could it be otherwise? Ukrainian bands in Canada sing Ukrainian with a Canadian accent. The thing about The Ukrainians, and a lot of other world music bands who create music from a hybrid of two or more cultures, is that we are a mixture. We're not trying to sound like a pure Ukrainian band – lots of bands in Ukraine are already doing that very successfully! We were and are a deliberate, self-conscious hybrid of East/West, Ukrainian/British, traditional folk/post punk indie music.

(clockwise from top left) Len Liggins through the years: with mum Ellen & dad Len, 1958ish; aged 11 in 1968 in Campion school uniform; 1969 family holiday in Bexhill-on-Sea; student ID from Perugia University, Italy; 1981 membership card for Leeds University Union Music For The Masses Society; with now wife Rebecca at a 1960s-themed party

(clockwise from top left) Peter Solowka through the years: Ukrainian community Whit Walks about 1966 (Peter Solowka); sat on his dad's knee in Middleton Ukrainian Club, c1968; playing out in Hollins Estate, c1967; with his mum, dad & sister Norah, c1968; aged 10; aged 13; in 1992, with his first music room

UKRAINSKI VISTUPI

DAVID GEDGE, THE WEDDING PRESENT

I've known Peter for decades. I met him in Manchester when we were both eleven years old and became school friends. I also met his parents, so I knew that his father was Ukrainian. He didn't seem to be that bothered about his Ukrainian heritage for the first few years that I knew him but, when we started doing The Wedding Present, he began voicing a growing interest in rediscovering his roots, particularly Ukrainian music. I'm sure it wasn't being played on the radio, but you could buy records from specialist shops like Foyles, in London, who imported that kind of stuff from eastern Europe. But also, we would play in both East and West Berlin in the 1980s and, on those occasions, Peter would often disappear to look round the local record shops and come back with a bag full of Soviet pressings of traditional music from the Eastern Bloc.

I used to find most of the music a bit dreary, if I'm honest. He'd play me tracks and I remember thinking that it was just a load of sombre-sounding blokes going 'oy-oy-oy-eee', quite slowly. It didn't really fill me with much enthusiasm. But then he did play me the occasional song where I'd go: 'Oh, yes, I *know* this!' It was music you were familiar with without quite knowing why. Well, apart from the Ukrainian version of 'Those Were The Days', of course, which Mary Hopkin had made famous in the 1960s. But there were others where you thought 'perhaps I've heard this on a film or something'.

I suppose it was to be expected that Peter would end up learning how to play some of those Ukrainian songs on the guitar, and there was one in particular that he used to play us during breaks at Wedding Present rehearsals. He called it 'Cossachok' at the time, but then I think he later found out it was actually called 'Hopak'. We ended up joining in; I played rhythm guitar, Keith Gregory played bass and Shaun Charman played drums. It was just for fun, really. We would play it faster and faster until it fell off the rails, which is what The Wedding Present tended to do with everything in those days.

In October 1986, we were invited to record our second session for John Peel at the BBC's Maida Vale studios in London. The producer was Dale Griffin, who was, excitingly, the ex-drummer of Mott the Hoople. Usually, a Peel session would consist of four songs, but we said to Dale, 'We've been messing around with a little instrumental thing. Can we record it quickly and add it on, as a fifth song? It's only a minute and a half long!' Dale said, 'Yeah, sure! Peel loves that kind of thing.' So we knocked it out. And, in a way, I guess that's how The Ukrainians were born. It was from The Wedding Present covering Ukrainian folk music.

MAIDA VALE STUDIOS
26 OCTOBER 1986, LONDON, UK

PETER

The first Peel session we did had Shaun on it, so Simon must have moved into the house before he was part of The Wedding Present. He then introduced me to Len and Simon then became our drummer. The very first Ukrainian music we recorded was where we just messed around at the end of the Peel session. 'Hopak' is one of the most famous Ukrainian tunes and one of the songs I remembered from when I was a kid. In downtime in practice and rehearsals, people would be talking and I'd just get on my guitar and start playing Ukrainian tunes. I used to play 'Hopak' to annoy people, and once or twice the rest of the band would join in. I just started playing it at the end of a Peel session and they all joined in for about a minute and a half. No one said anything about it and it was just left in the session tape.

REBECCA WALKLEY

The first time I heard of Ukraine was around 50 years ago when I had to dress up in a traditional Ukrainian costume with three other 14-year-old girls and pretend to dance like a cossack on the steps of Luton Town Hall in front of a *Luton News* photographer. We were there to promote a play set in the Soviet Union that was being performed at Luton Library. I hadn't realised at that young age the significance of dressing up as a Ukrainian dancing girl and that I would hear Ukrainian songs played in the background to my life for the next 50 years.

At the age of 19, I met Len at Leeds University. He was a student of Slavonic languages and I was studying art. After leaving, in 1980, I remember us both sitting on Woodhouse Moor, a park in Leeds 6, thinking about what we were going to do with our lives and Len said he wanted to be a musician.

Six years later, we were both still in Leeds, living in Brudenell Mount. We were in a rundown terraced house in a sea of rundown terraced houses in the city, with its rich subculture of unemployed ex-students, artists, musicians and migrants. Len at the time was writing and performing in the bands The Marvellous Roofs and The Sinister Cleaners, and playing his own solo gigs while working as a sound engineer at Lion Studios recording studio in the city centre.

Sometime in 1987 Pete Solowka knocked on his door and asked if Len could play fiddle and sing some Ukrainian tunes, knowing that Len had studied Russian and Czech and that he played in bands. So although Len didn't speak a single word of Ukrainian and hadn't played the fiddle since he was at school, he welcomed the opportunity and the two of them began working on songs once a week at Pete's house. That eventually led to Len recording three John Peel sessions with The Wedding Present, after which Pete, Len and Roman formed their own band, The Ukrainians.

PETER

We were doing more gigs as The Wedding Present than we'd ever done before and John Peel liked to get sessions on his show all the time, to show that he was current with the bands that were going on. And we were very into that, because we loved the idea that John Peel liked us. And he said, 'Are you up for another session, lads?' David said, 'Yeah, yeah, yeah, we'll do another session.' And then we sat there and we didn't have enough new songs. We had been so busy gigging we hadn't had time to write any new songs. And what you don't do is turn Peel down, because if you turn him down once, he might not ask you again. And The Wedding Present were between publishing deals at the time and so didn't want to broadcast new songs.

So I said to the others, 'Look, me and Len have been working on these songs, you know what we've been working on. We've played 'Hopak' a few times and you know what it sounds like. Why don't we do something really weird? Let's just do four Ukrainian songs in a Wedding Present style and see what happens.' I said it as a jokey thing and I can't believe they went for it, but they said 'yeah, go on then.' They weren't our songs. They were basically traditional Ukrainian songs that we punked up to make them different. I said, 'Look, the Pogues have done it with Irish music. Let's do it.' I loved what the Pogues did with traditional Irish music in the early '80s. They gave it energy. You still felt the energy of the traditional songs. If there was a song about drinking and dancing, you were drinking and dancing. If it was a sad song, you were sad with them. They could use the English language to help with that expression, of course, which we couldn't do.

MAIDA VALE STUDIOS
6 OCTOBER 1987, LONDON, UK

DAVID GEDGE

Peter went on to play me some other Ukrainian tracks that were quite tuneful and rhythmic. They weren't unlike The Wedding Present, in a way, especially if you sped them up and played them aggressively to create a more exciting arrangement. As a result, we discussed the idea of doing a Peel session of *entirely* Ukrainian folk music, but using a more traditional sound. It was kind of a radical idea but I'd been a massive fan of Peel's programme since the late 1970s, and I was well aware that he was fond of stuff which surprised or challenged his audience.

Neither Peel nor his producer, John Walters, knew we were intending to play Ukrainian folk music when we turned up to record the fourth Wedding Present session in October 1987. I didn't think there was any need to tell them in advance because they were used to all sorts of weird line-ups and musical experiments, anyway.

By then, Peter had learned to play the accordion, but he'd also bought a mandolin, which

THE UKRAINIANS

wasn't too dissimilar to a guitar. We also had a friend called Len Liggins, who was in other bands in Leeds round that time. Len had studied Russian at university and had spent some time in the Soviet Union as part of his course. Most importantly, in a perfect twist of fate, he could sing and also play the violin! So Peter asked him if he would be interested in taking part in our little project. He said he would and he came to the rehearsals. In this way, The Wedding Present evolved into a strange hybrid. Half Western Indie Rock band and half eastern European Folk band!

We rolled up at Maida Vale and, as far as the session engineers and producers were concerned, it was just going to be another Wedding Present session. But that was the great thing about Peel Sessions. You could do whatever you wanted! There was never anyone saying, 'You've got to do this' or 'You can't do that.' Funnily enough, it was exactly at the same time that *George Best* was being released and Red Rhino – the distributor and financial backers of our label, Reception Records – assumed that we'd go in and do tracks off the new album to promote it. But I knew Peel didn't really like it when bands did that, and we didn't want to do it, anyway. And, what do you know, Peel loved the Ukrainian session! I remember him saying that he couldn't think of any other band who had two such diverse sounds but did each of them as well as we did. We took that as quite a compliment, obviously, because it was clearly quite a different type of music.

Well, to be honest, it wasn't *that* difficult for me, personally, because I was just playing chords and it was not dissimilar to what I would do in The 'normal' Wedding Present. So I suppose I was taking credit where it wasn't completely due. I think Keith actually might've accused me of that at one point! But Peter had to learn new instruments and work out all these parts, and there was no end of intricate arrangements and harmonies.

Funnily enough, we squeezed five tracks onto that October 1987 session, too! The producer was Dale Griffin again but he wasn't quite as accommodating on this occasion. I remember that one of the songs wasn't coming together; mistakes were being made, probably because we weren't that familiar with playing violins and accordions and stuff. After a few false starts we heard Dale's angry voice in our headphones saying, 'Can't any of you cunts play your instruments?!' That obviously intimidated us slightly, so we were too scared to ask permission to record a fifth song. Instead, we just played two of the other songs in a row – without a gap – and pretended it was just one long song which kind of 'changed' half-way through. If he noticed that we'd done that, he never said anything!

LEN

It was daunting working with The Wedding Present. They were very focussed, and worked very quickly. I wasn't used to that level of discipline. The Sinister Cleaners could sit around John's kitchen table for hours talking about music while consuming endless tea and biscuits before going down to the cellar and plugging in.

The first Ukrainian rehearsal must have been a bit strange for David, Keith and Shaun as well as me and Peter though. Here was some speccy-looking southerner (Keith called me 'the professor') turning up with a fiddle that I hadn't played since school, and taking David's place at the mic in order to sing in Ukrainian. But it was amazing how quickly everything gelled. We'd spend an hour or so on each song, discussing arrangements and then go through them all again at the end to fix them in our memories. I think we only had about two more rehearsals before driving down to Maida Vale studios to record that first Peel session.

The scariest thing for me was being in the studio itself. We had five songs to record and mix, so we had to work quickly. There wasn't a lot of time for re-doing things if somebody made a horrendous mistake or if we played a version of a song that wasn't quite up to scratch, so the pressure was on. My overriding feeling was of not being able to move, partly out of sheer terror, and partly because I was fixed in front of a mic and all wired up. The others were much more relaxed, this being their fourth BBC radio session, which made me feel even more nervous.

I remember the session engineer, Dale Griffin, who used to be Mott the Hoople's drummer, saying 'can't any of you cunts play your instruments?'. I brought this up with David recently and he said, 'I think he was just referring to you, Len.'

PETER

If The Wedding Present hadn't done that Peel session, there's no way the band The Ukrainians would exist. Because there wasn't a door to open. But they said yes and we said to Peel 'this session is going to be so different. It's not like anything we've done before. Are you going to go for it?' And he said, 'Yeah, go on then.' The band saying yes and Peel saying yes opened two doors.

Keith was the one who was into the musical Indie culture and the vibe and getting it right. He knew everything about every band in the genre that we were in. What they were doing. What their releases were. David might have said yes to the session because we were old schoolmates. And David stepped back to let Len sing. That was a big thing when you think about the egos of lead singers, letting someone else sing on a Wedding Present session – a really big thing.

The first session was a success. Peel repeated it more times than he did any normal Wedding Present session. I don't think that was particularly because of listener feedback, more that he liked it. He knew he had something that hadn't been played on his show before.

THE UKRAINIANS

LEN

At first, I thought we were doing a one-off session of Ukrainian folk tunes as a stop-gap while David wrote some more English-language Wedding Present songs. I expected it to get played once and then be forgotten. I couldn't believe it when Peel repeated it over and over on his programme and asked us if we would do another one, which he played multiple times as well.

It was round about this time that we got approached by the makers of Snub TV, a new and very lo-fi music programme aired by the BBC. They were curious about the Ukrainian project and so me, Pete, David and Simon quickly prepared a version of a song that Pete and I had just written called 'Ty Moyi Radoshchi' (You Are My Joy). They filmed us playing the song along with a short interview in Pete's room in Brudenell Road and it appeared in the last episode of series one.

DAVID GEDGE

We really enjoyed recording that session – and we thought it sounded great – so we decided that we'd like to do a second one. In the meantime, Peter had met another Leeds musician called Roman Revkniv. He had a Ukrainian surname so, for his musical endeavours, he'd decided to go by the hilarious moniker of Roman Remeynes.

Roman had been round to Peter's house and said, 'I'm hearing you playing all this Ukrainian music, but I don't think you're doing it authentically enough.' I think that was maybe partly because there was some Russian music in amongst it! So Peter said, 'Well, okay, do you want to join us, then?!' So, for the second session, Roman came along and also played the mandolin and a Ukrainian flute-like instrument called a sopilka. That freed up Peter to do a second mandolin and concentrate more on the accordion. The second session was, again, very well received – although perhaps not by *all* Wedding Present fans, I guess, some of whom just wanted normal service to be resumed. But it was well received by Peel, anyway! Besides, we were back in Maida Vale doing a 'normal' session a couple of months later. However, for our seventh session, the following year, we decided to revert to Ukrainian mode yet again. I can't remember why, but we only recorded three tracks on that occasion. The other main difference this time was that the songs were written by Peter, Len and Roman, rather than us covering traditional music. So that was another pivotal moment.

LEN

I felt more confident for the second session. I'd had time to learn a bit more about the Ukrainian language and to remember how to play the fiddle! Also, we had just four songs this time and we were better rehearsed. The producer, Dale Griffin, was a formidable presence and could be quite intimidating. Nevertheless, when he asked us to run through all the songs, he could tell that one of them, 'Verkhovyno', had a lot of potential to be a great track. It was already a long song, but he encouraged us to lengthen the ending even more, and to speed up even faster. The result was an eight-minute epic and Dale very kindly stayed until midnight mixing it. Peel loved it, of course, and the session became one of his all-time favourites.

PETER

'Verkhovyno' is such an iconic Ukrainian folk song. Set in the far west of Ukraine in the Carpathian mountains and a great example of the *kolomeyka* folk style. The quiet bits, so gentle, the fast bits so furious, yet it blends so well. Then in the studio Roman shouted Ukrainian phrases over the most passionate part of the dance sequence. Just magic - it really shows how we were bringing out the passion, the energy in Ukrainian music - and bringing it to life.

EUGENE CZAUDERNA

I wouldn't say I was in right at the beginning of the band The Ukrainians but due to my very long-standing friendship with the Legendary Len, and the interest I have always had in his varied musical career, it must have been quite early on. So it was that I had my finger poised on the record button of my tape recorder, when the first John Peel session was broadcast (should I admit to this?). This later became *Ukrainski Vistupi V Johna Peela*, but of course this was actually by The Wedding Present, so I'm not sure if it counts.

I have now seen The Ukrainians many times, in various incarnations, in multiple venues, notably several times in the Ukrainian Club in Holland Park, London and even in the National Trust property of Polesden Lacey. I have heard of their exploits in Europe and other parts of the globe, but regrettably have never seen them outside Britain, and indeed, have mostly seen them in London.

My parents were both Polish and so I was steeped in the Polish language, music and culture from the cradle. The relationship between the Polish people and Ukrainian people has been long and often stormy. As we might discover from certain Hollywood movies, which may star Yul Brynner, the Poles lorded it over the Ukrainians and were all cruel tyrants. Listening to the band The Ukrainians has flagged up both the similarities and the differences between the two cultures. In the end the similarities are what stay with you. So, if you want a wild rush of energetic punk-inspired music, suitable for energetic dancing, in a language you (probably) don't understand, you can't do better than listen to The Ukrainians!

THE UKRAINIANS

PETER

Peel always survived on difference, something new that's different, and that's why he asked for a new session only a few months later. And the second one involved another person, Roman, who had a massive effect on the band. He heard the first session, found out where I lived, knocked on my door and said, 'Hi, I'm Roman and I'm Ukrainian and you're doing it wrong.' I said, 'We're not doing it wrong. We're doing it the way we do it.' He said, 'Let me show you some things.' He brought an instrument to the band that we'd never used properly, one which I'd played but not very well – the mandolin. He was in a few bands in Leeds and played bass and ordinary guitar, but he said, 'I grew up playing the mandolin. Listen to this…' and it was amazing. He'd grown up playing it in a way I'd never heard before. The way he trilled it, the punctuation, and the way he expressed the tunes was really, really good. I wasn't doing it right.

Roman came from a very different background to me. His was a traditional Ukrainian background, living in Leeds. Both his parents were Ukrainian, which was very rare, because most of the people who came to Britain were like my dad. I have a funny feeling that his parents may have been political refugees, rather than just happening to be in the West like my dad. I think their upbringing of Roman was so intensely Ukrainian because of that. They spoke Ukrainian to him at home when he was a child and his parents still spoke Ukrainian to him in his 20s and 30s. If you went into his house, the English spoken in his house was pretty poor because they spoke Ukrainian all the time. To Roman, being Ukrainian was a political thing. 'You're Ukrainian. You're special. Remember, the KGB will always try and get you, they'll try and stop you. And we escaped. You're special. You've got the culture.' I got that message once or twice from my dad. Roman would have got that every bloody day. So for him Ukrainian culture was really, really important. That's why he knocked on the door of my house saying 'You're not doing it right'.

He didn't like the idea that some of the influences, the chord sequences and the melody lines, weren't quite Ukrainian enough and that the language wasn't pronounced properly. He felt they were too Russian-influenced. He'd have heard them in Ukrainian clubs. There would have been some songs that he wouldn't have heard, because we took them from other sources. But he said, 'You're calling it Ukrainian but your music sounds Russian.' I said to him, 'In my opinion, Ukraine is a multi-cultural place.' I disagreed with him that there was only one way to be Ukrainian. The Ukrainian territory contains people who regard themselves as Ukrainian and people who regard themselves as Russian, along with people who are Jewish and people who have a Crimean Tatar or Muslim background. These people still call themselves Ukrainian. For me, Ukrainian music is the music of that land and not one particular (although majority) ethnic group. But I said to him, 'If you can make our music sound better, I'm happy to hear what you say.'

First me and Len, and then me, Len and Roman, started to write our own songs. In the early days, we started off using a traditional Ukrainian tune or Ukrainian style and putting songs together with our new interpretations and it felt okay. But that never feels as good as when you compose your own stuff. Rather than writing about what it was like to be Ukrainian in Leeds 6 though, we took on historical ideas from Ukrainian folklore. We were creating more songs in our Wedding Present-inspired style, but the source of our material in the early days was the romantic images that you were given in Ukrainian clubs as a kid: the beautiful farmsteads, the cherry orchard, the brave Cossacks going to fight to defend the land.

I knew nothing of Ukrainian myths and history when I was a kid. The only thing I knew as a kid was that Ukrainian wasn't Russian. I learnt the history partly because I was a frustrated intellectual. I'd finished my degree course in environmental biology and I'm very well qualified if you ever have a colliery spoil heap and you want to grow grass on it. But I wasn't working and I didn't want to work. But even when I wasn't working, I was doing GCSEs and A-levels for fun. I did a GCSE in psychology just to keep my brain ticking over. I also did some research via the Ukrainian Bookshop in London, to learn about the history of Ukraine and its background.

And when you get folk songs and you start to translate them, and you realise what the subject material is, those are the ideas that we tended to use. Me and Len started doing that after the first Peel session, and Roman was always interested in doing as many Ukrainian things as possible. He already had some lyrics, and sometimes we'd adapt those to the music that we'd written. A lot of times, Len and Roman would collaborate on words. Roman's vocabulary was much larger because he used to speak Ukrainian at home, but he wasn't as experienced a songwriter. The collaborations between Len and Roman brought about the best of our early material.

 JOHN PEEL SESSION, MAIDA VALE STUDIOS
15 MARCH 1988, LONDON, UK

PETER

The chance for us to do another session was another door being opened. I still don't know why we did a second session, but it was far more sophisticated and more of what the Ukrainians became, because once the session was booked, we expanded from being a five-piece to being a six-piece. The arrangements were far more complicated and Roman was an extra musician who came in with extra ideas. This was another point at which The Wedding Present could have said 'no'. I don't know why Keith in particular thought that was a good thing to do. Keith was all about the history of pop culture. He was aware of everything that the Velvet Underground had ever said. He was super cultured, Keith, and yet he'd do this.

You can hear a real difference in quality between the first and second sessions. It's not just the fact that you've got extra musicians there. The band also spent more time arranging and thinking about what was going to make a good song, so it wasn't just the fact that me, Len and Roman worked on this. The others were working too. They weren't just passively there. They were actually trying to make the songs sound good, which is really weird considering where we were as a group. We could have been the big new Indie thing. The Smiths had gone, people were saying, 'Who's our next champion?' and we're doing this stuff. It's almost like self-destruction. Maybe the band saw a little bit of the energy, the excitement, the difference and the truth behind the music. That there was something there and that it's not a joke. It's not a gimmick. We never had that discussion, though – we just did it.

I was surprised by the first session, but I was more surprised that they were willing to work and lift the second session to a level above it. David, Keith and Simon, who was on drums by the time of the second session, all wanted to make it as good as possible. We played 'Verkhovyno' on that second session and we never played it better live than we did then. Dale Griffin, who engineered the Peel sessions, always had his little line of coke, to make sure he was perfectly cued in.

The first session was a stopgap, a fill-in, a space-maker. It was almost a joke, a challenge to Peel. 'How different can you take our music?' And he said, 'Fine'. After that, it was, 'Let's make it better'. That's even more interesting to me. It was never part of the band's plan, and even when you're in that hard working zone, you don't discuss everything. You only focus on the things that you work well together on. You work on the guitar parts. You work on your drum parts. We'd be in the practice room for three or four hours, and two or three days later in a tour bus, you'd sit and read your book. You'd do your gig. You don't always talk about why you do the things you do. But reflecting back on it, they were massive decisions. They might even have done it consciously. Without those two decisions about the Peel sessions – 'let's do it' the first time, and 'let's upgrade it' the second time – The Ukrainians would not exist.

UKRAINSKI VISTUPI V JOHNA PEELA
RELEASED 3 FEBRUARY 1989

PETER

We did the second Peel session and it went down as well as, if not better than, the first. Red Rhino Records got the rights from the BBC to release them as an album and we got all the artwork together. It was going to be a ten-inch record, which is a really weird format that you find a lot in eastern Europe, and the packaging was meant to be distinctive and rough-looking, like eastern European cardboard. The two Peel sessions came in at just over 30 minutes, and one of those was an eight-minute song. I don't know why the rest of the band agreed to do it. I think it was just to say, 'We are different. We can do any music we like, and we can get away with it.' The album cover had the band's name in Ukrainian and the record title translated as 'Ukrainian Sessions For John Peel'.

It was all in the Cyrillic (Slavic) script that is used in Ukraine rather than the Latin script we use in western Europe. It didn't even have The Wedding Present (in English) printed on it (apart from on the spine), and it was about to be released in the record shops when Red Rhino went bankrupt. I think we bankrupted them actually! We were their biggest band. They had so much faith in the fact that we could sell records. I don't think they were great business people. They never turned round and said, 'Are you sure you want that expensive artwork? Are you sure you want to do that video?' The person who ran the label, his house was a guarantee to the business and he lost his house.

You had Ukrainian tracks appearing on the Peel Festive 50. That was absolutely bizarre, having those songs appearing amongst the Indie elite of the UK in Thatcher's downtrodden '80s and people choosing songs from what most people thought was Britain's enemy in the Soviet bloc. It's so hard to put a reason on why people like that. Maybe it's just the music of rebellion. 'I've heard this band. It's so different.'

LEN

It seemed to take an eternity to come out. The album's distribution was handled by Red Rhino. They had pressed up a few DJ promo seven-inch singles with two tracks from the album, 'Davni Chasy' ('Those Were The Days') on the A-side, backed by 'Katrusya'. Incidentally, 'Davni Chasy' isn't a traditional eastern European folk song, as a lot of people think. The tune and original Russian lyrics were written by a chap from St Petersburg called Boris Fomin, probably sometime during the 1920s. It was then called 'Dorogoy Dlinnoyu' ('By The Long Road'). The English language lyrics by Gene Raskin, an American musician from the Bronx, weren't written until 1962.

As well as the promo singles, Red Rhino had also pressed up a batch of the ten-inch vinyl LPs, ready for release in late 1988, but the company went into receivership before it could release the album. A tiny number of these original pressings managed to 'leave' the warehouse and a small number were sold via The Wedding Present's mail order in a matching promo plastic bag! Looking on the Discogs website, it seems these initial pressings are sought after nowadays. Luckily, I managed to procure two copies for myself and got everyone playing on the record to sign them at the time, so I'm guessing these would be particularly desirable. (You can tell I'm a record collector, can't you? It's a sad affliction and I'm only too aware of it.)

Two other versions of the vinyl album exist. When the band signed to RCA the company bought all the unsold albums (about 15,000 copies) from Red Rhino. These had a sticker on the back with the RCA logo and a new catalogue number and barcode. When they ran out of those, RCA pressed up the third version with their own catalogue number (RCA 74104) printed on the labels and sleeves.

Pete pretty much put the booklet together on his own, except for the bits which explained what each song was about. It included some folk images and a brief introduction to certain aspects of Ukrainian history and culture. The whole thing, including the sleeve and labels, was designed by Jonathan Hitchen, known as 'Hitch', who also did the graphic design for a number of The Wedding Present's other releases, including *Seamonsters* and the string of twelve *Hit Parade* singles. Oh yes, and the photo in the centre spread of the booklet was a still from us performing 'Verkhovyno' on the BBC TV's *On A Personal Note* programme.

Anyhow, the album sold 70,000 copies and got to number 22 in the chart, not the Indie chart but the 'proper' national 'pop' chart. Who would have guessed it possible? We had a lot of support from the music press, with the *NME*, *Melody Maker* and *Sounds* all running substantial interviews with the band. The run-out grooves of the vinyl carry the message 'Should I worship at the feet… of this god-like ferret?' This message, which was David's idea, is a cryptic reference to Pete. The Wedding Present played up Peter's northern working-class heritage, where ferrets would be kept as pets. On The Wedding Present's merchandise stall, there were even cardboard cut-out 'Grapper' dolls (Peter's nickname is allegedly southern slang for 'Old Man') where you could put a ferret on a lead, or stuff the ferret down his trousers!

DAVID GEDGE

We decided that it would be nice to release the first two Ukrainian sessions on a mini-LP on Reception Records so we approached the BBC to license the recordings and asked our usual record cover designer, Hitch, to create a sleeve. Unfortunately, this was the point at which Red Rhino – our financial backers – famously started having financial problems which eventually sent them into liquidation, although not before they had pressed up stock of our *Ukrainski Vistupi V Johna Peela* ten-inch vinyl and CDs.

However, just before Red Rhino went into liquidation, The Wedding Present had decided to sign to RCA Records. After Red Rhino had gone bust, we persuaded RCA to purchase all the stock from the liquidator and also to repress it, if it sold out, which it did. So – and, again, this is typical Wedding Present – after signing our fantastic new record deal, our first major-label release was a mini-LP of Ukrainian folk music! It's absolutely not what you would describe as an ideal marketing plan. The executives at RCA certainly had to be persuaded that it was a good idea. But, to their credit, they went along with it. They bought all the stock from Red Rhino, re-stickered it with their logo, and it became our first release on RCA.

PETER

That's when we signed to RCA. They were the only big label that were really interested in us, and that was because they'd just made a shitload of money the year before on Rick Astley and Annie Lennox (from The Eurythmics). And you either pay tax on the money you've made, or you reinvest it in an asset and the band is an asset, so you sign bands up with the money you've made. I think they signed up four artists in the '86/'87 period, and we were one of them, so I don't want to big ourselves up too much. Other labels weren't really interested! Korda Marshall's job at RCA was to try and invest some of that money and he chose us, which was interesting because RCA had never really gone down the Indie route at all. It was new territory for them. But he thought we were a band they could sell records with.

We didn't really want to sign to a major. We wanted the independence that we had with Red Rhino Records. The arrogance of youth is unbelievable. You imagine that nobody else can tell you how to sell records or how to do well. As an artist you want to get your music out. You just want to play your music, and we'd done it all ourselves so far. The idea that someone could tell us how to do it better? 'Ha, ha, ha – get lost! We're 30 years old. We're top of our game. You're not telling us anything.'

So we really negotiated on the contract and they gave us everything. They gave us full control on what the artwork looked like, and full control of what the final mixes sounded like – just as long as it reached a certain standard that could be broadcast on the radio.

We were just going through the normal signing process and they said, 'The first thing we want to release is your Ukrainian record.' Even I said, 'No, no, this is not what the band is about. We're an Indie guitar band. We don't want to do Ukrainian music.' And they said, 'Well, we've heard the Ukrainian stuff and we think it's great. You've done that version of 'Those Were The Days'. We think that's going to chart. We can get it out as a seven-inch single with the album release. It'll get played on the radio and, honest, you'll sell hundreds of thousands of records.' And even I said, 'I don't want to do that. That's not what we're here for.'

The deal we had with them was that we could make a record not in the normal style of The Wedding Present. If your first album does well, they sign you up for a second. And if that does well, they sign you up for a third. But if your first record doesn't do well, they drop you. Our album was a three-album deal and we said, 'It's not fair to put the Ukrainian stuff on there (in the contract), because we don't know if it's going to sell or not.' So they gave us a concurrent deal and a budget to make an album of Ukrainian music, and it didn't make any difference at all to the main Wedding Present contract. As far as I'm aware, that was an absolutely unique arrangement. Can you imagine, say, someone with a Turkish background negotiating a contract to do their English language stuff and their Turkish stuff as well? They really must have had a load of money to get rid of!

THE UKRAINIANS

As far as we knew, this was the first time anyone had ever recorded any Ukrainian-style music in a proper professional recording studio. The Wedding Present Ukrainian LP was brought out by RCA in the three formats – vinyl, cassette and CD. And we were convinced that this was the first ever CD to have Ukrainian music on it, until we found one group who got there about a month before us. It was an American duo called Darka and Slavko, two first-generation Ukrainian Americans based in New York. It was disappointing to hear this, but not actually surprising considering the large number of Americans and Canadians with Ukrainian heritage, and how technology works a bit faster over there.

I contacted Darka and Slavko to find out exactly when their album had been released. Unfortunately, we still couldn't work out who was first, but then disaster struck! Darka found a catalogue reference to a group called Cheremosh from Canada who released 'Encore', a CD to celebrate their 20th anniversary, in 1988. If that's true, this makes our debate with Darka and Slavko redundant! However, our record was definitely the first Ukrainian language CD to appear on a major record label.

When The Wedding Present had spare time while recording the second album, *Bizarro*, me and Len would be working on Ukrainian tracks that we'd written with Roman. And when we'd got time, we'd go into the studio, with a producer under RCA Records, and record the same way as we would record as The Wedding Present.

DAVID GEDGE

When RCA discovered that one of the Ukrainian tracks, 'Davni Chasy', was a cover of 'Those Were The Days', they proposed releasing it as a single and insisted we'd have a big hit on our hands. When we were still with Red Rhino, we'd pressed up promotional singles of 'Davni Chasy' – specifically to give to radio DJs – but RCA wanted to go the next step and release it as a proper, commercially-available, single. They were saying things like 'we could do a great video for this' and 'is Mary Hopkin still alive? Maybe we could get her involved!' All that kind of stuff. But it all kind of appalled us and we ended up saying, 'No, no, you're going too far!' We didn't want a joke hit! So we turned all that down. It was already a bizarre project and we didn't want it to be made even stranger by having our RCA catalogue be heralded by a novelty record. They were fine about it. In the end, the first single we put out on RCA was 'Kennedy', which wasn't particularly commercial either, but that's another story.

LEN

Korda Marshall, the A&R guy at RCA wanted to lift 'Davni Chasy' ('Those Were The Days') from the album and release it as a single. He said it was guaranteed to go to number 1.

DAVID GEDGE

Mick Houghton was our press officer at the time and, when the mini-LP was coming out, he arranged for us to be on the front cover of *Melody Maker*. We knew the interviewer, Ian Gittins, because Keith had been at university with him and he'd interviewed us before. He and the photographer, Tom Sheehan, came up to Leeds to do the feature. But it didn't really go to plan. While we were doing the photo session, my memory is that Tom said to me, "Ere, son, grab a violin and stick it under your chin,' and I said, 'Well, no, because I'm not a violinist!' He insisted that it would look good but I said, 'No, I'd feel stupid. Surely it would be better to have the whole band on the front cover, anyway, since it's a Ukrainian folk music band?' And he said, 'No, that'd be too many people. The editors typically only want one person on the front cover, and that obviously should be you because The Wedding Present is *your* band. You're the most recognisable face so, like I say, stick this violin under your chin!' And I said, 'No, I'm not doing that.' He replied, 'Well, if you don't do it, you'll lose the front cover.' I said, 'I think we'll lose the front cover, then, because I'm not doing it!'

And so we lost the front cover. Mick Houghton and RCA were probably disappointed with that, because it's obviously an exciting thing to get, but I just didn't feel comfortable with the idea. And I don't blame Tom for suggesting it, either; he was just doing his job. The shoot still happened and the feature went out, but it just wasn't on the cover anymore. It was actually quite a substantial interview and there were lots of photographs of all the band. We did interviews for all of the papers for that Ukrainian release – *NME*, *Sounds*, etc. – but that was the one where we'd been 'guaranteed' a front cover. And I'd blown it!

IAN GITTINS, *MELODY MAKER* JOURNALIST

I certainly remember Tom asking David Gedge to pose with a violin, David declining and Tom being pissed off. I don't personally remember Tom saying, 'You won't be on the front cover then', and that wouldn't be his decision to make. I don't know if that's why the Ukrainian (Wedding Present) line-up was bumped off the cover – I wrote the feature but I wasn't party to that editorial discussion or decision. (Allan Jones, the editor, says he remembers the fuss about the photos, but doesn't think it led to the feature being bumped from the cover.)

MICK HOUGHTON, THE WEDDING PRESENT'S PR

I can imagine Tom saying that a shot of David with the violin under his chin might put them in with a chance of a front cover in order to try and get the shot. The front covers weren't always set in stone and a great photo did sometimes make a difference. I just think it would have been unlikely because – at that time – there was so much antipathy towards The Wedding Present at *Melody Maker* (especially amongst the main staff writers and editors). We didn't get a cover till *The Hit Parade* and that was giving the *Melody Maker* an exclusive interview about the 12 singles concept. By then the band was a lot more successful.

Plus, the Ukrainian stuff was pretty left field. It also charted, getting their highest chart position to date, which didn't go unnoticed.

So my main memory of the precursor to The Ukrainians is that (against the odds) the band got away with it. It was such an outrageous and unlikely thing for the band to do that it worked in their favour. As I remember, the LP got pretty good reviews but it was the live shows that took people by surprise because the Ukrainian set worked so well. For some it was an antidote to the usual, more dour presentation. It was fun, after all. More than anything, it got people talking positively about The Wedding Present because the band wasn't afraid to do something that could easily have been a disaster. It was a one-off and then they wisely moved on.

I was always pleased The Ukrainians carried on with Len and Pete and successfully carved out a good niche audience, shifting from Indie to Folk.

CHRIS PALAHNIUK

I grew up in Winnipeg, Manitoba, Canada where the internet says 13 per cent of all Canadian-Ukrainians live. In my family it felt like more (both father and mother had large Ukrainian families) as we attended St. Basil's Church where I was an altar boy. After a few run-ins at public school, I was made to attend Immaculate Heart of Mary Ukrainian School in Grade 5. I tried to learn the language and the dance, but only rebelled against it as a teen. It was all too much Ukrainian for a boy who just wanted to listen to Iron Maiden (my first concert, in 1984) and play hockey (I never made it.) I regret feeling that way now (but don't regret listening to Iron Maiden).

Fast forward a few rebellious years. I went to the University of Winnipeg and listened to their in-house radio station CKUW, 'the best thing Winnipeg will never hear.' My musical sensibilities were exploding with college radio, going to shows and very cool new friends who had the best alt music at their fingertips. I saw Billy Bragg and Weddings Parties Anything at the 1989 *Winnipeg Folk Festival* and had the *Bizzaro* cassette in rotation in my 1978 VW Rabbit, showing off 'Brassneck' whenever new folks needed a ride somewhere.

I had friends who knew CKUW DJs (the real cool of the school) who knew music I could never dream of hearing. I was introduced to one such very nice senior student, Hartley Odwak, at a party and got to talking about being Ukrainian. (He wasn't, but was interested in those of us that were.) He told me he had this cassette of The Wedding Present singing in Ukrainian that was good but not his thing and that he'd be willing to sell it. I could barely afford gas in the Rabbit, never mind a rare cassette I could only get from Hartley. Would he be willing to trade? (What could I have that he would want anyways?) Hearing The Wedding Present sing in Ukrainian seemed lost before I'd even heard it.

I would run into Hartley around school and we would talk. One day he brought in the prized cassette and then I knew it was on. I just started listing everything I owned. What could he want? Well, there was that *Captain Fantastic* poster I had up in my apartment hallway, originally from my father's copy of the album. Hartley was very interested in this and so the trade was made and my Ukrainian-ness was amplified.

I played that new Ukrainian music wherever I went, professing my Ukrainian-ness proudly from my Rabbit and telling whoever would listen that Ukrainian music was truly as cool as it gets. My friends listened, my family listened and my Ukrainian wife listened with her Ukrainian family to The Wedding Present and then The Ukrainians. (The Ukrainians sing the Smiths? Fuck!) I was indeed Ukrainian cool now and proud of it.

A lot has happened since 1989. I now live in Minneapolis and am married to a Norwegian. I have never been to Ukraine and, although so very upset with the current war, am no more Ukrainian than I have ever been. I do however still have The Ukrainians and that feeling I get of being 19 and discovering that there are lots of new things to try to discover, but your pierogi roots are where it is all really at.

The Ukrainians made me a prouder Ukrainian, a cooler 20-something, and truly an appreciative human for other humans willing to take a chance. I still cherish that original cassette, the artwork and the feeling, and can even play it again thanks to the resurgence of cassettes.

 RIVERSIDE
17 APRIL 1989, NEWCASTLE, UK

DAVID ARMSTRONG

It wasn't long to wait before on walked the support band. 'Hello, we're the support band' jokingly said Mr Gedge, leading Peter, Keith and Simon on stage to blast through an unadvertised short set of their 'normal' tunes, primarily consisting of songs from their yet to be released *Bizarro* album. 'That's a bonus,' we all thought, giving ourselves a metaphorical pat on the back for getting there in time.

After a short break (and another pint) the band returned, this time joined by Len Liggins and Roman Remeynes, and pretty soon the whole place was bouncing to a unique mix of folk and alternative music. The fact no one knew the words was neither here nor there. You could pogo to it. You could join in the 'ois!' that punctuated what seemed like every other song. You could punch the air at all the right parts. It was loud. It was fast. It was mental. With the two guests taking centre stage, the lads stepped back, seemingly enjoying the experience as much as we all were, if their massive grins were anything to go by. The gig flew by, presumably as the songs were short and there weren't many of them, but it was long enough to be soaked in sweat, my new Ukrainian t-shirt destined never to be quite as white as it started.

BIERKELLER
19 APRIL 1989, BRISTOL, UK

GUY RUDRUM
'You *do* know it's Ukrainian?' the lady on the ticket counter asked me. I was 15, loved *George Best* and *Tommy* and wasn't going to let the fact I wouldn't be able to understand the songs stop me. The evening finally arrived and I excitedly entered the Bristol Bierkeller. One nervous underage pint of lager later and on stage walked the support band. Nobody particularly paid any attention. 'Hello, we're the support band' came a distinctive voice, before launching into a ferocious guitar intro. The crowd rushed to the front and the pogoing began. That night was also the first time I ever heard 'Kennedy'. The Ukrainian set began with 'Davni Chasy' with its singalong chorus. I had got a place right at the front and more enthusiastic pogoing taught me a valuable lesson about getting too close to the stage when it is only about thigh-height! No Wedding Present gig is complete without a trip to the merchandise stall. I came away with a massive Ukrainian tour dates poster that never stayed up.

TOWN & COUNTRY CLUB
20 APRIL 1989, LONDON, UK

DAVID GEDGE
When the mini-LP was released, we did a tour of the United Kingdom under the title 'An Evening of Ukrainian Music by The Wedding Present' but we also supported ourselves, secretly, as the 'normal' band. We'd written some new songs that we wanted to try out, and we thought it would be good to have a little half-hour set. We didn't want to broadcast it too much, so we just advertised it as 'plus support'. You couldn't do that these days, because the first time you appear opening for yourselves, everybody's going to be on social media saying, 'Hey, everybody, The Wedding Present's support band is The Wedding Present!' But, back then, you could get away with it because,

unless people rang each other up, there was no way that anyone would find out. It was quite funny, actually, because people had bought tickets to see the Ukrainian version of The Wedding Present and, if they'd arrived early, would be milling around the venue, when, suddenly the 'normal' version would take the stage. You could see the penny gradually starting to drop.

There was a really good concert in London, at the Town & Country Club – which is now Kentish Town Forum – where someone had contacted a local Ukrainian society and managed to persuade them to bring a troupe of Ukrainian dancers to join us on stage. It was quite spectacular. I wish I had footage of it. Oh, and also spectacularly, I had a different type of curry every single night on that tour!

LEN

We played eight live shows, most of which were packed to the rafters with incredulous, sweaty, screaming fans.

PETER

We did a seven or eight-date tour of Britain, playing places that – apart from the London Town & Country Club – were nowhere near as big as the places we would normally have played. These were smaller venues which held 500 or 600 people, when we'd been playing venues of 1,000 plus. The idea was that we were playing the Ukrainian album and about five or six more songs – some of which me, Len and Roman had written – and which were getting their first airing as songs that the rest of The Wedding Present played. But they were essentially what were to become Ukrainians songs and some of them eventually appeared on the first Ukrainians album.

Two of the most classic ones that came from that period were 'Cherez Richku, Cherez Hai' and 'Zavtra', both of which have since been adopted as part of the repertoire of what is now considered Ukrainian folk music. People sing them, people know them. We've even  seen nursery schools in Lviv teaching their kids 'Cherez Richku, Cherez Hai' as Ukrainian heritage. Because we used traditional themes and traditional song structures, they can take that away from the fast guitar Wedding Present approach and sing it with an acoustic guitar and an accordion and it sounds like a Ukrainian folk song.

This was the tour where The Wedding Present supported The Wedding Present (Ukrainian-style). We thought, 'Fans won't really want to see the Ukrainian music, they'll want to see The Wedding Present, so we'll have to support ourselves.' So The Wedding Present played a very short set of mainly six or seven new songs which we were working on and which people hadn't heard. Then we went off stage and 15 minutes later came back on and did the Ukrainian set. It was very strange. The main thing I realised was what a difference it makes if you are a support band and not the main band. The hall is only half full because most people are in the bar chatting to their mates and thinking, 'I'm not bothering to see the support band', because they didn't realise it was us. It took me back a bit to when we were starting out and reminded me how difficult it really is as a support band.

But what made me realise there might be something in this was the response of the audience. It wasn't a novelty thing, with people sitting back with a little smirk on their faces. They were full on down the front. Maybe it's because it was The Wedding Present that was delivering it, but you looked at people and you could see that they were enjoying this music in a way that I didn't recognise. Maybe they were enjoying the difference of it, and enjoying it because it was fast and furious. Maybe they were enjoying the emotions of it, with all the eastern European music tricks we used, going slow and speeding up and taking it even further because we were good at going fast, so that just gave it the extra edge. But it was that reaction which made me think, 'Yes, we could do something with this'.

We never toured it again, and I never expected the rest of The Wedding Present would do it again.

ANDREW WHITING

I was a guitarist/singer and we were called Thrilled Skinny. We were a basic noise band – very trashy, not at all like The Wedding Present when we started, but we released records in late 1987 and early 1988 and started gigging widely. We were really young and naive and just all packed in our jobs, bought a van and that was it. We played loads of seriously hardcore Punk gigs and benefits, and although we sometimes landed gigs with quieter bands such as Television Personalities, CUD, Lush and others, we didn't fit in with that crowd. John Peel got us to do a session and played us loads in those days, and so we started to get lots of gigs. C86 bands had been a massive influence on us (as well as more Punk stuff like Ramones, Wire, Swell Maps, US hardcore, etc.) and our singer and bassist Simon was already a massive Wedding Present fan, as was our drummer Elliot and his brother Tim, who roadied for us. We cheekily wrote to The Wedding Present asking if they wanted to release a record by us! I think they found that amusing and were intrigued.

We played a gig at Leeds Duchess of York and all The Wedding Present turned up to see us, including Sally and Justine (who were both selling t-shirts for them at that time, as well as being romantically involved with David and Keith, of course).

A few weeks later they phoned our Simon up and asked us to play the Town & Country in Kentish Town with them. It was really short notice so I don't think we were even listed on any gig press releases, tickets or posters, etc. It was so nice of them to do that, but they

Через Річку Через Гай

Через річку, через гай
Ластівка летіла
Через поле, через край
Тирса шелестіла

Вставайте козаки! вставайте козаки!
У лісі калина, червона калина
Вставайте козаки!

Поїдемо разом! поїдемо разом!
Гей, святкувати! гей випивати!
Поїдемо разом!

Швидко готуймося! швидко готуймося!
Ще раз захищати, ще раз воювати
Швидко готуймося!

Через річку, через гай
Ластівка летіла
Через поле, через край
Тирса шелестіла

Cherez Richku Cherez Hai
(Across The River, Through The Grove)

Across the river, through the grove
The swallow flew
Across the field, thoughout the countryside
The rye grass whispered

Arise Cossacks! Arise Cossacks!
In the woods is a cranberry, a red cranberry
Arise Cossacks!

Let's ride together! Let's ride together!
To celebrate! To drink!
Let's ride together!

Let us prepare ourselves quickly! Let us prepare ourselves quickly!
Once more to defend, once more to fight
Let us prepare ourselves quickly!

Across the river, through the grove
The swallow flew
Across the field, thoughout the countryside
The rye grass whispered

Завтра

Хочу доживати віку
Тільки із тобою
А любити я не можу
Перед війною

Ой, миленько за мене молися
Завтра я буду під небом чужим
Завтра я буду під небом чужим

Чую голос Марусеньки
Від Дону до Карпат
Личенька не забуду
Від Волги до Дунаю

За країну, за славу
За волю, за правду
Треба мені боротися

За тебе, за славу
За волю, за правду
Завтра я буду під небом чужим

Zavtra (Tomorrow)

I want to live my whole life
Only with you
But I cannot love you
Until the war is over

Oh, my dear one, pray for me
Tomorrow I will be under a foreign sky
Tomorrow I will be under a foreign sky

I hear the voice of Marusya
From the Don river to the Carpathian mountains
Her little face follows me
From the Volga to the Danube

For our country, for glory
For honour, for truth
I must fight

For you, for glory
For honour, for truth
For tomorrow I will be under a foreign sky

pretty much have done similar favours for small bands their entire career. The gig itself is a bit of a blur – The Wedding Present went on unannounced and it took quite a few minutes before people realised it was them playing. I was at the t-shirt stall with Justine and Sally and we kept having to tell people that instead of buying t-shirts they should check out the band on stage!

We went on next and were so shambolic and Punk we thought we went down pretty badly. (Our songs were all about one minute long and so odd.) But afterwards we completely sold out of t-shirts and sold loads of records too. The Wedding Present went on last and played their Ukrainian set and they were wonderful. It was incredibly danceable.

Afterwards we were a bit shell-shocked and turned down an invitation to a party with the band as we'd had trouble with our van dying and we had no idea if we were going to get it going again. We didn't. Nine of us slept in the van and it got towed back home to Luton, whilst we caught the train home with all our gear.

DAN WHALEY

I'm proud to say I've been along for the ride since that very first Wedding Present Ukrainian gig at the Town & Country Club in Kentish Town in 1989. Since then, I have collected all the records. I must have at least three copies of the *Ukrainski Vistupi V Johna Peela* ten-inch. (And speaking of Peel, it'd be lovely if the '91 session containing the otherwise unavailable 'Leeds Waltz' would get an official release.) I've seen them countless times at venues including The Mean Fiddler, a church/art centre in Salisbury, a place that may have been a squat in Leytonstone, and on multiple occasions at the band's spiritual home – the Holland Park Ukrainian Centre.

Most recently, I had the pleasure of DJing before and after their set at the *Endorset Festival*.

TOM STANLEY (INVISIBLE TOM)

I was a fan of The Wedding Present and the alternative music scene in the late '80s. When The Wedding Present did their Ukrainian John Peel session tour, I went to see them at the Town & Country Club in London. I was blown away by the brilliance and excitement of the music and also by the Ukrainian dancers. It was one of the best gigs I have been to. Massive inspiration. I got the album and listened to it repeatedly.

There was already an interest in eastern Europe as we had a Polish family friend when growing up and as a young man I wrote (and still write) to another Polish friend. My first visit to Poland was in 1990 and I have visited several times since. I have learned to speak a bit of Polish and can sing some songs.

Musically, I had played guitar in bands since Punk times. I have played and still do play

Indie music. I wanted to learn this Ukrainian/eastern European music and got a mandolin. I was always fascinated by the balalaika but didn't know how or where to get one. I did see one in a London market but didn't have the money at that time.

Many years later, my wife (who was with me at the Wedding Present gig in 1989) kindly bought me my first balalaika. I taught myself to play it with the help of YouTube videos, the book *Complete Balalaika* by Bibs Ekkel and anything else I could find. I played balalaika live at open mics and small gigs around my home town and occasionally further afield, for example at the Mercato Metropolitano in London.

In 2020 I released an album of balalaika songs. The album is called *Luna* and was released under the band name Atom Mirny: myself (Invisible Tom) and my son, Jem Stanley. I have released other balalaika songs on my Invisible Tom page on Spotify and Bandcamp. The balalaika also appears as a backing instrument in my Indie music and that of my band, Stanways. Sadly, it's a difficult issue nowadays playing the balalaika in public due to the terrible conflict, so I rarely do so, and only thoughtfully chosen songs if I do. Another welcome addition to the musical instrument collection is a Ukrainian Domra, made in Odesa.

Thank you to The Ukrainians for that awesome gig in London in 1989, for the many great albums you have released and for the inspiration you have given me and others.

ROOTS GO EAST: BACK IN THE USSR
20 APRIL 1989, *THE INDEPENDENT*

MAREK KOHN

The message has got across. There were no cries of *George Best*, or 'Why Are You Being So Reasonable Now?' For this tour, The Wedding Present have taken a break from sounding like The Smiths without the preciousness, and are performing an evening of traditional Ukrainian music.

Two senior figures stand out behind this unusual project. One is John Peel, the focus of the culture in which the Leeds based band have thrived – they now feature strongly in the upper reaches of the Festive Fifty, chosen annually by Peel's listeners, up there with The Smiths and New Order. The other is guitarist Solowka's father, who is Ukrainian.

This was Solowka Junior's night. Frontman Dave Gedge remained on the sidelines, bent gravely over his guitar, while the tousled Slav stood centre stage with mandolin and a beam of delight that never seemed to leave his face. The rough-hewn four piece was upgraded by the addition of Len Liggins and Roman Remeynes, instrumentalists, who concentrated on fiddle and mandolin.

The concerts had their genesis in a session recorded for Peel's show, later released as a mini LP *Ukrainski Vistupi V Johna Peela*. The recording itself does not quite do the idea justice. On the evidence of the show, however, all that was missing was the spirit of live performance.

The songs themselves come in two modes; the poignant, yearning ballad and its exuberant, rollicking antithesis. Both combined in the Ukrainian song, best known here, 'Davni Chasy' – recorded some time ago as 'Those Were The Days'. In the hands of The Wedding Present, it had a thrash inflection absent from Mary Hopkin's interpretation but that seemed to do it no harm.

It would be easy to dismiss this all as a bit of a joke, like the source of Ruritanian amusement that many Britons find in Albania. What is actually going on here is, surely, the essence of how a culture renews itself under conditions of migration; the new generation, playing the old melodies in its own idiom. The cultural exchange between Solowka and his fellow musicians was certainly effective; the audience has rather further to go. One crop-headed youth did leap onto the stage and succeed in executing some rudimentary Cossack-style kicks. His achievements paled, however, beside the display put on by the genuine article. At the climax of the show, on strode the men and women of the Reading Ukrainian Dance Troupe. The men wore square-cornered black hats, boots and baggy trousers. They leapt, kicked, and reminded the crowd who really invented break-dancing. The audience gave this magnificent display the applause it deserved. Their own performance was largely limited to individuals climbing on stage and dropping back onto their peers. But it is an infant culture. Ukrainians showed them what you can manage with a few hundred years' practice.

*

The Ukrainians weren't ahead of their time when they began their project, before modern Ukraine achieved independence. The need for what they do already existed. Ukraine needed explaining to the British public back then, when it was not appreciated as a nation with an identity of its own, and Ukrainian culture in Britain needed to be sustained. But those weren't pressing needs then. They became vital more than thirty years later, when Ukraine's independence was imperilled by an aggressor that denied its nationhood and its identity. Though nobody could have foreseen it at the time, what The Ukrainians were doing in 1989 anticipated what needs to be done today.

Looking at my account of the band's 1989 show, what leapt Hopak-like out at me was how similar the content was to that of the Ukrainian community events that I've been attending since refugees began to arrive from Ukraine in the spring and summer of 2022: traditional songs, modern ones in traditional idioms, and dances that speak of the nation too. These are communal performances, their spirit embodied by the choirs that seem to have come together in every town where Ukrainians have found themselves. Through performing their culture, the new Ukrainian communities are sustaining themselves and their nation far from their homeland.

They are also trying to share that culture with the wider communities around them, and trying to explain who they are as a nation, which is exactly what The Ukrainians were doing in the late 1980s. The point of noting that 'the' Ukraine was an imperial ploy, the definite article implying the country was merely a region, is certainly clearer now. It was a start, at least.

The Ukrainians also developed understanding among themselves, bringing together British musicians of Ukrainian heritage and ones without it. They brought contemporary musical styles to traditional forms, which is the kind of intercultural exchange that helps to renew diasporic cultures and to sustain them, enriching the connections between them and the wider communities of which they are part. The *Together For Ukraine* compilation of cover versions, by performers from a remarkable range of countries, backgrounds and musical genres, illustrates the richness of the connections they have made. And they haven't just kept on repeating themselves, either. They have deepened their understanding of Ukraine, engaging reflectively with the real country, rather than a sentimentalised image of it.

That's another respect in which they offer an example for supporters of Ukraine to follow. So is the simple fact that they have stayed with Ukraine for all this time. It shows commitment, and it also shows how rewarding an engagement with Ukrainian culture can be. The need for commitment will continue, and so will the rewards. Hopefully The Ukrainians will too!

THE WEDDING PRESENT: FROM RUSSIA WITH LOVE
22 APRIL 1989, *MELODY MAKER*

IAN GITTINS

How have four normal people from Leeds become the most successful Indie band of the late-eighties? Why have the trusty Punksters just released an album of Ukrainian folk songs called *Ukrainski Vistupi V Johna Peela*? How are they going to take this oddball venture on a major British tour this week?

Tell me, David. Do you have faith in The Wedding Present?

David Gedge: I have a complete lack of faith, really. To be honest. I live my life one day to the next, worried about what we're doing. I worry if it's good enough, if it's worth doing when I could be doing other things that might be more rewarding to me. On the whole, I've been satisfied. But this is an odd thing to do, isn't it? I do feel nervous about whether it'll actually work or not. It has to be a strange idea, to go on tour with folk music and play it to a rock audience, on strange instruments with lyrics they can't understand. I'm very apprehensive about how it's going to go.

There's a pause, a deep sigh, and then a grin.

David: Oh, I'm sure it'll be OK!

FROM KYIV TO THE KOSMOS

It was last November when *Ukrainski Vistupi V Johna Peela* was first due out. A huge, swelling, pathos-laden burst of energy, it comprised The Wedding Present, trusty Punksters, re-arranging old Ukrainian folk songs into their own zealous ways. Jagged, itchy and frenzied, the LP was like the band's normal hi-octane pop, and also like nothing on earth. The record was all set to appear when Red Rhino folded, and it had to spend five months locked in a warehouse.

Luck can sometimes work like that. Now the album is finally out, to a world where *glasnost* and Gorbachev's trip to Britain have made Russia a happening place. A topical media event. Where Simon Mayo plays The Wedding Present at breakfast time and new label RCA, bless 'em, want to fill a London record shop window with Russian dolls (the band don't agree). Where The Wedding Present are about to take their odd venture out on tour, and get their nerves tested rather severely…

It's not as odd as they think it is. *Ukrainski Vistupi…*, while obviously a departure from their usual tales of boy-meets-girl, bears all The Wedding Present hallmarks. The story in brief: guitarist Pete Solowka spent years listening to his Ukrainian father's old records, learnt to play some, and the band loved them. Push came to shove, a Peel session gave them the chance to air a few, and the idea of a record soon followed. Len Liggins, cult Leeds figure, ex-Sinister Cleaner and Slavic student, was called in to sing and play skrypka, balalaika and sopilka. Roman Remeynes brought his mandolin.

Onstage this time round, David Gedge will be standing at the back with his guitar and a bemused expression… So Peter, how hard was this stuff to record?

Peter: Easier than our normal stuff! Definitely! It's totally different. The normal Wedding Present stuff is very hi-tech now — well, you mightn't think so, but we do drums, bass, guitar all separate, go over it all again and again. The Ukrainian stuff, all we do is fix the mics up and play it straight off!

Len: And that rough live feel is crucial.

He's right. Critically, there's little to say about this venture. Musically, The Wedding Present have accurately mimicked the frenzied spirals and huge comic rhythms of the originals, the best being a breathless version of 'Those Were The Days' called 'Davni Chasy'. It's great party music. The live shows will be a riot. This is all they hope for, despite the educational booklet which comes with the LP. Did they do much research into all this?

Peter: Yeah, 'cos in our set we're doing half-a-dozen of our own songs, written in the Ukrainian style, and to get ideas for words I've read story-books and history books. But they're mostly folk-songs, popular tunes for 150 years. We can't pretend ours are of the same ilk. That would be arrogant.

Is normal Wedding Present music folky?

Len: I'm not sure people will be singing 'My Favourite Dress' round a camp-fire in the countryside in 200 years' time.

He has a point.

Peter: And we thought of taking this music to Ukraine, to play there, which would be great. But it's hard to find the time to do it. And I think it'd be quite strange, us playing Ukrainian pop songs in Kyiv. It could end up just like a Russian band coming to London and trying to play 'Greensleeves'.

The Wedding Present have no idea at all how this strange fare will go down with their followers, and are more than a little nervous. I'd guess it'll be just fine, but one last question, Pete. When you play this rowdy, exaggerated music, with its sense of high seriousness… won't it be hard to keep a straight face?

Peter: I haven't played it live yet. But I think it's all relative. When I play our normal stuff, I find it hard to keep a straight face…

UNIVERSITY OF EAST ANGLIA
29 APRIL 1989, NORWICH, UK

IAN MOXON

I have distant memories of a cracking Ukrainian Weddoes gig at the University of East Anglia, with my then-girlfriend Mandy and my mates Roger Denton and Pete Wylie. I bought the EP and played it to death.

CIVIC HALL
30 APRIL 1989, MIDDLETON, MANCHESTER, UK

HELEN MCINTYRE

I first heard the Ukrainian set done by The Wedding Present on John Peel's BBC radio programme and was immediately smitten. At my first opportunity to go to Manchester, our nearest big city, I bought the record and have loved it ever since. (I now own two copies of it, alongside all The Ukrainians releases.) I was 21 at the time and lived a very sheltered life in a small mill town in the Rossendale Valley in Lancashire and knew no one else who could possibly share my interest in Punk Folk music (or Folk Punk music) of the Ukrainian variety. To rectify this, I exposed my youngest brother to the music and he soon became a fan too. He was 15.

When The Wedding Present toured in 1989 to promote the Ukrainian songs, the nearest place I could see them was Middleton Civic Hall, two bus rides away from where I lived. Undeterred by the threat of multiple public transport journeys, I decided I would take my youngest brother with me so he could see the wonders of the music being played more live than the live studio sessions that John Peel had had a hand in. It would be the first concert experience for both of us and I knew it would be brilliant.

The only problem was I hadn't asked my mother's permission to take my younger brother, and as the concert grew closer and she found out that he was coming along with me on what seemed like an epic journey out of the Rossendale Valley, she banned me from taking him, stating that I was irresponsible and couldn't be trusted to keep him safe from harm. My response was to use the only bad language I ever used towards my mother, and I called her a 'silly cow'. The Folk Punk or Punk Folk influence was turning me rebellious and foul-mouthed.

On the evening of the concert, and disobeying my mother, I took my brother on the first bus which took us to Rochdale and then one from Rochdale to Middleton. We arrived at the venue and I was surprised to find it was seated, and that the seats were tiny wooden chairs bolted to the floor.

Although I hadn't been to a concert before, I'd often seen pictures of people standing at concerts in the *NME* and *Melody Maker*, so I was surprised that we would be expected to sit throughout such a lively set. However, as the music started up all of my mother's fears about my younger brother's safety were realised, when everyone in the audience stood on their infant school-sized chairs and began to push and shove and start up what I now know is a mosh pit. But it was a more precarious mosh pit than the average as it was raised above the ground and people were falling over the backs of the chairs in front and falling to the floor with gay abandon.

To my untrained concert-going eyes, it appeared to be a biggest fight I'd ever witnessed. (And I'd witnessed a few, being from a small northern town where fights started up if a pub played U2 in a Simple Minds-favoured area, or if you went to a pub a mile and a half up the road and were discovered to be 'out of your area', which could be detected in a very slight difference in the accent.) Sadly, the more I instructed my little brother not to join in, the more he did and the more he enjoyed it. The music was fab. The stress of ensuring my brother didn't come home covered in bruises not so much.

My mother was proved right about my irresponsibility levels once more that night, as I had forgotten that last buses usually all stop about the same time. The set went on longer than expected, to everyone's delight, and I did manage to get myself and my brother on the last bus from Middleton to Rochdale. But then we were left stranded in Rochdale, as the last bus from Rochdale had long since left.

I wrote a letter to the *NME* about the rough and tumble – well, the fighting nature – of the people attending the concert which Steve Lamacq responded to, though he must have wondered which stone I'd been living under not to expect a Punk experience to involve some pushing and shoving.

The moral of the story is that mothers are always right.

I moved to Leeds in 1991 because The Ukrainians had formed in 1990 and were based there and a lot of other bands were coming from the same area, and I wanted to be nearer to the music's source. I saw The Ukrainians at the *Heineken Festival* with my older sister in Roundhay Park in 1994, but there were no wooden chairs bolted to the grass and my sister drove us there so there was no danger of us missing our ride back (and we were both in our mid to late-20s by then, so Mother had no clue what we were up to). It was a very pleasant surprise to discover that my sister had discovered them and loved them as long and as heartily as I had over the years, and that we both still feel the same to this present day.

ADRIAN WHITE

In April 1989 The Wedding Present toured the Ukrainian stuff, playing the songs that no one could ever type up on a cassette sleeve! I was not happy when my mates said they weren't bothering to go and see them on this tour, as it wasn't really The Wedding Present.

That night I returned home from some dodgy part-time job to be called by one of my mates to tell me to dress up as we were going ten-pin bowling. Ten-pin bowling?

We were cool Indie lads – why were we doing that? 'Dress smart,' they said, so I went for the Eighties staple of white shirt, black shoes and black trousers – attire largely connected with 'lads' that liked Wham! and Dire Straits. When my mates picked me up they were all in jeans and t-shirts, so I took this to be an advantage to me in case we met any girls at the bowling alley. I was looking good!

The car headed towards Manchester. Surely there was a bowling alley closer than that, I thought? We eventually ended up in Middleton, just outside Rochdale. As we parked up, nowhere near a bowling alley, it suddenly struck me. My mates' laughter then confirmed everything – we were going to see The Wedding Present doing the Ukrainian stuff!

In we went and took up our usual place in the middle, in David's eye-line, where the hard action was. But my joy was tinged by the embarrassment of my attire and the funny looks I was getting – I looked like some sort of newbie, and when you are a hardened Wedding Present gig-goer that's not a good feeling. My white shirt was ripped to shreds and my posh black work shoes scuffed and crushed beyond repair. Which made it even sweeter in the end.

CHARLIE BRIDGE

The Wedding Present played my – and Gedge's – hometown, and supported themselves with Pete's Ukrainians. David had a brand-new guitar that night, still with the price tag on – £115. After the gig, me and my mates – Andy Royle, Chris Pomfret and Dean Heywood – were outside the venue when some guy approached us trying to sell us said guitar. He'd managed to steal it. We liberated the guitar and took it back into the venue to give it back to David. David came out and thanked us and we had a good chat. We were all a bit pissed and teenagers but – fair play to him – he had a chat nonetheless. I'm certain to this day he thought we'd nicked the guitar and then had a prick of conscience, but I can assure him that wasn't the case.

ALARIC NEVILLE, THE UKRAINIANS SOUND ENGINEER

The first member of what would become my touring buddies that I can recall meeting was Pete Solowka back in 1982 or '83. We were both at Leeds University then, Pete a few years ahead of me. There was an Indie music night at the Student's Union, 'Music For the Masses', which put on bands before switching to an Indie and Goth DJ set. Pete's pre-Wedding Present band The Chorus, who also featured Simon Smith on drums, headlined one such night and my own modest Punk funk outfit, The Maracas, supported them. In your late teens or early 20s, a couple of years' seniority still counted for a lot, but beyond simple age, Pete and his band appeared like proper musicians because they had that holy grail of the wannabe rock star, their own proper seven-inch 45rpm single. The cachet of being on nodding terms with members of The Chorus was soon inflated by first Pete and then Simon becoming members of The Wedding Present, a band who would go on to have many more vinyl releases to their name.

In 1986, I opened a 16-track recording studio in Leeds with a large live room, drum booth and control room. One of the local bands that booked out the studio primarily to rehearse in was The Sinister Cleaners, featuring two ex-Chorus members, Simon Smith and Johnny Parkes. Alongside them was 'The Legendary' Len Liggins on guitar and vocals. Len then turned up again as a producer of a session for another local band, Ket Kolomper, and a friendship developed.

I first met and spoke to the third member of the founding triumvirate of The Ukrainians, Roman Remeynes, at the legendary long lost Leeds venue, The Duchess [Of York] on 31 August 1989. By this time, I was managing Leeds band The Bridewell Taxis, who were on tour with The Inspiral Carpets during August and September. We put on our own headline gig at The Duchess in the middle of their *Find Out Why* tour as a way of subsidising the paltry £50 a night we were getting as support act. As a promoter, I stumbled across an opportunity too good to pass up when a friend happened to mention he had a pen pal staying with him who was a real Ukrainian musician from Kyiv, Gennady Rabatsiev. The Wedding Present had released their Ukrainian John Peel sessions LP in February that year and were the hip, happening, bankable band in Leeds at the time, just about to release their first top 40 hit, 'Kennedy'. Cheekily, I added Gennady to the Duchess line-up billed as a 'Genuine Ukrainian Musician from Kyiv'.

Sure enough, the speculation everywhere was that this might be code for a guest spot from a member of – or the whole of – The Wedding Present. We sold out the venue, cramming as many punters as was physically possible into the steaming sweaty pub and bankrolling the rest of our own support tour in the process. Gennady had no idea what he was in the middle of or why he had been offered a chance to play a packed-out venue in Leeds. He was a sweet guy who sang some songs with a guitar borrowed from me and, once the audience got over the disappointment of him not being David Gedge, he was actually cheered and applauded.

One member of the audience who was not applauding was Roman. Although Gennady considered himself Ukrainian, he wrote and sang in Russian like many of his contemporary countrymen at that time. Roman came backstage grumbling, huffing and puffing, spoiling for an argument as he felt he had been cheated into listening to songs in the despised Russian language. All I could do was introduce him to Gennady and leave them to it, glancing over now and again to see Roman in full declamatory flow berating Gennady's unpatriotic choice of language.

Touring with The Ukrainians and visiting Ukraine itself in the following years, I came to understand the cultural politics of language was a defining one for the newly independent nation. I also got to know Roman very well and valued him as a friend; I know the one thing he enjoyed more than playing Ukrainian music was arguing about Ukrainian music along with anything else he had an opinion on, so I'm sure he enjoyed his night backstage at The Duchess pointing out in great detail all of poor old Gennady's errors.

WLODEK NAKONECZNY

My adventure with The Ukrainians started on a summer afternoon in 1989. On Polish radio, I heard sounds that intrigued me. These were fragments of the 'Ukrainian' session for John Peel by The Wedding Present.

The Wedding Present were known in the alternative community. But to take specifically 'Ukrainian' folk songs...? It was strange. I use quotation marks consciously because there were also Russian hits of the Soviet era ('Katrusya' and 'Davni Chasy'). For Ukrainian-centrics and patriots it was jarring; along with the conclusion that the musicians knew something, but not quite what.

I didn't have high expectations of Western musicians, even if someone there was discovering their roots, because the historical and cultural nuances of this part of Europe with a bit of Asia might have been too complicated for them. For me, the Ukrainian part was more important. And even – and I don't hide it – the fact that the album was not tainted with the Russian language, which would have ruined it by positioning it as an ignorant joke with a lousy, political subtext. So there was not Russian language, because the Soviet hit 'Katyusha', Ukrainian-ised into 'Katrusya', was 'muttered' and 'Davni Chasy' was 'la-la-la-la-ed'. This compromise was acceptable to me, because the rest, although with a foreign accent, was already sung in Ukrainian.

The last track – 'Verkhovyno' – had me on the edge of my seat with its trance drive and toasts 'for the freedom of Ukraine!' – a timeless message, which the world did not understand then, but seems to understand more today... The freedom of Ukraine, which I had been waiting for so much, still seemed vague against the background of the decaying but still active Moscow empire.

In 1989, I used to study Ukrainian Philology at the University of Warsaw. I was a Ukrainian born in Poland, raised to respect my own tradition and culture. My sensitivity and tastes were also shaped by Punk rock and alternative music. In the mid-'80s, I was involved in animating the Ukrainian alternative scene in Poland around the band Oseledec (1985-87), the world's first Ukrainian-singing post-Punk band. From 1988, together with my then partner Larysa Szost, we implemented her idea of publishing a 'zine' called *Vidryzhka* (which translates as 'Burp' in English!) in the Ukrainian language, and a year later releasing Ukrainian underground music on the Koka label (later Koka Records). In 1990, we had already published several editions of the magazine and released several albums, including both Oseledec and other bands from Ukraine: Vopli Vidopliasova (aka VV), Kolezkiy Assesor, Braty Hadiukiny and Banita Bajda.

While searching material for the 'zine, I started looking for contacts for The Wedding Present. A journalist from the UK, Taras Kuzio (now Professor of Political Science at the National University of Kyiv-Mohylan Academy), gave me an album and contact for the mandolinist Roman Revkniv aka Roman Remeynes.

I wrote a letter to Roman about our label and zine, asking him to write something about the project. He scribbled something about The Wedding Present and a little more about his own band, Idiot Gods. To our delight it was in Ukrainian! He included press materials, an Idiot Gods audio-cassette and a VHS of The Wedding Present concert. We printed his text and were able to spread the information to people.

THE UKRAINIANS

REBECCA WALKLEY

Between 1987 and 1993, the three members of what was to become The Ukrainians – Pete, Len and Roman – were feeling their way around their new project, singing and playing traditional songs but also starting to write their own material. At the time Ukraine was inching itself away from Soviet control until, in 1991, the country proclaimed its independence. In the same year, The Ukrainians brought out their first eponymously-titled album on Cooking Vinyl Records.

Len, Pete and Roman's first experience of Ukraine was in 1990. When they arrived in Kyiv, they were met by a couple of people in a car at the airport. They had to stop for petrol and joined a long queue of cars. However, their car screeched to the front of the queue and immediately got served. When Len asked how they managed that, he was told that they had threatened to set fire to the petrol station if they didn't give them petrol.

It wasn't just the organisers they had to worry about. The food in Ukraine had been contaminated by the fall-out from the Chornobyl nuclear power station accident a few years before, in 1986. They were told in particular not to eat fish or mushrooms as these foods were highly contaminated. They were also advised not to go out on building rooftops as the dust was still highly radioactive. When they arrived in the capital their hosts served up… you've guessed it… dishes of fish and mushrooms, and the film maker travelling with them insisted on shooting footage of the band out on the atmospheric dusty rooftop of the block of flats where they were staying.

While they were in the country, the band had planned to make a video. They smuggled in a VHS video cassette player to pay the film makers, as these were impossible to buy in Ukraine. The band was driven to the The Museum of Folk Architecture and Way of Life on the outskirts of Kyiv where the alleged Miss Kyiv arrived to be filmed with them. Their filmmaker proceeded to make a video of the Ukrainian beauty queen and the three Yorkshire musicians, dancing together while singing and playing 'Oi Divchino' over and over again. To an onlooker, it must have looked very surreal.

LEN

Peter, Roman and myself flew out to Ukraine in October 1990 to make a video for 'Oi Divchino'. Shot in Kyiv's outdoor Museum of National Folk Architecture and Way of Life, it was the first pop video to be produced entirely in the east for a Western band. We asked the crew if they could find a female dancer and we were told, 'We will find you the most beautiful girl in Kyiv.' 'OK,' we thought, but the next day Miss Kyiv herself turned up for the shoot… or at least that's what we were told.

(clockwise from top left) Peter Solowka, Len Liggins & Peter, Len & Roman Revkniv visiting Ukraine in 1990; Len explaining to one of the locals about why they were in Ukraine; in Kyiv whilst students & hunger strikers were demonstrating; Roman & Pete

(clockwise from top left) Ukraine 1990: witnessing demos in Maidan (now Independence Square), Kyiv; Peter makes the call; Peter, Len & Roman in Kyiv; Peter & Len; Peter being filmed for the 'Oi Divchino' video; Peter

PETER

When we were still The Wedding Present, we thought it would be a great idea to film what would have been the first ever music video in Ukrainian and to shoot it in Ukraine. Korda Marshall said, 'That's a great idea – can you set it up?' Someone managed to contact somebody who was part of an independent TV company in Ukraine. The Soviet system was falling apart at this time. With Perestroika coming in and countries fighting for independence, you could start to travel all over Europe and an 'independent television company' in Ukraine just meant that a group of people had control of the state TV assets which meant, 'We can make a video for you.'

We said, 'How do you want to be paid?' and they said, 'There is no real facility for us to take any money from the West. Instead, we would like a VHS-to-VHS recorder.' These didn't exist in the Soviet Union, but having a machine like that would enable them to do tape-to-tape copies and distribute films, etc., even do bootlegs. We said, 'How would we get it to you?' and they said, 'You bring it through customs.' We said, 'If we bring it through customs, it's written on a roster of stuff and we're supposed to leave with it or we get charged,' and they said, 'Well, if you get charged that's just the price you pay for the video. And if you don't get charged, you've not paid for the video, have you?' So we got RCA records to buy the VHS-to-VHS recorder.

Me, Len and Roman went out to do the video. I'd never been to that part of the world before and when we landed at the airport, they had arranged a welcoming party for us. This was probably one of their first contacts with the West and they gave us some Ukrainian embroidered shirts as a gift. Roman spoke Ukrainian very fluently, Len spoke a bit and I'm looking round, going, 'What is going on here?'

They took us back to this great big block of flats, which looked like something you might see in East Germany, but the flat itself was quite nice and spacious inside and very well heated. Someone brought out an accordion and played music, and they cooked food for us and got the vodka out. The only person who spoke any English was the director of the video. He was telling me his ideas for the video and he said, 'I will do this' and 'I will do that', but I had no idea what the video was going to be like, and it ended up being far more folky than we ever wanted it to be. They were interpreting the lyrics literally, which were taken from folk themes. The song 'Oi Divchino' is about someone who is in love with a young woman, and he wants her to kiss him and then fly off into the golden sunshine together on the back of a horse! The director's interpretation of the video was very close to that. We would have gone for something a little more dark and more industrial, but we couldn't change it by that stage.

Then they took us the National Museum of Folk Architecture and Way of Life, just outside Kyiv, in a minibus with their crew and their cameras, and they'd arranged for some musicians to be there and some people in national dress. In Soviet times, the only way you could express yourself in the Ukrainian culture was as a jokey peasant. Anything that was modern or contemporary was just not allowed. In their view, Ukrainian culture belonged in the villages. It was in the past. It was going to die out and be replaced by modern Russian culture. So in the video you had these folk musicians with double basses and people doing folk dancing to our music in these old village scenes with straw-roofed buildings and old windmills in the background. It wasn't what we wanted. The video never got played anywhere.

We were only there for two nights. But we gave them the video recorder and they were very happy about it, and when we went back through customs, they said, 'Have you got your documents?' They didn't speak English and we said we didn't know what they were talking about. After a few exchanges where the border guards did the "they don't understand us – let's shout it louder" technique, we kept shrugging our shoulders. Eventually, they gave up and waived us through. If we'd tried that two years before, we'd have been locked up, but because the whole system was falling apart, no one cared.

LEN

What we didn't realise when we were presented with an official document in Ukrainian legalese by the customs people was that we were supposed to bring the video recorder back with us on our return to the UK. We came back through customs without it of course, and all we could do was shrug our shoulders at them when they very officiously questioned us regarding its whereabouts. It was really intimidating but what were they going to do? Put us in prison? Eventually they let us go.

PETER

It was on that trip that Roman's paranoia came out. Considering the stories he'd grown up with, about how the KGB were always watching him, it was very brave of Roman to come to Ukraine with us. But he was really, really suspicious and anxious all the time. He was thinking everyone was listening to him and that at any minute he was going to be taken away because this was some sort of trap to capture Ukrainian nationalists. Instead of coming back with me and Len, when he was supposed to get on the train home he did a runner and disappeared. I think he went to visit family or villages near to where his family was from, but no one's really quite sure. He got back to the UK five or six days later, and when he arrived back he was completely changed. He was really paranoid.

He started avoiding people and hiding from people, and he eventually got to the stage where he was hospitalised for that. Actually visiting Ukraine brought all those "they're out to get you" fears that his identity had dictated to him, and those phases of going in and out of being able to socialise with people characterised his four years of membership of

(clockwise from top left) Ukraine 1990: Roman, Peter & Len in the Maidan, Kyiv; Peter & Len; Len, Roman & Peter pose amongst the posters in a pedestrian underpass; Peter; Len

(clockwise from top left) Ukraine 1990: Len, Roman & Peter in the Maidan, Kyiv; Roman, Len & Peter; Len; Len & Peter; Roman; Roman, Peter & Len

the band. There were times when he would play with us and times when he just couldn't because he thought he might stand out too much. It was bordering on schizophrenia. So although he was involved in the very early days of The Ukrainians – in '91 and early '92, he did the recording for the *Vorony* album – he then faded in and out of the band.

So we had another mandolin player for the shows after that, who was Miroslaw Stebiwka, who was from the Ukrainian community in Wolverhampton.

JOHN BOOCOCK, MUSIC REVIEWS, *LEEDS OTHER PAPER*

In 1991, my friend Dave and I were very keen to climb Jebel Toubkal which, at over 13,000 feet, is the highest mountain in North Africa's Atlas Mountains. I took with me my newly purchased Dixons (remember them?) Walkman-copy cassette player. Limited to two cassettes, I decided to take two recent review copies sent to me by Cooking Vinyl.

At one point in our trip we shared our taxi with an assortment of locals including a woman who had a chicken in a wooden cage. The taxi turned up and to our amazement it was a 1959 pink Cadillac convertible. Morrocco never disappoints. The roof was down, it was a bright sunny May morning, and we were heading north – excellent! The driver kept fiddling about with the car radio but failed to find a station which was even barely audible. The Cadillac did have a cassette player and I offered the driver one of my cassettes. He shoved it in, turned up the volume and the chicken in the wooden cage went loopy. The driver plonked the Cadillac in a ditch after swerving all over the road. The cassette player had turned itself off and spewed out lengths of the offending tape.

Feathers flew, a woman sat next to me started shouting at the driver and kicking me. Two small children started crying. I suggest this is the first and last time ever a Ukrainians song had frightened a chicken, caused a minor road accident, and made children cry on a sunny May morning in southern Morocco. The song? Appropriately it was 'Dity Plachut' ('The Children Are Crying') from an album which still reminds me of my trip to the Atlas Mountains. (I wonder what effect my other cassette, Andy White's 'Himself', would have had on the chicken…?)

PETER

There was a little bit of time between working on *Bizarro* as The Wedding Present and other things we were doing, so we went into the studio and recorded five of those Ukrainian songs that we'd been playing live – 'Oi Divchino', 'Cherez Richku, Cherez Hai', 'Zavtra', 'Hopak' and 'Tebe Zhdu'. They ended up appearing on the first Ukrainians album, because The Wedding Present were the rhythm section that started The Ukrainians off. So when we talk about the first Ukrainians album, the rhythm section on half of the album was still The Wedding Present.

We did one more recording session under the RCA contract with Len and Roman and a session musician, Yuri Babchuk from Stockport, who played the tsymbaly (a form of Ukrainian hammer dulcimer) on the track 'Slava Kobzarya'. That produced slower, more atmospheric tracks and those two sessions went together to form what would've been another Wedding Present Ukrainian-style eastern European album, but ended up being The Ukrainians because I was no longer with The Wedding Present.

The last Wedding Present album I worked on was *Seamonsters*, which was recorded in the winter of 1990 near Minneapolis with Steve Albini and released in 1991. Trying to be in The Wedding Present and The Ukrainians clouded things. You do your music and you get your marketing ready. You do your press interviews and your publicity and you do your tour. And the problem we found was that because the first record that we did on RCA was the Ukrainian one, that was the reference point for a lot of journalists. Journalists who had followed us all the way through weren't distracted by it, but when you get into the major league you attract a different set of journalists and a different set of media, and even if you tell people you're not going to talk about it, they want to talk about the Ukrainian stuff so you can't avoid it. I found it really frustrating. Me and David would do interviews and we wanted to talk about the best album we'd done, which was *Bizarro*, and halfway through the journalist would be talking about the Ukrainian record and its effect, and say, 'Is there any more Ukrainian music coming out?' It doesn't help you. It was a psychological thing where it was definitely having an effect on the way The Wedding Present was perceived. I don't think anyone cared about it at the start of the Ukrainian story, but it was becoming a hindrance and not a help.

Another frustrating thing was that I knew it was something I wanted to develop. There was no band name. It was just Ukrainian music, 'the Ukrainian project'. And you could feel the tension in the band. It wasn't being in two bands. It was having two personalities, two faces, two sides in a world which didn't fit together. Maybe it would be easier today, because the world is a more diverse place. But it just created a tension that you didn't want. Because you have this ethnic background and you feel that it needs to be expressed in some way. It means that you end up not sitting in the place that you were very, very happy being in, which was The Wedding Present. There was nothing about The Wedding Present that I was unhappy about at all.

DAVID GEDGE

Peter, Len and Roman had started writing original music in the Ukrainian folk style and so, somewhat inevitably, they decided to form their own offshoot band, which they called The Ukrainians. This was while Peter was still in The Wedding Present, so when they went to record an album, they featured Simon Smith and Keith Gregory as the rhythm section. I also played on a couple of tracks, but obviously Peter can play the guitar so he didn't really need me to do as much in the studio.

Sometimes, artists record material for major record companies which the label doesn't think is commercial enough. If that happens, they can just refuse to release it. You hear these horror stories of bands making an album which then never comes out. And, because the record label owns it, they can stop anybody else releasing it, too. But The Wedding Present had a clause written into our contract with RCA which said that if they didn't want to release something we'd recorded, we were free to go to a different company. I don't think they wanted to release that Ukrainians album, even though they'd funded it, and so that's why it came out on Cooking Vinyl Records.

Keith, Simon and I asked Peter to leave The Wedding Present in 1991 because we'd decided that we wanted a change in the band. It wasn't totally amicable but it was friendly enough for him to continue working with us, even after we'd replaced him with a new guitarist called Paul Dorrington. He was doing our accounts for a while. I'm sure he'd say he was disappointed to be leaving The Wedding Present but, at the same time, he did enjoy doing the Ukrainian stuff and this obviously freed him up to do that.

LEN

A 'Those Were The Days' single by the Weddoes' Ukrainian line-up would have been great as far as I was concerned, but it would have completely altered the trajectory of The Wedding Present. They didn't want to have to be asked to play that for the rest of their career, and understandably so. There was no way the band could go on with the two different musical identities and the runaway success of the Ukrainian "side project" was confusing the fans.

RCA had already asked us to record a studio album of Ukrainian material and half of it had already been completed by the Ukrainian line-up of me, Pete, Roman, David, Keith, and Simon. However, halfway through putting that together, it was decided that The Wedding Present and The Ukrainian Wedding Present line-up would need to go their separate ways. It was all discussed very rationally. There were no meltdowns or bricks through windows. The Wedding Present really isn't like that.

PETER

The Wedding Present had this album of Ukrainian music ready to go but the frictions between myself and The Wedding Present came to a head. They said, 'We don't think you're an asset to this band anymore,' which was understandable in retrospect, but it meant that RCA Records had this recorded album and didn't know what to do with it. Because I was no longer in The Wedding Present, I no longer had a contract with RCA Records.

The contract is worded in such a way that the label signs the concept (The Wedding Present) and although the individual band members sign the contract, there are clauses within the contract which say that if a person isn't in the band anymore, they cease to be on the contract. So if you're out of the band you're out of RCA Records. Which technically meant that if The Wedding Present didn't want to release the album it wasn't going to get released. RCA could have released it anyway, but they decided it was too much of a gamble and so they sold the album rights to Cooking Vinyl Records, who had a reputation for taking on bands who had left major labels. And they released a lot of world music, so it was definitely the right place for The Ukrainians. Martin Goldschmidt, who runs Cooking Vinyl, is quite excited by anything new. Korda Marshall may not have negotiated with Cooking Vinyl himself, but he would've directed somebody to do so because he would've thought, 'We can get some of our assets back.' Several thousand pounds had been spent recording the album.

LEN

So, we had to think of a name for this new group that Peter, me and Roman were going to launch. We had a few in the pot, some of which were truly awful, but I really liked the idea of 'The Ukrainians' because it sounded confident and definitive.

PETER

Retrospectively, The Ukrainians isn't a great name for the band. But when we were deciding on the name and the artwork, we were considering lots of different world music names that you couldn't get your head around. 'How do you say these words if you are from the West?' These names were going to put us into a pigeonhole when no one knew who we were. Then Korda Marshall from RCA said, 'Why don't you call yourselves 'Ukrainian' or 'The Ukrainians'?' We said 'that's really simple' and he said, 'Yes, but it symbolises what you've done.'

There wasn't even a country called Ukraine then. It was still part of the Soviet Union, which was going through Perestroika and the independence movement, so calling ourselves The Ukrainians seemed quite reasonable and almost quite rebellious as a name. It would be like calling yourselves 'The Kurds' or 'The Kurdistan Music System'. Nobody could've known in the spring of 1991 that there was going to be an independent country called Ukraine after years of struggle. But just before the album came out, there was a referendum in which the people of Ukraine voted for independence, so Ukraine officially announced its independence just before the record came out. Some people thought we were jumping on the bandwagon calling ourselves The Ukrainians. We had the same problem in 2022, when we started doing the benefit concerts after the war started, and got quite a few negative comments on social media. In hindsight, it would've been better to have a world music sort of name. But back in my 20s, if you'd asked me if I thought there would ever be an independent Ukraine, I would've said, 'Not in my lifetime. It won't happen in the next 500 years.'

'OI DIVCHINO'
RELEASED 29 JULY 1991

LEN

The Ukrainians were going to have a twelve-inch vinyl single out! Hooray, our first release. I couldn't wait! We chose 'Oi Divchino' and 'Zavtra' from the album plus a track called 'Kolyadka', which was an experiment in writing a song for the Christmas season based on the festive songs of the ancient Ukrainian folk tradition. There was also a live version of a song Pete and I had written called 'Sertsem i Dusheyu' ('With Heart And Soul'). It was a desk recording from a gig at the Middleton Civic Hall in Manchester on 30 April 1989, the last of the eight UK shows we did to promote the *Ukrainski Vistupi V Johna Peela* album.

I must admit I didn't expect too much in the way of music press reviews in the UK, because this release was technically by The Ukrainians and not The Wedding Present. However, some weeks later I walked to the Merrion Centre in Leeds and bought an *NME* just in case the single had been reviewed. It had, and it was 'Single of the Week'!

PETER

The first Ukrainians album was just called *The Ukrainians*. We released a twelve-inch single from it which got into the Indie charts, almost certainly from Wedding Present fans buying it as a collector's item.

The artwork for the single, and the album that followed it, was done by our friend Tony Gresko. He was actually on stage with us at The Town and Country Club gig in 1989 as a dancer. The album cover had a stylised Kozak in the front of some phrases from a Taras Shevchenko poem (Ukraine's national poet – the equivalent of Shakespeare to the English). The script roughly translates as 'teach yourselves' and is meant as a motivation to learn about your history and roots. We use the lyric in the track 'Slava Kobzarya' on the album.

LEN

The Kozak occupies an important place in Ukrainian history and folklore, which is why we used an image of one on the front cover of our first album. The Ukrainian word 'Kozak' comes from the same Turkic root as our word 'cossack'. Kozaks were an eastern Slavic people, many of whom were descended from runaway agricultural labourers escaping their feudal landlords. They set up a semi-independent military republic in Ukraine in the 15th and 16th centuries.

GORDON CLARK

Oi Divchino - A

The Ukrainians brought a whole new genre of music to the world. The world is a better place as a result. My favourite song is 'Oi Divchino'. It was the one we'd always sing along to when we'd had a few. I still listen to The Ukrainians every night. Some of those songs I listen to 200 times in a year.

WALDEMAR JANUSZCZAK, ART CRITIC & TV PRODUCER

The first song I remember hearing by The Ukrainians was 'Oi Divchino'. I don't remember where I heard it. All I remember is that once I heard it, I couldn't stop listening. Over and over and over again, I played it. Someone was speaking to my heart. And they were doing it in a language my heart understood immediately, even if I didn't. Not all the words anyway.

I'm ethnically Polish not Ukrainian, but the two languages are pretty similar and certainly similar enough for me to know that 'divchino' must be the Ukrainian equivalent of 'dziewczyno', which means 'girl'. 'Oi' is a standard Slavic grunt meaning something like 'oh' in English. So 'Oi Divchino' would be 'Oh Girl'. I was listening to a love song. Of course I was!

Not that I actually needed the words to tell me this. It was obvious from the singer's soft opening smooch that the guy was dreaming about a woman. And the typical Slavic way the song gets faster and faster and faster was the way that Slav blood always starts to pump when love enters the door.

Did you know that the English word 'slave' comes from 'Slav'? A couple of millenniums back, we Slavs were the go-to slaves of Europe. The Vikings would sail down the Volga and sell us to the Turks on the Black Sea. Our memories don't remember this. But our hearts can never forget. When a girl enslaves us, we know it and we show it. 'Oi Divchino, yaka zh ty mylen'ka'. 'I love you girl. You're so dear to me. I need to protect you.'

So there I was, unable to get the love music out of my mind, obsessed with The Ukrainians. What The Pogues had done for Irish music, The Ukrainians were doing for us Slavs: mixing folk and Punk; quickening the pulse to vodka speeds; transporting us from over here to over there. I played *The Ukrainians* EP so often I scratched it out, and had to go on Discogs to find another.

Fast forward a couple of decades and it's February 2022, and that bastard Putin has ordered the invasion of Ukraine. He's already annexed Crimea in 2014. Now the pool of putrescence is back to finish the job.

As it happens, Poles and Ukrainians have what is known as a "chequered past". For much of their history they have mistrusted each other and fought. My mother, who grew up near Lviv when it was a Polish city, loved some Ukrainians, but was unsure about the others. Her memories were sometimes cruel.

But there is one glue so strong, so utterly unbreakable, that it will always cement our two nations together: Russia. If you are positioned where Ukraine and Poland are positioned in Europe, you have no choice but to hate the Russians. The bastards are always invading you, diminishing you, partitioning you, trying to subjugate you. When the Russians invaded Ukraine in 2022, they forced Polish hearts into the conflict. We stand by our Slav brothers. We feel your pain.

A few weeks after the invasion, I was sent to Ukraine by my newspaper, *The Sunday Times*, and asked to make a short film about the visit by the Polish Cultural Institute. It's not the kind of gig I would usually go on – I'm an art critic for Christ's sake – but this was beyond choice. The brain whispered 'no', but the heart screamed 'yes' as loudly as Len Liggins in a Ukrainians encore.

The film I made was about art – how the Ukrainian people were transporting their precious national treasures from the East to the West. Hiding them where it was safer. How art, in times of war, gets to mean something special.

I needed music for the film. Something that grabbed the heart. The moment I crossed the border I knew what it had to be… 'Oi divchino, divchino divchinon'ko…'. Because love conquers all.

THE UKRAINIANS
RELEASED 26 AUGUST 1991

LEN

The first album was released on vinyl, CD and cassette in 1991. Five tracks ('Oi Divchino', 'Hopak', 'Zavtra', 'Cherez Richku, Cherez Hai' and 'Tebe Zhdu') were recorded with The Wedding Present at Great Linton Manor studios in Milton Keynes. It was a residential studio built into a 17th-century manor and was pretty impressive. The studio was downstairs, with a huge window overlooking the grounds, and our accommodation was upstairs. My biggest surprise was being told there was a chef on hand and that each day we should let him know what we would like to eat. I remember saying to him, 'What if we want a vegetable curry at three o'clock in the morning?' 'Just ask,' he said. It seemed so decadent!

The second set of tracks ('Ty Moyi Radoshchi', 'Slava Kobzarya', 'Dity Plachut', 'Pereyidu' and 'Son') were recorded at Woodlands studio in West Yorkshire's Castleford, right next to a very stinky meat rendering plant. Our producer was Harri Kakoulli, who used to be the bass player in Squeeze. Harri had a fondness for baggy woollen clothes and drove a Capri like my Dad's. He had me and Paul captivated by his story that his second car was a big pink American Cadillac, but he wouldn't drive it from London to Leeds because it only did 8 miles to the gallon! He's a lovely guy – a proper Londoner with a Greek Cypriot background. In the early days my violin playing was a bit tentative and basic, and when Harri first heard me play it in the studio he said to the other guys, 'I like Len's fiddle playing. It's sad, innit?' and then he roared with laughter.

PETER

With the first Ukrainians album, the one I call the transition album between The Wedding Present and The Ukrainians, Korda Marshall wanted to lift the standard a little bit and we were quite happy with that, because the record that had been released as the Peel Sessions album was just recorded live and fast and furious. It has a certain dynamic to it, but it wasn't quite as good as what you'd expect a world music album to be.

And Korda suggested that we use a producer. Now with the Wedding Present set up, the idea of using a producer was a scary thing. As soon as someone mentions a producer, you feel that someone's imposing a style on you, and the only time we didn't feel like that with The Wedding Present was when we worked with Steve Albini on *Seamonsters*, because we chose to work with him.

We didn't know anyone who made world music albums, let alone produced them, but Korda suggested someone who had worked on the pop music side but had a very eastern ethnic background. He said, 'I know someone called Harri Kakoulli. He used to play bass with Squeeze in the early days.' He said, 'He doesn't play with the group anymore but he's been involved in all sorts of music projects to do mainly with his Eastern and Greek and Cypriot backgrounds, and I think he'll be a really, really good mix for you.'

We met him and I was really surprised, because if you didn't know he had a Greek background, he just sounded to me like somebody from the East End of London with his accent and the way he talked. But as soon as he started talking about music, and he'd obviously listened to a few of the things that we'd done, we realised that he was as excited about the idea of working with some eastern European musicians as we were about trying to raise the standard of what we did a little bit.

He had a very, very smiling, relaxed idea of working with us, but he was very firm as well.

He was particularly keen on making sure the melodies were really clear in the music and he said that sometimes in the music that we'd used the melodies didn't come through the thrash as much as they should. I couldn't criticise that opinion, so we worked very much on making sure that the melodies and harmonies had a clarity that enhanced our music.

He particularly liked the sessions when the rest of The Wedding Present weren't there. When they were, and we were playing the fast and furious stuff, that was almost pre-determined. You couldn't really move that because it had The Wedding Present's machine behind it. But when he got into a situation where he was working on songs with me, Len and Roman, there was a lot more flexibility and dynamism. And Harri was really good at pulling out the sounds on some of those more sensitive tracks on the album.

One of the best phrases that he used was about Len's violin playing. Len was always a little bit insecure, unfairly I think, about his violin playing, because a lot of people that you see on the world music scene are often superbly accomplished Celtic fiddle players. Len never thought that he was in that league but he was absolutely fine. Harri was in the studio with us and he listened to Len playing the violin part and he said, 'I like your violin, Len. It's sad, isn't it?' It was one of those beautiful double-edged phrases.

LEN

After we lost the RCA connection, Cooking Vinyl agreed to release the album, which would have been towards the end of 1991. It did well, selling in a lot of territories outside the UK. If I remember rightly, it even sold 6,000 copies in Israel.

We might have been getting records sold on the other side of the planet, but our recording experiences revolved very much around the aforementioned West Yorkshire town of Castleford. Castleford suffered greatly during the 1980s when Margaret Thatcher ensured that Wheldale Colliery closed following the 1985 miners' strike. Proud grown men were reduced to tears when their livelihoods suddenly disappeared. Tough rugby league supporters became shadows of their former selves, emasculated by unemployment. They were hard, Castleford blokes, and they weren't keen on people from that London, like me. My first personal experience of this was late one night after a hard day in the studio. I was so tired that I couldn't find my way out of the town and back to Leeds, so I thought I'd better ask for directions. Luckily it was pub chucking out time, so I drew into the car park of the Prince of Wales' Feathers and approached a small gang of very drunken lads. 'Excuse me,' I asked politely, 'Would you mind directing me to Leeds Road, please?' They all stared at me, and quick as a flash one blurted out, 'Fuck off you soft, southern, four-eyed cunt'. It flowed like poetry.

Another window onto the world of the Wakefield district was a lunchtime visit to a Castleford sandwich shop. I took a list with me with the band orders on. You need to remember that down south at this time, fillings like smoked salmon and cream cheese or avocado with chilli jam were pretty standard fare. There were two grim-faced old ladies standing behind the counter wearing aprons and hairnets. I walked up to the counter and started to read out the orders.

'Cheese or 'am,' one of them interrupted.

'Er, OK, cheese please. Could I have three on brown…'

'White,' she barked.

'… with salad?', I asked nervously.

She fixed me between the eyes, took a deep intake of breath, and through gritted teeth angrily muttered one single, solitary, monosyllabic word…

'NO!'

My best memory of Roman during the writing of the first album is going round to his house one Saturday morning. Pete had given us a tape with chord sequences and a melody on. Pete wanted to use a folksong chorus and I remember saying, 'I think it would be good if we had our own tune using those chords.' I went round to Roman's with the express idea that, by lunchtime, we would have the lyrics for the whole song. Being more fluent in Ukrainian, speaking it at home with his mum and dad, Roman was better at throwing out phrases than I was, because my Ukrainian was much more academic. So I had a piece of paper and a pencil, and he suggested phrases and I would write them down. And when we had all these phrases, we kept the best, threw some out, assembled what was left and, sure enough, by lunchtime we had the finished lyric. It was an interesting process and we never did that for any other song. That song was 'Cherez Richku, Cherez Hai', which became an important song for the band. It now gets sung and played in Ukraine itself, taught in schools as if it were a folk song that had been around for hundreds of years.

That was the only song where we collaborated. Roman wrote the lyrics for two of the other songs on our first album, *The Ukrainians*, and I wrote the rest. Roman's biggest contribution really was that he was a fantastic mandolin player.

PETER

One of my favourite songs from the first album is 'Dity Plachut'. It's prayer-like. Even if you can't understand the lyrics, you can feel the pleading, the hope for a better future. When Roman wrote this, and we recorded it, Ukraine was nowhere near being an independent country. This song asks for a time when evil is no longer imposed on the country and freedom reigns. We revived it on our social media when the full scale invasion started in 2022. The theme of the song seems just as relevant today.

WLODEK NAKONECZNY

Roman sent us the EP *Oi Divchino*, then my sister brought CDs from Berlin, first *The Ukrainians* and then *Vorony*. The first one was already 'kosher', without any Soviet-Russian element and entirely Ukrainian. Interestingly, most of the material was original works. From a textual point of view, it may not be stunning, but grammatically it was correct and had its own charm. Most important was that these lyrics were created entirely by a Briton for whom Ukrainian was the language he had discovered at university (although at that time we were sure that Ukrainian was his native language!) In the melodic sphere, however, these songs were very deeply and solidly rooted in Ukrainian musical folk music; so deeply that for a long time many people were convinced that these were 'rock' versions of folk standards. Three songs were especially bright spots on the first album: 'Oi Divchino', 'Cherez Richku, Cherez Hai' and the instrumental 'Hopak' – a cool version of a traditional Ukrainian dance.

DREW MILLER, OMNIUM RECORDS

I heard about them first from the John Peel session with The Wedding Present, but what got me into it was my own progression as a musician, turning into a record label guy. My band, Boiled in Lead, got signed to Cooking Vinyl and we put out two records with them. By 1990, I was very disillusioned and disappointed with the original label we were signed to in the US, so with a couple partners, I started my own label, Omnium, and we were looking for similar types of world music that rocks. The Ukrainians are clearly that, they've always been that. I've always loved rock 'n' roll music not sung in English, from Turkish psychedelic onwards, and they consistently rock. It's consistently melodic yet heavy, and they're a very fun band. Plus we already knew the people at Cooking Vinyl, so we were able to get The Ukrainians record released on CD as part of our first releases in 1991.

PETER

In the early days, we used the same manager as The Wedding Present, Brian Hallin, and with the same deal. I don't know why The Wedding Present had a manager because we basically managed ourselves. But we had signed a contract with him so we just ended up paying him. Most managers take ten or 15 or 20 per cent off the top of everything you earn, but the deal The Wedding Present had was that the percentage would be of the profit not of the overheads. There would've been no profit otherwise, because we kept ticket prices, record prices, etcetera as low as we could so that we could engage people and do fun things. If he'd taken 20 per cent off the top, we couldn't have survived. But he was good in the early days of The Ukrainians, because he knew all the people to contact and start us off.

For the first three Wedding Present albums, we were basically just an English band that only did a few gigs abroad. The Wedding Present would play in halls in Britain to between 1,500 and 3,000 people and then go across to Germany and only play to 200 or 300. It just hadn't spread in that way. The one or two American shows The Wedding Present did were also very poorly attended.

But Cooking Vinyl and Brian were both very good at finding us international contacts, where they would take an interesting sounding world music band abroad, so we found it quite easy to get to places which The Wedding Present could never do. There were no giant shows, but we found it easier to break out. By the time we got to Germany in 1992, we were doing 16 to 17-date tours playing to audiences of 200 to 300 people and it would be non-stop for three weeks. The Wedding Present might be doing two or three shows in Germany in similar-sized halls. It was a really funny feeling at that time, to go and play somewhere as The Ukrainians and be more well known than The Wedding Present. It was very unexpected.

Germany was more accepting of and understanding of eastern Europe because they're closer to it. There's probably more curiosity in Britain about Eastern music, whereas half of Germany was run by the Eastern Bloc so there was a lot of knowledge of what life was like there, and what the restrictions were like. People in Germany would know Russian folk songs, because you'd hear the equivalent on East German TV.

THE ADELPHI
3 SEPTEMBER 1991, HULL, UK

STEPAN PASICZNYK, FIRST UKRAINIANS ACCORDION PLAYER
Our first ever gig. I seem to remember a pillar in front of the stage. It was strange playing into a pillar.

JOHN PEEL SESSION, MAIDA VALE STUDIOS
24 SEPTEMBER 1991, LONDON, UK

LEN

We'd already had a boost from John Peel. We got asked to record our first Ukrainians Peel session. It was so well received that even thirteen years later it was listed as one of *MOJO* magazine's '20 Landmark Peel Sessions' in their December 2004 issue, alongside classic sessions from Pink Floyd, The Buzzcocks, Nirvana, Billy Bragg and Joy Division!

ROCK / Roots go east: Marek Kohn on The Wedding Present at the Town and Country

Back in the USSR

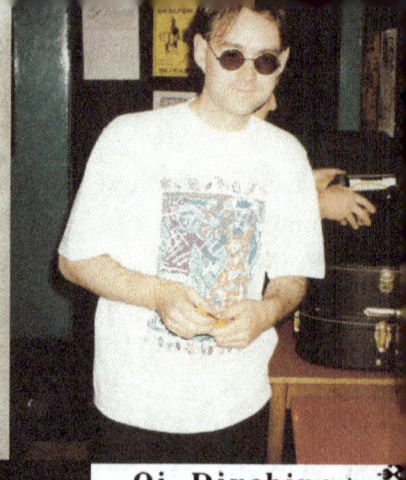

THE message has got across. There were no cries of "George Best", or "Why are you being so reasonable now?" For this tour, The Wedding Present have taken a break from sounding like The Smiths without the preciousness, and are performing an evening of traditional Ukrainian music.

Two senior figures stand behind this unusual project. One is John Peel, the focus of the culture in which the Leeds-based band have thrived — they now feature strongly in the upper reaches of the Festive Fifty chosen annually by Peel's listeners, up there with The Smiths and New Order. The other is guitarist Solowka's father, who is Ukrainian.

This was Solowka Junior's night. Frontman Dave Gedge remained on the sidelines, bent gravely over his guitar, while the tousled Slav stood centre stage with a mandolin and a beam of delight that never seemed to leave his face. The rough-hewn four-piece was upgraded by the addition of Len Liggins and Roman Remeynes, instrumentalists who concentrated on accordion and fiddle.

The concerts had their genesis in a session recorded for Peel's show, later released as a mini LP *Ukrainski Vistupi Johna Peela*. Its underlying respectfulness is demonstrated in the accompanying booklet about Ukraine (the definite article, it says, was "a linguistic ploy first used by an 18th-century Tsar in order to lower the status of Ukraine within his empire"). The recording itself does not quite do the idea justice. On the evidence of the show, however, all that was missing was the spirit of live performance.

The songs themselves come in two modes; the poignant, yearning ballad and its exuberant, rollicking antithesis. Both are combined in the Ukrainian song best known here, *Davni Chasy* — recorded some time ago as *Those Were The Days*. In the hands of The Wedding Present, it had a thrash inflection absent from Mary Hopkins's interpretation but that seemed to do it no harm.

It would be easy to dismiss this all as a bit of a joke, like the source of Ruritanian amusement that many Britons find in Albania. But what is actually going on here is, surely, the essence of how a culture renews itself under conditions of migration; the new generation playing the old melodies in its own idiom.

The cultural exchange between Solowka and his fellow musicians was certainly effective; the audience has rather further to go. One crop-headed youth did leap onto the stage and succeed in executing some rudimentary Cossack-style kicks. His achievements paled, however, beside the display put on by the genuine article. At the climax of the show, on strode the men and women of the Reading Ukrainian Dance Troupe. The men wore square-cornered black hats, boots and baggy trousers. They leapt, kicked, and reminded the crowd who really invented break-dancing. The audience gave this magnificent display the applause it deserved. Their own performance was largely limited to individuals climbing on stage and dropping back onto their peers. But it is an infant culture. The Ukrainians showed them what you can manage with a few hundred years' practice.

(clockwise from top left) Marek Kohn's review of The Wedding Present's 'Ukrainian' gig at London's Town & Country Club in *The Independent*; Len at the Adelphi in Hull, September 1991 (Karl Kathuria); press ad for 'Oi Divchino'; the first Ukrainians' gig, at Hull's Adelphi (three images - Karl Kathuria)

(clockwise from top left) Len in late 1992 or early 1993; The Ukrainians in 1992 with Carlos Fleischmann from Bremen's Blue Star Booking Agency, December 1992; Roman & Paul in 1992; producer Harri Kakoulli at the mixing desk, Castleford, West Yorkshire c1992; Peter in Woodhouse Studios, Leeds (Alaric Neville); 1992 Bremen gig ticket

BANGOR UNIVERSITY
2 OCTOBER 1991, BANGOR, UK

LEN

We began our first UK tour in October 1991. Pete was characteristically confident but I was full of trepidation. As the days went by, I got more and more into it and my nervousness began to drift away, especially after we got a live review in the *NME* saying, 'This is POP and it blows your trousers off!'

Our first album, *The Ukrainians*, definitely established us as the exponents of a brand-new World music hybrid, combining traditional Ukrainian Folk and Western Rock music. That was our unique selling point and music journalists were really keen to write about it. 'A new genre has just been born,' said *Rock 'n' Reel* magazine, 'Cossack thrash!' The album received fantastic reviews in the UK and in mainland Europe. As a result, an agency approached us to play a tour in Germany. Little did we know, it was to be the first of many.

In fact, word had even begun to spread to the US, resulting in the band being approached by NIKE to record the soundtrack for a TV advertisement for training shoes. Our brief was that the music was to accompany footage of the world champion pole vaulter Sergey Bubka working out at a gym in his Ukrainian home town of Donetsk. So, we got sent a rough cut of the footage, recorded the music in a studio in London somewhere, and sent it by satellite to the US. The footage then got edited to the track. That was the easiest money we ever made - $10,000 for 29 seconds of music!

The ad went on to be screened in the UK by ITV, Channel 4, MTV and the Sky Sports channels and by countless TV stations in Europe, America, Canada and Australia. My auntie Nora even rang my mum from Perth (in Australia, not Scotland) to let her know it was regularly on the telly over there!

We should have made a small fortune in royalties, too, but in a cruel twist of fate they 'disappeared' as a result of 'inadequate paperwork' being submitted to the PRS (Performing Right Society) by the publishing company. There was a rumour that seminal punk figure Malcolm McClaren, who did another NIKE ad at the same time as us, may have got our royalties 'by mistake'. Who knows?

READING UNIVERSITY
3 OCTOBER 1991, READING, UK

STEPAN PASICZNYK
We were the support act for The Levellers at Reading Uni. We got the gig, they got the power cut. I would have liked to have watched them as they really do make a great sound, and looking at where they are now, that episode didn't affect their success!

RILEY SMITH HALL, LEEDS UNIVERSITY
4 OCTOBER 1991, LEEDS, UK

ALARIC NEVILLE
I owned and ran Woodhouse Studios in Leeds from 1986 to 2000, but from 1989 I spent more time as a live touring sound engineer as I started managing and producing The Bridewell Taxis. That band's career ran its course by the end of 1992 and although I had other regular or irregular sound jobs with the likes of CUD and Chumbawamba, my MU [Musician's Union] work diary now had some gaps which needed filling.

I was aware of the break between The Wedding Present and the three members who would become the nucleus of The Ukrainians; the Leeds music scene was a small village where you are only ever one mate removed from any act. One such muso mate was Chris Harrop, whose band Third Party recorded at my studio. Chris's next band turned out to be the newly-formed, full-fat touring line-up of The Ukrainians.

Consequently, I was on the guest list for what my memory has framed as their first ever gig, or maybe their first gig in Leeds at the University Riley Smith Hall. I remember standing with Simon Smith to watch the set and, again, from memory David Gedge was there too on the edges of our huddle, although I didn't know him to speak to.

My reaction must have been positive as I subsequently asked them to contribute a track for a compilation of Leeds bands I was putting out on my label Stolen Sounds Records, *Knowing Where It All Leeds*. Not long after that album came out, I was asked if I wanted to do some live dates with the band as their Front of House sound engineer. Chris had actually left The Ukrainians by then and had spent a year playing bass in the last line-up of The Bridewells before concentrating on his own new musical project, Black Star Liner.

Personal chemistry is a crucial part of being in any band and that includes the larger crew that lives, works and plays together on tour. For some people the music industry is a job like any other. One simply offers up one's time and expertise in return for a wage. Others, like me, are also looking for something more, a fellowship of friends engaged in a common cause, fun and intellectual stimulation in all its myriad forms and if possible, exotic travel to faraway places. The Ukrainians in 1992 offered all this, and very soon I felt completely at home in the company of a band of brothers careering around Europe surfing the rumbustious wave of world music and Punk rock.

In some ways touring with The Ukrainians was a similar experience to touring with any other band of the era; hours cooped up in vans and tour buses, sticky-floored venues with cramped dressing rooms covered in graffiti, a different PA every night, fanatical fans and those just curious to see the latest novelty act on the circuit, hotel rooms of questionable quality, dubious bars, flights, fights, fun and frolicking mixed up with the unavoidable tedium of travel between the brief bright moments of magic. In other ways The Ukies were a very different proposition to the usual bands I had been in or worked with.

The line-up seemed to be made up of a random mix of misfits and oddballs. It is often the case that band members are drawn together from a close-knit scene, an age group, or a sub culture. The Ukies, on the other hand, were and remain a gloriously ramshackle collection of individuals whose back stories might have led any of them in other directions far away from a Slavic, Post Punk, Proto-World Music, Indie band based in Leeds. Early dates were based on the first album with its mix of Wedding Present line-up rock songs and acoustic trio tracks. Soon the new line-up began to develop its own sound and the second album, *Vorony*, with the near contemporaneous Smiths EP, came over as a much more cohesive product. A band's sound is often a unique composite of all the styles and influences its members bring to the creative process of interpreting and presenting a set of songs. Chris was a fine classic bass player but his replacement Paul Briggs used his bass as more of a lead instrument, complete with an overdriven chorused tone and a cheeky, annoying habit of turning himself up song by song during a gig. This was the final piece of the jigsaw which created The Ukrainians' sound and set the style the band has followed ever since.

Being a part of a creative endeavour that knows it is producing something new and of consequence has its own particular thrill and it certainly was a thrilling time to be with The Ukies.

PETER

The first big gig we played was during Freshers Week at Leeds University. There were six of us on stage playing. During Freshers Week, people are just there to get drunk and it was a really weird atmosphere, with a lot of people just walking in and out all the time. But there was a hard-core there in the middle of the audience who knew all the songs. It was the first time we got to play outside of the Wedding Present machine. It didn't sound or feel particularly different. There were a few songs that were a bit more intricate and a bit more eastern and therefore it sounded a bit more like us. And there were more vocals from Len, because with The Wedding Present we tended to do more instrumentals because the vocals took a bit longer. It did feel weird playing these songs without The Wedding Present being there, although some of them were in the audience watching us. That was quite strange, but it was a kickstart to our career.

We'd had to recruit new members to replace the Wedding Present members. Chris, our new bass player, played with us for two or three years. But a friend of his called Dave Lee tried out for the drums and he was very like Shaun was in the early days of The Wedding Present. Shaun never claimed to be a drummer. He was always happy to be a bass player, but he learned to play the drums. And he was great because he put so much power and energy behind it, but not technique. I think it helped us to drive that fast-and-furious-but-almost-falling-to-bits style, because it was almost falling to bits. Dave's drumming felt similar to me. From the way he hit the drums and the intensity of it, I just knew he was going to do it right. He loved the speeding up and the slowing down.

We decided to get someone who could play accordion permanently and so we advertised for an accordion player, ideally from the Ukrainian community, because we didn't want to have to tell people how to play the accordion. We advertised in Ukrainian newspapers and in Indie places that we knew in London, in Leeds and elsewhere in the north.

We had four or five people wanting to do the job. We went for an accordion player called Stepan Pasicznyk, whose nickname was Luddy, after Ludwig van Beethoven! In some ways he had a similar background to me, although he was a lot more Ukrainian than me. He grew up at home with a Ukrainian dad and an Irish mum so went to Catholic schools. He didn't learn to speak Ukrainian until his early twenties. He learnt to speak it absolutely fluently and he also taught himself Ukrainian tunes on the accordion. He was a really good accordion player, one of these people who can play and sing at the same time, which I could never do. It's hard enough playing the accordion because you can't see the buttons when you're playing. And he was a really big imposing personality, a big fella, six foot two and about 16 stone. He was jovial and good fun to be with, and he was our accordion player until 1994.

 DUCHESS OF YORK
31 OCTOBER 1991, LEEDS, UK

BILL BAILEY, NUMBER ONE GROUPIE 1990-94

It was after I'd heard 'Yuri's Hair Salon' on the John Peel show in the late 80s that I knew I had to meet 'The Legendary' Len Liggins. Coming from Bradford, and with hardly any money or knowledge of Leeds, I got on the X48 bus to the unknown world of Bramley. I'd spotted Len's address on the back of an AAZ record that he'd put out, so I headed round to see my new best friend, without knowing if he was home or not. Unfortunately for Len, he was.

During the next couple of months, I managed to blag a few more cheap records off Len, a free ride to Leeds train station in Peter's dodgy Fiat (I can't recall what, but something major didn't work), and a job selling a lot of large sized t-shirts for The Ukrainians, who had just played a kind of secret debut gig in The Duchess of York. Much to the band's disappointment, I think I was their first groupie.

Over the next few years, I would follow them all over the UK, again mainly due to the fact that I was small of frame and didn't take up too much space in the tour van. And I loved being in that Ukrainians Mk1 tour van. Gordon, one of the roadies, just had a mad face, Luddy and Chris made me giggle constantly, Peter's brown leather jacket was a source of amusement, Dave and Roman were just cool, and Len was – well – just Len. And I discovered cherry vodka.

By 1994 I was in my own band, and if you'd told me, four years earlier, that Peter would be playing guitar on our first album, then I would have spat borscht in your face. All because I heard Len's 'Yuri's Hair Salon' on the radio.

I, like many, have a lot to thank John Peel for.

JOHN BOOCOCK

Over 30 years ago I was living in the far North of Scotland. I had left my native Leeds for the undoubted joys of the Scottish Highlands, safe in the knowledge that the only way out was via the A9 and an as yet underdeveloped A74. Even though my self-imposed relocation meant a distance by road of 430 miles each way, I still kept my eye on things in Leeds and made regular trips to Elland Road to see the beauty that was Howard Wilkinson's creation. It also meant that when I was in the Holy City I looked out for interesting gigs.

In late 1991, I saw that The Ukrainians were playing in Leeds. I had never witnessed The Ukrainians live although there was vinyl on my shelves. I knew Len from my days at LOP (*Leeds Other Paper*) and I was also a fan of The Wedding Present, so I was keen to see the combination this would throw up played out on stage.

On the way down from Scotland, we decided to stop in Grassington and then go for a leisurely stroll up Trollers Gill in search of its famous ghosts and spooky things. When we arrived back in the car park we were disappointed to find that my car was no longer with us.

I reported the theft at Skipton nick and all was revealed. My car had been stolen and had been used in a post office job somewhere in Keighley that very afternoon and was now a heavily damaged wreck in Bradford. When the detective dealing with the crime asked me where I was that afternoon, I had no choice but to tell him that I had been looking for ghosts and deranged goblins at Trollers Gill with my mate. He was not impressed but assessed the chances of us being at the post office in Keighley, then Bradford and back to the Dales would be a bit far-fetched. A short statement would see me on my way.

I turned up at The Duchess at about 9pm, wearing a very muddy cagoule, walking boots and gaiters and a Leeds United bobble hat. A woman asked me why I was hiding in a corner, dressed like a very sad member of the Ramblers Association. I responded: 'It's a long story but me and my mate were up Trollers Gill looking for ghosts and spooky things like deranged goblins…' At which point she pointed out the date and what this meant for Ukrainians.

The Ukrainians were great and yes it was the 31st of October. And the moral of the story is don't go searching for ghosts and deranged goblins before going to a Ukrainians gig, especially if it is Veles's Night.

Veles's night is a pre-Christian Slavic holiday that falls on the same day as Hallowe'en in the west. The tradition is for candles to be lit so that ancestors' souls can find their way back home.

KING TUT'S WAH-WAH HUT
19 DECEMBER 1991, GLASGOW, UK

STEPAN PASICZNYK

We played Newcastle University the night before, going on after a pretty well-known drag act at the time called Divine. The stage was flooded in beer from half-empty plastic pint glasses that had been thrown at him. I wish I'd had wellies for that one. Newcastle felt like the best part of 100 in a big hall. But due to some promo or whatever breakdown in communications, King Tut's had an audience of about five people.

SONNECK
9 JANUARY 1992, KEMPTEN, BAVARIA, GERMANY

STEPAN PASICZNYK

We played a small venue on a mountainside. The owner was a dwarf with a big Alsatian. The audience was shall we say, sparse. There was a blizzard outside. What looked like two skiers watched us, and the owner skipped around as we played. Meanwhile John our driver had a placard saying something derogatory about Pete and was holding it up behind him as he strummed away.

DAVE LEE

After the gig we had a rowdy bottle-walking contest in someone's bedroom in the B&B, which was brought to a premature halt when someone screamed 'ENOUGH!!!' from the bottom of the stairs.

 GLASTONBURY FESTIVAL
28 JUNE 1992, GLASTONBURY, UK

REBECCA WALKLEY

By the summer of 1992 the band had been driving its usual zigzag route over Europe, playing gigs from Heidelberg to Haarlem to Hackney Empire. They were on top of their game. Len had given up his nine-to-five job and being on the road was his place of work. There was pressure from the band manager, their booking agent and the record company for the band to keep busy. Their 34th gig that year was Glastonbury.

We drove down from Leeds to the Somerset countryside on the Sunday afternoon. I was the van driver on this occasion. We arrived at the festival site and I couldn't find anywhere to park. I asked people for directions but many of them had been getting high on their chosen substances since Friday evening and all I got was glazed-over looks. Grumpy, I rocked up at the VIP area and asked someone who looked like a festival organiser where to go and he very helpfully gave me detailed directions. Len pointed out that I had just asked Richard Thompson (of Fairport Convention fame) where to park my van!

The festival was very different back then compared to today's highly-priced chic event. The cost for the three-day event was £49. The place had an edge to it, dealers walked past you mumbling the names of various drugs you could purchase. There was no TV coverage, no glamping tents with ensuite toilets, no technology, no TikTok. People just sat around and talked to each other. Unthinkable for today's youth!

The Ukrainians were the headline act on the New Bands Stage on Sunday evening. I knew the routine by now and this is what happened. The crowd, not knowing what they were getting at first, began by enjoying the energy, then the musicians connected with everyone. The songs started speeding up and the sounds swirled high around the canopy, pulling the audience up higher. Already on their feet, they leapt up off the ground to reach something higher, floating on the rhythms playing at an ever-quickening pulse to the final climax. This was the band's alchemy at work and at its best. This, combined with the magic of Glastonbury, a place where hundreds of people party each year on a ley line, an ancient invisible pathway linking prehistoric monuments across the world. And we were at the centre of it all, in that tent that evening.

Printed on the *Glastonbury Festival* poster in 1992 was a William Blake quote, 'For everything that lives is holy, life delights in life, Because the soul of sweet delight can never be defil'd'. Everything is connected and the band and the audience was at one that midsummer's evening.

This is what a young journalist called James Hall had to say when he wrote about the gig in the *Daily Telegraph* 15 years after the event in 2007 and again in 2020:

> *Take the guitarist from The Wedding Present, Peter Solowka, and get him to form a band playing insanely fast Ukrainian folk music. Stick them in a far-flung tent on the last night of one of the hottest ever festivals, and what do you get? One hell of a party. The best end to a Glastonbury ever.*

James ranked The Ukrainians' gig the fourth best performance ever at Glastonbury, beaten only by Radiohead in 1997, Love with Arthur Lee in 2003 and David Bowie in 2000.

Glastonbury was unforgettable. The band was even invited back to play in 1993. I remember many years later when I mentioned to a colleague of mine that my significant other played in a band called The Ukrainians, they said they had seen the band and immediately recalled the gig in 1992 and how much they enjoyed it.

Before writing this, I asked Len what it was like playing at Glastonbury. I realise it was a few decades ago and Len and myself had had a few beers at the time. He replied, 'You know, I can't remember a single thing about it.'

SHEFFIELD UNIVERSITY
3 JULY 1992, SHEFFIELD, UK

STEPAN PASICZNYK

After doing our gig in the Student Union bar, I did an impromptu karaoke performance of 'Like a Virgin' by Madonna translated in real time to Ukrainian. It went down quite well due to its clumsy translation at some points. Len mentioned to me that a forte of mine is putting comedy into music. Perhaps I need to act on that some time.

BUMBERSHOOT FESTIVAL
5 AUGUST 1992, SEATTLE, WASHINGTON

DAVE LEE, DRUMMER, THE UKRAINIANS

If it hadn't been for The Ukrainians, I wouldn't have left this sceptred isle, because I was absolutely petrified of flying. The first gig we did abroad was in Berlin. I couldn't bring myself to fly so I went on the bus two days earlier and waited there for the rest of the band to turn up. On the return journey I got back two days after everyone else. The day that I left, Roman – God bless him – came into my room in Berlin and said, 'Dave, we're off to the airport. Take a look at these pictures,' and he gave me two pictures of the view from the aeroplane when it

UKRAINIANS TOUR
MARCH '92

Sat. 14th	Colchester · Essex Uni
Fri. 20th	Sheffield · Polytechnic
Sat. 21st	Newcastle · Riverside
Sun. 22nd	Middlesborough · Arena
Tues. 24th	Derby · The Warehouse
Weds. 25th	Lampeter · St. Davids
Fri. 27th	Northampton · Roadmenders
Sat. 28th	London · Middlesex Poly
Sun. 29th	London · Mean Fiddler
Mon. 30th	Stoke · Wheatsheaf

THE UKIES' VEGGIE COOKBOOK
Hакипляк - NAKYPLIAK – CABBAGE SOUFFLE

This dish is not easy to get right, but it's worth a try!

Preparation time : 5 days!   Serves 3 Hungry people!

INGREDIENTS:
- White Cabbage (360grm/12oz)
- Onion
- Eggs, separated
- Gruyere cheese (150grm/5oz)
- Milk (½ litre)
- Butter (75grm/3oz)
- Flour (3 Tbsp)
- Breadcrumbs (2Tbsp)
- 1 Clove Garlic
- Cayenne pepper
- Paprika
- Caraway Seeds
- Black pepper (Freshly ground)
- Salt (2Tsp)

PREPARATION:

Remove outer leaves of cabbage, remove core and cut remainder into 3 wedges. Shred as thinly as possible and place in a large bowl. Sprinkle salt over the top and toss! Squeeze the salt into the cabbage, thus softening it. Place a weighted plate (not too heavy!) on the cabbage and a tea-towel over the top of the bowl. Leave for a few hours in a warm place (such as your neighbour's illicit horilka distillery) until it's juicy!

Pour boiling water over cabbage until plate is just submerged. Put the tea-towel over bowl. Leave in a warm place again and go to bed for 4 days.

Get up. Drain cabbage. Rinse it in cold water then drain again. Mix cabbage with ½ teaspoon of caraway seeds and a little water and cook for 20 minutes in an uncovered pan. Stir intermittently until cabbage is soft and water has evaporated. Drain in colander and press cabbage to remove as much liquid as possible. Allow to cool.

Melt butter in a casserole dish and sauté onion until light brown. Add garlic and cook for 2 minutes, then stir in flour and cook for a further 2 minutes. Take off the heat and stir in cayenne pepper, paprika, salt, pepper and, little by little, the milk. Return to heat, bring to boil and stir 'til it thickens. Remove from heat again and beat in the cheese and egg yolks.

Preheat oven to 190 c. (Gas mark 5). Stir cooled cabbage into the sauce! Whisk egg whites until stiff (but not dry) and fold into cabbage mixture. Spoon the mixture into a greased soufflé dish and sprinkle the breadcrumbs on top. Bake in the oven for 40 minutes until risen, lightly browned and set.

Sing 3 verses of 'Rospryahaite Khloptsi Koni' (or the first verse 30 times - Len) and serve immediately.

DID ANYONE SPOT THE DELIBERATE MISTAKE IN OUR RECIPE FOR BORSCH IN NEWSLETTER #1? THE MISSING INGREDIENT WAS BEET!

UKRAINIANS SOBER UP!!

It seems hard to believe that it's 11 months since Newsletter No.3 — but it is!! A lot of that time was spent touring — navigating the autobahns of Europe in a tired, alcoholic haze — but we finally managed to take a couple of months off (if you can call it that) to sober up and write and record our brilliant new L.P., 'Kultura'!

UKRAINAMERICA...

When you see translations of (most of) the new songs (i.e. when you've bought the record!), you'll notice that the subject matter of cossacks, gypsy girls, horses and ye olde Worlde Ukraine have been replaced by more contemporary concerns (with the notable exception of our bar-room version of 'Suhanochka'!). Songs like 'Polityka', 'UKrainAmerica' and 'Kievskiy Express' are directly inspired by our experiences on tour in Ukraine last year. We found an impoverished people there, struggling to find an identity after three quarters of a century of political, economic, social and cultural suppression. Unfortunately, instead of creating a new, modern culture, Ukrainians are succumbing to the attractions of Western consumerism and to the thought of being able to partake in the American dream. Thus McDonald's, hamburgers and Marlborough cigarettes everywhere. Sad, but totally inevitable.

EUROPA....

After this U.K. tour, we'll be taking 'Kultura' to Germany, Holland, France and Belgium — and probably well beyond — wearing down the autobahns again and generally destroying our eating and sleeping patterns till Christmas! Oh how we suffer!!

Enjoy the new album. Love & Kisses, Len x

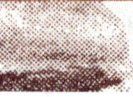

Assorted Ukrainians' newsletters (in English & German)

the ukrainians NEWSLETTER

LENS: UKRAINIAN LANGUAGE LESSON
EASY TO FOLLOW STEPPE BY STEPPE GUIDE TO THE UKRAINIAN TONGUE

1. "AND THIS IS MINE... INTERVIEW ROOM"

2. "THE QUEEN IS DEAD..."

3. "WHEN I SAW THAT THE FLAMES ROSE TO HER ROMAN NOSE... AND THE WALKMAN STARTED TO MELT"

4. "SWEETNESS, SWEETNESS I WAS ONLY JOKING WHEN I SAID... IT'S DEATH FOR NO REASON, AND DEATH FOR NO REASON IS MURDER."

TRANSLATIONS & TRANSLITERATIONS

1. У всіх секрети і ці мої
   OO FSEEKH SEKRETY TSEE MOYEE

2. Королева померла
   KOROLEVA POMERLA

3. Коли я зуб, що римський ніс
   і Волкмен полумяні
   KOLY BACHEEV SHCHO REEMSKIY NEES EE WALKMAN POLOOMYANEE

4. Мила, мила, я просто жартував
   з тим, що смерть без причини
   смерть без причини — убивство
   MILA, MILA YA PROSTO ZHARTOOVAV Z TEEM SHO SMERT BEZ PRYCHYNY EE SMERT BEZ PRYCHYNY — UBIVSTVO

A WOLF CHASES A RABBIT. DO NOT SHOOT THE RABBIT BECAUSE THE WOLF WILL THEN TURN ON YOU

UKRAINIANS TOUR

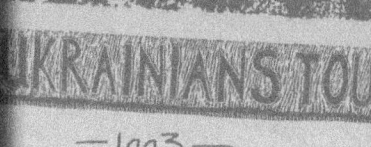

— 1993 —

MARCH
- LONDON ~ U.L.U.
- PORTSMOUTH ~ WEDGEWOOD ROOMS
- COVENTRY ~ THE GENERAL WOOL
- CAMBRIDGE ~ THE BOATRACE
- OXFORD ~ THE VENUE
- LEEDS ~ THE DUCHESS
- SOUTHAMPTON ~ THE JOINERS ARMS
- HULL ~ THE ADELPHI
- BATH ~ COLLEGE OF F.E.
- COLCHESTER ~ THE ARTS CENTRE
- LONDON ~ POWERHAUS

APRIL
- LONDON ~ THE VENUE

DATES CORRECT AT TIME OF PRINTING BUT CHECK WITH THE VENUES.

FEAR OF F!

Ukrainians sticks completely overcame his fear. This occurred as the result forced by the 5 other members board a British Airways in USA (to play the Rumbersho Once up in the air someone brought his a gutta to open all the doors and ! complimentary spirits. Wit the plane was gliding abov was sporting a huge conten last twelve hours.

Unfortunately, his itself mid-flight to pass so unnerved by his first that he vowed never to do again. "As far as festiva said, "it's just heading for me in future".

UKRAINI CROWS !

Anglo-S rockers THE U at last relea second LP, ! means Crows

The al tracks, a ni and yellow c available on cassette. Th includes a s with song tr other infor

When about the n record, man commented: woke up one was there! Profiles' — joke!" — ed

Those who Indie world stars, have ...with mile on dean to promote inians, in France, ver ten, is learning how to of time on dry cheese strong coffee ot to top it off with in chocolate, beer and

BAND PROFILES

PAUL BRIGGS — **REAL NAME:** Unknown **HEIGHT:** Unknown **HAIR:** Yes **FIXATION:** Being enigmatic **ON STAGE ANTICS:** Doing the mystery dance **MUM:** Unknown **DAD:** Unknown **SAYINGS:** 'No comment' **ANNOYING HABITS:** Being a riddle wrapped in a mystery inside an enigma. **FAVE FOOD:** Unconfirmed reports suggest Bananas. **BEST COLLECTION:** As much printed matter as he can stuff into his suitcase whilst on tour.

ROMAN REMEYNES — **A.K.A:** The Sleeper (The doziest Roman of them all' W.Shakespeare) **HEIGHT:** Medium **HAIR:** Long, black and flowing down his back (none on his head, just down his back.) **FIXATION:** Must get at least 24 hours sleep per day or he gets grumpy **MUM:** Ukrainian **DAD:** Ukrainian **SAYINGS:** Zzzzzzz ! **ANNOYING HABITS:** Waking up **FAVE FOOD:** Horlicks **BEST COLLECTION:** 1000 'Do Not Disturb' signs **ON STAGE ANTICS:** Amazes audiences by smiling and playing in his sleep.

HELLO BOYS AND GIRLS

PETE SOLOWKA — **A.K.A:** The Grinder **HEIGHT:** Medium **HAIR:** Has recently taken to wearing a pair of rabbits on his head (from a distance they look like hares — (aural joke-Ed.)) **FIXATION:** The Ukrainians **ON STAGE ANTICS:** Crouches down towards the end of gigs and steals beer off people at the front. **MUM:** Austrian **DAD:** Ukrainian **SAYINGS:** T.Shirts are available at the back of the venue! **ANNOYING HABITS:** Being habitually annoying.

COMPETITION TIME!

AN EASY ONE FOR YOU THIS TIME. SIMPLY GUESS THE COMBINED WEIGHT OF THE UKRAINIANS IN POUNDS AND SEND YOUR ANSWERS (ON A POSTCARD PLEASE) TO THE MERCHANDISE ADDRESS (SEE ABOVE, RIGHT) THE LUCKY WINNER WILL RECEIVE 6 UKRAINIAN VODKA GLASSES AND A BOTTLE OF UKRAINIAN VODKA. GOOD LUCK. (NO SCALES BACKSTAGE PLEASE

was in flight. And I thought, 'Oh, maybe I should have gone on the plane.'

Then we were playing in Seattle so I had to go on a plane. I was absolutely petrified. I drank a couple of cans of really strong full-strength Tennent's lager and took some paracetamol. And when we got to Los Angeles, I just jumped on the next plane and my fear of flying had gone.

Seattle was one of my favourite gigs. We played in a football stadium. There were so many people on the bill – Joan Armatrading, They Might Be Giants, Little Feat. I didn't see any of them. We got looked after like we were rock stars. We had minders who looked after us and they would do anything for you. I had friends coming to see us and I couldn't remember my friend's wife's name, so I said, 'Can you find her name out for me?' and they said, 'Yes, of course, of course.' And then, as soon as we'd finished the gig and done our bit, the minders just ignored us!

And then we had to get work permits to cross the border and go to Canada, and we had to be out of Canada by midnight after the gig. Otherwise, I don't know what would have happened. Perhaps they would have kept us there.

LEN

Playing the enormous *Bumbershoot Festival* in Seattle was our first incursion into the USA. The line-up also included John Lee Hooker, Michelle Shocked, Joan Armatrading and John Mayall & The Bluesbreakers. We were in good company. Unfortunately, I missed John Lee Hooker's set, but our lives momentarily interacted at the hotel we were staying in when he and I both passed through the revolving doors at the same time!

THE UKRAINIANS

VORONY

PISNI IZ THE SMITHS EP
RELEASED 21 SEPTEMBER 1992

LEN

We wanted to do something different after the first album, so we hit on the idea of reworking some classic Indie pop songs. We had a brainstorming session at a rehearsal and Paul Briggs, our second bass player, and myself tried to convince the rest of the band that The Smiths would be perfect. We could see that the way Morrissey sings and Johnny Marr's chord changes somehow leant themselves to being "Ukrainianised". I loved The Smiths, and still do, and I was ecstatically happy. So, we chose 'Bigmouth Strikes Again', 'Meat Is Murder', 'The Queen Is Dead' and 'What Difference Does It Make?'. They were recorded in Castleford along with all the other songs we'd written for our *Vorony* album.

For the front cover we decided to reference Morrissey's tendency to play gigs with a handful of gladioli stuffed into his back pocket, so all we needed to do was get a bunch from the florist and we could pop over to the park and take the front cover photo. Easy! Unfortunately Castleford's only florist didn't have gladioli, but they did have a nice bunch of daffodils, so we bought those. We traipsed over to the park and Pete proceeded to take some snaps of my rear end with a bunch of daffs sticking out of the back pocket. When we looked at the image later though, it was a bit blurry, so we pixillated it, a technique that was quite in vogue at that time anyway. The Ukrainians have had a canny knack of turning disadvantages into advantages at many stages of our career, and this is a very small example of one of them.

The reaction to Pisni Iz The Smiths was incredible. As we were signed to Cooking Vinyl Records at the time and the CEO Martin Goldschmidt was chuffed with the recordings, so the EP got a lot of promotion and airplay. And so many reviews. Someone even sent us a cutting in the post from Germany with a chart compiled by a panel of Berlin DJs showing the record at the number 1 spot, ahead of big established artists like Depeche Mode. It was licensed to record companies around the world and was even released in Australia (Festival Records).

WLODEK NAKONECZNY

The EP, *Pisni Iz The Smiths*, with songs by Morrissey and his crew was brilliantly played in Ukrainian style and language. They sounded more interesting than the originals. I was amazed and so was my friend Marcin Borchardt (now a respected documentary maker). He started playing these songs at a local radio station in Elbląg and we started thinking about how to bring the band to Poland.

LEN

It was all happening so fast. A month later saw the release of our second album, *Vorony*, featuring twelve new Ukrainians' original compositions plus an optimistic version of the Velvet Underground's dark and moody 'Venus In Furs'. *Vorony* extended our popularity to almost every country in Europe. To promote it we played an extensive 110-date tour ranging from Leon in western Spain to Kharkiv in eastern Ukraine, covering most of the countries in between. These included festivals at Glastonbury and WOMAD in Britain and a host of Indie, World Music, Folk and Rock events throughout mainland Europe.

PETER

We did a few shows, including a few abroad which was down to Martin Goldschmidt's Indie world music connections with other labels. In particular, there was a world music forum in Berlin where every year each label would bring over one or two new artists for this one or two-day festival. We went to that and I think we did really well. We were able to license our records to a lot of places in Europe and met agents from France and from Germany who took us on to tour. That was one of the things that really helped a lot. That's something RCA Records would probably not have done because they would not have had the same structure. If that album had been released on RCA Records as another Wedding Present album, it would almost certainly have disappeared because the band would not have wanted to tour. It would have been a novelty thing that just sat on the shelf.

We did quite a few international shows. We played in Seattle at the *Bumbershoot Festival*, which was three days of mainly world music, and that did really well for us for meeting agents in Canada in particular, because of the Ukrainian community there.

Back then you couldn't listen to all a band's music before you went to the gig. You saw the posters, you saw the press release and, if you were lucky, you might have heard it on the radio. You might not even be able to find the record in the shop, so when you used to go out and see bands in the '80s and '90s, a lot more of it was based on what people have told you and what you've read rather than what you actually knew the sound to be.

The audiences we were playing to ranged from people who had bought the first record (as Wedding Present fans) to people who saw the word Ukrainian and thought, 'That's eastern European.' There were people with Ukrainian heritage and people saying, 'I've always loved Russian music.' It was such a very, very eclectic mix of people. In the UK in the

THE UKRAINIANS

'80s and '90s, we'd get people from the late teens to their late-30s. The age range was very restricted compared with the age range that you see at gigs now. Whereas when we went to play in Germany, it was quite a wide age range. I think what made it big and sustainable for us was doing something different for the second album. We now had a new three album deal with Cooking Vinyl because Martin Goldschmidt was happy that we had sold enough of the first album.

Martin could see it growing and he was getting really positive contacts everywhere, so we recorded a second album. From recording the first album in 1990 until 1992 we had accumulated two years' worth of songs that we had written so this was quite a long album. We recorded them and played them to Martin and he said, 'These are really good. There is no doubt the quality has increased. But how am I going to sell it? I need more than just great music. Why don't you do something that you've never done before? Make it as Ukrainian as you like, but why don't you do cover versions of Western songs in Ukrainian, because then I've got a hook? You've got to give people a reason to buy your second record.'

We chose The Smiths. We changed some of the chord structures in some of the verses and choruses, translating the lyrics into Ukrainian and replacing the Western instrumentation – the electric guitar and so on – with mandolins and accordions. I listened to it and thought, 'This is weird, we can't do this. This isn't going to work.' But we played them to Martin and his team and he said, 'You've got to go with The Smiths. You've got to cover Smiths songs.' I can't remember which one we gave to him, but it did sound very eastern. There's something in the way Morrissey wails, his voice, which is very eastern and almost Arabic rather than anything Slavic. It sounds so different. Martin said, 'People will recognise it from the original but it's so different. You have put a mark on what you do.'

It took a bit of time to get used to the idea but he was right. So we went back to the studio and we worked on four Smiths songs that we could make sound as eastern European as possible.

That single preceded the second album, *Vorony* (which means 'crows'), which I think of as our first album anyway, because the other one was the transition with The Wedding Present. The artwork was designed by us this time. The main logo looks like two birds, head to head – they could be crows. The image is based on ancient jewellery designs, going back to the Scythians (the ancestry equivalent to Ukrainians as celts are to the British).

We didn't create the single for Smiths fans. It was meant for people to play on the radio. And it worked. The songs appeared on the Indie charts and DJs played them, all over Europe. We were doing 16, 17, 18 gigs in Germany back-to-back and 12 to 15 dates in France. It had never been bigger than playing venues of 300 to 400. But that record put us on to that level.

LEN

'The Queen Is Dead' video was mostly shot next to the bronze Queen Victoria memorial statue on Leeds 6's Woodhouse Moor. A musician friend of ours, Alan Thomas, shot and edited the video with help from his other half, Jenny Alexandrowicz.

ALAN THOMAS, DIRECTOR, 'THE QUEEN IS DEAD' VIDEO

Myself and Jenny had a great time filming the video for 'The Queen Is Dead'.

LEN

Having a zero budget for videos, Alan, Jenny, Pete, Dave and myself sought out some low-cost 'props'. They included top hats and overcoats which I believe we borrowed from Leeds Playhouse, and a pile of large (but free) cardboard boxes from Morrisons supermarket – that we struggled to carry from the city centre on foot. Someone procured some vintage-looking crocheted blousy tops and flouncy pink and black bonnets that we used in a few shots. The only

things we paid for, I think, were three cardboard Queen Elizabeth II face masks that we shelled out about 25p each for from a local newsagent's.

There is some live footage thrown in too, but where the gig – or gigs – took place is anybody's guess now. Looking back at it now, it's so of its time. It's Indie, lo-fi, DIY and full of clunky 1980s video effects. I love it!

VORONY
RELEASED 25 JANUARY 1993

LEN

1993 was another busy year for us. In fact, that's probably an example of Great British understatement! We performed about a hundred gigs, touring Ukraine, Germany, Austria and France, as well as the UK. It would be fantastic to be able to say I remember all the various wonderful places we visited but in truth it's a massive blur. We were tired, hungry and a tad worse for wear due to the demon drink a lot of the time. Get up, sober up, go for a run, shower, eat breakfast, get in the van, travel hundreds of miles down endless motorways and autobahns, get out, unload the gear, soundcheck, drink beer, play our hearts out for an hour and a half, sell CDs and t-shirts, eat pizza, get back in the van – and repeat, repeat, repeat for days or weeks on end. It was gruelling. People think being in a band is glamorous but it's very, very hard work.

Vorony was an interesting album for us to do. Pete and myself somehow found time to write a lot of songs, with input from Roman and Luddy. There were lots of rehearsals, many at Bradford Ukrainian Club where we were helped immensely by three people in particular: Wally, Bohdan and Mick. They really deserve their namecheck here – they gave us a lot of encouragement, as well as a constant stream of cassettes of Ukrainian folk songs and carols. They also had an amazing audio-visual archive which they kindly opened up for us. In return, we'd play gigs to help them to raise funds to keep the club going.

Vorony was very successful. It was an 'Album of the Month' in *Vox* magazine (which was later replaced by *Uncut*). Pete and myself had got into our songwriting stride and I was soaking up the language more. We were writing about a wide range of topics and I started writing lyrics that were more impressionistic. Folk songs tended to be stories, with a developing narrative, but I wanted to introduce tangential, open-to-interpretation words that you might find more commonly in Western pop and rock songs. You didn't really get that in Ukrainian folk music, or any other folk music for that matter.

We thought it might be good to do another cover version for the album, too, so we stumbled on the idea of The Velvet Underground's 'Venus In Furs'. Lou Reed got the title and idea for the song from a short story by a chap called Leopold von Sacher-Masoch, who was born about 200 years ago in Lemburg, the Germanic name for the present-day Lviv. The song infamously has S&M undertones, you know, 'Shiny, shiny, shiny boots of leather, whiplash girl child in the dark,' and all that. We loved the melody and the Ukrainian connection but wanted to have a lyric that celebrated Ukraine in some way, so we came up with words that described the beauty of Verkhovyna, the stunning Ukrainian highlands. Roman sings the lead vocals, wrote much of the lyric and arranged the track. He spent so much time in the studio putting it together, directing parts and overdubbing mandolin that work on other tracks was squeezed a bit.

Listening to it now, I think *Vorony* stands up as a fine album. It has a coherence to it, sound-wise. I think that's due to Harri Kakoulli's production. He's a gifted guy and he clearly enjoyed working with us on those songs.

PETER

Harri Kakoulli worked on *Vorony*, and if you think about how the sound of The Ukrainians developed from the Wedding Present thrash to be a little bit more subtle and a little bit more melodic and a little bit deeper in the subject matter that we use, there's no doubt that Harri Kakoulli's influence is really strong there.

WLODEK NAKONECZNY

Vorony I perceived as a musically perfect album from the first to the last beat. To say that it seduced me is to say nothing: I swallowed it in one gulp, whole and many times, and the enthusiasm it evoked didn't want to fade away. It was a great album with great music! If not a masterpiece, then at least a little masterpiece.

HARRI KAKOULLI, PRODUCER OF *VORONY* & *PISNI IZ THE SMITHS*

When I first started working on the *Vorony* sessions in Castleford the band would have their own meetings outside the studio control room. There might be a question about the level of the bass, for instance, and the band would say 'give us five minutes' and they'd disappear off. It'd be like a trade union meeting – they'd be all huddled together outside, then they'd come back into the control room and say 'yep, that's alright!'

I think 'Chekannya', the band's version of The Velvet Underground's 'Venus In Furs', is an amazing track. It's one of their best. I know what it's about, the beautiful Ukrainian mountains, and the way it's put together is magical and timeless. I often play it on my radio show, which I do every Saturday.

There are five or six songs from this album that I really love, and I'm proud of them because I produced them and put a lot of work into them. The band came to trust me and that felt so good. In the end they weren't going out so much saying, 'Give us five minutes…'! I felt like I was an extra member of the band, they made me feel that comfortable.

I'm pretty hands-on as a producer. There was an engineer, Pat Grogan, at the studio and he liked to get the recordings up and ready before we got into the studio, but I had to say to him, 'What are you doing?' I'd have to strip the mixing desk down and start again. I wanted to do my own EQing and all the rest of it. He'd say, 'It's rock 'n' roll, Harri. We want it to sound rock 'n' roll, don't we?' and I'd say, 'No, we don't!'

There's very little compression on the tracks because The Ukrainians' music goes soft then it goes high and it makes you fall off your chair. Compression would make it all sound the same.

I always said Len's violin playing makes me cry. It does. I don't know what it is about it, but his playing has got this effect on me that makes me feel tearful. It's not that it's crap – it's good! And it reminds me of a lot of sad things! He plays it really well. Less is more, you know? When people play fancy stuff it means fuck all to me. I love Len's playing, and Pete's, too. I love Pete. They're all like brothers to me.

For one week during the sessions, I was doing a digital diary for BBC2. I was taking footage of everyone in the studio and Pete was getting pissed off with me. Even in the B&B where I was staying, I was going into the kitchen in the morning and pointing the camera saying, 'Hey, what's cooking, chef?' He wasn't too pleased either!

THE UKRAINIANS

TIM BOURNE (AGED 62¼)
Ode to The Ukrainians

Of band The Ukrainians I'm a big fan
And have been for 35 years since when
I first heard them broadcast a John Peel session,
Though back then still part of Peel's faves, Wedding Present.

But no mere side project out on the edge
They gained independence beyond the boy Gedge.
And over the years I've kept up with their journey
Though I can't speak the lingo, their music still stirs me.

Their albums I prize in my vinyl collection,
Both covers and own songs of equal affection.
Though having said that, I have to concede,
Their 'Venus in Furs' I prefer to Lou Reed's.
I'll play it again and again and forever,
It raises my spirits whatever, whenever.

And as for their shows of rip-roaring fun,
Traditional sounds through amps of Punk
Three decades on and they recharge me still
To dance and sing, though I'm over the hill.

You'll find more layers in their catchy airs,
Meanings profound, stark truths, hopes and fears.
Ukrainian club gigs across the UK
Now seem more poignant when Russia invades.
Like the country from which the band take their name,
May all carry on and thrive with acclaim.

JAKE THRUSH

My favourite song by the band is 'Rospryahaite'. I love the part in the middle with the violin solo – so, so uplifting. It has helped me when things have been a bit tough over the years, that message of just keep going. So for this, and for the sheer joy of their music, a massive thank you.

JIM HOWE

One of our older songs that I love to play on the bass is 'Vorony', or 'Crows'. I love the melody and the semi-chord structure of the bass line.

PAUL BRIGGS, UKRAINIANS BASS PLAYER 1992-94

I was The Ukrainians' bass player from 1992 to 1994. My most memorable and favourite experiences in the band? We were recording the *Vorony* album and the idea came up to do a cover version, but we didn't know what and there were lots of ridiculous ideas going round. We tried a couple of things and they weren't really working but we were sat around Len's one night and in his living room he has this fantastic record collection. I mean – everything's in there, the whole lot. We went through it to see if anything would jump out and inspire us and we found his Smiths' collection (plus something else which was our second choice, maybe Len can remember what it was). We only wanted one song but we couldn't choose, so we did a bunch of them, and of course after we'd chosen a few and had a couple of good ideas, Len said, 'In the studio the next day, the band will absolutely hate this idea. They really will…'.

And they did. They couldn't stand it. They were moaning and whining. It was quite funny really, so job done! But once we started doing the arrangements and rehearsing it and practising it, it turned out really quite good, and those that were kind of complaining really enjoyed it in the end and could see the value in it. That was a really memorable moment.

I don't have a favourite track. I think people should listen to the *Vorony* album. It's incredibly well written and incredibly well arranged and some of the ideas on there and the execution are phenomenal. I suspect it's incredibly underrated, and we worked really hard to rehearse the album and get everything well mixed. It was done somewhere in Yorkshire – Castleford? The producer was Harri Kakoulli from Squeeze. Can you believe that? He had a Ford Capri 2.8 injection, I seem to remember – a man of taste!

I really loved the Germany tour in 1993 because we had a lot of new members and we got really settled. We rehearsed, we were tight and it was a good group with a great set list. And the audience over in Germany just absolutely loved us. There's just nothing like it; they're really into their music. And it was a proper tour. We had a tour bus and we had a crew and support band and it was a lot of laughs.

LA SALAMANDE
10 FEBRUARY 1993, STRASBOURG, FRANCE

PHILIPPE BARON

When I heard that a 'Ukrainian' band was covering songs by The Smiths, I felt it was something worth discovering. So when The Ukrainians announced a gig in my town of Strasbourg, I went to see them and I was not disappointed. Me and my friends had a great time and I purchased a few things from the merchandise shop after the concert – an audio cassette, a CD and a t-shirt. I loved that t-shirt, it just had the letters UKR on the side and gold and blue stripes.

In 1996, I was drafted into the French Army where I met a guy from Ukraine. He had managed to get a French passport and so had to serve his ten months just like the rest of us. He had a hard time understanding French, so I helped him during his first days. We were playing chess and listening to music – The Ukrainians, of course! The guy loved it. It reminded him of his country and he got to discover a bit of our Western alternative pop culture at the same time. Eventually, I gave him the t-shirt, and he was so happy! (I wish the band would reissue that particular design.)

I wonder where that guy is now. Maybe still in the army, and maybe he joined the glorious TDF (Territorial Defense Forces) of Ukraine. Slava Ukraini!

JOINERS ARMS
18 MARCH 1993, SOUTHAMPTON, UK

GORDON CLARK

The Joiners in Southampton was always my favourite gig. It was a very small venue with very enthusiastic crowds. The crowd just wouldn't let the band off the stage. And there was no backstage. You had to go through the crowd to get off, and every time the band tried to get off, the people just picked them back up and plonked them back on the stage.

The Ukrainians were always really, really good mates and we got on so well, like family rather than just a band. I always felt like I was part of the band as much as any of the musicians.

THE VENUE
2 APRIL 1993, NEW CROSS, LONDON, UK

STEPAN PASICZNYK

A crowd of fans from Germany turned up! There was a contingent known as The Mülheim Crew who would follow bands on tour at home and in different countries then hop between their tours from town to town. Obviously, we first encountered them in Germany so it was a pleasant surprise and I take this opportunity to mention them here and thank them for their loyalty. They were also into New Model Army.

(clockwise from top left) Len & Stepan (aka Luddy) at ULU, March 1993 (Steve Drury); Len & Peter at ULU, March 1993 (Steve Drury); on tour with Rev Hammer, Osnabruck, Austria, April 1993; WOM record store signing, Hamburg, Germany, April 1993; Len & Luddy on stage September 1993; Len, Paul, road manager Gordon & sound engineer Alaric, September 1993

(clockwise from top left) Roman, Len, Luddy, Gordon & Alaric, September 1993; La Sainte College Students Union, Southampton, October 1993 with Paul Briggs (left), Dave Lee (centre) & Len (right); Nigel Morton (live gig agent) & Len, Borderline, London, October 1993 (Dave Lee); tour bus luxury (Alaric Neville); producer Harri Kaoulli enjoying a curry after one of the Vorony sessions; what is Peter drinking?

SCHEUNE
11 APRIL 1993, DRESDEN, GERMANY

STEPAN PASICZNYK

The Dresden gig was hilarious. Len and Roman's debate about something or other boiled over and they went off stage right to shout it out with each other as we were playing 'Teper My Hovorymo'. Pete, Dave, Paul and I just played it on and on and on until eventually the two came back out on stage, to which we rounded the tune off and ended. The audience loved it. It reminded me of the Spinal Tap moment when the bassist eventually broke out of the malfunctioning pod prop once the song had ended.

THE LOFT
12 APRIL 1993, BERLIN, GERMANY

PETER

A lot of tour stories with The Ukrainians involve a lot of drinking and too much laddish stuff. But when we went to Berlin in 1993, we played this club called The Loft which used to be a theatre. It had a flat area with a stage in the corner and it made you think that it had a bit of an old-world history to it. The gig was as normal a gig as you could imagine, but the promoter was somebody called Monika. We never saw her until the end of the show. She had some legacy association with the venue, and she must have been in her eighties. She turned up dressed like someone from the 1930s burlesque nightclub Berlin scene that everyone associates with musicals. She had a sparkly silver dress on and the way she behaved was all to do with that time. She'd turned up at the end of the gig, at eleven o'clock at night, with a big bouquet of flowers and a bottle of fizzy champagne, and just came up to us all and said, 'Boys, that was beautiful, that was a fantastic performance, well done, well done, well done. So great to have you here. So great to have you in this wonderful artistic city that we have.'

I wasn't sure at first if it was real. I felt like I was on the set of a musical. But after I spoke to a few people they said, 'Oh yes, that's Monika. She's famous, she does that to all the artists who come here. She appreciates all the art, she comes and watches the end of the show, and then basically what she does is go out clubbing in Berlin.' The club scene in Berlin starts at eleven o'clock at night and goes on until four or five in the morning. Monika would walk around different clubs in the middle of Berlin and just socialise with people until four or five in the morning. She probably spent the next day recovering. And I think that's what her lifestyle had been ever since the 1930s, since the days of the KitKat club and those sorts of things. She was an absolutely amazing character. It was a real flavour of what Berlin would have been like, a real-life slice of the movie *Cabaret*.

STEPAN PASICZNYK

I can't remember exactly where we were in Southern Germany when a big rosy-cheeked, tipsy groupie jumped into our van with her Alsatian dog on the way back to the venue, making it plainly obvious I was her intention. Sound man Jem laughed and said, 'Luddy, it's your problem!' Outside the accommodation, she promptly squatted in front of me, peed on the pavement, then motioned as if to come into the building with us. I managed to bundle her into a waiting taxi and told the driver to ask her here where she was going. Phew!

EASY SCHORRE
13 APRIL 1993, HALLE, GERMANY

ARMIN SIEBERT, EASTBLOK MUSIC, BERLIN

It all started with the Ukrainian John Peel Sessions, of course. I am from eastern Germany, from the GDR and in the late Eighties our John Peel was called Lutz Schramm, who played The Ukrainians on his radio show *Parocktikum*. Western Indie music combined with eastern European folk and sung in Ukrainian? That was confusing and exciting at the same time. Folk and Russian – or its relative, Ukrainian, in this case – was something we were force-fed all the time and it was uncool. So, why were our Western heroes The Wedding Present doing this? This made me listen to it with an open heart and, of course, it fell on fertile soil.

After the Wall came down shortly afterwards, it became cool for some time to remember our very own past in the Eastern Bloc and combine this with our new Western freedom. Former GDR underground bands like Feeling B (a predecessor of Rammstein) or Herbst in Peking were doing Punk versions of Russian Folk or communist songs. Some German bands, like Apparatschik and 44 Leningrad, were defining their whole concept on this mixture. But The Ukrainians – first as part of The Wedding Present, then on their own – were the first to do it. And as they continued on that path, people in the GDR became faithful fans, only out-loved by the Ukrainian and Polish fans, maybe. With anything GDR and Soviet being erased at light speed, this was some coding that we could understand better than our Western brothers and sisters – at least, something that we were better at.

In the early Nineties there was no private party without Ukrainians' songs. We were dancing on the tables to 'Durak', 'Cherez Richku, Cherez Hai' or 'Oi Divchino'. At one of these parties, I met two boys (twins) who later became my best friends. They were a diplomat's sons and had spent their childhood with their parents in Kyiv in the Eighties.

For them, The Ukrainians were a revelation, combining their childhood memories with their wild student days. With them, I was even learning and translating the lyrics, which was pretty hardcore even for diehard fans. And we could finally even watch our idols play live! The Ukrainians were quite big in Germany, filling 600-1,000 capacity venues.

My favourite track by The Ukrainians is their cover version of 'Venus In Furs'. I like the delicate atmosphere and the dark underbelly, preserved from the original Velvet Underground track, combined with the heavenly mandolin sounds.

 CAFE DANEBEN
24 APRIL 1993 JENA, GERMANY

LEN

It all started pleasantly: we arrived at the café on time, unloaded our gear, set up our equipment on stage... and we even had a chance to sit outside in the sunshine and drink a few beers before doing the gig. Perfect! What could possibly go wrong? Well, what we didn't know, until somebody tipped us off, was that this particular Saturday was smack bang between Hitler's birthday (20th April, in case you wanted to know) and the anniversary of the day of his suicide, 30th April. 'OK,' we thought, 'but how can that possibly affect us?'

'Well,' our new friend confided, 'once or twice in the past, on the Saturday nearest Adolf's birthday we've had a busload of fired-up neo-Nazis turning up looking for trouble. And, of course,' he added, 'you're foreigners.' We quizzed the owner, who was beginning to look a bit worried, and he confirmed that it would probably have been better not to have booked us that weekend. So, we had an emergency band meeting to discuss whether we should pull the gig and find somewhere else to sleep. Being the people we are, it was a no-brainer – people had travelled and paid for tickets to see us, so we weren't going to let them down.

Then it dawned on us that the frontage of the venue was made entirely from glass, and worse still, there was no exit. The only way in and out of the café was through the main entrance, a set of glass double doors. The thought of what could happen in a worst-case scenario made it difficult for us to eat the hot meal provided for us, but we bravely jumped onto the stage at the appointed time and played a blistering set. The crowd loved it. They cheered loudly, clapped enthusiastically, and queued up in droves to buy CDs and t-shirts. We were overwhelmed.

And then, within an hour, everyone had drunk up and gone home. It was so quiet in the venue that you could have heard a pin drop, and outside there wasn't a person to be seen anywhere. Phew!

LEN

In April 1993 we were getting claustrophobic and ratty in our van and occasionally we needed to find ways to let off steam. I'm not proud of this, and apologies to cyclists everywhere, but when driving our oily old vehicle in the Netherlands, we came up with a game to pass the time. There was no shortage of very fit, healthy-looking cyclists to overtake, and we soon discovered that if Gordon took his foot off the clutch and suddenly pushed the accelerator to the floor, you could engulf one or more in a thick black cloud of smoke. Success was judged by how many cyclists you could get in one toxic cloud, whether they looked like they were going to choke, and how angry they got. Oh, the fun we had.

In our defence, we'd already done 21 gigs so far that month before crossing the border into Holland, so we were tired and wired and unfortunately we took our frustration out on them. Mind you, the memory of it still makes me laugh.

BEVRIJDINGS FESTIVAL
5 MAY 1993, LEUWARDEN, NETHERLANDS

STEPAN PASICZNYK

I remember us getting quite excited about the venue being decked out with blue and yellow bunting everywhere, until we realised it was just the local coat of arms colours. I've never been to a place where everyone was so tall. Most people there were my height at around six foot two inches, which I only noticed when having a wander round and watching the acts prior to us performing.

LA TELECORESCA FESTIVAL
7 MAY 1993, BARCELONA, SPAIN

STEPAN PASICZNYK

Never scratch your bum in public, or even look like you are picking your nose, as I discovered when Alaric our sound man reminded me we were being projected on huge screens at this concert. It was one of the massive gigs.

ALARIC NEVILLE

Barcelona is always a special, alluring destination but this gig seemed to have it all for me: the evening was warm, the venue spectacular, the PA, desk and crew were first rate, the stage huge, the crowd receptive and enthusiastic and the band raised their game, delivering a great set brimming with confidence. I don't think this gig was recorded, unlike other smaller ones, which means I have never heard a tape that contradicts my glowing memory of the night.

I had been a guitarist and performer before I drifted into sound engineering, coming from the creative side of the game while many engineers have technical backgrounds. I always enjoyed using the mixing desk as an instrument, manipulating the sound to enhance and embellish the band's performance on stage. I loved painting rich soundscapes with different reverbs and I particularly enjoyed timed repeat echoes on vocals and lead instruments, bringing elements of dub into some song arrangements.

In Barcelona, the stage had two giant video monitors on either side which were fed by roving cameras picking out various members of the band and audience. At one synchronous moment, the camera focused in on Roman as he played a mandolin solo and I flicked a long repeat echo on his last few lines and then spun it around the stadium left to right. Roman's face was around the size of house so I clearly saw him break into a huge beaming smile as he heard himself bouncing about the speakers. He peered out at me, what to him must have been a tiny dot in the distance, and started ad-libbing little lines designed to tempt me into more fun and games on the desk. For the next few bars, we played off each other over the heads of thousands of people, me doing ever longer echoes while he pulled more mandolin hero poses with each lick, beaming in that special way he had where his whole face smiled from his mouth to his eyes. Roman was always an old show off, and so was I. This remains a magical memory of The Ukrainians live and, particularly, the best of Roman Remeynes.

Sadly, not all our memories of him were so happy and carefree. Roman was always ready for an argument and would stand his ground on any subject, great or small. While he wasn't the easiest going member of the band to tour with, he could also be the wittiest and most mischievous. You would forgive him his ways because he also brought a charisma and musicality and was a natural performer when on form. Sadly, his mental health started to decline and there were many days when he barely got out of his bunk for anything but the actual gig. When on stage during one of the last German tours he managed to do, he didn't smile, speak or interact with the audience or the rest of the band. I remember patiently trying to coax him out of the tour bus to do the soundcheck but he just couldn't face it and our roadie Gordon had to set up and play his mandolin.

Not long after, Roman suffered a full-blown breakdown which effectively ended his career with The Ukrainians. After he left the band, he would sometimes turn up at my house for company. Some days he was lucid and positive, on others he would just sit and stare which was OK with me, he could do that if that's what he needed. His was a slow and laboured recovery but he did get himself back together and went on to other projects and a different, fulfilling life. The cruellest blow of all was that he then developed cancer and died far too young on 4 March 2014.

PETER

I don't think Roman did a lot of lyric writing in Ukrainian before us. I think he just wrote songs in English. I don't think he ever thought about composing songs in Ukrainian before that. I think we opened the door for Roman in that respect. His mandolin playing was brilliant.

LEN

Peter and I had a working relationship but I felt that Roman was trying to edge me out. However we're all human and we've got our faults as well as strengths and that's all part of how bands work. The tension made me feel uncomfortable but you could argue that positive results came out of it in the sense that it pushed both Roman and myself to be more creative.

HAYES ISLAND BANDSTAND
15 MAY 1993, CARDIFF, UK

DAVID COUNSELL

I first found The Ukrainians through the John Peel Wedding Present sessions, but then forgot about them. But they played in Cardiff on the bandstand in Hayes Island (it's not actually an island) in the spring of 1993 and I totally loved them. I bought up all their music straight away. Then I saw them in the acoustic tent at *Glastonbury Festival* the same year, where I should have died from frantically dancing to every song.

In 1996 I moved to a small village on the west coast of north Scotland, so I haven't been able to see them live since, but I've continued buying and loving their music. It's almost impossible to pick favourite tracks but... they are 'Oi Divchino', 'Pereyidu', 'Vorony', 'Teper My Hovorymo', 'Tsyhanochka', 'Arkan', 'Vykhid', 'Koly Ya Tantsyuyu' and 'Lito u Lvovi', plus one of the best cover versions *ever* (and it beats the original), 'American Idiot'. Their music is so joyous and uplifting, even on the not-so-uplifting subject matter!

ROCK AM SEE FESTIVAL
22 MAY 1993, LAKE KONSTANZ, GERMANY

STEPAN PASICZNYK

Another massive gig. Backstage before going on, we were eating food provided courtesy of gig organisers, as at every gig. Another band, the German rappers Fantastic Four, were on.

They were one of those bands using low frequency huge bass. I watched my drink and plate vibrate their way around the table due to the bass vibration on stage and wondered what it was doing to those in front of it.

 FESTIVAL MUNDIAL
13 JUNE 1993, TILBURG, NETHERLANDS

STEPAN PASICZNYK
Len and I had a debate about how we are perceived. Len insisted we are a Rock band with Folk influences. I thought it would be a good wind-up to insist we were a Folk band. As we approached, the banner outside the venue said in big letters 'Tilburg Folk Festival'. It was just funny but having said that, I also saw us as a Folk-Rock band, 'Folk' being the adjective, 'Rock' being the genre. After the festival, we were delighted to find untouched crates of beer in the backstage tent. It was only after we'd loaded it onto the van and driven off that we realised it was alcohol-free beer.

 GLASTONBURY FESTIVAL
25 JUNE 1993, GLASTONBURY, UK

STEPAN PASICZNYK
I recognised a friend from the Ukrainian community in Reading. He was at the front of the crowd near the stage and shouted to me that the bar had closed. I replied something like 'no problem, John' and lobbed a six pack of beer to him from the stage. All the people round him were of course surprised. 'Do you know him?' Perhaps it's not every day performers at Glastonbury 'reach out' like that!

 YMCA
27 JUNE 1993, GDYNIA, POLAND

GORDON CLARK
Gdynia was a fantastic place. It was Poland's seaside resort near Gdansk. We spent some time in Gdansk as well and saw the shipyards where the Solidarity trade union leader Lech Wałęsa made his famous speech. But Gdynia just reminded me of my childhood in the 1970s in the Isle of Man. Even all the pinball machines and games were still from the

THE UKRAINIANS

1970s. It was just really, really magical.

Before the gig the backstage crew shared some of their herbal infusion with me, smoked in a squashed-down Coke can with a hole in it. Needless to say, by the time the gig started I was on a different plane from the rest of the band. I remember that the lights started pulsating, going down and up, down and up, and I thought it was my brain about to break down. A few minutes into the gig, Pete started breaking strings and he was throwing his guitar at me and I was grabbing it, changing the strings, giving it back to him and then he'd break another string and it seemed to go on for the whole gig. Years later, I saw a video of the gig and it wasn't me – the lights actually were going up and down! It was very surreal, but not as surreal as one of the gigs we did in Ukraine, where the pyrotechnics were set off by the guys at the front of the crowd just with their matches.

At the time, Polish złotys were worthless so we were all carrying around big clumps of money. One night, Dave and I went out to some dodgy nightclub in the middle of nowhere and we ended up spending a million złotys in an evening. We were millionaires for a night. But a million złotys were only worth about £9. But even so I think we were still ripped off, because drinks and everything were so, so cheap.

The promoter of the Gdynia gig was an ex-naval radio operator who seemed to be involved with the local mafia. As well as putting on events, he had an Irish-themed pub which served real Guinness, which he was very proud of. Just before we caught the train back to Berlin, he took us to his pub. Some of his "business associates" were there and we had a drinking session. Now he thought he was going to drink us all under the table, but he didn't realise that Luddy was half-Irish and half-Ukrainian and could drink for both countries. At the end of the evening, I'd drunk about eight pints of Guinness and I don't know how many Luddy had drunk, but I couldn't drink any more so I started drinking vodka.

By the time we got on the train to Berlin, we were pretty much the worse for wear. I tried to get to sleep but that wasn't going to happen because Luddy and Roman decided to have a party and they were going absolutely mad. Dave was very, very drunk and at one point he managed to get himself locked between the carriages, having a panic attack and breaking one of the windows.

When we came to the border, it really kicked off because Luddy started getting mouthy with the guards, abusing them because they were Poles. I think they understood what he was talking about because there are similar sounding words in Ukrainian and Polish. At one point, they were dragging him off and were going to take him off the train but we managed to talk them round. We managed to get to Berlin station in one piece but I was tired and emotional after that day.

PETER

The first time we played in Poland was a spare day we had on a German tour. Someone said, 'Do you want to go and play at a Ukrainian festival in Poland?' We drove overnight and when we got there it was absolutely tiny. There were perhaps 40 or 50 people in an old school hall but they'd put a stage up for us. And, since then, that Ukrainian festival has become a really big thing, a two-day music and arts festival, bringing in artists from Poland, Ukraine and Canada. It's now held in nearby Gdansk where the main shipyard, where the leader of Solidarity Lech Wałęsa worked, has been converted into an arts theatre.

STEPAN PASICZNYK

For breakfast the rest of the band ordered in English. I thought I'd order in Ukrainian, with it being close to Polish. The hotelier was quite off, not serving me, repeating, 'I speak Polish, English and Russian.' Perhaps he thought I was some sort of provocateur. I got fed eventually but it was a weird experience.

LEN

We would probably never have got to tour in Poland had it not been for our friend Wlodek…

WLODEK NAKONECZNY

Details are blurred: Dates, places, faces, names. I never cared about documenting my own activities, so now I suffer from the lack of photos, films and reports that constantly capture the fleetingness of moments; moments that determined, diversified and enriched my life for many years.

I'm combing back through my memory – starting with a thorough audit of my archives and the Internet. I've counted at least 38 concerts of The Ukrainians in which I participated, either as an organiser, co-organiser, manager, tour manager, sometimes just as an intermediary. All this in the years 1993 to 2014, in Poland and – occasionally – in Ukraine. I have never done so many concerts with any other band.

The opportunity was provided by the Festival of Ukrainian Culture in Sopot in the summer of 1993. In previous years I had been involved a little bit in organising concerts supporting the festival with underground bands from Poland and Ukraine, which attracted crowds of people. The concert was called 'Ukrainian Nights' and was the first of its kind in Poland, a joint initiative of Ukrainian youth and Polish anarchist communities. I proposed

THE UKRAINIANS

The Ukrainians to the organisers of the festival, and they agreed.

But I didn't know how to manage that. All my experience was focused on eastern Europe and was based on private contacts. Marcin offered his help. He was a fan of The Ukrainians, spoke English very well, and knew how to talk to Western agencies. Marcin not only negotiated the details of arrival, but also found a sponsor willing to finance the organisation of 'Ukrainian Nights', at which both The Ukrainians and the Kyiv bands Viy and Zhaba v Dyryzhabli were to play.

The Ukrainians were also supposed to perform in front of an audience of several thousand people on the stage of the Forest Opera, where the festival was held. But they arrived too late to do a soundcheck and didn't want to go on stage without it.

'Ukrainian Nights' turned out to be an attendance failure. The festival organisers simply overdid it by organising a Polka dance party near the Forest Opera and a rock concert several kilometres away, in Gdynia. Only a handful of the most persistent ones arrived at the concert – at the same time, hundreds of the less persistent ones were cavorting at the Polka dance party.

This was the last chord of the concerts called 'Ukrainian Nights' – one of the most beautiful initiatives of the early 1990s in Tricity. I also had the questionable pleasure of meeting a disappointed sponsor. He looked like a gangster and was threatening Marcin, because there was supposed to be a crowd of people who were supposed to buy a lot of tickets. I was devastated, but Marcin remained silent with a stony humility etched on his face, which still cheers me up when I remember this moment. Because the sponsor wasn't a nice sponsor…

What I remember most from the concert was the stage charisma of Peter and Len and especially Roman, who writhed and danced spectacularly with his mandolin. We invited the musicians to an after-party the next day at the Ukrainian Club in Gdansk to which Roman and the accordionist, Stepan Pasicznyk, came. They were very communicative, open and natural. We communicated freely in Ukrainian, which was invaluable in the context of the times. And it was great, as if yesterday's flop had not happened, but then, around 6pm, Marcin said: 'Wlodek, Jacek is dead!'

Jacek Magdziak was my and Marcin's close friend from Elbląg, with whom we discovered the music. Jacek, heart of gold, was fucked: in 1983, he was kicked out of school for anti-communist leaflets and his life was poisoned. He never gave up. He and his girlfriend had had a car crash near Gdynia on their way to the Ukrainians concert that we, his friends, had organised. I didn't go to the funeral – I felt guilty, I couldn't bear it – and it took me a long, long time to get over. I still see my 'debut' with The Ukrainians as a disaster.

LIVE IN GERMANY
RELEASED 28 JUNE 1993

LEN

This was a run of just 1,000 copies, each one hand-numbered, and is now almost impossible to find. It was released on a German label called Blue Records, which was run by a very friendly guy called Michael Wille. He was a big fan and wanted to release a vinyl of us playing in Germany to raise money for Shelter, the campaign for homeless people, which was a cause close to his heart. We compiled the album from live tracks recorded from the sound desk onto cassettes at various German gigs. Unfortunately, information about the dates and venues where each song was recorded has been lost in the mists of time. To keep costs down, the cover was printed on fairly thin high-gloss paper, folded in two, with the vinyl inside, and the whole was slipped into a transparent plastic sleeve. One of my favourite photos of The Ukrainians from that time, taken by a great photographer called Waldemar Scholtysek, was printed across the inside of the cover.

TANZ UND FOLKFEST
2 & 4 JULY 1993, RUDOLSTADT, GERMANY

CHRISTIAN PLETZ

It was in 1993 when The Ukrainians played in Rudolstadt at the 'Tanz Und Folkfest'. I was visiting a friend in that deep dark eastern jungle part of Germany and we decided, spontaneously, to visit the festival. We didn't know The Ukrainians yet. (Sorry, guys.) Mea culpa. But what we found is that God is alive and that The Smiths were living like the UK-Ukrainians Jesus. Flash! Superflash! Kaboom! That's why I have followed your activities over the years. You are still resident on my turntable and deep in my heart.

THE UKRAINIANS

OFFICIAL TOUR OF UKRAINE

LEN

In August 1993 we undertook our first tour of Ukraine as guests of Ukraine's Ministry Of Culture. We played theatres and festivals in Lviv, Kharkiv and Kherson, as well as playing a set on the Lesya Ukrainka cruise ship, which was rammed with mafia types in shell suits carrying massive mobile phones. The ship was also host to the most jaw-droppingly stunning beauty queens from all over Ukraine. The tour culminated in a nerve-wracking performance in Kyiv's Independence Square in front of more than 70,000 people, an internationally-televised event to celebrate the second anniversary of Ukraine's independence from the Soviet Union.

You have to remember the political backdrop to all this. Although two years into its independence, much of the infrastructure in Ukraine was still run by the Russians. Ukraine wasn't getting the aviation fuel it needed, the Ukrainian language was only just being taught in schools again, and, because the Russians also controlled the paper supply, the only books you could get in the Ukrainian language were children's books. All the other books in the bookshops were in the Russian language.

PETER

We did about 80 shows in 1992 on the *Pisni Iz The Smiths* ('Songs of The Smiths') tour and somebody in Ukraine said, 'Your music sounds great – would you like to come and tour Ukraine?' We said, 'OK, but how much will we get?' He said, 'Oh, it'll cost you £3,000' and we said, 'It'll *cost* us £3,000?' He said, 'Well yeah. There's no money out here. People have got no money.' There was no national currency. They had something called coupons which were like IOUs, Monopoly money. He said, 'If you want to come here and play, we've got the venues, we've got the sound systems, we've got food, accommodation and transport. But you can't expect the people to pay for it because the people have nothing. If you want to do a tour, you've got to pay for the tour.' We said, 'It's absolutely mad… but let's do it!'

The summer of '93 was the busiest year for the Ukrainians. We did over 100 shows in that year. We were practically never home when you think about the travelling time involved. We'd be at a hotel and we'd get a call saying, 'Oh, in five or six weeks' time, can you do four days in Spain?' It never stopped. We made almost nothing from it. It was always at a small level, small clubs where you could just about pay for your food, pay for a few beers, and carry on.

The Ukraine trip came in the middle of that. So we paid the money up front. It was absolutely superbly arranged. We did six shows altogether and they were very, very

(clockwise from top left) The Dnipro River cruise, Ukraine 1993: talking to a fellow passenger; the Lesya Ukrainka cruise ship (Peter Solowka); on board with (left to right) Dave, Len, Paul, Alaric & Gordon; The Ukrainians ashore with VV, crew and tour guides; Roman, Gordon & Sasha (now Dave Lee's wife); Pete & Luddy in Kyiv (Dave Lee)

(clockwise from top left) Ukraine tour 1993: (left to right) Alaric, Dave, Sasha, Roman, Luddy & Pete, Independence Square, Kyiv; at Kharkiv Station; Len aboard the train from Kyiv to Kharkiv (Dave Lee); recording the video for 'Ty Moyi Radoshchi' on a street in Nova Kakhovka (Paul Briggs); Independence Square, Kyiv; Independence Square, Kyiv

different. We did a show in the west of Ukraine, in Lviv, which is the most European city in Ukraine, a show in Kharkiv, which is a Russian-speaking city right on the Russian border, two shows in Kyiv and we did a music festival right in the bottom of Crimea. There was a different feel to practically every one of those shows. They were seated venues with balconies, etc. There were no rock venues of any kind. We took a filmmaker out with us as we thought we might be able to make a documentary out of it, or videos or something.

ALARIC NEVILLE

The tour had been organised as part of the national celebration of two years of independence from what was the Soviet Union but in practice meant Russia. Clearly such an honour must have carried so much emotional weight for those members of the band with Ukrainian heritage. Growing up in the UK with parents who had fled the country after World War Two, waiting decades for the politics in the region to change and their country to become an independent nation once more, keeping alive the language and culture in exile. How magnificent and heartwarming for all of us involved as well.

In the weeks leading up to the flight to Kyiv, the grand return to Ukraine was the main topic of conversation at any gig or rehearsal. Pete, Roman and Luddy were bursting with pride and eagerly anticipated the welcome they would receive. Kyiv Airport in the summer of 1993 was still very much a Soviet-era establishment, far removed from the polished designer slickness the modern air traveller has come to expect. When we landed, there was no baggage reclaim carousel, just a huge pile of suitcases and electronic goods dumped in a concrete-floored hanger. Passengers and crew from the plane had to climb over each other to get their luggage or gifts for the folks back home from the materialist West. Each band member's instrument and personal bags were buried deep in this teeming ant hill of chaos, unattended and unorganised by any airport official.

The one exception in our party, which also included a freelance documentary film crew, was me. As a sound engineer, I had no instrument to carry and as a seasoned traveller I had long learned never to trust my personal kit to the lottery of airline baggage handling. As the time ticked on and the chaos continued, Pete suggested I go through customs ahead of the rest to make contact with our tour agent on the other side. This was clearly a sensible plan but it still filled me with trepidation as an Englishman speaking absolutely no Ukrainian beyond the rote learning of songs like 'Rosprydhayte'. How useful would urging a Kalashnikov-toting border guard to unharness his horse be if challenged?

I stood in line with my old blue UK passport in my sweaty hand, praying I would just be waved through but as I got to the desk and presented my documents, the officials appeared to take a particular interest in me and started asking questions I had no way of understanding. Then one of them beckoned me away from the queue and into a closed small room, just him and me. Obviously, I had no idea what he was asking me to do or say. If it wasn't about horses, cherry orchards or beautiful young girls I was lost. All I could do was repeat the basic phrase Roman had armed me with: 'Ya anhliyets, ya ne volodiyu Ukrayinoyu.' I am English, I don't understand Ukrainian, while pointing to my Ukrainians band t-shirt.

Exasperated, he produced some paper money and started waving it at me. All I could think was that he was after a bribe, or was just going to rob me of any money I had. I took out the roll of dollars we were told would be the best currency to take on tour and meekly offered him the lot in a 'Please don't hurt me, have it all' way. To my surprise he finally smiled and put the five pound note he had been waving in my hand, took four dollars from the pile on the table and urged me to pick up the rest. I had just been an unofficial Bureau de Change and, boy, was that a relief!

Still shaken from the money changing episode, I was then escorted through a pair of double swing doors by my new best friend in the Ukrainian border force. As the doors opened, he called out something to a group of people on the other side. Clearly this was a signal for everything to start kicking off; camera bulbs flashed, people cheered and slapped me on the back or shook my hand, and a pair of beautiful women in traditional dress pressed forward to offer me trays of food and drink before standing either side of me posing for all the cameras. Microphones were thrust in my face and a babble of Ukrainian questions were shouted at me. Yet again I fell back on my trusty response which seemed to be understood, and after a bit of discussion one reporter who spoke English was pushed forward to interpret. A series of questions followed such as, 'What are you looking forward to seeing in Ukraine?' and, 'What instrument do you play?' I have no idea if Sound Engineer was translated correctly but everything seemed to be going just fine. The beautiful women were smiling, the reporters were smiling, the crowd around them were smiling. For five minutes I was the centre of everyone's attention and my every word was translated and then taken down to murmurs of respect and admiration. Then my interrogator asked, 'How does it feel to set foot in the land of your forefathers?' I could see a consternation come over the faces of those around me when I informed them my forefathers came from Northampton in England and that I was not Ukrainian, not even a little bit.

Thankfully this was the moment that the doors behind me opened again and I caught sight of the rest of the band coming through with their instruments and bags. I quickly pointed everyone toward the real English Ukrainians and the multitude moved on to their intended targets, my brief time in the spotlight came to an end.

As an opening to the tour, I couldn't have asked for anything more memorable and unusual, chaotic and comic. Life on the road with The Ukrainians was peppered with such bizarre incidents.

PETER

We were treated like visiting dignitaries. There were people in national dress waiting for us in embroidered attire, and they had bread and salt wrapped in a rushnyk – a decorative, ritual cloth – for us, because that's what you do to people who come to your village or town. You break bread and salt with them. We were treated like celebrities, even though we were just lads from Leeds 6 in our jeans and leather jackets.

DAVE LEE

I don't think I've ever drunk so much for such a long time as when we were in Ukraine. We were drinking for a whole week. There was a lot of anticipation but a lot of nerves, and Roman was somewhat paranoid about Russian spies and Russian agents in Ukraine. On the plane over there he was giving us all a lecture about, 'When you get there, what they'll do is they'll try and separate you and try and take you to separate apartments and find out things about you, so you've got to be very careful. Be careful about what you drink. Don't drink too much. Be on guard.' So we were all a bit, 'Ooh, really?' and worried about it. But we had a few drinks on the plane. And when we landed in Kyiv, it was absolutely packed with people who could now travel anywhere, so they'd all come back from trips outside of Ukraine with hi-fis, TVs and electric kettles. There were trolleys piled high with electrical goods and huge queues to get through customs. When we got to the head of the queue, the customs bloke said, 'Have you got anything to declare?'. Roman – who'd had a few by then – pointed and said, 'Well, the guns are in that bag and the drugs are in that one!'

When we got into the arrivals lounge, there were all these bright lights and we thought, 'Oh God, there must be somebody famous on the plane.' And it was us! This music started playing and people ran towards us. The people who'd met Len, Peter and Roman from the time when they'd come before were all hugging and kissing. People were bringing out bread and salt, which is a traditional thing to do, and everyone was in national costume.

PAUL BRIGGS

Ukraine was both wonderful and utterly bizarre and weird, like nothing I have ever seen. I was still very young back then, and I hadn't really been anywhere, certainly nowhere where the values and the culture were the complete opposite of what I was used to. We arrived at the airport and – I don't know why – but there were all these TVs everywhere on the floor, people buying TVs from another country and flying them in. That was the first thing I ever saw there. The second thing was that we got through Customs and the whole airport was just full of people, with girls with flowers around their necks and everything, and TV cameras. There was a real sort of euphoria for something. We were looking round at each other and thinking, 'Well there must be a football team arriving or something. Or the Rolling Stones or someone like that?'

Then we realised it was all for us, and the whole thing about us being the first Western band in Ukraine suddenly hit home. They put all the flowers around our necks and we were being filmed and interviewed and everything; it was just absolutely incredible, and very strange indeed. That was quickly followed up by witnessing the incredible depravity there and the lack of value for life and infrastructure and things. Some of it was really quite horrid. I came back a completely different person. I never whined or complained about anything ever again when I came back. It really changed me. I think it's important for a lot of young people to go and experience something like that. You'll come back very different. The actual gigs that we did? Apparently, we did quite a few, and I really don't remember any of them, apart from vaguely the one in Independence Square because there was euphoria about playing in a location like that. But the rest? I'm afraid it's gone…

DAVE LEE

They whisked us away from the airport in this bus, at the back of which were ten drunken journalists who had come to see us, and we drove off into the darkness. I remembered Roman's warnings on the plane and thinking, 'What's happening? What's happening? Where are they taking us in the dark?' But it was all dark because there were no street lights.

We were taken to two or three different flats. Each time there'd be a huge spread, and we had to drink vodka and eat caviar and salo (which is basically cured bacon fat; it's very nice) and then it was time to go and we were told, 'You're going with these people and *you're* going with *those* people' and we thought, 'Right, they're trying to separate us now.'

Me, Alaric, Luddy and Paul went with this nice young lady called Alexandra who Pete and Len knew from their previous visit. She took us to the block of flats where she lived with her parents and her sister. We were in this dark corridor on the sixth floor of this block and she said, 'OK, here we are, this is my flat,' put her key in the door and couldn't open it. We thought, 'This is a bit weird, why can't you open it?' And she said, 'My sister's in there and she's drunk with her boyfriend and they've locked the door. I think they've fallen asleep.'

Alaric said, 'Let's just phone a taxi and go somewhere else,' but she said, 'There's no taxis to phone. I'll tell you what, I'll just phone some neighbours.' So she arranged for Alaric, Paul and myself to go to a neighbour's upstairs. We got in there and they said, 'Let's have a drink!' But we were ready just to crash out because we'd been drinking all night. So Luddy said, 'You lot go to bed. I'll take care of this. I'll stay up and drink!'

PETER

That tour of Ukraine was the single most significant thing we did in terms of its effect on the politics of Ukrainian music being promoted in the West, and for me personally in terms of what I saw and from what I know of the response of the people who were in the crowd. But even in Kharkiv I remember someone coming up and saying, 'I love your music. It's just like my grandma used to sing to me when I was a kid.' And someone else at the same show said, 'I really like what you're doing but can I give you a tip? If you want to make money, sing in English. That's what the people want. Nobody makes money singing in this language.'

This was the first time these people had seen somebody making an international career of any sort with their culture but with that Western element to it. And there was a respect amongst people that we'd done something with their music which no one else had been able to do.

SLAVKO M

Whilst working as an artist in Kyiv, I managed to meet up with The Ukrainians on their first tour of Ukraine in 1993. I was quite fortunate to know the entire band prior; I once shared digs as a student with Stepan, the first accordion player.

DAVE LEE

We met a couple of friends from Wolverhampton, Fred Syvij (who has sadly now passed away) and Mick Cos, who just happened to be bumming around Ukraine. They were in Lviv, came to the gig and followed us for the rest of the tour, as did another guy, an artist called Slavko Mykosowski.

SLAVKO M

It was a hot summer in Kyiv, and I recall my excitement when I first saw posters advertising their pending concert in Cyrillic, transliterated from the English as юкрейніанз. When the concert day arrived, the venue was in a Soviet-styled cinema merged into a concert hall. Kyiv back then was very much a dreary place where time had stood still. It was in slow transition politically and economically. There was an oppressive film noir greyness to it all, as if the Cold War hadn't left and Nikita Khrushchev or Brezhnev were still in power. The Ukrainian summer fashion appeared like progress for many people to express their individuality, but it was rather eclectic, with vintage Teddy Boy haircuts worn by aspirational guys parading their glinting oily hair creams contrasting with the iconic '70s longhair look which was once frowned upon by the authorities. They were all mixing together, expressing many identities without cultural prejudice.

There was evidently a lot of Kyiv press attention about this British band that sang in Ukrainian in the official corridors. People need to understand that the Ukrainian language had been historically subjugated and banned throughout the Soviet Union and the Russian empire. However, things were changing in this country for the better! After a raucous show, I was kindly invited to tag along for the next stage of the tour. A night train to Kharkiv departed, and we were singing and drinking in one of the rickety carriages into the early hours. I became an adopted crew-member, but I can't recall doing anything but partying.

 LESYA UKRAINKA CRUISE SHIP
20 AUGUST 1993, RIVER DNIPRO, UKRAINE

REBECCA WALKLEY

In 1993, the band was invited to play in Ukraine by the country's Ministry of Culture. Their tour took in Lviv in the west, Kyiv the capital, Kharkiv in the north east (which at the time of writing is under Russian control) and Kherson in the south (which again at the time of writing is under Russian control). The tour also included a trip on a cruise ship, the Lesya Ukrainka, named after Ukraine's foremost female poet and playwright.

Although Ukraine was a poor country compared to western Europe, the mafia (all men of course) displayed a decadent amount of wealth (to Ukrainian and The Ukrainians' eyes). Apparently, they spoke loudly into the oversized mobile phones pressed to their heads and dressed in shell suits. The ship had its own casino, bars and restaurant and the other  passengers were what appeared to be contestants for the national Miss Ukraine competition, who paraded around the boat daily in their swimsuits. You're right in what you're thinking; it's not always easy being the wife or girlfriend of a musician, especially when they are away on tour, on a mafia-run boat full of booze and beauty queens.

ALARIC NEVILLE

We were transported down the mighty Dnieper river in a large cruise boat whose funnel still displayed the outline of a hammer and sickle. Our fellow travellers were all the performers and staff who were part of the national Independence Day celebrations the Ukies were performing at. Stunning models due to stage a beauty contest mingled with local Punk rock bands, a German heavy metal act and the newly emerging strongmen and their henchmen. Law and order in the country at that time was nowhere to be seen so our group was protected by large, surly men in anonymous dark clothing carrying guns, a strangely unnerving experience for any Brit used to a police force that doesn't even carry guns on the beat.

FROM KYIV TO THE KOSMOS

On the top deck of the cruise ship was a casino, perhaps one of the aspirational symbols of Western decadence the emerging oligarchs were proud to show off to their Western guests. The idea that any of the impoverished scruffs in The Ukrainians' party frequented such places back home was comical but we were all ushered in with an ostentatious show of welcome from the big man in charge. Part of his display of power and position was to theatrically hand out crisp bundles of US dollars to every member of the band with a flamboyant invite to play the roulette table.

It is worth noting that at the time we were in the country, there wasn't actually a functioning national currency. The rouble had gone with the Russians and the modern hryvnia currency didn't arrive until 1996. In between, the state issued small coupon-style notes called karbovanets. When we first arrived we were given daily spending money, PDs (per diems, or daily handouts), in denominations of one, two, five and ten karbovanets. By the time we left, the denominations were 20s, 50s and 100s as hyperinflation tore through the value of this currency. Consequently, the stable US dollar was the preferred way of getting paid or spending for those that could get their hands on them. What was also peculiar to this situation was that there was no exact exchange rate; it was all barter and deals. A clean fresh dollar note would get you more than a creased or dirty old one and a clean bundle of notes with a bank wrap around them was worth more than the same number of loose dollars bills.

Turning back to our visit to the casino; we all stood around the roulette table, dollars in hand, happy to play our well-armed host's game to while away time and avoid any fuss. The one exception to this was Pete, always a financially prudent fellow and not one to literally toss money about when he knew the odds of winning were heavily stacked against him. As far as Pete was concerned, he had been given a bundle of dollars and he cheerfully announced he would be keeping them safe in his pocket and had no intention of losing them on any silly game of chance, thank-you-very-much.

This development did not go unnoticed by our host and his entourage. Most of them were standing behind Pete but from my position around the table it was clear there was some agitation brewing in the room. The protestations by the rest of the band that Pete should bet with the money fell on deaf ears and he proceeded to head off back to his cabin, dollar rich and seemingly oblivious to the offence he had given. The big man and his lieutenants glowered in our direction and started a heated conversation with Yulia, our translator and tour guide. It became clear the matter was not going away and it appeared as if some of the muscle was being dispatched to find Pete and bring him back to the table with his dollars. Len and I stepped in and said we'd have a word first and went down to see Pete to plead with him to return and play. Thankfully he grudgingly agreed to come back, although to this day I don't think he is aware of how close he came to getting all of us into a sticky predicament. As a general rule, I would suggest that the smart money choice was for not pissing off a casino-owning gangster in front of his hangers on and henchmen with AK47s, especially if we are all cooped up together on a slow boat for a couple of days.

PETER

When we played the festival in the south, right near the Black Sea in Kherson, we couldn't get there by train so we travelled down on a cruise ship that housed 400 to 500 people. It had restaurants, a little bar area with a stage and a casino. I said to the organiser, 'How did you get us on this?' and he said, 'Oh, this is the music industry boat. All the officials from state TV and the film industry use it, anyone to do with arts entertainment. This boat is hired by the state and they travel from Kyiv on the River Dnipro all the way down on a three-day cruise, stop off at the festival that you're going to be playing at and then cruise back.' I said, 'Well, who pays for that?' 'Oh, the state pays for it. It's a government cruise.' For Ukraine it was absolutely top-notch, with three course meals with waiter service, proper cutlery and champagne on the table, or the equivalent of it. But it was really, really dodgy.

The language we heard being spoken was all Russian. The people on the boat were part of the ruling elite, the ones who controlled everything, and it was so sleazy. There were groups of people in the bar area who were prostitutes and there were loads of lads, aged 18 to 20, in suits with this money that was coupons, folded over wads with elastic bands. They also had American dollars. They were sitting around in the casino area, just throwing money on the table. But those piles of coupons would have been gold dust to people in the villages. I don't know who these people were or where they were from.

STEPAN PASICZNYK

Being a fluent Ukrainian speaker, Len and Pete suggested I do the press conference on the ship. A load of microphones were stuck in my face and the questions started in English. I thought I'd impress so replied to all in Ukrainian. We were met with confused faces. We then realised they were from other countries, notably the Baltic States, so didn't understand a word I said and it would have made more sense for a band from England to just do the interviews in English anyway!

SLAVKO M

The band had a cruise ship booked for the next stage of the journey with some other rock bands, VIP passengers and a 'Miss Ukraine' beauty pageant on board. I was rather lucky to sneak onto the cruise ship carrying a guitar case shielded by the band, as it all seemed official at the checkpoint. No questions were asked by the ticket inspector who was a bit humdrum waving people on.

The 'Miss Ukraine' ladies were unfortunately under strict cabin curfews as a TV contest promotion was underway at the next concert. Anyone approaching them for a chat was simply ushered away. Understandably, British bands had a reputation! However, we all cruised merrily down to the next city in relative luxury, surrounded by morose Lenin banners in the stern, a casino in the amidships lounge, and all types of booze and tacky cocktails in various bar locations. I recall seeing the dark satanic chimneys of Zaporizhzhia bellowing rancid smoke; the dusk sky appeared like an eerie orange and purple haze.

The next day, it was full steam ahead onto Kakhovka for a stadium event. An enthusiastic but well-behaved crowd embraced it all but they were made to stand well away from the stage.

STEPAN PASICZNYK

There were various other performing acts on the cruise ship. Dave, who is very dry witted, was humouring a drummer from one of the other bands who couldn't seem to 'get out of band character'. He asked him his name and he said 'Ace', to which Dave calmly replied 'Ace? How do you spell that?'

PETER

Later on during the cruise, our tour guide said, 'The sponsor would like to have a word.' I didn't even know we had a sponsor. The tour guide took us into this cabin on the boat and it could have been a scene out of a movie. There was a bloke sat at a desk in white trousers and white shirt, grunting as he signed the paperwork spread out in front of him and not looking up from the desk. Behind him a bloke in a black suit, arms folded and wearing shades, was staring at me. I was stood there and the tour organiser said something in Russian to the bloke behind the desk like, 'He's here now', because he hadn't looked up. The translator said, 'Is the food all right?' I said, 'Yeah'. 'Tour been OK?' I said, 'Yeah'. He said, 'Fantastic.' He then pushed a piece of paper over towards me, still not looking up from the desk, and the tour organiser said to me, 'Your sponsor would like you to sign this piece of paper.' I said, 'OK. What is it, by the way?'

He said, 'It's a piece of paper that says the sponsor has covered all your costs.' And I said, 'Just a minute, he hasn't covered all our costs. We paid for it.' And he said, 'I know, but the sponsor would be very grateful if you signed this.' I said to myself, 'This is a fiddle'. He was going to claim this letter back as expenses from the state, even though we'd already paid him. So I said, 'Well, what's in it for us?' And the bloke behind the desk lifted his head up from the table, looked at me and said, 'Vot do you vont?'

If I was clever, and into the way that business worked in Ukraine, I'd have said, 'Well we're really enjoying this. Maybe next time we come back we could do some TV shows? Or a tour of festivals? Or we could write the music for any films you've got coming up?' He'd have said yes and he'd have made that happen. We could have gone on to be national TV stars in Ukraine. But I wasn't thinking like that because I wasn't into that world, so I said, 'Can we have a crate of your best brandy please?' and he said, 'OK,' whilst probably thinking, 'What a bunch of dicks.' I signed the piece of paper – if I hadn't have done, I might have been disappeared off the end of the boat and nobody would ever have known – and later that evening I was looking out over the balcony of this cruise ship when I saw this giant army truck with massive wheels turn up. Two soldiers got out of the truck, pulled the back of the truck down, picked up this big crate and brought it onto the ship. They knocked on my door and said, 'This is for you.' It was the crate of brandy, delivered to my cabin by two soldiers with guns strapped to their backs. And I was thinking, 'Shit, who have I just been dealing with?' It was one of the Mr Bigs, one of the corrupt Mafia-types. But that's what the whole country was like, when independence came in 1991 and the old Soviet structure disappeared. It was really scary. If Mr White Suit could have a soldier make a crate of brandy appear, he could just as easily make a troublesome Western musician disappear. The brandy was excellent though!

 INTERNATIONAL FESTIVAL 'TAVRIYS'KI IHRI'
21 AUGUST 1993, KAKHOVKA, UKRAINE

PETER
Kharkiv is a really scary-looking city, with a huge central square full of really big and imposing government buildings and where you imagine they might hold parades. We played in a theatre. It was a mixture of old traditional songs, our own compositions and a few Smiths songs thrown in and it went down really, really well.

DAVE LEE
One of the biggest things we did was called Tavriys'ki Ihri which was a festival by the sea or by a lake. We went there on a boat, which we caught from the boat station in Kyiv. Again, we weren't exactly sure what was going on or what sort of boat it was. But it was specially commissioned for people who were going to this festival. So there were loads of really famous Ukrainian entertainers, musicians and singers on this boat – and us! We had nice cabins and the cruise took over a day and again we were drinking eating and indulging on the boat, and in the evening, there was a cabaret. We reached the festival the next day and played there. The headline band was our mates VV. And we went back to the boat after

the gig and all these famous entertainers entertained us. We made some friends and some lasting relationships on that trip, relationships which still last today.

ALARIC NEVILLE

The distances involved in touring Ukraine were vast, like the country itself. Apart from flights and river trips we also let the train take the strain. One particular leg of the tour was from the *Kakhovka Festival* to Lviv, an epic day and night train journey. Not only was it a 600-mile trip, the erroneously-named sleeper train appeared to be crawling through the countryside at little more than walking pace.

Our party took over three compartments of sleeping bunks as the local Punk band VV was on the package as support act. The idea of a quiet carriage had not made it to Ukraine in 1993 and our plucky chaps did their best to liven things up for every poor sod on board, whether they welcomed such entertainment or not. During the vodka-fuelled session that went on and on and on, I lay in my bunk wondering just how many Ukrainian folk songs I had to endure before I would be allowed to attempt sleep. The answer appeared to be that there is always one more Ukrainian folk song to sing.

The other aspect of that journey that lingers long in the memory is the toilet at either end of the carriage. I say toilets, but a more accurate description would be a small room with a hole in the floor that had been the site of a dirty protest by a well-fed but incontinent herd of elephants. When the Russians left, they clearly took the state toilet brush with them.

As a lifelong vegetarian, I had my concerns about the range of food I would be able to find in Ukraine. It seemed sensible to use a good portion of my precious baggage space for a tightly-packed stash of protein bars along with a vital jar of Marmite; clean underpants were an optional luxury compared to actually eating. My Anglo-wholefood supply drew some comic mockery from the carnivores in the band at the beginning of the tour, but part way through the train journey from hell I was being offered silly karbovanets amounts for a bar or a knifeful of Marmite by vodka-rich, food-poor musicians. By the time we arrived at Lviv, I was close to being a karbovanets millionaire although my fortune was wiped out by the ever-crumbling value of the currency just over the course of one train journey.

DAVE LEE

That evening we were supporting the group VV, Vopli Vidopliassova, a very famous Ukrainian group in a round theatre, with a typical Soviet stage with a grey/beige backdrop. There were no lasers or lights or anything. And straight after the gig, we had to go and catch a train. Everything was running late so they said, 'Quick quick, follow us this way.' People got in taxis and they said we'll meet at the station. But when we went to the station it was worse than the airport. It was absolutely jammed with thousands of people and we completely lost each other in the crowd. Julia (or at least I think she was called Julia), who was one of the people looking after us, said, 'Follow me' and she took us to the train. We were saying, 'Where is everybody else?' and she said, 'Oh, they'll be here soon. Get on the train, get on the train!'

So we got on the train with our gear but there were only the two or three of us and we didn't know if anybody else had got on or not. The train started chugging away and we thought, 'We could be going anywhere. We don't know where we're going and we don't know if anybody else is on the train.' But then Pete and Len appeared from the other end of the train carrying guitars and stuff. Somebody brought out the vodka and somebody else brought out the watermelon and somebody had brought some salo and black bread. We sat on the train with the security guard who'd been assigned to us. We said, 'Can we see your gun?' I don't know if he had a gun. I didn't see it.

LEN

We were partying away on the train but we had been warned that this particular route was notorious for gangs holding up trains and stripping the passengers of their belongings. So, we had been assigned a "private guard", a thoroughly scary and humourless individual who was positioned on a pull-down seat next to the carriage door. He had a 24-hour stare and his hand was fixed permanently on what I can only assume was a gun of some sort "hidden" in the inside pocket of his jacket. He never slept, never ate, and certainly never spoke. Meanwhile we sang and made our way through endless bottles of illicit spirit that could be bought cheaply from an equally scary but enterprising chap in carriage 8.

PETER

The tour itself was very, very strange. We flew out and back, but all the transport within Ukraine was by train, because the motorway and road systems were absolutely terrible, so we had to change the way we did things. We'd have to set off for the town we were playing the day before the show, so most of our gigs started at 5pm or 6pm and finished at 7pm or 8pm. Then we'd unload and get the slow overnight train to the next venue, arriving the next morning. There was no zooming into cities. It was stop after stop after stop on the train, with loads of people getting on and loads of people getting off. It was almost like being on the Tube, it was that crowded. All the stuff we took with us – the cameras, the guitars, even some of the amplifiers – was carried on and off the train. Getting on a crowded train is difficult enough anyway, but making sure we had all the gear on board and nothing had been left on the platform was quite stressful. But it was an absolutely brilliant thing to do.

And you'd get up in the morning and go to the next venue, and you're supposed to have slept before you played. But we were The Ukrainians. We didn't sleep! We'd be on the train singing and playing, and people we'd never met would come up to us carrying  bottles of vodka and start singing along with us. One time, someone even brought their accordion along and started playing with us. So we would stay on these trains in the evening and carry on drinking until two or three in the morning, then get two or three hours sleep and then it would be time to disembark from the train.

INDEPENDENCE SQUARE
24 AUGUST 1993, KYIV, UKRAINE

REBECCA WALKLEY

The icing on the cake for the band was performing in Kyiv's Independence Square in front of 70,000 people as part of the country's second anniversary of independence celebrations. I would have loved to have gone on this trip but I couldn't take the time off work. Len recounted that it was probably the most bizarre tour they ever did.

ALARIC NEVILLE

Touring Ukraine in 1993 was a unique experience, and witnessing an independent state emerging from decades of Russian dominance was such a particular and peculiar moment. Evidence of the recently departed regime was still around: red stars, hammers and sickles, statues of Lenin. Alongside those were the shadowy marks where other Soviet symbols of oppression had recently been removed. When we played the central square in Kyiv, the stage was set up over the plinth of what had been a giant Soviet statue of Lenin striding resolutely into the glorious collective future, forever. Now all that remained visible beneath the stage floor boards was the imprint of the bronze and marble statue's feet.

The symbolism of this location was poignant. Before independence the square had gone by the catchy name of Ploshcha Zhovtnevoyi Revolyutsiyi (October Revolution Square) but had been renamed Maidan Nezalezhnosti (Independence Square) in 1991. The memorial to Lenin had just been taken down but the imposing statue on a 61-metre column celebrating the birth of independent Ukraine was not built until 2001. This was a period of transition for a nation looking back to its past in order to fashion an identity for the future.

Literally onto this stage strode a band from the West called The Ukrainians, playing traditional folk tunes and modern western rock songs sung in Ukrainian, a language that had at best been a second class tongue behind Russian for many decades. This event drew a huge audience, probably the largest crowd I have ever done the sound for in my life. As is usual at such events, the sound desk was situated in the centre of the stone paved square, high up in a tower built of scaffolding poles. It was effectively an island in the middle of a good-natured and exuberant sea of locals clearly enjoying the moment. All was right with the world.

As the band took the stage and began their set, the crowd took notice and began to grow as people from the surrounding streets pushed into the square while those at the back moved forward to see and hear. I became increasingly aware that the PA tower was not built to the rigid health and safety standards we are accustomed to in Britain. It began to sway like the mast of a sailing ship in a heavy swell as waves of people brushed up against its spindly, un-braced poles. Other more adventurous souls had decided climbing up on the tower would give them a better view. I was already feeling slightly concerned for the safety of the mixing desk along with the mere trifle of my own bodily well-being when the band reached the point in the set when the traditional dance tune 'Hopak' was played.

Oh, my giddy aunt! This was the cue for the entire crowd to cast off any last inhibitions and throw themselves into the national dance with a fervour bordering on an epileptic fit. The people between me and the stage who had been packed tight front to back, now needed much more space to flail their arms and legs about whilst at the same time avoiding their neighbours' lethal limbs. At this point it became apparent that the PA tower was not securely anchored to the ground. We were being pushed backward by the crowd, the feet of the tower screeching and scraping along the stone flags away from the stage. All the barriers under me were down and the few PA crew left had lost control, some retreating up the ladder to my first floor platform. The further we moved, the more the thick multicore cable connecting the out-front mixing desk to the stage was drawn tight until it began to lift off the ground. Some in the crowd started to jump over it as part of their dance routine, but not all made it so the tower was tugged over one way and pushed back another. We then started to twist round as people on the right behind us pushed forward to join the mosh pit while on the left a channel of injured and bemused casualties escaped the mayhem.

While all this was going on beneath me, those who had climbed up the tower were also joining in the dance, rhythmically kicking their legs out in the air while hanging on by their arms. After 'Hopak' I remember absolutely nothing of how or what the band played as I spent the rest of the gig desperately clinging to the mixing desk screaming at the crew to do something, convinced I was about to die as the tower fell, bones broken by the PA gear, or speared on a scaffolding pole and then crushed under thousands of Cossack-booted revellers drunk on vodka and freedom.

DAVE LEE

We were invited to play in Maidan and it was a very moving experience. I don't know how many people we played in front of. (Every time Len writes the figure down it gets bigger and bigger.) But there were millions of people there.

We didn't know what was going on. On the day of the gig, we got taken to the Ministry of Culture and were deposited at the foot of a big Soviet-style marble staircase. We were tired and I remember Roman and Luddy stretched out on the stairs while we were sitting around. The employees of the ministry were just stepping over the bodies on the stairs. Then someone went to look for a toilet and there was this door next to the stairs and they said, 'Hey, there's showers in here!', and because nobody had had a shower for a couple of days, we went and had showers.

We were taken into a very narrow room that was about a metre wide and with a man at a desk at the end and with seats all down one side. We were all sat facing the wall, and someone said, 'Alaric, you go to the stage and look at the gear' and someone else got asked to go somewhere else. It was a case of, 'You might be on and you might not be on.'

We went for a meal and then we went to the Maidan in the evening. When we arrived, we were told, 'Right, you're on after (whoever) and you've got four minutes.' 'Four minutes?' 'Yes, you've got four minutes.' Which was time to play one song. And we said, 'Hang on, we've come all this way to Ukraine to play on Independence Day,' and so we got on stage and said, 'Let's do this, this, this and this', which was obviously going to be longer than four minutes, and we went down really well. The crowd was fantastic. They were independent and there was no cynicism.

Afterwards, we crossed Maidan to go to a bar somewhere and there was a line of police. An expat friend of ours called Slabka was with us and he approached the police line and said, 'Can we get through?'. They said, 'No, you can't.' He said, 'Come on, it's a free country now. People have voted for independence.' And the policeman went, 'I didn't!'

PETER

The great big official party hotel was at the head of Independence Square and it was where all guests who came to the capital stayed. It had a giant statue of Lenin in front of it. There are pictures of me, Len and Roman sat around that statue from when we first visited in 1990 and saw the demonstrators. These were students who were living in tents as part of a non-stop demo to try and get the Ukrainian language recognised as an official language in schools.

When we came back in 1993, some statues of Lenin had gone and Independence Day had become a celebration of Ukrainian culture in Kyiv. So this day was a festival of Ukrainian culture. There were stalls with Ukrainian food, people busking, even people on horseback dressed as old Cossacks wandering around the place. Ukrainian language bands played all day on a stage that had been placed where Lenin's statue used to be. It was really symbolic.

When we played there, it was late afternoon and we had to go and catch our train afterwards. There were thousands of people watching us. Some already knew we were coming and playing. Although we were singing in the Ukrainian language, we weren't trying to be a Western rock band. We'd turned up with accordions and mandolins, so we presented as an acceptable Western version of Ukrainian music. But every other band on that stage was trying to be Ukrainian versions of Led Zeppelin, thrashing away with their electric guitars and their grungy old leather. I was watching these other bands for a few hours, thinking, 'Why aren't they doing what we do? Why aren't they engaging with their own culture?' And it's because for generations they've been told, 'You can't succeed with Ukrainian language'.

We didn't open the door to millions of people, but we opened the eyes of many thousands. Nobody else had ever modernised the Ukrainian language in this way and they could see some degree of acceptance internationally of Ukrainian culture. I've no doubt that we contributed to what became the growth of modern Ukrainian culture. Even artists that we played with on the tour later went on to organise countrywide folk and roots-based music festivals – something pretty radical for the early '90s.

When the Ukrainian currency was established in 1993-94, they started trading internationally and started to get their own CDs and recording studios and do proper shows, and some of the first bands that came out were doing the style of music that we'd done in Ukraine in 1993. You did get bands with accordions, violins and mandolins. Before that, there'd been none. We must have influenced some of those bands. When we went to Ukraine to do that video in 1990, there were people with cassettes of the John Peel sessions. They were passing them around. The real in-the-know underground kids knew about the music. They knew it was going on.

We've done about four festivals or one-off shows in Ukraine since, but no more tours there. We're most popular in places where there's already a knowledge of Ukrainian culture such as Canada, Germany and Poland, but not necessarily in Ukraine. It's because they've got people with Ukrainian background who've gone through the same transition musically that we have.

SLAVKO M

Lviv was the next exciting departure, so we were back on another rickety train traversing towards the Carpathian Mountains with a few bottles of vodka. The concert in Western Ukraine was much wilder than previous, the reason being the crowd were near the stage and embraced the language and the Ukrainian spirit more. This set us off for our return trip to

Kyiv for the band to perform at their final date on the Maidan, better known as Independent Square. This was the all-important Independence Day celebration which was going out live on TV. There must have been 40,000 people crammed into this particular area. Years later, it has embraced many mainstream performers like Paul McCartney, Deep Purple and Gogol Bordello. It is also synonymous with the Euromaidan anti-corruption demonstrations, which culminated in a terrible massacre in 2014; all fingers pointing at the Kremlin.

The Ukrainians to their credit did a fantastic tour and helped to establish a musical kinship with the country and inspire bands to sing in their national language.

My favourite Ukrainians song that sums up this magical 1993 tour? 'Hopak' from their first album.

STEPAN PASICZNYK

As part of the tour, we were taken to the Museum of Ukrainian Folk Architecture and Way of Life near Kyiv to do some music video stuff. On the bus we shared with VV, there were music journalists from Russia. When the bus pulled up, we went into the open-air museum showcasing villages from all over Ukraine, and the Russians ran into the cornfield opposite and started picking the unripened corn cobs and eating them. I saw the museum's doorman guard grin, shake his head, roll his eyes, and say out loud (but to himself), 'Ah, Moskali' (ah, Muscovites) as if to say that is what he expected from them.

A truly unforgettable moment was the gig in Khreshchatyk, in front of Hotel Moskva which is now renamed Hotel Ukrayina. After a long stretch of Russian-language heavy metal, we blew the audience away with the following, all in Ukrainian:

'Good Evening Kyiv, Good evening Independent Ukraine, Raz Dva Try (One, Two Three)' and then launched into 'Cherez Richku, Cherez Hai', whose opening lyrics are 'Vstavayte Kozaky' ('Rise up, Kozaks!').

At that time (the second anniversary of Independence) Kyiv was still quite 'Russo-phone' and Russian was still common throughout popular music. For example, statues of Lenin hadn't yet been torn down. VV had a cheery roadie called Kostia Syromiatnikov. He said that as a resident of Ukraine's capital Kyiv, he had only been speaking Ukrainian regularly for three years, learnt at school, whereas I, born in the UK, was speaking it from birth.

I remember our roadie Gordon's face of surprise and disgust when he tried to quench his thirst with a bottle of mineral water that had a salty taste. It was around the Kherson area. He said, 'Why can't I just get a Coke or something?' I pointed to a huge statue of Lenin behind him and said: 'Because of him!'

THE UKRAINIANS

HARRIET SIMMS, PRESS OFFICER, COOKING VINYL

My tapes got worn out with all the playing of The Ukrainians' albums in my ancient car. My driving got worse and faster when I put their music on. Through the band, I learnt some things I hadn't known before about Ukraine. That the cranberry was the national fruit of the country and was a significant symbol in folklore – a house isn't a home without a cranberry bush – and that when talking about the country, Ukraine, you shouldn't put 'The' in front.

Very few bands of the time seemed to match the energy or intensity of this band's live performances. I loved seeing them live. A long (long) time ago, I worked for independent record label, Cooking Vinyl. It was the late 1980s, I was quite young and had arrived there, more-or-less by accident, not too long after they had signed Michelle Shocked. Shocked had propelled the tiny company onto the centre stage, but it soon faced a difficult period and I turned up as they were in the process of re-grouping. There were only a couple of people there, not like now. For a while, I looked after their international marketing but soon became a press officer, to which I think it's fair to say, I was a lot better suited.

Cooking Vinyl had already developed a distinct and eclectic roster of artists for which they're still renowned, then mostly artists and bands considered to have a "roots" base, but what I think they mostly really shared, certainly in those days, was a Punk ethos.

So it didn't seem too odd that into this mix arrived former members of The Wedding Present, Indie rock band, legends of Leeds, some of whom, it turned out, were second generation Ukrainian. They performed music mostly inspired by Ukrainian folk songs. They were accomplished players, the music was charming, but I think what set the music apart was being played at breathtaking, breakneck speed. When a four track EP of The Smiths songs, sung entirely in Ukrainian, arrived on my desk I didn't know what to think. I didn't know what anyone else would think. Shoot me down but I wasn't much of a fan of Morrissey, but then I listened to The Ukrainians' take on The Smiths. I thought it was brilliant and, nearly three decades later, I still think so. John Peel had been an early adopter of the band and *NME* were amongst those in the media who became fans. And with album titles like *Drink to My Horse!*, why not?

I loved working with all the bands at the label but my relationship with The Ukrainians became that bit extra when they were invited to tour in what was then pre-revolution Ukraine. My boyfriend at the time, an aspiring film-maker, put together a proposal to make a film about the band's touring experience. I got involved in trying to help make this documentary possible. I learnt that some of their planes at the time were not originally built for commercial use and were adapted from military planes, so had a tendency to "swoop". (Also, I learnt that the person I was speaking to only had a limited number of phone calls permitted and so when I casually asked if I could call them back in order that I could deal with something else, they were, understandably, put out. 'No, I've booked this call two weeks ago,' they said.)

Eventually, the band did tour Ukraine, travelling cross-country, playing to huge crowds and being accompanied by their film crew (of one). (Sadly, I wasn't able to go along and left Cooking Vinyl soon after, eventually moving to Topic Records for several years before setting up Glass Ceiling PR.)

The band supported Ukraine's biggest band of the time and they got a wonderful reception from audiences, by all accounts. I understood that they slept, squashed on trains, drank a lot of vodka, made a video featuring a woman dancing, in traditional dress, around a haystack and a bonfire, all of which seemed a bit too close to one another. I think they were one of the first Western bands to tour Ukraine and the first to make a pop promo there.

The band returned to the UK with some interesting stories and some great footage but, sadly, the film didn't get commissioned or finished. Which is a real shame especially as, with the benefit of hindsight, it was capturing a unique band on a pretty unusual sort of a tour, at a very particular point in Ukraine's history.

THE UKRAINIANS

KULTURA

LEN

When we got back from Ukraine we weren't done for the year as we still had some European dates to do, but the experiences in Ukraine were percolating in our minds and we started to think of themes for the next album.

 POTSDAMER ABKOMMEN '93
4 SEPTEMBER 1993, POTSDAM, GERMANY

DAVE LEE

I often sat in the front of the van, annoying everybody by smoking. I'd sit there puffing away on cigarettes with the window open. I used to enjoy stopping at service stations late at night and looking at what they'd got for sale, cassettes and stuff.

I remember Len's banter, and Luddy was a great banterer. I remember him getting completely sunburnt in Germany. He was bright red, like a lobster, and he was standing there saying it didn't hurt him at all – 'No it's fine, it's fine, it's the best way to do it, get it all over' – and then every time we went to a service station, he would douse himself with cold water and he was drinking and walking with his legs bowed and his arms away from his body. But still he was saying, 'No, no pain, no pain'.

Travelling was always fun but a pain in the arse sometimes. One of my favourite gigs was when we played in Potsdam. We'd sort of reached a peak. The place was packed, and everybody had definitely paid to come and see us. Apart from festival audiences, it was one of the biggest crowds we played to. I don't know how many people were there but it seemed like a lot. Everybody was really into it and afterwards somebody said, 'Look, there's the drummer!' That made my day. It made my life! And they were too shy to talk to me.

One of my pet annoyances was us going into restaurants and then out again and wandering around town for ages and ages while we decided where we were going to eat. This used to happen in almost every town we went to. We had per diems for the day – daily money to buy food and stuff – but for the evening meal, the drill would be that we'd gather together and wander around town in a tight group, looking in the windows of all the restaurants and wondering, 'Can we afford that?'.

In Austria one time, we found this very middle-class restaurant full of normal, respectable people. As we walked in, the room hushed and some eyes looked towards us and some looked away. We sat around a table in the window of the restaurant, in front of everybody. We'd been in the van for two or three days and we looked like crusties. Everyone was looking at the menu – have they got anything vegetarian? Ooh, it's a bit expensive, isn't it? OK, tell you what, let's go somewhere else, shall we? – so we said to the waiters, 'No, we'll go somewhere else.' We all stood up together to go, and as we walked out, there was a huge round of applause from everybody in the restaurant.

I enjoyed gigging and getting the roar of the greasepaint and the smell of the crowd but it was fun in the studio. When we went to Wales to record, we stayed there, with our engineer Phil Wright. It was the best studio I've been to, so we must have got some money from somewhere. The drum booth was surrounded by glass and you could see the garden. Sometimes the drum booth is in some pokey little hole but with this one it was like you were sitting in the garden. Great sound too! In the studio you can hear the drums. You can't always hear yourself playing when you're playing live.

 WINTERTHURER MUSIKFEST
11 SEPTEMBER 1993, WINTERTHUR, SWITZERLAND

GORDON CLARK
The Ukrainians were supporting Siouxsie and the Banshees, and Queen's Brian May was due to play the day after. Once The Ukrainians and Siouxsie had done their sets, Brian May's roadies decided to have a drinking competition with us – which they lost! We literally drank them under the table. I left those poor guys slumped in the bar. I don't know how they got on the following day – or whether they still work for Brian May!

 RUN AR PUNS
18 SEPTEMBER 1993, CHATEAULIN, FRANCE

STEPAN PASICZNYK
We would always launch into the *Magic Roundabout* tune when going around Place de l'Étoile roundabouts in Paris and indeed any other large roundabout in Europe. Parisian gig-goers were difficult to read. They'd sit or stand very still as if it was uncool to 'get into it', sipping their expensive small beers, and you'd get the feeling you were going down like a lead balloon. Then afterwards, they'd rave about how good it was. That was completely unlike some gigs we did in Brittany. I remember one that was an outside gig and a bit muddy. Cider was the go-to drink, everyone was gulping fair quantities of it, all dancing enthusiastically, some in Wellington boots, and there was an abundance of red-haired freckled people. One lady smiled at me with a charming gap in her upper front teeth. It

was a different experience altogether from "cool" Paris, but then again Brittany is Celtic, not Gallic. It was the Brittany Craic!

 FESTIVAL SAN MATEO
23 SEPTEMBER 1993, VALLADOLID, SPAIN

ALARIC NEVILLE

The life of a touring musician is not generally considered one of the healthiest or most conducive to living in a calm and centred manner. Days and weeks away from your own home, relying on the whims of promoters to serve up nutritional meals or cheap easy calories, avoiding the inevitable pull of a beer or five at every gig to get you in the mood, long periods of sedentary boredom interspersed with frenetic physical activity on stage. The lifestyle can take its toll on anyone and its effects aren't always the obvious ones of popular myth.

In the days before smart phones meant we can all carry digital diaries with us and have access to emails and messages 24 hours a day, we had to rely on the near universal Musician's Union diary or possibly a Filofax to keep a hold on our future plans. Len was always an organised chap, constantly planning the band's next move while on tour. However, after a few beers Len did not have the best short-term memory as he'd tell you himself if he could only remember. He had developed his own way of dealing with the problem of remembering vital band information; he always wore a black Levi's jacket with two big inside pockets. On one side he kept sheets of A4 paper with a spider's web of notes about each gig and tour day, fees, guest lists, interviews, hotels, etc. In the other were more sheets of paper for longer-term topics. Both were constantly updated, altered, re-copied and examined daily. We joked that these were in effect Len's brain in paper form.

At one wonderful engagement in Valladolid, Spain, the gig was done but the night was yet young. We all headed out into the town to soak up the Spanish fiesta atmosphere along with a fair amount of local alcoholic drinks. My memory is that it was bass player Paul's birthday and him being the original victim of the time-honoured British tradition of giving the bumps to a birthday boy. This ritual ended in him being thrown into one of the central fountains.

Len was in high spirits and had led the charge, which in turn meant Paul decided to return the favour and Len was then thrown into the fountain in a good-natured retaliation. Much hilarity ensued as the pair thrashed about in the warm Iberian spring night and both parties were soon soaked to their skin. This was all harmless fun until Len suddenly stood up crying out in anguish. From his soaking Levi's jacket pockets, he pulled clumps of ink-stained papier maché, all his careful life notes now resembling a Rorschach Test on porridge. His paper brain had melted!

Back in the hotel the paper pulp was spread out on towels and radiators with all the care of an archaeologist unravelling a dead sea scroll. Faint pencil notes, blushing biro marks and the nebular ink stains were examined like ancient hieroglyphs in an attempt to decipher their meaning. For the next few days, Len was bent over the remains of his brain, piecing back together his plans for the future and murmuring under his breath, 'Deary me, oh deary me.'

NIGEL MORTON, UKRAINIANS BOOKING AGENT 1991-1994

I once booked a really huge 30 or 40-date tour for the band. A big part of the tour had three bands on the same bill: The Ukrainians, Oysterband and Rev Hammer – all on Cooking Vinyl Records at the time. That was around Germany in 1994. They had a tour bus with them all on. I remember flying out the year before for a festival in Rudolstadt. I was with my partner Barbara then. We got roaringly drunk so many times, which was actually wrong for me and Barbara because we were both in AA at the time.

It's odd the things you remember. After one gig we were all staying in an East German dormitory and there were no plugs in the bathrooms, not even in the sinks. We asked about this and apparently it was to stop people stealing them. It went back to the communist era days. Strange things to nick. You can't imagine the East German equivalent of Joe Spiv angling up to you in a bar and saying, ''Ere, mate, I've got a real good one 'ere. Enamelled. Yours for 500 marks.'

Another Spain gig was the San Mateo festival in Valladolid. I wasn't at that one but it seemed like the gig went well and there was a generous amount of beer and vodka on the rider for the band to drink afterwards, which of course they did. My understanding is that Len and Paul ended up in the fountain in the main square, frolicking drunkenly, swigging vodka straight from the bottle. Just then – I was later informed – a long line of people came round the corner being led by a bishop carrying a cross. They got closer and closer… and as they approached the fountain, they looked horrified. Paul and Len had no idea what was happening. The gig was over and the clock had just struck midnight for heaven's sake. What they didn't know was that the San Mateo festival culminated every year in the bishop baptising all the new converts at midnight. I recall getting a fax from the promoter who went berserk because Len and Paul had, in his words, desecrated the fountain. There was also a fax from the mayor of Valladolid permanently banning the group from the city. This was a potential new promoter for the band in Spain. Unfortunately, the incident severed any possibility of us ever working together again.

Those are really my standout, and actually my fondest, memories of The Ukrainians. I mean, they're the ones that definitely stay in my mind. I look back on them warmly now. The band was very serious when it came to songwriting and recording, but it was very rock 'n' roll when it was on the road.

I enjoyed Len's company, and Pete's, and Dave's. Len was the serious, artistic, cultured one who led the band in that respect, but he could also be quite daft after a drink. Many years later, after my lung operation, it was Len who still showed an interest and concern for me. We hadn't worked together for years but he sent a package to me at the hospital, so I had that waiting for me when I came to after the anaesthetic wore off. There were new issues of all the monthly music mags. He knew that would help take my attention away from the illness.

I picked up more about the culture of Ukraine from Pete. He still had family over there and I picked up information about the nature of the country and its people from him. I just thought, like a lot of western Europeans, that Ukrainians were Russians of some sort. I soon learned that wasn't the case. I do remember all the guys in the band were very easy to be with. Pete was the man who looked after the band's bank account though, that's for sure.

PAUL BRIGGS

We flew there for just a couple of days. We went out for a drink after the festival, and I suddenly remembered it was my birthday, so our roadie Gordon pushed me into the fountain. I don't know how Len got in there, but most of us were in it at some point. I seem to think the police came, and some sort of letter went to our manager with our names and our passport numbers on it, with a ban!

As it was a one-off gig, most of us only brought the clothes we had on. There was no washing machine in the hotel, so we were all trying to dry our clothes on the floor and fighting over the only hair-dryer available. In the end we gave up trying to dry them. We got back on the plane the next morning with our wet clothes on. We absolutely stank by the time we got back to London. I made my way back to Norwich but I needed to stop at the pub first before going home – my mates were waiting for me as it was still my birthday and I was still in my stinky clothes.

PETER

With The Wedding Present, one or two beers would be enough. It was completely different with The Ukrainians. It was like seeing the other side of the music business. With The Wedding Present, being Indie meant being in control. And The Wedding Present was so controlled, business-wise but also personally. No drinking. No messing around. Make sure you get plenty of sleep. It was like a professional football outfit in many ways. They weren't naturally people who would drink and party and stay up all night.

But The Ukrainians were mostly people who were in their late twenties or early thirties who had probably spent a lot of time doing the most boring jobs or not had jobs at all and

Assorted gig posters

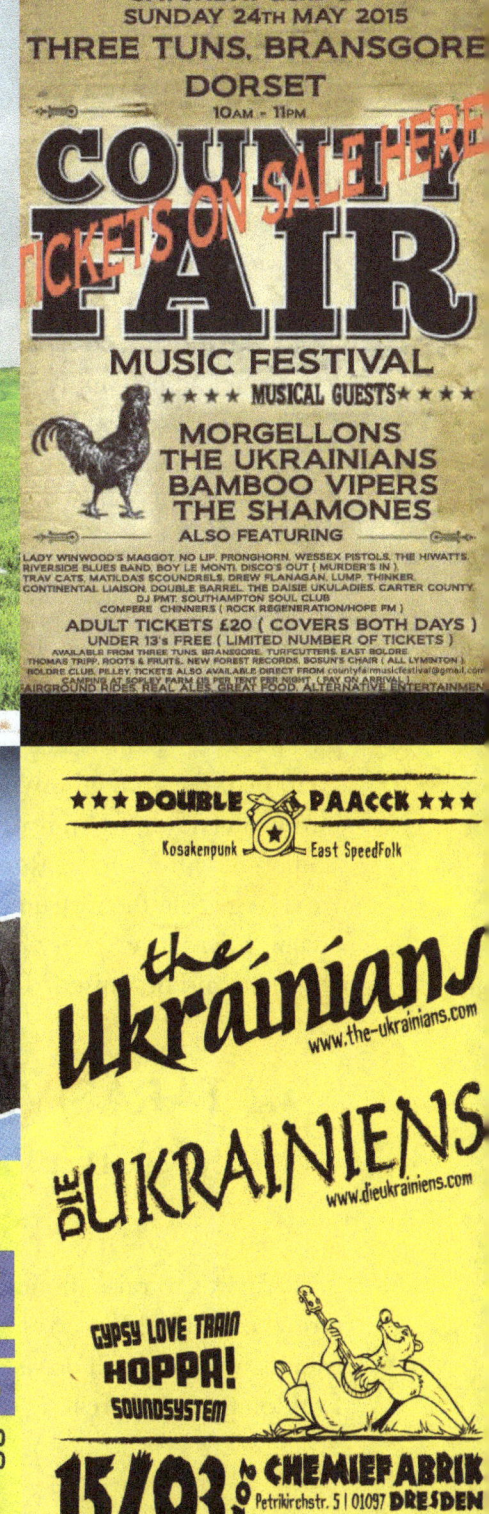

assorted gig posters

this was fun. You go out, you get driven somewhere, they feed you, they give you as much alcohol as possible, then they drive you to your hotel, you wake up in the morning and they drive you to another hotel and you do it all again. It was a completely different experience from being in The Wedding Present. The only thing that was similar was some of the songs that we played.

One of the things you would have to watch is the audience giving you drinks. They assume that drinking is what you do. There were many shows where I thought we were too drunk to play. But it didn't seem to make a difference because the audience were in the same condition. And the energy and the excitement feed off that.

The Ukrainians were a heavy-drinking outfit, particularly after shows. The promoters in Germany and France would know that and on our rider for gigs it would have 'so many bottles of beer, so much food… and a bottle of vodka.' And they'd never give us the bottle of vodka until after the show in case it wrecked the show.

The Wedding Present only did one tour with tour buses. The Ukrainians did quite a few. We'd take tour buses to Germany and France and just drive around and sleep on the coach. For the good of the driver, who needed to sleep once we were parked, we had to bring in a rule that once the coach stopped in a new town and parked up for the night, you had to go to bed. Because otherwise we'd have stayed up drinking until dawn and sleep until three in the afternoon, when it was time for the soundcheck. And it wasn't just people talking. Sometimes after shows, Roman and Luddy would start playing new folk songs to us and we'd be getting the instruments out and start jamming the songs and singing them on the coach. It was a very, very lively feel, whereas The Wedding Present was very cool, calm, collected and organised. This was a lot more dynamic and spontaneous and emotional.

 TARASIVKA UKRAINIAN YOUTH CENTRE
16 OCTOBER 1993, WESTON-ON-TRENT, UK

STEPAN PASICZNYK
This gig was to raise money for a Chornobyl charity and guess what? The Mülheim Crew turned up! I'm not sure if Carsten was in this 'crew' but bands create long lasting friendships and I still occasionally meet up with him for a few beers when he comes to London for short breaks.

PETER
Our pull amongst the British Ukrainian community was big enough now to organise this major music event. Tarasivka is a large camping / community field in the Midlands, where

an annual gathering of Ukrainian folk groups still happens today. There's a large building, a bit like a big school hall, and loads of space to camp or sleep in the car. We invited the most modern and uptempo Ukrainian artists for this event, which started mid-afternoon and went on till midnight. Around a thousand attended, mostly from the UK Ukrainian communities, but some fans came from abroad. I'm guessing that it's still the largest Ukrainian music 'festival' held there. I loved it.

LEN

The first major personnel changes were in 1993 and 1994 when both Luddy and Roman left the band. They were replaced respectively by Stefan 'Mr Steff' Tymruk on accordion and Mick West on mandolin, guitar and backing vocals, although there was a brief period when 'Stebs' Stebiwka played mandolin. Then Paul 'Dino' Briggs moved to Germany and bass playing duties were subsequently shared by 'the two Als', Alan Dawson and Allan Martin. In 1996 or 1997, Dave Lee left to live in Kyiv and Stephen 'Woody' Wood took over on drums. Jim was the last person to join our current line-up, becoming our permanent bass player in 2004.

While new players will always have their own personal styles which are really interesting to listen to, I don't think anyone came along and changed the direction of the band as such. Pete and myself had too much of a vision for the band to allow that to happen.

Woody is particularly vocal in the rehearsal room though – I'm sure he wouldn't mind me saying that! He knows the kind of thing he does and doesn't want to play and will let you know if he doesn't like something. That's a good thing, I think. It probably keeps some of mine and Pete's excesses in check!

MIROSLAW 'STEBS' STEBIWKA

It was 1993 when I joined the Ukrainians for the all-too-brief time I was with them. As a kid of Ukrainian parents, I was taught to play Ukrainian songs on the mandolin, so it wasn't a stretch to play that music with Pete and the boys. We toured Europe and England, including *Glastonbury Festival*. Fun times and high energy shows made playing the Ukrainian music I had grown up with a real adventure. I had many outstanding experiences in my time with The Ukrainians, and touring was especially fun. The guys were great to be with, including lots of ribbing going on in that particularly English caustic way, which some in my adopted home of the USA don't quite understand as being the kind of thing mates do. The music was already in my blood but the insane speed at which the songs were played was new territory for me. Was Dave not the fastest drummer of all time? In my experience, yes! Sometimes I wonder why I didn't continue with the band. I suppose I was chasing other youthful dreams at the time, but upon reflection I wish I had stayed in the band longer. Still, the experience has stayed with me, and I continue to play Ukrainian music to American audiences these days, with my wife Darka and The Borsch Beatniks. Once in a while, we play a Ukrainians tune.

PETER

We were quite prolific in 1993, playing over 100 shows and writing all those songs. Sometimes ideas for songs came out of those boozy jams on the tour bus or on the train, if we could remember them the next day. Len would write down sentences or phrases. When it comes to songwriting in The Ukrainians, 90 per cent of the melody lines and the chord sequences come from me. Very occasionally, if it was important to the music, I would add a phrase to the lyrics which I thought should be part of it because that's the emotion you feel while you're playing the guitar.

And then I would give the tune to Len or suggest to Len what I think the song should be about, and he'd go away and write the lyrics. And then we'd have a bit of a bounce back and forth about how we want the words to fit.

There may have been some occasions where Len was already working with some lyrics and ideas and concepts and I put a tune up and he modifies the lyrics to fit it, but I can't remember a situation where Len has said, 'Here's some lyrics – can you do a tune for it?' It's always been music first. If we were writing in English, it would be absolutely fine to start with the lyrics and I'd know where to go. With it being in Ukrainian, you've got to make the tune fit the stress of the word, and I don't know Ukrainian well enough to do that.

But we talk about what we should write a song about. Coming back from that tour of Ukraine we said, 'We should definitely write a song about those train journeys!'

Len has written some of the tunes, and because he writes fewer tunes, they tend to stand out more because he has a different way of doing it. His songs tend to be ones where the majority of the song is voices, because he's made the tune fit round the words he's written. The music tends to be a background accompaniment rather than a major driving force.

LEN

It's usually a collaborative process, but I'd say at least one song per album I write on my own. What normally happens though is that Pete's got chord sequences and tunes and he passes them on to me. I listen to them and see what mental images they suggest. Almost always a skeleton of words and phrases come into my head, and so the subject matter of the song is established. Then it's a case of filling in the rest of the words, which is a really absorbing task. I can find myself concentrating for hours and not eating until the lyric is finished.

I like to vary the subject matter, but generally there's a point to the lyric. It may be political, it may not; it might follow a traditional theme, or be about something contemporary; it could be a narrative or something more impressionistic. What I don't like are lyrics that are pointless, which is one of the reasons I really dislike most pop chart music.

In the early days I immersed myself in Ukrainian folk songs and was fascinated by how they worked, lyrically. I was really inspired by them and of course this laid the foundation for songwriting in Ukrainian for me. As a result my first lyrics were heavily influenced by these folk songs, but once I became good enough to read Ukrainian books and magazines I became more confident in using the Ukrainian language and started to write about a broader range of things.

Looking back now, some of those early songs were very naive, but they have a simplicity and purity to them. They work. It's amazing really.

REBECCA WALKLEY

The Ukrainians would often tour for two or three weeks at a time and they played hundreds of gigs. I would occasionally join them, selling merchandise. I remember long journeys cooped up in a sweaty van, Paul Simon playing on the stereo, driving past Dutch houses, on through Germany to Hanover, to Berlin, back over the border into France to Strasbourg. The gig venues unhelpfully zigzagged across the map of Europe as there seemed to be a lack of logic about where and when the band played but they didn't seem to care as long as they had a gig. It looked to an outsider like a rollercoaster of fun and frolicking (although I knew Len, Pete and Roman took it seriously). They were a mix of musically talented souls who probably wouldn't all fit comfortably into a nine to five job but given a bed and a quantity of alcohol every night for three weeks, they were happy to play.

Performances were fuelled by an addictive cocktail of adrenaline, sweat, the copious amounts of beer and vodka on their rider, mixed with adoring carloads of fans who would follow the van. Everything worked at these gigs; the band played with a manic energy that incited the audience to dance along, reeling, pogoing, fist pumping, mouthing the Ukrainian words, building to a crescendo climax, finally exhausted and wanting more. Amazing really, as the fans loved a band whose words they didn't understand, and yet somehow they understood. During this time, The Ukrainians lost two band members as they found partners en route. Paul Briggs, their bass player, met Sabine in Cologne and Dave Lee, their drummer, found love with Sasha in Kyiv. Neither band member returned home to live in England.

KULTURA
RELEASED 31 JANUARY 1994

PETER

That trip to Ukraine became the inspiration for our next album, *Kultura*. Most of the songs that were written there were about the clashes of culture and the way culture was changing in the country that we saw. The West had to get used to eastern European countries joining the European Union, so we wrote songs like 'Europa', expressing the views of people in Ukraine that we came across who wanted to be part of the wider Europe, and about the positivity of the things you can find in Europe – clubs in Berlin, sun in Barcelona, high culture in Vienna, all sorts of interesting things in Amsterdam. One of the reasons there's war now is because Ukraine is facing west instead of east.

'Kyivskyy Express' is about immigration, because people were travelling from Kyiv to the West and yet some people from my background were travelling east to try and discover their roots and set up a business in Kyiv. It was about the issues when you move from one culture to another. Can you cope with it, where is your home and what do you call your home? So there is a theme running through the album which is to do with that clash of cultures.

We always had a lot of support from the more aware media – Channel 4, some parts of the BBC like the World Service, *The Guardian* – but not the mainstream music papers. As soon as you sing in Ukrainian and it becomes a band that just doesn't sing in English, you don't get coverage. *Songlines* magazine has covered us sometimes and *Folk Roots* but that language issue is a massive barrier, and not one you find abroad. In Germany, for example, you get bands that sing in German and bands that sing in English. But in Britain we'd gone beyond the boundaries of acceptable music.

We chose to create the artwork ourselves again with this album. The cover says what we experienced in Ukraine in 1993. There's a blue and yellow statue of liberty breaking out from under a sea of "communist" hammers and sickles. This move towards a western idea of freedom was a process that we saw beginning, and one that would take many years to achieve. As we write in 2024, it's still going on now, but in a more deadly form.

The *Kultura* album was just as well received as previous albums but there weren't as many shows. In many ways *Kultura* is the album I was most satisfied with. It was like a transition. Our first album was reflections on a made-up world from the past, and what made us different because we've got this country and we've got these memories, and the *Kultura* album was about what it's like to be in that transition now to making your own country. We had started off writing songs based entirely on romantic Ukrainian ideas that come from historic beautiful pastoral village scenes. When we got to *Kultura*, we were writing songs about the real world as we saw it and the issues that people in Ukraine had. We'd been to Ukraine and played, we'd seen what it was like and we'd seen the country changing and our music had changed too. And if you understood Ukrainian, you would see that in our lyrics even if the change wasn't obvious in the music. For me that was the completion of a journey. I was and remain really happy with that album.

One of the songs was called 'UkrainAmerica', which was a real spoof of what people in Ukraine think the West is. Everyone wanted MTV, everybody wanted burgers and McDonalds. The country had gone through a transition and so had we. I couldn't have imagined writing a song like that when we started out.

LEN

We took our time over the *Vorony* album, but *Kultura* seemed to come out of nowhere. When the time arrived to deliver an album, we had the songs written and went into the studio to record them. It all seemed effortless. The producer was Phil Wright, who had been our live sound engineer, and we did the initial sessions at Monnow Valley studios in south Wales, where Black Sabbath recorded. My main memory of that now is that the studio was at the end of a long country lane populated with hundreds of rabbits. Funny the things you remember. I don't have any memory of recording anything there but I vividly remember the bunnies outside.

The second set of sessions was at Elephant Studios in Wapping. It was in a basement on Metropolitan Wharf, on the north bank of the Thames. The Smiths had demoed their first album there, so we were on hallowed ground as far as I was concerned. We had difficulty getting the sound we wanted though, so we took the tapes back up to Yorkshire and mixed the album at Woodlands in Castleford. The engineer was an ex-miner from Doncaster called Pat Grogan, who was a very funny guy but he took no prisoners. If you said anything vaguely intellectual, he'd either laugh at you or wither you with one of his looks.

Kultura was released in January 1994. A lot of the lyrics I came up with came as a result of the eye-opening experiences we'd had on tour in Ukraine the previous year. The politics, the desperation, the corruption, the fact that there seemed to be no dividing lines between government officials and the mafia, all seemed so alien to us. Even paper to print anything but children's books was still apparently controlled by Russia, and certain foods and aviation fuel were difficult to get hold of for the same reason. It was hard to digest such a reality, and we could see it was incredibly hard for Ukrainians to function in such an environment, especially when the rest of the world thought they were now truly independent. In so many ways they weren't. People we met told us that a lot of the infrastructure – and the people in control – were the same as in Soviet times.

Чекання

Вже приходить ніч туманна
Сумно, тихо на воді
Ледве чути голос пташенята
І не видно кораблі

А десь тече, тече спокійна річка
Та шумить зелений гай
Там тепер природа процвітає
До світанку почекай!

Я візьму тебе на Верховину
Там знайдем чудовий край
Поглянемо на полонину
На чарівний, безмежний рай

За горою сонечко лягає
Раптом зимно на дворі
Ой турбують ненадійні думи
І зменшаються дороги

Я візьму тебе на Верховину
Там знайдем чудовий край
Поглянемо на полонину
На чарівний, безмежний рай

Chekannya (**Expectation**)

The foggy night is already coming
Sad, quiet on the water
You can barely hear a small bird's call
And there are no ships

And somewhere, a calm river flows
But the green grove is noisy
Nature is flourishing there now
Wait until dawn!

I will take you to Verkhovyna
There we will find a wonderful land
Let us look at the landscape
A magical, boundless paradise

The sun is setting behind the mountain
Suddenly it's winter outside
Oh, hopeless thoughts trouble me
And the roads diminish

I will take you to Verkhovyna
There we will find a wonderful land
Let us look at the landscape
A magical, boundless paradise

Київський Експрес

Я їду поїздом
Їду до Києва
я на краю безнадії
Бо вдома нічого немає
І здається, на жаль, мені
що краще он там тобі
ну, звідкіля ця безглуздість
І моя нестямна душа?

Краще нам їхати поїздом
Краще на Україну поїздом

Ти їдеш поїздом
Їдеш на Захід
я на краю руїни
Бо вдома нічого немає
І здається, на жаль, тобі
що краще ось тут мені
ну, звідкіля ця наївність
І твоя невинна душа?

Краще нам їхати поїздом
Краще на Захід поїздом

Я, як і ти, бідний і безглуздий
Ми на краю руїни
Ми, як і всі, щось шукаємо
Бо тут нічого немає

А що це на обрії?
Привиди утопії?
Ну, хай живе існування і хай живе життя!

Краще нам їхати додому
Краще нам їхати поїздом
Краще нам їхати додому
Краще нам їхати поїздом

Kyivskyy Express

I'm going by train
I'm going to Kyiv
I'm on the brink of despair
Because there's nothing at home
And it seems to me
It is better over there
Well, where did this nonsense
Come from - and my restless soul?

It's better that we go by train
Better to Ukraine by train!

You're coming by train
You're coming to the West
You're on the brink of ruin
Because you've got nothing at home
And it seems to you
that it's better over here
Well, where did this innocence
Come from - and your naive soul?

It's better that we go by train
Better to the West by train!

I, like you, am poor and stupid
We're on the brink of ruin
Like everyone else we're looking for something
Because there's nothing here

And what are those on the horizon?
Spectres of Utopia?
Well, long live living and long live life!

It's better that we go back home
Better to go by train!
It's better that we go back home
Better to go by train!

One song, 'UkrainAmerica', anticipated the effect that multinational corporations and advertising would exert. Now Ukrainians would be taught to consume certain brands of Western soft drinks, beef burgers and cigarettes, and to think of them as 'cool'. 'Polityka' described the new breed of manipulative politician who had appeared in the country, cynically exploiting a naïve and inexperienced electorate.

PETER

I like the song 'Europa'. It is such an optimistic song. When we first started playing lots of European tours, we realised there was just so much to see in this fantastic continent. The whole song is a list of clichés of what you can experience in each particular country, but together it paints a picture of all the wonderful things that we experienced when we were on tour in the early '90s.

At the time, Europe was opening up, trade was easier, the Schengen agreement for freedom of movement was coming in, everything looked rosy. Even from a Ukrainian point of view, the possibility that the newly independent country could become part of a new open and free Europe was being talked about. Eventually, the revolution of 2014, and arguably the invasion of 2022 were due to Ukraine moving towards the European sphere, but at the time we wrote the song (1993), everything was pointing to a bright and free future. I still feel that optimism when I hear the song.

PAUL BRIGGS

What most people who are not in a band don't realise is that not much of it is really anything to do with music. You're travelling and doing other stuff and get to play live for a couple of hours a day, but the rest of it is something else. I really liked doing the musician stuff, whether it was playing live or particularly rehearsing. I used to like rehearsing with the band because we were a good unit by then. The band was kind of

Europa - A

settled and we had some new members. I remember particularly the *Kultura* album. We were rehearsing in a room in Bradford somewhere, and we worked really hard, trying to get that right and working on the arrangements. Both Len and Pete had some great ideas for songs, so that when we went in the studio, we were really quite tight.

ANDREW DARLINGTON, *KULTURA* REVIEW & BAND INTERVIEW

This ain't no Disco. This ain't no Country Club either. This is… a rain-silted night in run-down inner-city Leeds where they even steal the street signs to confuse intruders. But,

THE UKRAINIANS

appropriately, it's Czar Street. Besieged by overgrown dereliction, we are in a converted chapel subdivided into sound studios. Every now and then Tamla Motown pulses through insulated walls from semi-pro noisemakers in some adjoining suite. While The Ukrainians are gnawing around what their PR handout claims to be a cultural collision of 'chord progressions and melodies commonly found in ethnic Ukrainian music with the dynamics and rhythms of Western Rock.'

More concisely The Ukrainians' current album is a healthy indulgence for your ears, a positive glut of transglobal Pop-U-Like. The CD cover has the Statue of Liberty resprayed in the Ukrainian national colours – blue and yellow, and it's thrusting up through a junkheap of discarded hammer-and-sickles, the lure of McDonalds and Coke. While the insert lists titles such as 'Polityka', 'UkrainAmerica' and 'Zillya Zelenenke' which all surf a fine line between the rival theses of East and West; and, brothers and sisters, The Ukrainians excel in being both.

'In some journalists' eyes, this kind of thing labels us a folk band,' explains Pete Solowka. 'They don't understand that you can be a contemporary musician and have a band like The Ukrainians.' He looks at you intently as you fire your questions. Then glances away while he thinks up an answer. 'I've been in a variety of bands,' he adds. 'Probably the most notable being The Wedding Present. You do get a certain amount of confidence when you know you're a person who can create music. And as my confidence grew, I realised that the one thing I really wanted to do was perform in the Ukrainian image, with Ukrainian themes, lyrics and song-structures…'

Co-conspirator Len Liggins likens what they do to what's happening in other second-generation immigrant communities. 'A lot of people, like Apaché Indian (who had a 1993 hit with 'Boom Shack A Lak'), Monsoon (who had a 1982 hit with 'Ever So Lonely'), the Bhangra bands and so on, sell huge numbers of records and tapes. But they're not readily available in traditional British chart return record shops. There was one quoted recently which, over a period of time, actually outsold the then-chart-topping single. If the sales samples had included Indian and Pakistani shops it would have been number 1. Which is bizarre, because it obviously got no media attention at all outside their own community. It would be really nice to hear more of that music, but we're not exposed to it. In the same way, we're trying to expose people to music that has Ukrainian content.'

Kultura is just the latest manifestation of this process. An album that captivates, and sometimes holds you to ransom.

There are six sartorially thrown-together members of the current Ukrainians line-up in attendance, rehearsing for a tour that will – as you read this, be 'navigating the autobahns of Europe in a tired alcoholic haze' and 'playing World Music festivals where you can't even pronounce any of the other names on the bill.' There's Pete, and the 'Legendary' Len, who acquired his well-deserved epithet from the equally legendary DJ John Peel. Sometime-

Європа

Ми музиканти - їдемо з Києва
У далекий кр**ай**
Щоби заграти тай мандрувати,
Це **є** наш звичай **є** наш звичай

Хмари **у** Лондоні, сонце **в** Барселоні
В Мюнхені **є** добре пиво – і акордеони!
Кохання **в** Парижі і високі вежі
Вид Віденської класики кращої нема

Ми ще поїдемо дальше
Ми ще не знаємо, що нас дочекає
Що побачемо

Європа, Європа
Ти не молода
Європа, Європа
Вже нова пора

Історія **в Афінах**
І також **у** Римі
Шоколад **у** Брюсселі
А що **є в** Амстердамі?

Ґіннес **у** Дубліні
Клюби **у** Берліні
Там не можна спати аж до самого дня

Europa (Europe)

We are musicians, we come from Kyiv
To a faraway country
To rove and play
That's what we do!

Clouds in London, sun in Barcelona
In Munich there is good beer – and accordions!
In Paris, love and high towers
And there is nothing finer than the classic style of the Viennese

Yet we will go further
We still do not know what is waiting for us
What we will see

Europe, Europe - you may not be young
Europe, Europe - but it is a new time

History in Athens, and Rome too
Chocolate in Brussels and what have you in Amsterdam?
Guinness in Dublin, clubs in Berlin
You can't sleep until morning!

Політика

Поблизу нікого нема
крім на екрані чоловіка
зовсім ясно, чому він тут
я без нього, як без рук
Нібито я його слуга

нам потрібна політика

Він людина, що політикується
Досягла всього сама
Він цинічний, а мені здається
Це державна зрада

Він і гадки немає
"Що вам бракує", питає
«Весь народ – на Майдан!
Пора! Биймо в барабан!»
Але нам тільки мріється

нам потрібна політика

Він людина, що політикується
Він сам себе обслуговує
Він жадібний, а мені здається
Це державна зрада

Polityka (**Politics**)

There's no-one near
except the man on the screen
It's quite clear why he's here
Not having him would be like having no arms
I am his slave

We need politics

He's someone who plays games
He's a self-made man
He's a cynic
And to me that's treason

He has no principles
"What do you need?", he says
"Come to the square, it's time to beat the drum!"
But we can only dream

We need politics

He's someone who plays games
He serves himself
He is greedy
And to me that's treason

poet and former Sinister Cleaner, Len's solo career includes the strange and wonderful *New Musical Express* Single of the Week 'A Remedy For Bad Nerves' and its low-rent nervy follow-up, 'A Headful Of Ants'. Such projects came before his stint as part-time vocalist and fiddle-player for Leeds' Wedding Present during their brief but innovative Ukrainian guise.

That's where Len first plotted with Pete to make the Weddoes' eccentric spin-off into the full-time venture it has since become. Len is so forward-thinking even his watch is set five minutes fast. The other Ukrainians include mandolin-playing Mick West, who also provides 'female backing vocals' and is loosely based in Hebden Bridge on the Pennine steppes. Then there's bassist Allan Martin, accordion-player Steve 'Mr Steff' Tymruk, who has half-German half-Ukrainian genealogy and corkscrews of black hair hung in defiance of gravity. And drummer of long standing and some sitting, 'Country' Dave Lee, supporting the Ukrainians merchandising division by wearing a band-logo'd t-shirt.

Vorony, The Ukrainians' second album, came via the Cooking Vinyl label in 1993. And although the bulk of the material is made up of Pete and Len originals, they also do mutant revisions – not only of The Smiths' 'The Queen Is Dead', but also The Velvet Underground's 'Venus In Furs' in a suitably Ukrainian retread. A smart and attention-grabbing strategy for opening out their market, or is there ethnic vindication for such coverology?

'I'd better get the story straight now,' grins Len. 'The original Lou Reed song was inspired by Sacher-Masoch's book, and writer Leopold was actually born in what is now Ukraine – even though it wasn't Ukraine at the time. There are also connections with The Velvet Underground's then-mentor Andy Warhol. One of his parents, and the original spelling of his name – Warholla – are Ukrainian. And quite genuinely the chord sequences in the song wouldn't be out of place in a traditional Ukrainian tune. So, for various reasons, it seemed like a really ideal song to do.'

So can you fabricate an equally convincing justification for doing The Smiths' song? 'Well, that's probably a little more difficult, but it wasn't a contrived PR thing… I don't know why I'm going on the defensive here,' he laughs. 'The Smiths are the band that reflect the England of the Eighties in the best way I've ever heard. And in the same way that the traditional tunes we've covered are traditional Ukrainian folk songs, the Smiths' songs we've covered are traditional British/Western Indie rock songs. The whole thing about The Ukrainians is that we have a foot in both camps. Obviously, our music is inspired by being exposed to traditional Folk music in the east, and classic Indie music in the west.'

On *Kultura*, there's 'UkrainAmerica' which goes, 'The multinational corporation has come to visit us, we will build their new beefburger stores together, the multinational corporation has come to visit us, we will buy up all their heavy metal records.' All of course written and performed in the Ukrainian language. To most people they could be singing it in the Klingon that it closely resembles (and judging by the size of 'Star Trek' fandom, in marketing terms it might be better if it were!).

THE UKRAINIANS

'How many words do *you* understand when you actually go to a Rock concert?' parries Pete. 'If the music is emotional and expressive, that's what appeals to people most.'

The Ukrainian nation gave the world violinists such as Nathan Milstein and the Oistrakhs. Its roots can be found in Ukrainian-American Folk violinist Pawlo Humeniuk. But the public perception is Chicken Kiev, the Red Fleet, or possibly Chornobyl?

'Kyivskyy Express' is a track carried on railroad noises, and illustrates the *Kultura* theme by using the train as a metaphor for two-way possibilities. Its passengers travel west, but are drawn to the east. It's a sound to bite your face off, with an eye for the dark as well as the bright side.

'There's no resistance to creeping Americanisation in Ukraine because they're very poor, and because they've suffered at the hands of the Soviets. They've never really had a chance to walk their own culture,' explains Len. 'The Russians have Russified it and not allowed the Ukrainians to develop in directions where they could have evolved modern culture. So the culture they tend to hang onto is a very old Folk-and-Dance culture which is the same now as it was pre-Revolution. If people wanted to get on and become writers, they learned how to speak Russian. All the books – technical books, scientific books, works of literature from abroad, philosophical works – were all in Russian, they weren't translated into Ukrainian. They still aren't, in fact. We've been to Ukraine twice now, between recording our second (*Vorony*) and third (*Kultura*) albums, and I was gobsmacked in the middle of Kyiv to go into bookshops looking for books in Ukrainian ('cos I'm trying to teach myself the language) and the only ones I could find were children's books and two others – a selection of Agatha Christie short stories, and a very thick edition of Isaac Asimov's *I Robot*. And that's two years after independence from the Soviet Union.

'So – the people in the bookshops are pretty reticent, but on the second anniversary of independence there were loads of people gathering and they had stalls out on the main square. I went over to a massive great big bookstall and the vendor explained to me that there is a strong underground of writers, but it's always been what they call "samizdat", or "self-published". And he said, 'Yes, it might be two years after independence, but the Russians won't let us have any paper.' And you see that the ex-Soviets still have quite a stranglehold on the country. In the same way that when we travelled around doing a five-day concert tour (the very last gig was in Kyiv on Independence Day, organised by their Ministry of Culture and televised on national Ukrainian TV), we had to go everywhere by train because the Russians didn't allow the Ukrainians any aviation fuel. All internal flights were completely grounded.'

This ain't Kyiv. This ain't no Independence Square either. This is a converted chapel in rain-silted inner-city Leeds. And a band called The Ukrainians is 'trying to expose people to music that has a Ukrainian content.' A music that roars and bites with the dynamics and rhythms of Western Rock. A music you could Folk-Dance to, if you knew the steps, with the chord progressions and melodies found in ethnic Ukrainian music.

Between numbers, off at one side of the studio as Allan picks out crawling bass runs and Mick serves up toxic machine coffee and slices of home-made carrot cake, Len confides: 'We do get quite a few letters from people who have come to our gigs, saying, 'My dad (or my mum) is Ukrainian and I've been down to the Ukrainian Club with them once or twice. And it's like, a bunch of old blokes sitting in the corner playing dominoes and reminiscing about the old days in a country that doesn't exist anymore, because it's all changed.' And the letters to us say, 'I've listened to your music, and for the first time I saw something exciting from Ukraine that I could relate to. And now I've been asking my dad for stories and things'.'

The 'Legendary' Len sips toxic coffee. 'I find that really moving. The fact that what we're doing can actually regenerate second generation people's interest in their parents' country of origin.'

Pete Solowka has 'Wedding Present' stencilled on his guitar case. He drinks machine coffee that's as addictive as crack. You can almost see the caffeine beneath the glaze of his eyes, behind his gold-rimmed glasses. 'It's only weird if you look at it from an English perspective.'

He's parrying my accusation that his band – the Ukrainians – operate from a weird concept. He moves constantly while he formulates his response. His fingers twine and twist. 'Every English artist has influences, Western and Pop, that are considered normal. There are bands around now who were just babies in their prams when The Beatles were on the go. Yet they say, 'Oh yeah, the Beatles were fine.' But if I say to you 'I'll play you songs that were written in Ukraine in the 1960s,' you say, 'Ah, that's weird. How can that be relevant to you?' Of course it's not relevant to you if you're – I won't say "ordinary", but if you're from mainstream English culture. But it is relevant to you if you grew up with it and if it's part of your culture.'

'It's like being called 'The Celts'.' Len, with shoulder-length black hair and a mauve tie-dyed t-shirt, nods his assent. 'Irish traditional music and Ukrainian music have a similar tonality, and sometimes even the same chord progressions. But the Ukrainians? Maybe people only think of the Ukrainians as a fiery eastern European nation? One that's hanging onto its nuclear weapons…?'

To fill in those gaps; the emergence of Ukrainian independence from the ex-USSR is very much part of what has been called a 'Europe of the Nations', in which all the submerged ethnic groups from the Celts and Basques to Azerbaijanis and Chechnyans are reclaiming and reasserting their cultural identity. And the appearance of the band The Ukrainians neatly coincides with the liberation of Ukraine, which is a pretty astute marketing device. Can we now expect to hear from other bands like The Armenians, The Belarusians, and The Lithuanians?

'It *is* weird from that point of view. And it *does* sound a bit strange,' Pete concedes. 'But it was quite a radical name when we chose it initially. We took the name 'The Ukrainians' a year before independence and all the possible wranglings of the splitting up of the Soviet system. It was the name of a country which most people didn't recognise. A country of 40 million people which most people here had never even heard of. But we released our first record about two weeks after the declaration of independence. Which was a complete coincidence. That was the really weird part.'

'TO ALL BANDS. DON'T FUCK WITH THE LEADS IN THE BACK OF THIS PA' it says on the wall of this rehearsal space in Chapel Studios, Leeds. And here the new Kultura Klub are running through material from their current album *Kultura* for the tour that commences tomorrow. Hamburg. Berlin. Then further, 'Tearing down the autobahns again and generally destroying our eating and sleeping patterns.'

Within the surround-sound of static, their songs are Natural Born Thrillers, with a feel-good factor high in a Pogues-y hoedown sort of groove. But bringing my sophisticated sensory apparatus to bear on the music, there's a problem too. Was it Byron who said, 'Critics have just enough learning to misquote'? Well – within the CD insert, it's all there in the small print. A toe-tapping explosion of a track called 'Horilka' is supposed to be about 'a very potent illicit brew'. It has a mandolin intro, with Phil Wright's slide guitar and a jaunty swing suggesting a potential Eurovision candidate.

But it has lyrics that go, 'Przed rankiem samogonke naganiajmy, tylko szklanke samogonke pije…'. And that's one of two translations. The original Ukrainian text is in Cyrillic lettering. There aren't enough asterisks and exclamation marks on my keyboard to do justice to this material.

The speaker burps.

Doesn't the fact that The Ukrainians sing in Ukrainian limit their potential audience?

'How many words do *you* understand when you actually go to a concert?' counters Pete. He sinks down into a studio chair with the grace and inevitability of a building collapsing under its own weight, in slow motion. And we engage in a full and frank exchange of views.

I say, 'That's the obvious come back.'

'It is. But if the music is emotional and expressive, that's what appeals to people most.'

Isn't it an option to do English language versions of the songs while retaining the Ukrainian musical elements?

'We haven't really thought of doing that. It doesn't really appeal to us. It seems a little bit of a crass marketing thing. I'm not saying we wouldn't do it, in the right environment, but it's not a natural thing for us to do. We don't think, 'Hey, let's appeal to an English market by singing in English. Let's appeal to the German market by singing in German.' It's just, we are what we are, and people accept us as we are.'

Kultura opens with a horn fanfare, with mandolins over solid Rock rhythms. It's an extraordinarily non-ordinary album. A music reflecting the seismic political and social changes shocking eastern Europe, apparently resting on two opposing musical tectonic plates, grinding together tremulously, throwing out sparks.

'If someone took a photograph of our audience you could mark all their heads with different coloured felt-tip pens,' relates Len with some amusement. 'This one's an Indie kid, this one's a World Music buff, this one's a Folkie, this one's a Wedding Present fan and so on. It's quite amazing.'

It's a sound that originally evolved in late-1987 around a Wedding Present spin-off project. David Gedge's Leeds band indulged then-member Pete's Ukrainian family roots, allying them to Len's useful Slavonic languages degree to formulate a hybrid one-off Wedding Present *Ukrainski Vistupi V Johna Peela* (Ukrainian John Peel Sessions*)* album.

'We've laid ourselves open a bit since this band began with those Wedding Present sessions,' leers Len. 'I'd been teaching myself Ukrainian and how to pronounce it for about two weeks before we did that, and all the songs that we did were traditional songs. Then we went on to our first proper album and we wrote some fairly simple songs in Ukrainian Folk style using Folk subject-matter. Then we did the second album (*Vorony*) on which we developed a more current style but still with Folk subject-matter. Since that second album we've actually *been* to Ukraine twice, and basically we've all been quite moved by the experience. So now we're wanting to branch out and write about more contemporary themes, which on *Kultura* we feel we've done.

'Songs like 'Polityka' (with Chris Walton and Andrew Stocks adding trombone and trumpet), 'UkrainAmerica' and 'Kyivskiy Express' are directly inspired by our experiences in Ukraine. We found an impoverished people there, struggling to find an identity after three-quarters of a century of political, economic, social and cultural suppression. But unfortunately, instead of creating a new modern culture, Ukrainians are succumbing to the attractions of Western consumerism and the thoughts of being able to partake in the American Dream. Thus, McDonalds burgers and Marlboro cigarettes are everywhere. Sad, but totally inevitable.'

It was not until August 1993 that they got to tour Ukraine properly, climaxing the jaunt with a performance in Kyiv's Independence Square – formerly October Revolution Square – before a live audience of 75,000 people in a nationally televised event organised to celebrate the end of Soviet dominance.

'That event was kind-of interesting. There were quite a few bands playing. We were just one of them. The Ukrainian authorities – their Ministry of Culture – had invited us and those other bands over, and they alternated Western bands with Ukrainian ones. And *all* of them, including the Ukrainian bands, played music that was definitely 'American' Rock music. Some of it was from Germany. Some of it from Finland. Some from Ukraine. Some of it from America. Some from England. But it was all very definitely American Western Rock music. And then we came on with mandolins and accordion, a British group singing in Ukrainian, and they couldn't quite work it out. It's as if, over in Ukraine, if you want to be cool musically you play guitar solos and you play loud and you have Marshall stacks and you play Rock music. You don't play mandolins and accordion, that's very uncool. But we were absolutely amazed by people coming up to us afterwards saying, 'It's weird, you're throwing our culture back at us, and we really like it!' That felt good. It made us very aware that we're not stuck in a little cocoon over here in the West.'

'A few journalists there have kept in touch and they've sent us some tapes they're playing on the radio,' adds Len. 'And we've heard stories that since we've been over there, there are bands out there now basing their style on the Ukrainians from England. Now *that* is a weird concept.'

CORN EXCHANGE
1 FEBRUARY 1994, CAMBRIDGE, UK

LEN
We supported Fairport Convention at this gig, so it should stay in my mind, but it doesn't. The only thing I remember is being starstruck when I saw Coronation Street star Geoffrey Hughes, who had played binman Eddie Yeats, in the foyer afterwards. Actually, at the time he was playing Onslow in Keeping Up Appearances and went on a few years later to play 'Twiggy' in The Royle Family. Oh yes, and he also voiced Paul McCartney in the Beatles' 'Yellow Submarine' film! Respect! Anyway, that night he was grinning away with a pint in his hand, so I'm guessing he enjoyed himself.

NORWICH ARTS CENTRE
25 APRIL 1994, NORWICH, UK

STEPAN PASICZNYK
I got locked in a toilet cubicle in this church converted into gig venue. I simply couldn't open the door with minutes to go before we were due on stage. I broke the door lock to get out. Luckily the manager saw the funny side of it.

ROCK AM SCHLOSS
30 JULY 1994, FÜRSTENAU BEI OSNABRÜCK, GERMANY

MATTHES KERSTING
My personal highlight was the *Rock am Schloss* festival in Fürstenau, Germany, where The Ukrainians were in the line-up. It was a warm and sunny night, I was there with very good

friends, and I remember it as if it was yesterday. The festival started with an unknown opener, and I remember seeing Immaculate Fools, a band I'd loved since the eighties. The Ukrainians then played a spectacular show, giving the festival a special vibe. The Bates were headliners and were quite famous in Germany at the time, but they couldn't top the two special sets I had just seen. I have attended hundreds of gigs and concerts, and played a lot of shows myself, but I will never forget this festival.

I was also a DJ for a total of 35 years. Whenever there were people at parties in the region who had attended the festival with me, I played 'Vorony'. Everyone would immediately jump up and dance their hearts out. So I thank The Ukrainians for their music. I have every one of their albums on either vinyl or CD. They've been my constant companions for 30 or so years now. They don't know it, but we're getting old together…

 BANDSTAND
12 AUGUST 1994, CARDIFF, UK

CHRISTOPHE VAN ROOY

It doesn't seem like that long ago, the summer of 1994. I was young. Well, at least younger than today, but who wasn't in those days? Anyway, my career as a student didn't go as smoothly as my parents had planned so they sent me to my aunt in England, to improve my English. Just to clarify: I'm Belgian, and Dutch is my mother tongue. My aunt had a friend who had a daughter whose boyfriend played in a band, so I hopped on a bus from Luton to Leeds. (Being a Fischer-Z fan I was expecting Lisbon, but lucky enough the trip didn't take that long.) And so it turned out I was to stay with Rebecca and Len for a couple of days, but maybe I would like to join Len and his band on a two-day trip to Cardiff festival? 'Sure! Sounds exciting!'

I set up a stand with CDs and t-shirts next to the stage and sold a few… CDs and t-shirts. One bloke tried to tell or ask me something, but I really didn't understand what he wanted. Then he went away. The audience wasn't all that big, but it was very enthusiastic. One person with a kilt on was dancing quite energetically. (I'll spare you the details.) After the gig, we were invited to a nightclub. We got to pass in front of the line of people waiting to get in. That was a first (and last) for me.

Back in the hotel, we appeared to have lost Len. (He and I shared a room.) The others told me he was notoriously bad at finding his way. Looking out of the window, I saw him down in the street. He tried to take a taxi to the hotel… which was right across the street! I seem to remember the cabbie's loud laughter.

The next day, after the roadie managed to get the towed van back, we set off back to Leeds. On the way, I got to listen to the Ukrainians' next CD, *Kultura*, which I liked a lot. I compared their mix of traditional music with rock to The Levellers, which they took as a compliment.

Back in Belgium a few weeks later, I'm afraid I resorted to vandalism in an attempt to promote The Ukrainians in Belgium, writing their name on several seats in different auditoria at the university (I'm not telling as to which one, but it wasn't the one I graduated from.)

I still tell people of the time 'I went on a road trip with the band.' I can tell people (especially my daughter) like my story, as they show me their appreciation by rolling their eyes!

 UKRAINIAN SOCIAL CLUB
23 AUGUST 1994, HOLLAND PARK, LONDON, UK

MARTIN GOLDSCHMIDT, CHAIRMAN, COOKING VINYL

My favourite memory is the launch party for *Kultura* we did at the beautiful Ukrainian Club in London's Holland Park. It was a disaster. The band had managed to blag a large quantity of a variety of incredible different Ukrainian vodkas. We had a fantastic media and industry turnout but the vodka was so popular and strong that it wrecked the event. I checked in with loads and loads of people afterwards and no-one was able to remember a thing that happened after the first hour, and couldn't remember anything about the music. It's well up there amongst my favourite industry parties…

LEN

I was told that before the gig our drummer Dave Lee staggered onto the stage and fell over his drum kit. He got up and slowly found his way to the mic to announce, 'If you think I'm pissed, you should see the singer!'

STEFF TYMRUK, UKRAINIANS ACCORDION PLAYER

I grew up in the Slough/Windsor area, and was playing in a local Celtic folk rock band around 1989/90 in Windsor. I knew The Ukrainians existed and I heard on the community grapevine that Luddy, the original accordion player, wasn't going to stay in the band much longer. His last gig was at the Ukrainian Club in London, which I went along to. I remember particularly Len, Luddy and Dave being totally plastered! This was in the days about five years before email, and during or after the gig I wrote down Pete and Len's phone numbers and got in touch with them. I'd never seen them live, and I didn't have any of their records or CDs. I probably borrowed a CD off someone before I came up.

In April 1994 I met Pete and Len at the café in Hyde Park, Leeds for a cup of coffee on a Wednesday or Thursday afternoon. It wasn't really an audition, more of a 'hello'. I was pretty convinced that this was what I wanted to do.

LEN

We held auditions, to which Steff came, and there were also a couple of other people, including one chap called Bohdan. Anyhow, we settled on Steff and introduced him to the rest of the band.

STEFF TYMRUK

First of all we did about 20 gigs around the UK, followed by a load more dates in Germany, with several more in Poland, Belgium, Austria and Switzerland, plus a couple in France. This was spread over from 1994 into 1995, and then in 1996 there were more UK and European dates followed by a twelve-date tour in Canada. That's where I met Roman, in that crossover period. I had just joined the band and that was my first foray into Canada.

I hadn't yet written or recorded any stuff for The Ukrainians, so I had three albums worth of stuff to learn, which was quite a tall order. We spent the best part of ten days rehearsing in the Bradford Ukrainian Club before we played a few German and Polish dates and then we went to Canada.

We hired a van and drove ourselves to gigs all over Canada. Me and Peter shared the driving and we covered a lot of territory. We also did a couple of one-off gigs in Toronto. We spent more time on the plane on one of those trips than we actually spent out there.

IN THE CITY FESTIVAL
19 SEPTEMBER 1994, MANCHESTER, UK

STEFF TYMRUK

My very first gig was the *Michelob Acoustic Festival* in Manchester, with Big Country as headliners. Over the years we played some weird and wonderful gigs like in Whitby and at Bridlington Arts Centre, and the marvellous Trades Club in Hebden Bridge. I always liked the Yorkshire gigs. I lived in Leeds for a couple of years after joining the band and then returned to Slough in 1997.

KULTUURKAFFEE
3 NOVEMBER 1994, BRUSSELS, BELGIUM

JEAN-PIERRE PONCELET

We had a booking agency in Verviers, Belgium called JCT Product. Len's band The Sinister Cleaners was on the agency's roster. I've known Len all the way back to 1987. In 1989, the year I got married, the album *Ukrainski Vistupi V Johna Peela* (the Ukrainian John Peel sessions) was released. Len presented me with this album at my wedding. Immediately, I was hooked!

Their music is bathed in a magnificent atmosphere. We come across absolutely jubilant soaring songs like 'Verkhovyno' and 'Oi Divchino'. Other titles like 'Ty Moyi Radoshchi', 'Chy Znayesh Ty?', and 'Pereyidu' are of a melancholic beauty – very eastern. The violin, mandolin and accordion are extremely present; however, The Ukrainians do not forget to be a rock band. The bass purrs wonderfully, the almost martial drums print the cadence, and there is no lack of rhythm changes!

Their music is energetic, festive. I have seen The Ukrainians several times in concert including twice in Morecambe during the WOMAD festival and twice in London in 2016 and 2019. Their performance has always been of high quality. The audience is very receptive, dancing and having a great time during their gigs.

In 1994 they had a tour in Belgium. Before their Brussels gig, we managed to get them an interview on the national radio (RTBF). For Verviers, we had contacted Mr Zenon Kowal, who worked as cultural attaché at the Ukrainian Embassy in Brussels. With him, we agreed to organise a Ukrainian weekend in Verviers. On the Friday, there should have been a reception between the leaders of the city of Verviers and the Ukrainian ambassador, followed by evening dinner and a concert of classical music. Unfortunately, this did not happen, but on the Saturday we had the concert by The Ukrainians. What an enthusiastic audience. We had a great evening!

The Ukrainians allowed me to discover a new musical and cultural universe. There is something truly unique about The Ukrainians' music. Nothing seems forced in this marriage of cultures, everything works perfectly. It's hard not to fall in love.

GROßE FREIHEIT
15 NOVEMBER 1994, HAMBURG, GERMANY

STEFF TYMRUK

We did a three-week tour of Germany in 1994, with additional gigs in Holland, Belgium, Austria and Switzerland. It was promoted as *The Spirit of the Gypsies* tour but we soon nicknamed it *The Smell of the Gypsies* tour because we'd been sharing a tour bus for three weeks! It was always really a great buzz playing in Germany, as the audiences were less blasé and much more appreciative. We were young guys in our late 20s, early 30s, and the hospitality was fantastic. German gigs were always the best ones. We were always well looked after there and we built up a big following in Germany over a number of years.

Once we got into regular touring around Germany, we became really popular, playing to audiences of over 200 in small to medium-sized clubs, as opposed to 70 to 80 in English clubs. That heyday lasted for about five years and then started to fade away a bit (I think the German government introduced a live-gig tax for foreign bands) but then the gigs in Poland started picking up a lot. You know you're fading when it's harder to get shows, but even in Germany after a while there was a set of ardent fans who would travel a lot and come to a load of dates, and even put us up for the night around their houses in Düsseldorf. Poland was as awesome as Germany though.

DAVID CARMICHAEL (AKA 'RAT')

I first met up with The Ukrainians late in 1994, when I received a phone call from Pete asking if I would like to take the role of sound engineer on their forthcoming *Spirit of the Gypsies* tour in Germany. I was informed that there would be a large sleeping bus and accommodation for the tour (ha ha!). I was intrigued and was already good friends with Dave Lee the drummer, so agreed. The plan was to do three warm-up gigs in the UK before embarking on the main German/Austrian leg. The line-up for this would be Pete (guitar/mando), Mick (guitar/mando), Dave (drums), Alan Martin (bass), Stefan Tymruk (accordion), Len (vocals/violin) plus Irena Kuszta and Marika Humeniuk from Ukrainski Vovki (backing vocals).

I've always loved languages and connecting with people from all over the world, and to hear what seemed to me at the time to be a kind of eastern European version of The Pogues, sung in Ukrainian, using traditional Ukrainian rhythm, which encompassed both the sadness and the simple joy of life – seemingly entrenched in the mother country – was very moving. I didn't tell them that of course; and it wasn't something I really realised until I saw the audience reactions and Ukrainians fans in mainland Europe. The band's heavy leaning towards a Punk ethos was also right up my street.

What I discovered was a chaotic band of people playing out-of-tune instruments and burst accordion bellows, through underpowered amps, played with great passion and zeal – often fuelled by vodka. It was brilliant – so I signed up!

On some of the UK dates in October 1994, there was a Polish guy who followed the band to each gig with his own fridge filled full of Polish and Ukrainian vodka, which he would set up and sell for £1 a shot to the audience (free to the band, of course). There didn't seem to be any merchandise in the normal sense. Who needs it if you've got vodka? The usually staid English audiences certainly seemed to be tucking into it and whipping themselves into a fervour. Len, Pete and Mick quickly introduced me to the joys of Soplica, Żubrówka, Horilka and Spotykach among many other eastern European spirits. I was now in love with Ukrainian culture and continued working with The Ukrainians for the next 16 years.

We got absolutely ratarsed on the journey from Leeds to Große Freiheit, Hamburg – the first day of the *Spirit of the Gypsies* tour. It was a good way of getting to know each and everyone; something that happens with many bands starting a tour. The gig was great as were the staff and audience at Große Freiheit. We were sharing the sleeper bus with Rev Hammer, various musicians, merch and roadcrew/helpers. After about a week, the sleeper bus was sent back to England as nobody could afford it. It was replaced by a battered Mercedes box van with two hard wooden benches on each side and with a top speed of 50mph, or 28mph in the mountains and valleys of Southern Germany and Austria. It was late November going into December and it was uncomfortable and fucking freezing. This became the norm for the next 16 years.

The Ukrainians were flat broke, with any money earned being ploughed straight back into touring costs. We never had hotel rooms to go back to, or much food apart from that provided by gig promoters, and this is where I, and I am sure, Len, Pete, and everyone playing in, and working with The Ukrainians, were so grateful to the fans of the band for looking after us.

My first experience of this was The Mülheim Crew – an ardent group of Ukrainians fans, always dancing at the front of gigs and whipping up the crowd, who would travel hundreds of miles from their hometown of Mülheim an der Ruhr to see us.

Comprising Heike, Meike, Arno, and Marcus (among others) they warmly welcomed us into spare rooms in already cramped apartments, setting out bedding and mattresses for us to rest. This could be for weeks at a time, especially when we were gigging around the western parts of Germany. Many a bier and good time was had, and I can't thank them enough.

Pete was the main organiser – intelligent and, at times, enigmatic. A good conversationalist and a great musician. He had a terrible guitar amp though – a 75 watt Laney Linebacker into which was plugged a six-string electric, 12-string acoustic, a mandolin – and occasionally an accordion! Early in the tour, I asked Pete about my need to understand and anticipate (on the sound desk) the structure of traditional Ukrainian rhythms. 'They start slow and get faster and faster,' was his thrifty advice. I guess, in a nutshell, that was pretty much right. A year later, while Pete was sorting the complex bureaucratic process of getting us to Ukraine, I asked him what to expect when we eventually got there. 'Expect the unexpected,' came the cryptic reply. Again, he was pretty much spot on.

Assorted album covers

Assorted album & EP covers

SZENE
2 DECEMBER 1994, WIEN, AUSTRIA

ALARIC NEVILLE

After Roman bowed out of the band, his place in the line-up was taken temporarily by a chap called 'Stebs' and then more permanently by Mick West. Mick was another in the long list of colourful Ukrainian band members, a gifted musician who lived a dedicated counter culture lifestyle. Mick had not travelled abroad much before joining the band and one of the aspects of foreign travel that concerned him was maintaining an adequate supply of spliffs. In the heady faraway days of the UK's membership of the EU, what had once been a pain in the arse negotiating all the various border checks had been replaced with open borders and smooth unhindered travel within the single market. Mick had been assured this was the case, but given that he thought it prudent to take his whole supply with him for a long tour of Germany, he was still understandably wary of any encounter with any official. Going from Germany to Austria there was some hold up at the border and our van was asked to wait in a queue before passing through the border post. Mick was getting very nervous, sweating and agitated. I was sitting next to him in the back and suggested he put his stash in his mouth just in case, a standard strategy in such situations.

In the next moment, a man in uniform tapped on the van window and we all feared the worst. Happily, it was just a friendly Teutonic apology for the hold up before ushering us on our way. I turned to Mick to say 'there you go, everything's OK', except it wasn't. Mick had panicked and swallowed his whole supply, wrapped in tin foil. The main thing you expect from a Ukrainian mandolin player is fast and furious fretwork, but for the next few days Mick was like a 45rpm single played at 33.3 – slooooow. He spent most of the days asleep or on the toilet. Border crossing had certainly become a pain in the arse for Mick even before Brexit.

Tragically, like Roman before him, Mick died far too early on 31 March 2018.

ARRASATE FOLK '95 FESTIVAL
11 MARCH 1995, MONDRAGÓN, SPAIN

STEFF TYMRUK

I remember sitting with our roadie Gordon at the back of a plane on an Easyjet flight to Bilbao, on our way to the Mondragón music festival in the Basque region of Spain. The beer and wine were complimentary and the ashtrays brimming during the two-and-a-half-hour flight from Manchester. Nowadays, it's difficult and unusual to imagine smoking on a plane – although at the time I remember the very effective air conditioning meant that no tobacco fumes escaped to other passengers' seats. Every now and then you can still find these now long defunct retractable ashtrays embedded in the armrests, eg. travelling on a Boeing 737 to one of many various European destinations. That gig was one of only two we played in Spain over the last 30 years – and the unusual billing meant that we had the best part of the day to explore a bit of Basque country and culture before going onstage at about 1.30am. I think we played for an hour, stayed up until breakfast time, and then slept for a while on the return flight to England. A day in the life of The Ukrainians…

GIBUS
28 APRIL 1995, PARIS, FRANCE

DANIEL EDWARDS

I first heard The Ukrainians either listening to the John Peel show one evening with my friend, when we were 16 or 17, or hearing him play their first single after he'd heard it on Peel. We both already loved The Wedding Present: 'Brassneck', *George Best*, etc. I first got the chance to see The Ukrainians live when I was on a university placement year in Paris in 1994-95, at an underground venue somewhere. I bought a copy of *Kultura* that night and dropped it while dancing at the gig. The CD still plays fine… and the CD case is still cracked!

I recorded other Ukrainians albums onto tapes which I kept in my first 'proper' car – a red VW Polo. (My 2CV and campervan don't really count as proper cars.) In the early days of going out with my now wife, we ran out of fuel on the M3. I got a lift to the nearest petrol station with my petrol can, leaving her in the car with just the Ukrainians tapes to listen to. By the time I got back three hours later, she had decided she wasn't a fan.

We moved from Hampshire to Norfolk in 2001 and saw The Ukrainians at Norwich Arts Centre, playing the Sex Pistols and Smiths covers. It's a lovely venue and it was a brilliant, sweaty gig. I bought the Sex Pistols EP on CD that night, and didn't drop it either! Then we got married and had kids…

As lockdown lifted in 2021, I met my sister for a weekend in Brighton and got tickets for us to watch them upstairs in the Prince Albert pub. It was close and intimate, the music was as excellent as ever – and my sister loved it too.

When I saw they were playing in Cambridge last year, I cycled 60-odd miles to the gig and left my bike locked up in the youth hostel. Getting there early, I spoke to the wife of one of the band and discovered that they now live pretty near me. (I haven't stalked them yet!) I saw a really good Ukrainian support act that night, Iryna Muha, with a hurdy-gurdy type machine, singing Ukrainian poetry and telling her story. I bought a CD or two and a Tom Robinson-style blue/yellow clenched fist badge in support of the people of Ukraine.

Then the band came on and were fantastic. I took a few short vids on my phone and got a pic of the playlist as I hadn't heard all the songs they played that night until then – and I loved them!

I don't know if I could exactly claim their music to be the soundtrack to my life, but The Ukrainians are a band I have loved to listen to over the past 25-odd years, and I love to see them live whenever I can. The album *Kultura* is right up there with Weezer's *Pinkerton* as one of my favourites.

RAT

The band already had Ukrainian friends such as Sasha (the man) and Sasha (the woman) who had managed to leave Ukraine shortly after the collapse of Soviet rule. Sasha (the man) had been in the popular Ukrainian Indie band VV and had often been hauled in by the police, or fined, for the band's anti-Soviet lyrics and style of music. Both Sashas had taken their chances, despite having no money, to get across the border, working their way across Europe doing menial jobs.

Sasha (the man) ended up washing dishes in Paris and sleeping on the floor of Laurence and Phillipe's (friends of the band) small flat in Nanterre, Paris. Sasha was great; a humorous, and talented musician, and rebellious with it, and he was always able to whip up a crowd of local Ukrainians (and Russians) to come and see us when the band played Paris. He also introduced me to quatre-vingt-dix (90) – a kind of cheap medical alcohol bought over the counter at French pharmacies. This was mixed with about a litre and a half of Cola and after a few swigs, you could almost convince yourself it was vodka and coke… To ensure a good time was had by all, Sasha and friends would sneak bottles of it into French nightclubs, where drinks prices were extortionate and beer only sold in half glasses or 50cl bottles. The band would get as many eastern European and French friends on the guest list as possible so that we all had a good cheap night out. I remember us playing Gibus in Paris in 1995 and the band rider consisted of one 50cl bottle of beer per band member. It was £5 a bottle at the bar. None of us had that kind of money, so quatre-vingt-dix it was.

The band's first drummer, Dave Lee, once told me a story about how Sasha had gone back from his washing up job in Paris, to visit his family back in Ukraine. Ukraine was a very rural economy in the '90s and on arriving back at his home village, his excited family had welcomed him back as the 'Successful Son from the West' by offering him first milk from the cow. Quite an honour, and although Sasha was not a big milk drinker, he did not want to offend, so he downed the large tankard of milk proffered straight from the cow the family kept.

The next day, on waking up, it was discovered that the cow had died of tuberculosis (or some such disease). Sasha got really sick on the train back to Paris, eventually having to be admitted to hospital for some time. He did have his fair share of mishaps but, happily, he is now back performing and writing music in the band Attraktor, with Dave in Kyiv.

Sasha (the woman) ended up in Leeds, living in the same shared house as Dave Lee and Steve (Steff) Tymruk. Sasha was warm, although she didn't tolerate fools, and straightforward. Sasha also introduced me to proper Ukrainian borscht which is like a full meal. We all enjoyed a good borscht if available on tour. I had many a good conversation with her and Dave. They eventually married and moved to Kyiv in the late 90s. I miss them both dearly.

 FESTIVAL ALTERNATIVA
17 SEPTEMBER 1995, SPARTAK, LVIV, UKRAINE

LEN

We drove all the way from Leeds in a coach to play a 25-minute slot at a festival in Lviv and then got back in the van and drove all the way back to Leeds again. It was bonkers. We didn't have a bass player at the time and Paul, our old bass player, was living in Germany and got a train from Cologne. There was no rehearsal. He turned up ten minutes before we were due to appear. We were already on stage tuning up when he arrived. If he hadn't arrived in time, Gordon, our roadie, was going to have a go at playing bass even though he didn't know the songs!

Paul's journey was the most dedicated rock 'n' roll thing I've ever known – 23 hours on a train from Germany, then three hours to get driven from a train station to the venue, 25 minutes spent doing the gig, then all the way back to Cologne immediately afterwards including a three-hour drive and another 23-hour train journey. Amazing!

RAT

I can't begin to imagine what deals had to be done with certain organisations in Ukraine to stage Lviv's *Festival Alternativa*. I do know that it was the first festival I'd been to where the security was done by young army conscripts carrying rifles and where the hotel (which we quickly checked out of) was overrun by gangsters. It's a great testament to the resilience, vision and determination of people such as the organisers, staff, volunteers, and fans who supported that independent festival and to people such as Wlodek Nakoneczny for looking after us and getting things moving against impossible odds and bureaucracy. (Years later, Wlodek would become our Polish tour manager, although when we first met him he was selling bootleg Ukrainian music tapes outside the festival.)

RAT

The sun was up and a lively easterly breeze whipped through the open crack of the minibus window as we approached Lviv. At first the breeze was refreshing, but as we drew closer to our destination, it became tinged with the chemical sting of heavy industry. I imagined it blowing through the industrial areas of Dnipropetrovsk and Donetsk, hundreds of miles ahead of us, as the workers began their day shifts, pouring spirit and hard labour into propping up once proud Ukrainian industry.

There was much in-depth chatter between Sasha and Alexei as Sasha made several calls on his Nokia 232. Personal cell phones were a new phenomenon sweeping the world, but which none of us in the band could afford nor had use for at that time. I fell into a broken-necked sleep until I was awoken by the squeaking of the minibus brakes on crunching gravel. In front of us was a large dirt-splattered white gate topped with barbed wire and some hastily welded spikes. The gate was manned by two young men in shell suits. Sasha leapt from the van, immediately assuming an air of control in his dialogue with them.

The driveway was lined by some tired-looking trees, their branches sagging and grey, and the scrubby grass verge was pocked with what looked like the rusting metal parts of discarded white goods and cars. 'Doesn't look much like Lviv from what I remember,' observed Len.

Steff concurred. 'Doesn't look like the rag and bone man has been around for a bit either.' Our laughter broke the feeling of stupefied exhaustion we all felt.

Sasha returned. 'Okay, this is the hotel,' he said, as if confirming the fact in his own mind. The soiled white gate slid back, revealing a parking and drop off area, again filled with young men in shell suits displaying all colours of the rainbow in their garishly coloured nylon outfits. We crawled, slow and bent, from the interior of the cramped minibus and began unloading the gear under the curious gaze of the shell-suited young men. We did not exude any of the glamorous image associated with rock bands, looking instead like we had just been to sign on at the dole office (which was true for two-thirds of the band), our clothes a mix of charity shop and January sales purchases. Myself, Len, and Steff all sported battered denim jackets – in white, black and blue respectively. The sensible members, like Pete, wore a padded rainproof anorak.

Dave, our drummer, would be arriving the next day, travelling down from where he now lived in Kyiv, with his long-term girlfriend, Sasha. I could already picture him dressed in the battered, heavy suede, deep-pocketed half jacket – crammed with lighters and loose cigarette papers – which had got him through so many a cold winter tour.

The hotel was a three-storey, dark, timbered lodge affair of worn carpets and yellowing net curtains located, we were soon to discover, some 20 minutes' drive or more from Lviv. While we dragged ourselves and our gear up the steps and into the darkened hotel foyer, Sasha organised the room keys with the hotel receptionist, a young, beautiful and cheerful woman in her twenties, dressed in black skirt and white shirt.

THE UKRAINIANS

'Welcome, welcome,' she beamed. 'My name is Juliana.' Her English was excellent and she carried the beautiful Slavic twang which makes the language come alive, much more so than the guttural grunts produced by the average native English speaker, me included.

The low ceiling and worn, heavily-patterned carpets of the foyer were dimly lit by a pale orange light emanating from what looked like a converted oil lamp hanging above our heads. The only natural light came from a couple of windows at the far side of the room framed by heavy drapes, and footed by dusty knick-knacks and decorated vases adorning the window sills. Layers of shabby net curtains seemed to have suffocated the fresh smell of pine and birch hanging on the breeze outside, giving the light an unnatural, almost ethereal hue, as if time had stopped and the foyer was unaware that outside its dark wood doors there was a crisp blue autumn day where life was continually renewed.

On the two sofas against the wall behind us lounged more shell-suited young men, sporting wispy moustaches, making phone calls and flaunting their mobile phones as if the blocks of black plastic were a form of status symbol. All I could think was, 'Jesus, I'm trapped in Miss Havisham's boudoir with the 1986 Liverpool football squad!' Followed by, 'At least we're not kipping on someone's floor again.'

I didn't sleep much, waking after only half an hour beneath a thin top sheet heavy with homespun blankets. The room was small with two cot beds. I looked over at the other cot bed where Gordon, the roadie, lay prostrate, his feet and ankles sticking out far beyond the end of the wooden bed frame as if some form of Norse Action Man had got drunk and crashed at Barbie's doll house in her spare single bed. The blankets looked like postage stamps on him. His long reddish-blond hair splayed out on each side of his face as if he had been prepared for a ceremonial Viking burial.

After a quick cold-water wash in the small ensuite cubicle, I headed down the hotel corridor in search of the breakfast Sasha had managed to organise on our arrival. I found Pete and Len sat at a large table at the opposite end of the room. The smell of coffee pricked up my senses as I plonked myself down. Pete's face was swollen and puffy with fatigue behind his thick-rimmed glasses. Len didn't look much better.

'Well, here we are,' observed Len.

'Looks like we are the only hotel guests here,' I said, looking around the empty room.

'There's probably not much call for holidaying this time of year,' Pete added.

'Well, I'm glad we made it. There were times I thought we weren't gonna. Did you see the number of times the London-Kraków coach drivers fell asleep at the wheel?'

'Yeah. That was scary. Thank goodness for those two dear old Polish ladies sat right at the front, who kept leaning over and waking the driver up while he was driving.'

A beautiful waitress appeared and introduced herself, in English, as Tanya. We ordered coffee and she said she would bring food, although we couldn't get her to understand that we were vegetarians. We were joined by Sasha, Steff and Gordon. We tried to explain to

Sasha that three of us were vegetarians, so he could translate to Tanya. Sasha looked at us wide-eyed, seemingly wrestling with the concept. 'You eat only vegetables!?' As plates of ham, tomato and gherkins were placed in front of us, it became clear that vegetarianism was going to be a difficult concept to translate.

RAT

From the East, streaks of silver began to crack the blackened October night sky, as glistening and tempting as a rich seam of anthracite glimpsed through the suffocating black of the coalface. As dawn began to break in front of us, Alexei busied himself rummaging in a bag hidden somewhere in the depths of the driver's footwell as everyone else slept, steering the minibus with his left elbow, now and then looking over the dashboard to make sure we were still on the road. I had long since given up caring whether we lived or died on that mountain road – perhaps a combination of the Ukrainian brandy I had drunk and fatigue.

This feeling of resignation is not an unusual sensation experienced by band members on long and cramped tours across various continents. In fact, once used to it, it's altogether a healthier state of mind to adopt. If one was to weigh up the averages of touring Europe and eastern Europe in a minibus, then there will always be a healthy percentage of bad drivers, either on the road or assigned to drive the band by the tour company, and a percentage of near-miss crashes, breakdowns, the obligatory tour colds and flu, getting lost, missed meals, sweaty feet, bad smells, snoring, diarrhoea, broken or lost equipment, long delays, feeling too cold, feeling too hot, no toilet paper, and sleepless nights such as this one. Once you have accepted that this will be and there is very little to be done about it, then it becomes a lot more fun.

Alexei peered at me in his driver's mirror. 'You hungry? I have good Ukrainian sausage and bread.' From a small cloth-tied bag he produced a knife, a loaf of bread and a length of dried sausage, passing them to Maryska, who adeptly cut them both some bread and sausage before handing me the bag. Following Alexei's lead, I used my knee as a chopping board to cut some for myself as he passed me some fresh tomatoes. It was one of the most memorable and delicious meals I have ever eaten. The comfort of a simple meal rejuvenating my cramped body and mind and reminding me of the simple kindness of strangers.

The dawn broke slowly that morning and it was still dark as we pulled into a deserted truck stop comprising a weather-worn wooden hut and standing tables on some patchy forest land. We were all fatigued, and conversation was stilted as we stretched our cramped bodies in the first rays. I pensively considered the Ukrainians' song lyric from their song 'Zavtra' – 'zavtra ya budu pid nebom chuzhim' 'tomorrow I'll be under a foreign sky' – as Sasha diligently took our coffee requests before returning with ten black coffees and some sachets of sugar. Maybe the café hadn't had a milk delivery that early in the morning.

THE UKRAINIANS

I'd met Sasha briefly at the bus station in Kraków. He had come into the bus station anxiously looking for us but, as the band had not yet returned from their scouting trip, I had introduced myself and assured him that we were all present and ready to go now that the minibus had arrived. Sasha wore a brown terylene suit, slightly too large for his small thin frame, with creases in the trousers, a crumpled open neck shirt, topped by thin brown hair. He was handsome in his own way but, like so many people I would meet over the next five days, had that drawn look of someone whom life was pressing just a little too hard. Sasha held a more official demeanour than Alexei's swarthy and road-worn practical work jeans and jerkin look and I wondered if Sasha was governmentally connected or part of the Festival Alternativa organisation. Either way, he was animated, friendly, and organised when loading us and the myriad of bags and guitars into the tiny minibus, if not a little confused as to why we weren't speaking Ukrainian. Once we had passed the outer city limits of Kraków, Sasha quickly dozed off in the seat adjacent to mine in the minibus, and during that time Alexei and Maryska had managed to roughly translate to me that Sasha was 'The Fixer'. I took a hefty swig of the black coffee, only to get a mouthful of coffee grounds, which, on closer inspection made up about an inch of thickly layered grout at the top of the cup. The liquid, if there was any, was hidden beneath. Laughing, Sasha pointed out that you have to strain the grounds with your teeth to get to the liquid. This was a new experience for most of us and we had fun smiling broadly at each other with teeth full of coffee grounds.

A cold wind began to whip up from the East and as we stood and smoked looking at the horizon, I could hear Alexei rooting around in the back of the van. Presently, he appeared with a petrol can and began digging a long shallow trench with the heel of his boot into the scrubby ground in front of me. Into this he poured petrol. With a whoomph! I was engulfed in a face-roasting flash of heat and the gagging reek of gasoline fumes as Alexei lit it triumphantly proclaiming, 'Heat!' and smiling through his cracked teeth. We all jumped back from the initial explosion, but as the flames calmed, the rest of the band put their backs to the heat, as I stood rubbing my eyes. I watched as the flames gently began licking at the hems of Steff's bootcut corduroys. He didn't notice as the seams charred and blackened – and I was too tired to tell him.

It was daylight as Alexei announced that we were approaching the border. I had been enjoying the landscape, which gradually swept down from the higher climbs we had come from into broad sweeps of open land framed by wide blue skies and pockets of heavily wooded dark forest to the North and East. Sasha awkwardly roused himself from his broken-necked slumber and readied himself to take on an air of officialdom, straightening his crumpled shirt collar and tugging his suit jacket into place. The Polish border guards didn't seem overly concerned by our arrival and waved us through before we had even managed to pass all our passports to the front. I assumed that they had only needed to see one or two with the very official-looking visa stamp before waving us through.

FROM KYIV TO THE KOSMOS

At the Ukrainian side, we were signalled to a halt by an efficient looking guard dressed in camouflage uniform emblazoned with the bright blue and yellow arm patch of the Ukrainian national flag, and carrying what I assumed to be a Kalashnikov rifle held across his chest. As we Westerners all looked at each other ominously, Sasha sprang in to action.

'Give me all your passports to front please,' he said, making panicked waving gestures towards himself. Of course, we had all been prepared for this moment as the most important task we would have to undertake that night but there is always one band member who, despite hearing the same regularly announced instructions as the rest of us about having passports to hand at the border, realises that they do not have their passport to hand and so begins the frenzied pocket search ritual, before moving on to the tipping personal bag out on to the seat and floor ritual, before moving on to the 'I must have left it in the back with the instruments' announcement.

All this is usually done with a queue of impatient vehicle drivers waiting behind and under the steely gaze of the local border guards or customs officials who are rarely sympathetic to the mindset of the musician. It doesn't matter which border you are crossing or which band you are touring with, this ritual is guaranteed every time by at least one member of the touring personnel.

With much chaotic gesturing and some basic Ukrainian, Steff, the Ukrainians accordion player, managed to communicate that he needed to get in to the back of the van to retrieve his passport. Alexei nodded and deftly jumped out of the driver's seat only to be barked at to get back in by the guard, who had stepped back, readying his rifle at the sudden break in protocol. Sasha moved quickly into action, opening the sliding side door on his side, talking quickly and brandishing the passports he had in his hand. The guard stepped forward, taking the passports in one hand with his other hand firmly on the rifle trigger, although thankfully it was no longer pointing at us.

After Sasha had explained some more, the guard gestured that Alexei, Steff, and Gordon – our Viking-statured roadie – could go and look in the back. And so began the stage four ritual of band border etiquette, the fact that the missing passport is never near the top of the precariously packed instrument pile. Gordon and Alexei began lugging the instruments cases out onto the concrete. With each case, Alexei eagerly pointed, looking at Steff with hopeful eyes asking, 'Tse? tse?,' ['This? This?'] and Steff's gruff London accent replying, 'Nah, nah.'

All this was taking too long for the border guard, who ordered Alexei to get back in the van and drive it over to the passport office block 50 yards away. He had no option but to comply and drove off with back doors trailing open, bags spilling out, Gordon and Steff running after us with the cases they'd removed and, inside the van, Dave and Len, who had been sat on the back seats, desperately sprawling themselves over the top of the instrument pile to stop the rest of the equipment falling out and smashing.

Sasha must have been a good fixer because after only ten minutes he emerged from the passport office with some suited officials who smiled at us bemusedly and a guard who made only a cursory check of the bags and instruments in the back of the minibus, before checking our faces against our passport photographs and issuing us with the forms for listing all the possessions we had with us.

The minibus pulled across the concrete slab road surface of the border post, tyres clicking at every concrete joint, as we entered Ukraine. We all looked at each other, tired yet elated that we were finally here. We were in Ukraine and our excitement was tangible. There was a notable lack of traffic travelling in our direction, but as the road narrowed and the forest built up around us once again, I was horrified by the sight that greeted us.

Camped on the opposite road side, the road out of Ukraine, as far as the eye could see in the early morning mist, were people. Hundreds, maybe thousands, of desperate looking people queueing at the entrance to the border post. They had obviously been there for a long time. As we drove cautiously along, I could see hastily-erected tents, soup kitchens, washing lines sagging with cold and wet clothes and blankets of all colours, stacked furniture, cooking fires, and makeshift trading posts. Decrepit-looking vehicles had been dragged up onto the grass verge, while battered minibuses, cars, trucks, and motorbikes with sidecars all stood empty on the road surface. What was obvious was the poverty and the desperation (perhaps to leave Ukraine, perhaps to make a new life in the West). It was a harrowing and humbling sight, as all refugee camps must be when first experienced.

In the minibus, we sat quietly looking out the window, shocked, as the line of gaunt, dejected yet proud faces, stared back at us, pausing momentarily in their day-to-day grinding task of survival to look at the strangers coming in to their country. It was maybe two miles before the line of vehicles, men, women and children began to thin out.

PAUL BRIGGS

I was in Ukraine twice with the band. The first time was for the big trip, but the second time was actually my last gig with the band. I'd already left by that time, but they had a new bass player who couldn't make the gig and they asked if I would do it. I said yes and the plan was that we were all going to meet up and fly over together but for some reason that didn't work out and they called and said they had to go a couple of days earlier, and would I travel on my own to Ukraine? 'Yeah, alright then.'

It took two days to get to Ukraine but eventually I got there. They'd arranged for me to be picked up in a car from the train station by somebody that I knew, our agent or someone. So I got out of the train station and was looking for this person and I couldn't find them anywhere. And this guy walks up to me and says, 'Paul! Paul!' and I said, 'Thank God, that's my man, that's my man,' so I got in his car and we were about to drive away when there was a bang on the window. It was the person that I was supposed to meet, that I knew, and she said, 'You're in the wrong car. Get out!' so how the fella knew my name I don't know. It's the kind of bizarre stuff that used to happen there then.

So I'm in the right car with the right person and she says, 'You're late'. I said, 'I'm not late.' She said, 'The band goes on in ten minutes.' So we got to this huge stadium – I don't know if it was a football stadium or a basketball stadium or something – but it was a festival with lots of bands, and I got backstage. I thought, 'Thank God for that, I can have a shower, something to eat and rest a little bit after the journey.' No, it was straight on stage! They weren't expecting me to arrive so Gordon, dear Gordon, had got the bass and he was learning all the lines as quick as he could as he thought he was going to have to play the bass. So I got launched on stage with my coat still on, my bag over my shoulder and a bass thrust on me and that's it – we start playing the gig. I don't remember much after that because, as soon as we finished the gig, at two in the morning, they said, 'You gotta go back again. There's a journey planned for you to go home straight after the gig.' So I got onto this other bus, a tour bus with some of the other bands from the festival on there, mostly from Poland and eastern European, and – oh my God – you think you've seen rock 'n' roll? You haven't seen anything until you've been on a tour bus with eastern European bands. I cannot repeat some of the things that I saw on that bus.

I eventually got back to Germany where I was supposed to meet the train. That was a hellish trip. It was incredible.

STEFF TYMRUK

I got to visit my dad's relatives on that trip. My dad's family originally came from a district of Lviv, a remote village called Stanyn, near Radekhiv. When we went out to play the *Alternativa Festival*, two of my cousins came along and introduced themselves before the gig – I had no idea at all they were coming. We were sorting ourselves out and loading our stuff in at the venue, and Peter came up to me and said, 'A couple of your relatives are here. Do you want to go down to the hotel lobby and meet them?' I went down there and I was just stunned to meet them. I don't know how they found out I was in the band, because this was before emails and the Internet so there was no Wikipedia or anything. My dad and then my mum used to write regularly to our family in Ukraine, but my dad had died in 1984 so my mum must have told them.

My cousins said, 'You can come back to the village and stay tonight.' The band and the roadies and everybody were staying in the nearby hotel, but my cousins drove me about 30 miles to the village and that night I slept in the same bedroom that my dad slept in as a kid. I was treated almost like a deity. They laid on a feast for me – salads and meats – and they took me to see my other cousins, and every house we visited they had a table of food ready. I felt so humbled. It was great to have the opportunity to play a festival in Ukraine anyway, so getting to meet my family as well was a double bonus.

Ukraine had always been under Russian occupation and during the Second World War, my dad decided that he didn't want to support a very oppressive communist regime by fighting for the Russian army so he left home and was recruited by the German army. It was the lesser of two evils. He was taken as a prisoner of war in Italy in a platoon of Ukrainian soldiers. He was the only one who had a driving licence and when they came to Britain, he ended up as a driver for all the other guys, who had to work in mine detecting in Felixstowe, Dover and along the south coast.

Every other weekend, my dad's duties included driving a high-ranking army officer and his wife up from an army camp in Borden, Hampshire to their home in London. My dad would stay in London overnight and drive them back on Sunday. One Saturday night, he went to a ballroom dance in Putney where he met my mum. Mum is Bavarian-German and Swiss, and she was an au pair over here just after the war. My dad had the option of being repatriated to Australia, America or Britain and he chose Britain because he'd met Mum and *her* mum was in southern Germany.

I was more integrated into the German side of my background than the Ukrainian side to begin with. By the age of ten, I was speaking a bit of Ukrainian but mostly German. We had a small Ukrainian club in Slough, and it was a focal point for people to meet up. Every Easter and Christmas there would be a dinner and a dance that my parents would go to. I had about five or six Ukrainian friends that were in my age group, but most of the kids at school were British or Irish. Actually, the cul-de-sac we lived in on the outskirts of Slough had five Ukrainian families out of about 20 houses, so that was a micro-community as well as the wider Slough Ukrainian community that consisted of about 25 or so families.

A lot of the guys from my dad's platoon ended up staying in the south of England and marrying Italian, Spanish or other European women so it was a real melting pot. At home we had an English-Ukrainian dictionary but we also had Saturday school, which I went to from the age of eight until I was 14. I did French, German and Spanish at school and can converse in those languages quite easily, but I've forgotten most of the Ukrainian I learnt. But I think if I went to Ukraine, I'd pick it up pretty quickly. I was planning to go there for a few months after my mum died but the invasion put paid to that.

WINDSOR BATHS
16 DECEMBER 1995, BRADFORD, UK

WOODY, UKRAINIANS DRUMMER & PERCUSSIONIST
I must admit I didn't know anything about the Ukies before joining. I was in Leeds, having gone to college there, and was just hanging around trying to join a band or two. I remember going for an audition for a band called Fuzzbird which was fronted by a

guy called John Parkes. I didn't get the gig but weeks later got a call from Pete asking if I would be interested in learning the Ukies set. John Parkes was a friend of Pete and Len in the Leeds music scene and he'd passed on my number to Pete after the failed Fuzzbird rehearsal. So I got a cassette of some desk mixes of the band and dutifully went into my Leeds 6 cellar to learn the songs. I loved those Leeds 6 cellars. It was always the first room I looked in when moving house in those days, as it's crucial for a drummer. We had our first Ukies rehearsal in the very same cellar, for a gig in Bradford at some sort of baths, supporting Hank Wangford. That was my first gig with the band.

I remember Mick was playing freaky left-handed bass for that gig. He managed to play most instruments in the group at various gigs: bass, mandolin, geetar and shonky keyboard-like accordion. Luddy was on the accordion. The gig went generally fine although I did cock up the arrangement of 'Koroleva Ne Pomerla' ('The Queen Is Dead') and experienced Pete's stare for the first time. These many years later, and after many such stares, I understand more clearly the limitations of Pete's own musical prowess and so fear it no longer. Doesn't stop him staring, of course.

We were tiny little musical creatures in those days and Pete and Len were mighty musical warriors. That was the illusion, at least. I remember having gone to see The Wedding Present in Aberdeen in my youth and so must've seen Pete play there. We used to drink bottles of Becks and listen to The Wedding Present and then go out dancing at an Indie night in the north of Scotland, unbeknownst that years later the same guitarist would be telling me how to hit my toms properly.

There was a German tour the next year and a Polish one to follow so it was all exciting and new. I'd never really travelled so getting a first taste of foreign climes with the added bonus of playing to half decent crowds was pretty cool really. I played in another band in Leeds at the time called Slur, and we managed to get them on the bill for the *Radioactivity* tour as a support and general roadie/merchandise/drivers, to keep costs down and of course get some publicity for the band. It worked really well, I thought. Folks worked hard, but me and Al Dawson (bass player) were part of Slur and the Ukies and this caused a bit of a rupture in that band eventually. The Ukies got foreign gigs and had a much bigger profile that allowed me to see Germany, Canada, Poland, Latvia, Monaco, Portugal, Ukraine, France, Austria and a few others… places I hadn't seen before.

LEN

By this time the band was beginning to get exhausted. If we didn't slow the pace a bit, I felt the band would fall apart, such was the pressure on us, so we scaled down our activities. Nevertheless, we continued to perform a set predominantly featuring *Kultura* songs for a while, touring throughout the UK, Germany and France. *Kultura* was ultimately responsible for extending our popularity in Poland, and there were also extremely enthusiastic responses from college radio stations and Ukrainian emigre communities in the USA and Canada.

Also, we had a depressing meeting with Martin at Cooking Vinyl, who suggested we think of a new direction because 'another album of Folk Rock' wasn't going to sell. We had one more album to deliver to fulfil our three-album contract and the road ahead wasn't clear. What could we do that was different? This is when we made the worst decision of our career.

A dance album. Really? Martin loved the idea but neither Pete nor myself had any clue about dance music. So off we went back to our respective houses and wrote drum rhythms and keyboard parts on our primitive computers. I had an Amstrad 512 that boasted 512 kB, yes just half a megabyte of RAM! I invested in a 2MB upgrade, bought a stack of floppy disks and set to work. Personally, I felt completely out of my depth. It was an interesting exercise but a very bad idea. To cut a long and painful story short, we spent all our advance producing a dance album and an EP of Prince songs with producer Harri Kakoulli and Martin hated it. Luckily the album never saw the light of day, although we did a low-key release that included two of the tracks in 2014, which dribbled out as the *Revolutsiya* EP.

The dance album led us down a cul-de-sac that took us a few years to get out of. With the help of the Musicians' Union, we managed to extricate ourselves from the contract with Cooking Vinyl, but it was a long and difficult process. We didn't play live much, and didn't record any albums for five or six years and the band effectively became defunct.

PETER

Then we tried to experiment with techno, dance and the new technologies that people were using – sequencers and drum machines and stuff – and we did it, but not very well. We did a tour of Germany in '96 and tried to bring some of the technology into the set, using a drum rhythm to follow and play along to, to give us a bigger sound. But we couldn't hear what we were playing and went out of time. It didn't co-ordinate well with the out-front sound and so they couldn't really mix it properly. I think we were trying a bit too hard to be a bit too different.

We decided to cover another artist like we had with The Smiths to try and rediscover that momentum. We covered some Prince songs but the EP was released in a very slow way. And that, in 1996, was the end of the first phase of the Ukrainians.

ALAN DAWSON, UKRAINIANS BASS PLAYER, 1996-97

I joined in January 1996 and did the first two tours of Poland, including a couple of festivals there, and the tour of Canada. I also played the *Radioactivity* tour in Germany when me and Woody were also playing in the support band, Slur. I remember at one place Roman kicked the smoke machine to pieces during our set. The big Polish gigs were memorable, mainly because the crowds knew all the words to the songs. I also remember one in France where I got my tooth chipped by a bottle thrown in the middle of the gig. That was after twisting my ankle falling down some stairs and later setting myself alight and falling into a bonfire.

RAT

In the 1990s, both Ukraine and Poland were very different countries to what they are today. Imagine being released from 70 plus years of totalitarianism wherein you were indoctrinated and educated to think and act only within the ruling party guidelines. Thinking or acting in any other way would get you imprisoned – or worse – and the authorities expected you to report anyone you deemed to be acting differently. How could you advance yourself under such life restricting circumstances, especially when getting enough food on the table was a daily struggle? By being a good party member? Taking the occasional bribe in your bureaucratic day job? Dealing in the black market? Scant choices for any human being.

Now imagine there was a massive change, almost overnight, in 1991. Would you suddenly feel that you were be able to think freely and make life-changing decisions? How would you make those decisions considering you had been taught that free thought is a crime against the state and the people? Would you be able to organise yourself with like-minded individuals? How would you progress after years of disempowerment? Or, would you be suspicious that nothing was going to change, and that the next government would be more of the same dictatorial shit – so best not stick your head above the parapet? Maybe you would just go on the biggest drunken bender of your life before, or in case, the country was locked down again? Or maybe you would just try and get out?

It was into these confused circumstances that the band was thrust. We were probably the worst ambassadors for Ukraine and the UK. But, both in Ukraine and Poland, we found that many people we met were seriously committed to the possibilities of freedom and independence, and, importantly, using their love of music as a great catalyst for showing what could be achieved.

The same thanks and appreciation goes for our Polish friends like Maciek, Andrii, Ania and, again, Wlodek who pooled their day job pay cheques in order to get The Ukrainians (and Hitmen 3 from Finland) over for their first ever tour of Poland in January 1996 – and also to Polish Punk-ska band Alians for supporting us musically and showing us the ropes on that first Polish tour. It was tough for all involved, and chaotic, but it was a real experience, and meeting like-minded Polish and Ukrainian music fans in that pre-internet era was brilliant. We must be the only band who decides that touring in January is a great idea. It was so cold!

THE UKRAINIANS

PETER

Part of what is now Ukraine used to be in Poland before the Second World War. When the borders moved, three or four cities that were previously in Prussia, including Danzig and Breslau, became part of Poland, with those two particular cities becoming Gdańsk and Wrocław, and so a lot of people with German background were kicked out. These areas became quite depopulated and landless Ukrainian peasants were brought into these cities to be used as a labour force. So a lot of people in Poland with a Ukrainian background are not near the Ukrainian border at all. They're near the German-Polish border. And that's why you've got a flourishing Ukrainian culture there.

The second Polish show was part of a tour we did when Poland was opening up after it got its independence. It was the middle of winter. We got on a coach with all our gear and the support band. We were driving to the first gig, the biggest gig of the tour and the one that paid all the money, in a town called Przemyśl right on the border of Ukraine. They said, 'Don't worry, it's going to be OK,' and I was thinking, 'Why would they tell us it's gonna be OK? That's not usual before a gig.'

The coach broke down on the way there and we had to unload it and stand by the side of the road at this bus stop in the middle of winter in a howling gale, with snow coming down, while they went back and got another coach. They said it would take half an hour and it was two hours and it was going dark. There were about ten of us stood there, shivering by the side of the road with guitars, amplifiers and personal baggage, and we had no food or drink or anything. And when they came back, it wasn't even a proper coach that turned up. It was a van with no seats in the back. Three of us sat in the front and the rest of us were in the back, sitting on the amplifiers. It was another hour and a half to the venue. We were so late arriving that it was a case of out of the van, onto the stage, plug in the guitars and play. That was one of the toughest gigs I've ever done, with frozen hands!

It was a theatre-type venue and it was packed out. It was so noisy and so loud. Because we were late, people had been drinking and were noisy and raucous. The venue was full of steam and condensation. It was like walking into a tropical forest. And we went down a storm! The reason for the earlier 'don't worry about it' warnings was that, in the minds of Polish people, this is a place where there is ethnic trouble because a lot of the people in the town have a Ukrainian background. They've had more freedom than people in Ukraine and are a bit more standup-ish, so there've been fights between the people with Polish and Ukrainian backgrounds. There was a row of police at the front of the stage with a really big gap to the audience, in case anyone from a Polish background wanted to have a go at us because we were Ukrainian. Or perhaps they were there to stop a stage invasion? It was quite frightening to see police with truncheons at a rock gig. We didn't mean to be political, but our playing there made a statement to people. It meant something to them.

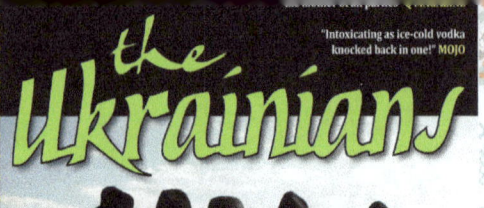

Assorted gig posters

Assorted gig posters

 NARODNIY DIM KOSCIUKS
31 JANUARY 1996, PRZEMYŚL, POLAND

WOODY

I liked Germany but I liked Poland too, where we went the following winter… It was shonky and lo-fi, the opposite of Germany, and cheap as chips, sleeping on floors as opposed to hotels, and the folks loved seeing the band. We were young and touring; even for a week or so, it's what you join a band for. Regardless of getting any payment, it didn't cost you anything so it was like a working holiday. God, I think we got the bus to Warsaw from London too – a fucking long way on a bus – but those were the cost-cutting ways to make these things happen. A frozen winter tour in an old bus, which conked out a few times, with two other bands. That old bus was pretty bloody cold. Some good gigs though, with people queuing to get in and five złotys to the pound.

WLODEK NAKONECZNY

After Jacek's death, I stopped doing concerts for a long time and focused on the record label, Koka. We were joined by Andrii Maruszeczko – friend, artist, owner of an advertising agency – who made us more professional. I met his colleague Maciek Kowalczuk, a lover of good music and a fan of The Ukrainians, and we started to dream about licensing their albums in Poland. Me and Andrii came from a Ukrainian community while Maciek was a Pole from Białystok, a multicultural area where the perception of eastern cultural threads was deeper than anywhere else in Poland. We were all sure that The Ukrainians could become known with their music, and integrate and inspire various circles, not just Ukrainians in Poland.

Koka released the first two Ukrainians albums on cassettes in 1994, and *Kultura* a year later, initially illegally, because we released the cassettes a little bit ahead of licensing them from Cooking Vinyl. But every cassette sold confirmed their potential and we started making concrete plans for a tour. Maciek took care of talks with the band, I the concert schedule and logistics, and Andrii the advertising, including the production of film material. We were planning on a grand scale.

A few months before the Polish tour, the band played in Lviv at the *Alternativa 1995* festival. I was there with a Polish band and came across Peter and Len in the hotel lobby. I spoke in Ukrainian and was misunderstood, then accidentally activated the remnants of English I had learned in primary school with similar results. I tried to tell them that I was going to organise a 'tour in Poland' for them in just 'a few months'. I wasn't sure they understood, despite the enthusiastic long, 'Oooh, ooo'keeeey, coool!'

We planned seven concerts throughout Poland, with support from the local folk-Punk

THE UKRAINIANS

band Alians and Maciek's friends from Finland, Hitmen 3, who played melodic Punk-rock, and set out to conquer Poland. We celebrated the arrival of The Ukrainians intensely, Maciek and Andrii sponsoring a nice restaurant for an 'acquaintance party'. Neither Roman nor Stepan were now in the band, and to my detriment, nobody in the band now spoke Ukrainian! And I only knew a few words of English, not enough for basic interaction.

We rented a bus for the tour in Piła. We left Warsaw for Przemyśl, 400 kilometres away, in good time for a soundcheck, lunch and a rest ahead of the concert. But the journey was quite slow and when the hills started, the bus began making strange sounds: snorting, groaning and puffing, with each hill getting harder and harder. During each difficult climb the team shouted a loud 'Allez!', but halfway through one... it didn't make it: the vehicle got stuck in the middle of nowhere.

I didn't think we were going to get to the concert. We stopped a car and it took few of us to the nearest village where we looked for transport for 20 people. With the help of locals, we found a van whose driver agreed to take us to Przemyśl. But one van wasn't enough, so he called his friends and found one more willing to take us. This one needed a little bit more time to organise. Kazi from Alians, who spoke English, arranged a meeting and we agreed that the van would take me, the sound man Rat (who had a cold) and all the instruments, luggage, etc., to put on the stage before the concert.

We arrived in Przemyśl half an hour before the scheduled start of the concert, which was to take place in the small theatre hall of a Renaissance castle, picturesquely situated on a steep hill. The crowd was thick near the castle, and it was impossible to squeeze through at the entrance. The organiser arranged a team to help get the equipment through the crowd, Rat started mastering the technology and I anxiously waited for the rest of the party to arrive.

Which they did three-quarters of an hour later, one of the longest times of my life. I breathed a sigh of relief, and so did they, although for a different reason. They were shaking like jelly and frosted over, but they were smiling. To this day, I can still see those broadly smiling, blue faces in my mind, and in my ears their joyful hoots towards me. I interpreted these as expressions of appreciation. It was only after the concert that I found out that the only vehicle that the friend of our driver – otherwise our saviour – had at his disposal was a refrigerated truck.

The concert was delayed by an hour and a half, but it was a big event. The hall was filled to capacity and there was an atmosphere of festivity; people danced, sang with the band and shouted out the titles of the songs they wanted to hear, the loudest being 'Horilka'. The concert in Przemyśl was organised by Mariusz Sidor, from the Ukrainian minority, and it was probably his first event.

It was a very important concert for Ukrainians. The city is unique due to its location right next to the Polish-Ukrainian border and the presence of a large group of Ukrainian 'autochthons', or original inhabitants rooted to the land. Mariusz was the first to organise an event not only for them, but one that was open to other communities. Today, the Przemyśl Ukrainian cultural centre ('Narodnyj Dim') is one of the most open institutions, with a very ambitious cultural programme for everyone. To some extent, this is the result of this previously unprecedented concert as well as several subsequent initiatives. There were very nice, enthusiastic reviews of the concert in the local press, emphasising, among other things the intercultural integration.

Mariusz also arranged transport back to Warsaw, where we were to change to another bus, hastily organised by Andrii and Maciek. It was a good start to the tour: 24 hours and four different types of transport, including a refrigerated truck...

KINOTEATR TĘCZA
1 FEBRUARY 1996, WARSZAWA, POLAND

RODZYN, BAD LOOK RECORDS

In 1996 I was 20 years old. Me and my friends mostly read the flyers which guys shared at Punk Rock gigs and on the Punk Rock market, which was in Warsaw every second Saturday. I knew that Alians were playing in Kino Teatr Tęcza, where I had never been before. I didn't realise that at that concert I would hear something better than the Polish band Alians – The Ukrainians. That was a blast! Punk, folk and it was so energetic! After more than 20 years, my friend Żaba who organises the *Rock Na Bagnie Festival* in Poland asked me to help him bring the band back to Poland. The Ukrainians one more time! After some email exchanges we finally 'got it!'. The Ukrainians came to the east of Poland. It was an honour for me to meet members of the band personally and again I heard these great songs. After all these years I still remember the 'Vorony' lyrics...

KINO FAMA
2 FEBRUARY 1996, BIAŁYSTOK, POLAND

WLODEK NAKONECZNY

At the Tęcza cinema theatre in Warsaw, the band was welcomed warmly and loudly. It was like an antidote for my stress-exhausted soul, and for the musicians' bodies, which were still chilled by the refrigerator.

The next day we went to Podlasie, to Białystok – Maciek's hometown. The event was organised by Andrzej Grygoruk aka Bazyl, a local master of ceremonies for alternative events. I knew this would be different from everywhere else; Maciek forewarned us, Bazyl forewarned us, and Ukrainians in Podlasie had been notified in advance. In Podlasie, Polish, Belarusian and Ukrainian ethnicities naturally coexisted and intermingled. Before the war there was also a Jewish aspect, which was then being discovered anew, and there was a community of Polish Tatars living nearby. It was a miniature republic of many nations and religions.

The Fama club, where we were supposed to play, was literally under siege. And amongst the besiegers were a lot of elderly people: the arrival of the Brits singing in Ukrainian became a great cross-generational and cross-community event. Bazyl took special care of the elders, setting aside part of the room for tables with chairs and armchairs where they could sit. They were there until the very end, bravely listening to the Hitmen and the Alians – and no one left early! The atmosphere was insane: hot and crowded in front of the stage, you couldn't even stick a pin in it. The Ukrainians' songs were accompanied by the choral singing of the crowd – everyone knew and understood the lyrics. I have attended many concerts, but I have never experienced such energy as the one in Białystok! We went back there several more times, and it was always unique and special.

ACK ESCULAP

3 FEBRUARY 1996, POZNAŃ, POLAND

WLODEK NAKONECZNY

The reaction in the Eskulap club in Poznań was also ecstatic, but less spontaneous and more restrained than in Białystok. The concert was great. But I more remember the second concert in Poznań, in 1997. It was an open-air event in the castle courtyard, with beautiful weather and a receptive audience of over a thousand people. And, after the concert, record sales of merchandise on cassettes, records and t-shirts.

Both concerts in Poznań were organised by Łukasz Minta, then a student, and after a few years the owner of a well-known concert agency; in 2007, he did one more concert by The Ukrainians as part of the 'Music from the Besieged City' festival in Lubin, where Len had the opportunity to talk to his idols from his youth, Misty in Roots, who played on the same stage.

KWADRATOWA
4 FEBRUARY 1996, GDAŃSK, POLAND

WLODEK NAKONECZNY

From Poznań we went to Tricity (the 'three ports' on Poland's northern coast) to Gdańsk to play at the Kwadratowa Club. This club already had its place in local Ukrainian history as Oseledec gave their last concert there eight years earlier! The club was now rebuilt, with a huge space under the stage and galleries around that were completely filled with people, about a thousand of them! The energy they generated could be compared to the energy from Białystok. Peter was full of admiration. I understood that I had done a 'good job', but I didn't understand any more.

SALA PKP
5 FEBRUARY 1996, WROCŁAW, POLAND

WLODEK NAKONECZNY

Steff played his last concert of the tour in Wrocław. He had to return to England because of a job he didn't want to lose. After the concert, I was supposed to send him by train to Warsaw, where Andrii was then to take him to the airport. After the concert, everyone said goodbye to him as if he was going off to war; hugs, songs, toasts, patting and comforting – the only thing missing was the mourning lasses. Steff really wanted to say something, but no one wanted to listen – everyone was noisily celebrating his return to work.

  At one point he managed to utter, 'Ticket!' and that's when I jumped into action! Shouting over the crowd, 'Yes, I know, I have your ticket!', I triumphantly waved the train ticket in front of his eyes, pointing out the carriage and seat numbers. But he wasn't happy! We got into a taxi and, amid cheers, set off for the short journey to the station. There, I forced Steff to eat a hamburger, because it was a seven-hour journey to Warsaw. With a growing pain in my heart, I tried to guess what was going on, because clearly something was wrong. Sauce was dripping down his chin, he was chewing the meat and still wanted to say something more, but the terror in his eyes was slowly giving way to resignation… I'm ashamed to say I was relieved when the train started moving.

  Steff probably wasn't. A few hours later it was finally understood: he had lost his… flight ticket! Andrii and his wife took care of him and after some time arranged for him to return home. Did he lose his job? I don't know. I didn't know English and I didn't understand Steff's problem. But the guys in the band spoke English, so how the hell didn't they understand him? Especially since it was apparently not the first incident of this type involving him. I have only one explanation: the scale of the tour's success clouded their minds and dulled their senses, including the sense of alertness.

CAFE TEATRALNA
6 FEBRUARY 1996, PIŁA, POLAND

WLODEK NAKONECZNY

The farewell concert in Piła was different from the others. Due to the lack of an accordion, Peter grabbed an electric guitar and the guys played everything in a Punk style. No one was bothered by the terrible sound system – at one point Rat waved his hand because he was unable to control the sound – on the contrary, many years later I met attendees of this concert who remembered it as legendary and unique. There's no accounting for taste!

We returned to Warsaw by another bus, because the one that took us through almost all of Poland in Piła refused to go any further. So we reached the end of this unforgettable adventure, having travelled 3,000 kilometres, breaking two buses and using a refrigerated truck.

As Maciek honestly promised at the outset, there was no money from this tour. Or to put it another way, it was 'very symbolic' and the musicians converted what little money they earned mostly into alcohol. If anyone made money, it was the organisers of the concerts, thanks to the unexpectedly high attendances.

BAD
26 APRIL 1996, HANNOVER, GERMANY

WOODY

The *Radioactivity* tour was the start of Pete and Len tinkering with electronic music and it was terrible to behold. Those gigs in Germany had new songs which were part electronic and the way we did it live was to play them through Pete's portable CD player from the stage. It was doomed to musically fail. Folk danced about on stage and the CD kept jumping, which was just embarrassing to try and stay in time with.

It was shocking really. Don't get me wrong – we didn't know at the time how to achieve this synthesis between live and backing track and we were trying to do it on a shoestring budget but the poor audience having to endure such an amateur spectacle... I feel for them all these years later.

Regardless of the technical issues there were good gigs on that tour. The band still had a decent following in Germany, regular folks came to multiple gigs and the band were treated to wonderful continental-style breakfasts. I liked Germany. We once were given a giant Kinder egg filled with someone's homegrown grass and such things only happen in dreams.

RADIOACTIVITY EP
RELEASED 26 APRIL 1996

LEN

We felt we needed to mark the tenth anniversary of the Chornobyl nuclear accident. The Association of Ukrainian Women in Great Britain were collecting money for the Ukrainian Children's Appeal Fund, which had been sending aid to the most affected areas of Ukraine since 1990, so we decided to record a version of Kraftwerk's 'Radioactivity' so that we could contribute too. It was a fairly simple affair, with a drum machine, keyboards and the nearest sample we could find to a bandura sound, and for the first time on a Ukrainians recording I sang in English. We added some appropriate words that I picked out from the Book of Revelation in my Ukrainian-language copy of the Bible, then our friends Irena Kuszta and Natalka Shiroka sang backing vocals and that was it. Easy!

The CD featured four mixes of what was essentially the same track, which a lot of people did in those days. One was a radio edit, another had a German language section because we had a lot of fans in Germany at that time, and one, called 'Revelation', only included our bits without any reference to the original Kraftwerk song. This last track also appeared on a double CD compilation called *No Compromize*, to raise money for the Campaign For Free Education. The album also featured, amongst many others, Suede, Zion Train, Transglobal Underground, New Model Army, and our Leeds mates Chumbawamba, Cud and The Wedding Present.

CALGARY FOLK FESTIVAL
27 & 28 JULY 1996, CALGARY, CANADA

PETER

We did a tour in Canada in '96 and Roman played with us again as he was living in Toronto at that point. Between ten and 15 per cent of the population in Canada have a Ukrainian background. In the late 1800s and early 1900s, immigration policies were encouraging people to populate the wide-open spaces, the prairies, and the weather in Canada is very, very similar to Ukraine. People would emigrate from Ukraine with a crate that included their farm implements and the seeds they were going to plant. They'd reach their railway station, disembark and head off with the number that designated their plot of land. The first year would be living in a turf hut they built out of the ground to survive the winter. Then they'd start building a house and growing crops. The Ukrainians that went there were pretty tough and knew what they were doing.

Ukrainian music in Canada has developed its own style. I can hear when a Ukrainian band is Canadian-Ukrainian. It has naturally melded with a country music style. The chord sequences and the fiddle sound are a lot more country.

LEN

When we did the *Kultura* album, we had Mick West playing mandolin with us instead of Roman. But Mick couldn't come to Canada with us, and so Roman came back for that tour. We'd recorded three albums by that stage, *The Ukrainians* and *Vorony*, which Roman had recorded with us, and *Kultura*, which he wasn't on. Our set was comprised of songs from all three albums. Roman played brilliantly on the songs that he'd originally recorded. If it was a song he liked, he'd dance around whilst playing the mandolin. He put everything into it. But as soon as it was one of the *Kultura* songs, he'd turn his back to the audience and wouldn't interact at all. He'd just stand there and look at the wall, just playing a D note all the way through. It was really extreme. I didn't challenge him about that, because we were pussyfooting around him at that time. We knew he had issues.

PETER

Roman did a few other one-off shows as well, but after the '96 tour, he didn't want to do it anymore. He just said, 'I can't do this, I'm not doing it.' I saw him on and off socially after that but then he died 18 years later. The last time I saw Roman he appeared unhappy and withdrawn. I found out later that he had decided a musical life was not for him. He spent the last years of his life in a vegan, drug-free world on the island of Crete, where meditation and mindfulness gave him the peace he was looking for. He was conflicted by the combination of being in The Ukrainians celebrating his Ukrainian-ness, and all the negative things that are associated with Ukrainian conflict and history.

BAMBOO CLUB
7 AUGUST 1996, TORONTO, CANADA

NESTOR GULA (AKA TONAL SURGE)

I first heard that there was a British band belting out Ukrainian songs back in 1989, when I was in a dingy room in a Soviet-style student residence in Poland. My friend Wlodek Nakoneczny asked me if I had heard of this British Ukrainian band. I had not. A month or so later, I was holding a rare import album in my hand, *Ukrainski Vistupi V Johna Peela*. This was by the band The Wedding Present, kinda… Len Liggins (vocals) and Roman Remeynes (mandolin) rounded out the members and added 'the element' to make this a classic collection of tunes. This was the start of The Ukrainians.

This was important for a number of reasons. Being Ukrainian was now cool. This was before Ukraine achieved independence – it was still widely considered some backwater in the USSR. Being a Ukrainian youth meant Saturdays spent in Ukrainian school and not engaging with friends on a football pitch, baseball diamond, ice rink or just hanging out. The only mention of Ukraine was in that horribly naïve Beatles song. The Ukrainians came at the right time – not just to showcase Ukraine to the world but to show the Ukrainian diaspora youth that being Ukrainian was not just a tale of woe, desperation and heartache. Ukrainian stuff was not just kitsch – there was passion and fun. And lots of rhythm.

Another reason is a personal one – The Ukrainians inspired me as a musician. At that time, I was in Вапняк Під Голим Небом / Vapniak Pid Holym Nebom / Stalagmite Under A Naked Sky. We were doing long-form experimental music for the larger part. Hearing The Ukrainians create their own original Ukrainian songs really lit a fire in me as a musician and songwriter. I heard The Ukrainians just after being in Ukraine where I met musicians such as Taras Chubai, Maria Burmaka, Braty Hadiukiny and VV amongst others. These all left a great impression on me. But they were all 'native' Ukrainians. They were not diaspora Ukes like The Ukrainians. The lyrics The Ukrainians came up with were poignant, humorous and oftentimes spoke of the Ukrainian diaspora experience and worldview.

Alas, until now I was only able to experience The Ukrainians live in concert once when they played the Bamboo club in Toronto in 1996. It was a brilliant high-end show. We billeted the rhythm section at our house. It was so long ago I forget their names, but we had a chance to hang out away from the festival. I will always recall one of the evenings where we were hanging out in a backyard in Toronto singing songs with a bunch of people. Peter Solowka and I would pass the guitar back and forth playing the Ukrainian songs that we knew. Occasionally Peter would get into a Smiths song, unbeknownst to us foreshadowing the *Pisni Iz the Smiths* EP. I would counter with a Nirvana tune. Quite a memorable evening.

While the Ukrainian diaspora had popular Zabava bands before, there was nothing like The Ukrainians. They were, and are, a proper band. They have their own tunes and they create a great energy.

 MUSEUM OF CIVILISATION
11 AUGUST 1996, GATINEAU, QUEBEC, CANADA

TONY PIDKALENKO
I had been following the Manchester and northern England music scene ever since the time of The Wedding Present before I discovered The Ukrainians. I instantly loved their music and their home area, as I have a fondness for Rochdale where my parents lived after World War II for five years before emigrating to Canada in 1952. I was born two years later in Montreal.

In the summer of 1996, The Ukrainians were on tour in North America and they performed at the Canadian Museum of Civilization in Gatineau (then called Hull) as part of the annual Canadian heritage celebrations in our capital city, Ottawa. A day before the show on a hot sultry summer weekend, I got a call from the organiser in the local Ukrainian arts scene who was arranging the show. She said that The Ukrainians were coming to Ottawa, that the fiddle player's bow had broken and he needed to urgently borrow one for the show as all the music stores were closed that weekend. Did I know where to get one? I did. A friend of mine, who was also a fiddle player as well as an accomplished local Ottawa watercolour artist, had a bow. She happily lent hers for the show.

The show organiser also asked me if I knew where they could stay in Ottawa, and without hesitation I offered my home in south Ottawa. We went out that weekend and in typical celebratory fashion enjoyed a wonderful time together as we took in the sights and nightlife of Ottawa. I remember, while drinking a few beers, the bass player Paul Briggs recounting bizarre stories of his experiences as a psychiatric nurse.

I would love The Ukrainians to tour Canada again.

PETER

And then people's lives were getting in the way. I was getting on a bit, in my late '30s, and you start thinking, 'What am I going to do?' I'd been doing this musical trip which many people never get to do in their lives, but there was also a realisation that you can't keep on doing it forever. You don't get the same buzz if you keep doing the same thing over and over. And I was thinking about families. I'd already bought a house with the money I had from The Wedding Present and so now I was thinking about the next phase of my life with my partner. And my first son was born in '97, and that does change your life quite a bit. If I could have earned £1,000 a night playing music and I could have paid my bills, I'd have kept it going. But if it's like a paying hobby, which it always was, you can't justify being away from family all the time.

Our gig rate had been falling anyway and it fell dramatically after that, but we didn't stop doing what we were doing.

When we brought out *Kultura* in '94, we did quite a few shows but then our accordion player, Stepan Pasicznyk, said he was retiring from the band because he was spending too long away from his partner. He said he couldn't justify all the time away with almost no money coming in and that he had to think about his future. We replaced him with Stephen Tymruk who's the accordion player we've got now and who's another person of Ukrainian background. He came up to live in Leeds.

We were already starting to be scattered, with a bass player in Norwich and an accordion player in London, which makes things harder. And Len had moved down to Reading, because his partner had a job down there.

While we were out on the tour of Ukraine, we met the people who organised our first video for us in 1990, and they followed us round and managed to get onto the dodgy cruise ship – they obviously knew people and knew how to get on there – and they managed to come across to England a couple of times as well. And Dave, our drummer, got on really well with one of them – Sasha, whose full name was Alexandra – and he left the band in about '94 or '95 to go and live with her in Kyiv, and he's been there ever since, in a flat looking after cats. And Paul, our bass player from Norwich, met somebody in Germany and they're living out in Cologne. He's a graphic designer and restores classic cars as a hobby. It seems that when you've been on this Ukrainians journey, it's a good way of meeting different people from other cultures.

In 1995 our drummer Steven 'Woody' Wood joined us. The line-up became amazingly stable from then for a six-piece line-up. It lasted for 16 years. Steff Tymruk sort of left in 1996 and we brought in an interesting multi-instrumentalist called Michael West from Hebden Bridge. He plays guitar, mandolin, trumpets and, instead of accordion, he played keyboards with an accordion sound for quite a few shows. And then we got Steff back again and Michael just played electric guitar after that. So we were actually a seven-piece for a while.

STEPHEN JUSYPIW

A thank you note. My father was born and lived in a small village in the Carpathian Mountains of Ukraine. At the age of 17, during the Nazi invasion of the Second World War, he was taken away from his family to the German labour camps, as happened to many Ukrainians. At the end of the war, he chose not to go back to a Ukraine under Soviet occupation and – like 65,000 other Ukrainians – came to the UK, where he married a good English girl, working hard to bring up a family.

My father's name was officially Iwan, pronounced 'Ivan' (he came to the UK with that spelling from his German documents), but he was known to all as John – or, at Leyland Motors, 'Johnny Clock', because he fixed everybody's clocks and watches for them, including all the factory timepieces.

By the time of Ukrainian independence in 1991, my father was too ill to travel, and he died in 1997. While discussing the funeral arrangements, the track 'Son' ('Sleep') from the 1991 album *The Ukrainians* struck us as something we would like for the funeral. It is a powerful and peacefully noble elegy. Pete Solowka readily granted us permission to use it for my father's funeral service, held in the UK, though we had already decided that we should try to return him home if possible. My youngest brother was eventually able to take my father's ashes to be buried in his old village in the Carpathians.

After the funeral, one of my father's best friends, another Ukrainian with an interest in traditional music, told me, 'I don't recognise the tune, but it reminds me of home.' A lost home, perhaps, but one to dream about.

KLUB GWINT
23 JUNE 1997, BIAŁYSTOK, POLAND

LEN
We got invited to undertake another tour of Poland in 1997, which we did even though we had no new recordings to promote, our main motivations being that we absolutely loved Poland… and also because we could bring back suitcases full of Bison Grass vodka at £1.50 a bottle!

KLUB GRAFFITI
24 JUNE 1997, LUBLIN, POLAND

PAUL WEATHERHEAD, UKRAINIANS MANDOLIN PLAYER
I first heard about The Ukrainians when my friend Mick West joined the band just before the *Kultura* album. He'd been looking for a band and went to two auditions around the same time – one for the mandolin player with The Ukrainians and the other playing guitar with PJ Harvey. He got offered both, and decided the road to wealth and success was with The Ukrainians.

I joined The Ukrainians on mandolin in June 1997 just before a two-week tour of Poland. By now, Michael was playing keyboards (though he also did a stint on bass and played electric guitar from *Respublika* until the time he left). I had an intense fortnight to learn the set, and then we were off. The journey was seemingly endless – we travelled from Leeds to Warsaw by bus. When we finally got to Warsaw, we had another two-hour drive deep into the forest to the artist commune where we were to stay for some of the nights on the tour. I thought the commune might be full of hippy girls in flowery dresses, though the only occupants were a couple of gay anarchists and an unhealthy-looking cat!

The tour was an amazing experience – I'd never played to crowds so big, and as the tour progressed the crowds just got bigger. It was pretty nerve-wracking with only a couple of weeks to learn a long set, so it was a baptism of fire of sorts. The second gig was particularly memorable. Mick imbibed rather too much Polish vodka during the soundcheck and during the gig tumbled off the back of the stage, pulling the keyboard on top of him as he went. It was quite a drop. He clambered back on to the stage only to fall off again. At the hotel, a member of the band who shall remain nameless covered Mick with hand-drawn heavy metal tattoos while he was sleeping off the excesses. He was not pleased to wake up with metal band logos covering his face and torso, especially when it became clear the marker used to draw the 'tattoos' was indelible…

Rock'n'roll shenanigans aside, Mick was my best friend and a huge part of the Ukrainians story and we still miss him.

PROXIMA
29 JUNE 1997, WARSZAWA, POLAND

WLODEK NAKONECZNY, PROMOTER

In the summer of 1997, we did a second tour of Poland. Another 3,000 kilometres, but this time all in one bus and with no refrigerated truck but several unforgettable concerts including Poznań Castle, the *Folk-Fiesta Festival* in Ząbkowice Śląskie, the Gwint club in Białystok and the Proxima in Warsaw. Warsaw was also memorable because the organiser hosted the musicians with a delicious vegetarian dinner when it was not yet a good time for vegetarians in Poland. Many bars were dominated by meat and I vividly remember a scene from a stop at a roadside bar when we were hungry where the meat eaters had their fill, while Peter and Len were forced to eat a roll with gherkin and a dollop of ketchup, because that was the extent of the bar's veggie menu. I suffered a lot when I looked at their plate; I still suffer when I remember it...

LEN

It has always been a principle of mine that if you're playing a gig in somebody else's country, you speak to them in their own language. I'm not a fan of the school of thought that suggests lead singers just shout 'Hello Warsaw' into the mic (especially if they're playing in Berlin) so I've always had a bit of chat for the audience in the language of our host country. In fact, I used to look forward to the odd technical malfunction at a gig because it gave me the opportunity to develop a stand-up routine, which I thought could be handy if the band packed in. In my case, the routine consisted of one joke that I mastered in English, French, German, Spanish, Polish and of course Ukrainian. The joke was, 'How many Ukrainians does it take to change a lightbulb?' 'Five. One to hold the lightbulb and four to drink vodka until the ceiling spins round.'

Maybe it sounds better in Polish...

LEN

After this there was a big hiatus due to the diversionary dance album debacle. By 1998, we were feeling older and had less energy for long tours. We had partners, relationships and – in Pete's case – children to consider. Also, some members of the band wanted to do things outside of playing in The Ukrainians, which is healthy musically. Woody, Paul, Mick and myself were involved in other projects: Woody with Tetchi, Paul and Mick with The Electric Brains and me with my English language solo records, which are very different in style from The Ukrainians.

There was also the fact that we didn't have a record company, a manager and a booking agent any more constantly feeding us stuff to do. When you're younger and full of ambition you'll do anything and everything to "make it", irrespective of how destructive that can be on your mental and physical health.

Once we had set up our own label, Zirka Records, we decided we'd take control of everything ourselves. That meant no-one was working on our behalf or investing in us anymore, so our public profile was going to take a dive, but at least we had control of our own careers and our own lives. Luckily, I'd worked in publicity and promotions for national environmental charities before the band came into being, so I was accustomed to writing and sending out press releases, editing photos and doing publicity campaigns. That was useful but because we almost always had an empty bank account, we didn't have much in the way of budgets to promote our new releases and gigs. But we could do whatever we wanted, whenever we wanted to do it, and that freedom meant that the band could continue to the present day. If we'd signed another record deal and continued the way we were going The Ukrainians would have imploded with the pressure years ago.

'NOTHING COMPARES 2 U'
RELEASED 14 SEPTEMBER 1998

LEN

Also known as *The Prince EP*, this was a further incursion into the dance music world, this time with *Vorony* album producer Harri Kakoulli. It was too much of a diversion from our usual style for me; an interesting one for us musically but one not destined to last very long. It featured English and Ukrainian language versions of the title track written by Prince but made famous by Sinéad O'Connor, who as we all know recorded a really beautiful interpretation of the song. There were also versions of 'Sign O' The Times' and an eight-and-a-half minute version of 'Purple Rain'. We had fun with the song titles… 'Purple Rain' was the 'Slavs in the Temple' mix and we dubbed the Ukrainian language version of 'Nothing Compares 2 U' the 'U Got the Uke' mix. Prince fans will get the references, I'm sure.

John Peel played the 'Nothing Compares 2 U' title track but was clearly a bit mystified by the radical change in direction. The EP dribbled out without much support from our label, Cooking Vinyl Records and remains one of the bizarre obscurities of our back catalogue.

DRINK TO MY HORSE!
RELEASED 20 OCTOBER 2000

LEN

Once Pete and I had our freedom from Cooking Vinyl, we decided to start up the band again. This time we would do everything ourselves. No record companies, no managers, no booking agents, nobody telling us what to do. It was going to be on our own terms. We set up our own record label, Zirka Records. We tried to think of how we might release something, bearing in mind we had a bank account with just one pound in it. I set about contacting ex-band members to see if they had any live recordings floating around. Occasionally we used to ask the sound engineers at gigs for cassette recordings from the mixing desk. I had a few and so did Mick. Dave Lee, who had been our drummer, sent me a few in the post, as did Paul Briggs, our previous bass player who now lived in Cologne. I went through about three dozen tapes and picked out 20 tracks, which became the *Drink To My Horse!* album. Our friend, studio owner and part-time live sound engineer, Alaric Neville, assembled the tracks and EQ'd them so that it sounded as near as possible to a coherent live album.

One of the things that tickles me about this album is the very end. We do (even though I say so myself) a fine rendition of 'Verkhovyno' that is taken from the Reading University gig we played on our first ever tour in October 1991. We were supporting The Levellers and had a very enthusiastic crowd. At the end of the track, we walked offstage and one clearly drunken fan shouts out 'come back yer wankers'.

It's nice to be wanted.

ROB BOWKER

I think it must have been early 2000 when Len walked into my life. He'd arrived at The Conservation Volunteers (then BTCV) in Wallingford to work on communications and I was graphic designer – you can see what's coming. My two earliest memories are being handed a bunch of inscrutable computer files for doing the artwork for the release of *Drink To My Horse* (Zirka Records ZRKCD1) and watching the World Trade Center receiving the second airliner in the attack of 11 September that year. Despite overlapping stays in West Yorkshire in the early 1980s and despite having worked on documenting the Ukrainian diaspora in Bradford, I'd never heard of The Ukrainians. Maybe that's the difference between Leeds and Bradford. I must have missed that particular Peel session.

THE UKRAINIANS

PATRICK LEE-THORP

I was with a Hamburg music distribution firm, New Music Distribution, for a while and we distributed the *Drink To My Horse!* live album in Germany. I remember presenting the album at our product meeting. Our firm had a little bit of a reputation for Punk music as well as several other Indie genres. Some of the sales force were indeed Punk musicians. But I made the mistake of not listening to the CD before the meeting and presented the record as being from an English Punk outfit. When the music started, my colleagues had a good laugh. But they liked it. I suppose this was because the music was lively and rousing, full of energy. What puzzled me was that the album had an English title and the songs were all in what we assumed was the Ukrainian language. We had no idea what the boys were singing about. But they must have had many Ukrainian fans in Germany so we were happy to meet the demand!

RESPUBLIKA

ANARCHY IN THE UK CD EP
RELEASED 3 JUNE 2002

LEN

In 2002 we regrouped and got back in the saddle. We had made enough money from the sales of *Drink To My Horse!* to record again, but not enough to spend weeks in the studio doing lavish productions, so decided to do something quick and Punky over a period of just a few days. We thought we'd research some traditional Ukrainian folk songs that were less well-known amongst the Ukrainian community that could be the basis of the album. But first we'd need to bring out a single as a taster for the album, and as we were going for a Punk vibe, we thought an EP of Sex Pistols' songs would fit the bill nicely.

   The choice of songs was easy. It's not like the Pistols left a legacy of hundreds of songs to choose from. 'Anarchy In The UK' was a must-do, and within minutes we'd agreed 'Pretty Vacant', 'God Save The Queen' and 'Holidays In The Sun'. It was a no-brainer. Then someone bizarrely suggested we do an acoustic version of 'Anarchy In The UK'. I just thought, 'How would I do a vocal on that? How could anyone express the concept of anarchy in a chilled and laid-back way, and why would anyone want to do it like that in the first place?' It seemed perverse. Anyhow, I'm the kind of person who's rarely unwilling to turn down a good challenge, so I gave it a go, the band liked it, and it ended up on the EP instead of 'Holidays In The Sun'.

ROB BOWKER

It is really hard to remember precisely but my first new album artwork was for *Respublika* (ZRKCD3), though I also did the EP that preceded it, *Anarchy In The UK* (ZRKCDS2). And that process set the tone for subsequent creative collaborations. I knew I was taking a brief from Len but there was always the sense that there were other voices chipping in with ideas and feedback. My best guess is Peter and Len's other half, Rebecca. So proposed designs can vacillate wildly from one idea to another and end up light years away from where they started. Which only with the cushioning of time elapsed seems like a reasonable way of working. Fortunately, from the start we agreed it 'isn't about the money' but by hook and by crook and often unexpectedly, I always seem to get paid. Sometimes cash, sometimes beer, sometimes CDs. But it is far from a commercial relationship and I'm certain Len knows I'd do it for nothing.

THE UKRAINIANS

ROB BOWKER

In a strange twist of events, my son Mr Robin, the little chap in the fur hat on the back sleeve of *Respublika*, grew up to bring home his very own Ukrainian *divchino* in 2022!

RESPUBLIKA
RELEASED 2 AUGUST 2002

PAUL WEATHERHEAD

Our 2002 album *Respublika* is one of my favourites. It was rehearsed and recorded in a super intense two-week period which I'll never forget. A few months earlier, we'd rehearsed and recorded those Sex Pistols tracks for a single in a similar intense fashion. Now we were recording a whole album of traditional Ukrainian folk tunes in a fuzz-heavy Punk style with just a few days to rehearse and a few days to record them. This meant that we spent nine to ten hours each day in a claustrophobic rehearsal room in Leeds working out the songs before going to Castleford to record them. It was an exhausting process. By the end of rehearsals, even my tinnitus was playing Ukie folk tunes…

Spending hour upon hour for day after day cooped up in a small room meant that tempers sometimes frayed. I remember at least two full-on sweary scream-fests that almost resulted in members quitting or being sacked. One was about having to pay 20p for a cup of coffee from the studio drinks machine and the other was about what to watch on the TV during a break. Football, or *Little House On The Prairie*? But the intense way the album was rehearsed and recorded in so little time meant that the urgency and tension really comes through in the music.

PETER

We were thinking about different things we could do and decided to do traditional Ukrainian songs in a very aggressive electric guitar Punk style. In eastern Europe, the Punk revival was big before it was big in the UK. We got distorted electric guitars and completely Punked up some Ukrainian folk songs. And we also decided to do Ukrainian language versions of Sex Pistols songs which worked really well. We decided we would do

it as Punk as we could, so we rehearsed it really quickly for four days non-stop twelve hours a day and then went in the studio again for just six days and belted them out, no messing about. It's got an energy to it. Some of the chord sequences in 'Anarchy in the UK' worked great. Those songs went down really well in eastern Europe.

The dance tune 'Arkan' was our biggest challenge. It's an instrumental track as fast as Hopak, but with a much more complicated structure. The arrangement took ages, and performing it takes lots of concentration. I love playing it live – it's so powerful, and watching the audience try to keep up with the speed and the dynamics can be fun!

LEN

Fans and reviewers commented that the ancient folk songs and the modern British Sex Pistols songs seemed to fit together perfectly on the album – it didn't sound like they had been uncomfortably forced together. I was pleased about that. To me, Punk was the Folk music of the time, and anyway, both the old eastern songs and the new western songs are

often about rebellion, so there's that subject matter and "feeling" that ties them together as well. We recorded the whole thing very quickly. We wanted to capture the urgency and spontaneity that was in our original Wedding Present Peel sessions. So, we had a few rehearsals and then went to the studio in Castleford, plugged our instruments in and went for it.

As a result of this album, we got a lot of interest in Poland, where there was a massive Punk scene. We played a lot of Punk and Rock clubs and festivals – and the audiences went nuts! We had a lot of hardcore Punks with mohicans, chains and tattoos, very different from our Indie and Folk rock UK audiences. As a touring musician that was very exciting.

LEN

Thankfully we started to attract the attention of record companies outside of the UK. This was very handy money-wise, as I'd loaned our label Zirka Records £7,000 so that we could get the album recorded, manufactured and out, and I needed to get it back. It was my life savings and all the money I had! Luckily, we licensed the album not only to Sonic Records in Warsaw, Poland, but also to Omnium Records in Minneapolis, USA, Umka in Ukraine and Soyuz in Moscow. Within 18 months, I had my money back and Zirka Records was afloat!

PETER

The band started going off and playing as a six-piece without me because I had family commitments and couldn't go. I didn't go abroad and do tours for a few years until the kids were a bit older and a bit more independent. The Punk/Pistols thing definitely enlivened us again.

KLUB RE
28 FEBRUARY 2003, KRAKÓW, POLAND

WLODEK NAKONECZNY, PROMOTER

The band got an invitation to the *Szanty in Wrocław* festival, so I sandwiched it between concerts in Kraków and Warsaw to make a mini-tour. Len warned that they would be coming without Peter and that... it would be like that for some time. Without a leader? I had concerns. What's more, it started badly: during the flight, luggage was lost, including Len's violin and Mick's guitar. We were stuck for half a day trying to locate the lost luggage, which had been flown to Germany. Mick insisted that he would not play with a borrowed guitar; he had to have a new one, and he tested the instruments in the store for an hour before choosing one. The bigger problem was the violin. I called all my violinist friends, but no one was able or willing to help.

We reached Kraków with great delay and without a violin. In the meantime, the luggage was redirected to Wrocław, where we were supposed to be the next day. The intimate Re Club in the Market Square in Kraków's Old Town was bursting at the seams. People waited for three hours to witness the strangest Ukrainians concert I have ever seen. Because Len not only sang, but vocalised the violin parts as well! They played the newly-released *Respublika* album along with their traditional Ukrainian repertoire and Sex Pistols classics. The songs were generally known, so the entire room supported Len with a full throat, drowning out the technical and arrangement deficiencies. Mick was charging around with the guitar as if he wanted to smash it for good. He didn't want to, because then he tried to sell it, but he achieved the effect. My friends who were seeing The Ukrainians for the first time were delighted, but I was a little less so. It reminded me too much of the concert in Piła in February 1996 when we had no accordion and had a terrible sound system.

The now found luggage was waiting at the hotel the next day, but the instruments arrived completely destroyed! At the Szanty festival, it was easier to get a violin, because every other band played one, and Len played on a borrowed one. He liked it so much that after the concert he made a deal with the owner and bought it. The seller was happy that he could sell his violin – which he had no intention of selling before – to 'Legendary Len' from the legendary Ukrainians!

The fears resulting from Peter's absence turned out to be exaggerated. After a great concert in Wrocław, this was confirmed by a concert at Warsaw's CDQ Club and a tour in 2004. In this line-up without Peter, but with Len, Paul, Woody, Mick, Steff and Jim, as well as Rat, The Ukrainians seemed more free and simply better. The sound was sharper, more electric, and the mandolin provided sufficient acoustic balance. You could feel the cohesion, the self-confidence and good atmosphere in the team. When Peter started appearing at concerts again, he had a completely different, better co-ordinated and more confident line-up.

(clockwise from top left) May 2001 gig ticket, Lublin, Poland (Wojtek Pe); Klub Graffiti poster, Lublin, Poland; waving the flag, February 2003; Polish gig ticket, February 2003; Steff & Len in Poland, 2003; Len & Mick on stage in Krakow, Poland

20 Landmark Peel Sessions

1. Pink Floyd
Recorded: September 30, 1967
The Floyd's first sets the agenda for future Peel sessions. Their second – aired on December 19 – was somewhat marred by Syd Barrett running out half way through.
Highlight: Apples & Oranges

2. Soft Machine
Recorded: December 5, 1967
Glorious testament to the sexy art weirdness of the Kevin Ayers line-up, and the beginning of Peel's 40-year bond with Robert Wyatt. Sadly unavailable on CD, but that's legendary for you.
Highlight: Clarence In Wonderland

3. Captain Beefheart & His Magic Band
Broadcast: January 24, 1968
Warped bluesfest subsequently prized by Beefheart bootleg boffins. Hear tracks at http://www.beefheart.com/filtered/peel.htm but don't say we sent you.
Highlight: Electricity

4. Son House
Broadcast: January 11, 1970
Blues legend beloved of Jack White, recorded at the Playhouse Theatre in London's West End.
Highlight: Death Letter

5. Roxy Music
Recorded: January 4, 1972
Roxy had no deal and Bryan Ferry gave their demo to Peel producer John Walters by hand. It was their big break, but guitarist Davy O'List was soon to get the elbow.
Highlight: Re-Make/Re-Model

6. Vivian Stanshall
Broadcast: December 22, 23, 24, 26, 1975
Stanshall reads the incredible Christmas At Rawlinson End (parts 1-4), accompanied by dulcimer. Top line: "The gathering outside the Fool & Bladder was swelled by elephantiasis and gossip".
Highlight: The Party's Over

7. Buzzcocks
Recorded: September 7, 1977
Mind-blowing version of Fast Cars enhanced by to expertise of original bassist Garth Smith. Punk's viral spread to "the provinces" was down to two things: the Pistols' Anarchy tour and John Peel.
Highlight: What Do I Get?

8. Joy Division
Recorded: January 31, 1979
Until its vinyl release in 1986, this remained most requested ever Peel session. And no wonder. She's Lost Control chills, Transmission thrills. The beginning of a beautiful friendship.
Highlight: She's Lost Control

9. Misty In Roots
Broadcast: December 6, 1979
Misty's second session confirmed Peel's support of British reggae, becoming a late night staple in the mid-'80s. Dig General Sparehead's toasting on Judgement Coming On The Land.
Highlight: Sodom and Gomorrah

10. The Fall
Broadcast: March 31, 1981
The fourth session by Peel's favourite band is the fans' pick, as Lie Dream Of A Casino Soul debuts and Mark E Smith declares, "Arthur Askey's been shot."
Highlight: Lie Dream Of A Casino Soul

11. Billy Bragg
Broadcast: August 3, 1983
Nasal tones and clumpy guitaring of the Barking bard reaffirmed Peel's show as a focus of political and musical dissent.
Highlight: Fear Is A Man's Best Friend

12. The Jesus And Mary Chain
Broadcast: October 1, 1984
Spectorish distorto-pop charmed ears accustomed to harsher Peel fare (Throbbing Gristle etc).
Highlight: You Trip Me Up

13. Half Man Half Biscuit
Broadcast: November 11, 1985
The world is rocked by DIY Scouse surrealism with a keyboard going "boink". Altogether now: "Every Saturday I get the Chigley Skins /And they always smash my windows 'cos the home side always wins."
Highlight: The Trumpton Riots

14. The Orb
Broadcast: December 19, 1989
Peel embraced electro, hip-hop, acid house and techno, maintaining his cutting edge when guitar rock waxed dull. Here Alex Paterson's mob get ambient on Minnie Riperton's ass.
Highlight: A Huge Ever-Growing Pulsating Brain That Rules From The Centre Of The Ultraworld (Loving You)

15. Nirvana
Broadcast: November 3, 1990
Like Sonic Youth before them, Nirvana had gut respect Peel. Their second session was a set of covers that embraced The Vaselines and Devo. The Peel sess at its unique best.
Highlight: Molly's Lips

16. Ukrainians
Broadcast: November 16, 1991
Peel the world music cheerleader helped inspire this side project by über-indie act The Wedding Present. Ukrainian folk tunes in a punked-up style.
Highlight: Teper Hovorymo

17. Ivor Cutler
Broadcast: 29 April, 1995
Retiring Scots poet (and trademark Peel enthusiasm) enjoys his twenty-first session. "Every evening about six he now, on the bridge and broke the arm of a passer-by."
Highlight: A Stuggy Pren

18. Blur
Broadcast: 5 May, 1997
Scintillating live set from Peel Acres with the Colchester foursome showcasing their Britpop-snubbing Blur album.
Highlight: Popscene

19. The White Stripes
Broadcast: 25 July, 2001
Gobsmacked to be gracing the same stage as Son House (see 4), Jack White delivers Death Letter and John The Revelator amid an incredible Gatling-Gun strafing of a session.
Highlight: Baby Blue (a Gene Vincent cover)

20. Polysics
Broadcast: October 12, 2004
The last studio session John Peel played on air, Japanese noise beserkers Polysics delighted young Mr Peel with Kaja Kaja Goo, their unique tribute to Limahl, Nick Beggs and co, plus New Wave Jacket as their delightful Knack cover...
Highlight: My Sharona

(clockwise from top left) Steff, Mick, Len & Paul, Wrocław, Poland, March 2003; Len, Allan Martin, Steff, Paul & Mick outside Wrocław station, Poland, March 2003; Steff on stage in Monaco, July 2004 (Steff Tymruk); The Ukrainians get a shout out in *Mojo* magazine for a landmark John Peel session, April 2004; Hebden Bridge, autumn 2004 (Steff Tymruk); outtake from photo shoot for Istoriya album cover (Tony Woolgar)

STEFF TYMRUK

The CDQ Club in Warsaw was a sweaty little club which held about 200 people. We've played there three times. The first time it seemed as though a bunch of art students decided to stick a load of condoms to the ceiling as an art installation. They were hanging there when we played the gig. During the performance, things got really steamy and we were fighting for air. I remember going round and kicking a fire exit door open because we were about to faint. And the condensation in the club began dripping down from the ceiling and off the condoms onto the audience.

MARSHALL'S BAR
16 APRIL 2004, HEBDEN BRIDGE, UK

JIM HOWE, UKRAINIANS BASS PLAYER

I was introduced to The Ukrainians by the late, great Michael L B West. At the time, I was in a band with Mick and Paul called The Babelonians, a band where every song was sung in a different language. Mick used to trawl through phrase books for "inspiration" to create the lyrics. The fateful day was in early 2004. Mick told me that Alan Martin had left The Ukrainians and they needed a new bass player for a couple of gigs in ten days' time. I said that I wasn't sure that I could learn 26 songs in ten days but Mick insisted that I could and said, 'You'll be fine. If in doubt, just play D.' There was a bit more to it than that!

So Mick supplied me with cassettes of live gig recordings which I played along to on my bass. After about eight days, I met Woody when I had my first rehearsal, with him on drums, Paul on mandolin and Mick on guitar and vocal approximations. The rehearsal went fairly well and, under the circumstances, I was as ready as I could be for my first Ukrainians' gig.

My first gig was a local one in Hebden Bridge, a warm-up in preparation for a bigger concert at the Ukrainian Club in Holland Park. I was quite nervous beforehand and when I looked at the set list, I didn't recognise most of the songs, like it was written in a foreign language or something. Oh, that's right – *it was*! All the song titles were written in Ukrainian and since I couldn't speak a word of it back then, I wasn't sure about which song was which. Luckily, as the band played the songs came back to me and I managed to play along without too many deviations. The audience loved it and I had some good feedback after the gig. I was buzzing. I believe several beers were consumed. I don't remember much after that.

LONDON UKRAINIAN CLUB
17 APRIL 2004, LONDON, UK

LAPIS COHEN

My first time at the London Ukrainian Club, on Holland Park Avenue, eastaways from Shepherds Bush. The date being April 17, in the year 2004. Wandering around, betwixt sets, trying to find the facilities – I spot a likely door, turn the handle and… Well, that is getting a wee bit ahead of ourselves.

My connection to the music of The Ukrainians goes back to the summer of 1990, when I was in Belgrade, in what is now Serbia. Investigating the local music (KUD Idijoti, Vis Idoli, Sarlo Akrabata), I heard a Wedding Present song being played on the famous local radio station B92 ('Nobody's Twisting Your Arm'). Returning home, I was not immediately able to source that single, and instead plumped for a ten-inch vinyl record whose cover was… not in English at all – the famous Peel Sessions! It was love at first listen.

Flash forward 14 years and I had managed to get myself from Madrid, where I was living at the time, over to London to catch The Ukrainians live for the first time. I still have the email from Peter Solowka in answer to my tour query: 'The London show is the only one. Tickets are £9 advance, £11 door. I suggest you get advance as the venue only holds 200.' Sound advice.

I remember the friendly fellow at the ticket table expressing surprise at the distance I had travelled for the gig. I also recall the kind gentleman from Poland (Lublin, perchance?) with whom I traded concert stories as we stood just along at the right corner of the stage. And then The Ukrainians came on stage and, alas, much becomes a blur, as I and everyone around me started dancing and singing along to each song (any jet lag was fully erased by the aural adrenalin provided by the band).

In between sets, I set off in search of the Gents and happened upon a door which seemed like a reasonable possibility, only to open it and come face-to-face with the band themselves! True gents (!), they helpfully pointed me in the proper direction, and kindly complimented me on my old, gig-battered, Ramones t-shirt. Quickly thanking them, both for the directions and, more importantly, for the unforgettable live show (remarking as I exited how the trip had been worth each and every mile), I left them to the peace of the intermission…

MIKE ROBINSON

What got me interested in The Ukrainians? A girlfriend with the surname Ugnivenko. I found out this was a Ukrainian name from this country called Ukraine. Also, a happy discovery of a CD in HMV on Oxford Street by a band called The Ukrainians. Fantastic music. I was intrigued. Where is this Ukraine? What is this music. I bought Anna Reid's book, *Borderland*, and decided to visit Ukraine for myself. This was in 2004, when a visa was still required and Ryanair had not discovered Kyiv. I travelled down to Odesa and across to Crimea. I tracked down more music by The Ukrainians plus The Wedding Present. Wonderful music that made you want to dance.

The highlight was a visit to the Ukrainian Club, Holland Park. My wife and I turned up around 7pm, thinking it would start soon but there was a bit of a wait and nothing happened until after 9pm, but there was lovely home-made food available on site which kept us going until the music started. We danced and danced until it was time to leave, when we drove home exhausted but happy after a great evening. One day we will have to do it again.

 GRIMALDI FORUM
29 MAY 2004, MONTE CARLO, MONACO

ALARIC NEVILLE

All good things come to an end and there is a time to everything under heaven. I had always done other work while doing sound for The Ukrainians and in early 1994 I took up the sound engineer position with The Oysterband at short notice after their man had family issues that kept him off the road. Although he returned for a while, he soon reduced the number of dates he did before leaving completely. For a while, I juggled both bands' live gigs but eventually there were too many clashes and by late 1995 a choice had to be made. These choices aren't always just about money and conditions, there is a creative angle to consider. The Oysters offered me a chance to contribute more to their music than I could with The Ukies, producing, playing and songwriting with them, so I sadly stepped down as The Ukrainians' main sound engineer. However, I remained and remain on call if needed and have stepped in a few times to help out live.

I even ended up producing the track 'Telstar' for them which oddly saw my only appearance on a Ukie track, playing that most Ukrainian instrument, the bandura.

One of the odd Ukie dates I did was in Monaco in 2004, the only time I have ever been to the playboys' principality. I have an old university friend who is an accountant there. After the gig, we had a hotel room and an early flight back to Blighty the next day but I decided to grab the rare opportunity to burn the candle at both ends while the band got their beauty sleep. I headed out into the Monte Carlo night with my old mate, and after one of those magical debauched nights of exotic excess and wild adventure, I crawled back to the hotel in time to get the morning airport bus with the band, regaling them with tales of the time they had missed before crashing out on the plane: You only live once!

There the matter would have ended but for the invention of the internet and the modern requirement for everyone everywhere to post an endless stream of selfies and status updates. In his role as chief band publicist, Len took it upon himself to let all the loyal Ukie fans know about the latest gig in Monaco. For reasons known only to him, he tacked on a spiced-up report saying, 'Our sound engineer Mr Al went out partying and ended up on Keith Richards' yacht doing lines of coke on the naked breast of a supermodel.'

The first I knew of this was when my silver surfer mother phoned me up to inform me that she had a few of her refined lady friends round and had decided to show them the band her dear son was out in Monaco with. It took some time to diffuse the situation and calm everyone in the family down, Mother included. I can only repeat here again that Len's story is categorically not correct. It definitely wasn't Keith Richards' yacht…

ISTORIYA - THE BEST OF THE UKRAINIANS 1991-2002
RELEASED 2 AUGUST 2004

LEN
This was really a stopgap until we recorded some new material. We wanted to include something new so Alaric and Roman finished off a version of the Tornados' 1960s classic 'Telstar' that we'd started and abandoned years earlier. It came out well though, and Gideon Coe played it on BBC 6 Music. Also on the disk, if you put it into your computer, are our song lyrics in Ukrainian with English translations, which is something fans often ask for.

PETER
'Telstar' was the last recording to feature Roman. Although he wasn't part of the band then, he volunteered to work with Alaric to upgrade an old demo version of the song.

ROB BOWKER
Music-wise my absolute favourite Ukrainians track is one of their first, 'Oi Divchino' ('Oh Girl') from *Drink To My Horse*, though 'Telstar' from *Istoriya* (ZRKCD4) is snapping at its heels.

RAT
We had a succession of drivers who would hire a van and drive us around Poland on each tour. Mirek was our favourite and probably the safest driver on the pitted Polish roads of the 1990s and early 2000s. He came from a village near Białystok and was in a band called

Czeremszyna with his wife Barbara – who played the biggest balalaika I have ever seen.

Mirek made his own vodka from the long forest grasses surrounding his village. He showed us a sample, which he kept in an aftershave bottle, while we were playing a gig in Białystok. Later in the tour, we were staying in the chalets of a summer holiday camp which had closed for the winter but which rented out the rooms to travellers such as us. Mirek joyfully produced a gallon demijohn of his dark green home brew vodka, wished us well and went off to bed.

 STANSTED AIRPORT
11 OCTOBER 2004, STANSTED, UK

LEN
In October 2004 we undertook a six-date tour of Poland.

MICK WEST
A day of travel – lots. Laden with assorted instrumental and personal clobber, the Hebden Bridge cell of the band (minus Paul, who had to go into work the next morning) hopped onto an early train to Bradford Interchange. After a bewildering succession of National Express coaches we disembarked at Stansted Airport. We met up with Len, Steff and Paul, who had somehow managed to make the drive south without breaking down, being struck by lightning or any other disaster.

We checked in, boarded the plane and started harassing the air hostesses (for coffee, that is). What could possibly go wrong? And nothing did. All our equipment and luggage landed present, correct and intact at Warsaw Airport. After meeting up with our Polish agent Wlodek (who seemed uncharacteristically relaxed), his pal Mirek (the lucky soul charged with the task of driving us all over Poland for the next few days) and Natalka, we repaired to a hotel (of sorts) for food, Żubrówka and sleep.

WOODY
Mirek's minibus had already been pretty much filled with our gear at the airport when we were told that they were going to pick up the backline the next day and that we – and it – were going to be packed into the same little bus. We went off to our hotel thinking 'a drum kit and amps fitting in that little bus? He'll never do it.' Back at the motel, such clouds of concern drifted away after our first bottle of Żubrówka.

UCHO

12 OCTOBER 2004, GDYNIA, POLAND

WOODY
Mirek had managed the impossible and fitted three amps, a drum kit, merchandise, personal bags and seven hulking musicians (apart from the very petite drummer) into his magical bus…

JIM HOWE
I remember Mick telling me dark stories concerning Polish roads and drivers. At one point on our first drive, we were behind a van and Mick said, 'Right Jim, you're about to see some Polish overtaking.' Mirek hung back and waited until it was safe to overtake. Nice driving.

STEFF
The drive to Gdynia was four to five hours, and we were all happy as we'd rested and slept properly. We arrived at the venue and there immediately followed a balloon blowing contest with Jim and Paul. Luckily the putting up of Woody's new backdrop was dealt with by the venue; it was nice to get help. After that: coffee, sandwiches, soundcheck, beer…

MICK WEST
The last Ukrainians backdrop weighed more than Pavarotti on Jupiter and had been stolen from a Munich venue in 1996 by a lunatic, a weightlifter – or both. Our new, prized, Woody-made possession was made of gossamer-light rubber… er, silk… and should in theory be much easier to hang. Theory can piss off. We struggled for hours to make it look vaguely symmetrical before conceding defeat and getting on with the soundcheck.

PAUL WEATHERHEAD
The club was packed with our regular fans and a new generation who really enjoyed themselves. This made a great start to the tour. I was a bit nervous because the first song was 'Spivaye Solovey' (The Smiths' 'What Difference Does It Make?') and I had only played it once live before, in the Hebden Bridge warm up gig the previous Sunday, and the song starts with the mandolin. It was the first time we released balloons in the concert and the crowd went wild. The balloons were batted between the audience and the stage, causing

a few spilt beers and the odd bum note, but it went down well. It was one of the most enjoyable Ukrainians gigs I've played.

JIM HOWE

This was a surreal event. A Ukrainian school in Biały Bór, 185 kilometers from Gdynia, had bussed in some coach-loads of Ukrainian teenagers who filled the front rows. There was lots of screaming, leaping about and chants of 'slava'. It felt a bit like being in a boy band. There was a stage invasion towards the end with teachers and pupils dancing around us as we played. After the gig, we got mobbed for autographs and one kid asked me if I was the lead singer from REM. I didn't know whether to be flattered or offended. Not that I have anything against Michael Stipe or REM. When I think about this today, though, I feel sad because I wonder how many of those kids are OK. I guess they will be around 36 years old now, maybe with kids of their own and impacted by the war to a greater or lesser extent.

MICK WEST

A good number of these largely female sixth-form students had positioned themselves at the front of the stage and were energetically formation-dancing in front of an effervescent sea of Punks and even some outwardly normal looking human beings (yep, these turn up occasionally). The gig was tight (in the 'together' sense, rather than referring to being inebriated or careful with money, allegations occasionally levelled at certain members in the past).

BLUE NOTE
13 OCTOBER 2004, POZNAŃ, POLAND

MICK

It was a briefish drive to Poznań. Mirek appeared reassuringly unwilling (or unable) to risk life and limb in pursuit of doubling the national speed limit. This could be because nine people, a drum kit, three amplifiers and sundry instrumentation were crammed Tardis-like into a glorified people carrier, which was consequently unable to exceed 55mph.

The venue was a 'jazz club' with black-painted walls. The electrics were shot to bits. The socket I plugged my amp into was hanging three inches out of the wall and did not appear to have an earth wire, perhaps explaining why it occasionally emitted worrisome 50Hz buzzes at sporadic intervals throughout the soundcheck, although serendipity made sure that the gig passed off OK without mains-farts or electrocution. The first two numbers were filmed for a local TV station. A gentleman from the Obolon beer company (clear, crisp and refreshing) came along with gratis t-shirts and a large crate of freebie beer, which we of course put aside until after the show in order not to be inebriated beforehand.

After the show was over and we had visited the nightshop for midnight munchies (pickled herrings for me), Mirek proved himself to be a man of infinite taste and discernment by unveiling a bottle of nettle samhonka (horilka, hooch) the size of a demijohn, from which us filthy brutes drank heartily.

PAUL WEATHERHEAD

After many toasts, I staggered off to bed to be informed after what seemed like ten minutes that it was eleven o'clock the next morning and breakfast was finishing. Poor Rat, our sound engineer, had been locked out of his room and walked up and down outside until 6am, when he helped the cleaners clean some of the rooms!

CENTRUM KULTURY – MUSA
14 OCTOBER 2004, LUBIN, POLAND

LEN

We woke up to find we'd stayed in a place that was part holiday camp and part barracks for sporty types. I went for a walk up to the main road to find a post office to buy stamps, but the queue was too long so I walked back. I felt vague, like I'd lost billions of brain cells. It was just past 9am and the group was collecting by the van.

WOODY

I felt extremely peculiar that morning... There was definitely something psychedelic in Mirek's beverage of the night before.

PAUL WEATHERHEAD

When we arrived at the venue, we were shocked to see it was a large restaurant with candlelit tables, not the sweaty clubs and halls we were accustomed to. The gig seemed very formal, with people sitting and watching us. Soon a few people started dancing, then a few more and by the second set it was much more enjoyable. The chef at the restaurant cooked us a great meal too.

LEN
After a slightly reserved and nervous first set I managed to swallow the contents of a 250ml sweet herb vodka. For some reason the second set seemed much livelier…

JIM HOWE
We may have gained our youngest fan at this gig, as a pregnant lady was telling us that her baby was dancing!

WYTWORNIA FILMOW
15 OCTOBER 2004, WROCŁAW, POLAND

MICK WEST
The PA system didn't arrive until 6.30pm, so we decided to go for a walk and some edibles. The Ukrainians have always been a rather odd-looking and somewhat disparate (if not dissolute) bunch of individuals, given their wildly differing dress sense and diverse ages, heights, etc. We must have looked strange in Wrocław, since at one point we were walking down the street as a pack and I realised that *everybody* in the tram opposite was staring at us!

    The evening was a great success, though I was a bit embarrassed at forgetting my words during 'Europa' and having them sung up at me word-perfect by a guy in the audience. When the food arrived afterwards, I realised I'd reached pizza saturation point. In our absence, it had obviously become the Polish national dish, since we seem to receive it almost every day. Come back pierogies, all is forgiven.

GWINT
16 OCTOBER 2004, BIAŁYSTOK, POLAND

MICK WEST
It was a looooooong drive, 330 miles overnight to Białystok. I managed to spend most of it in a Żubrówka-fuelled reverie. This was one of the few times I have seen Paul appear visibly drunk.

PAUL WEATHERHEAD
I can't usually sleep in buses so I bought a beer and small Żubrówka, hoping they would help. The next thing I remember is waking up in the van at around 9am. I was later told

that I'd consumed much more vodka and fallen out of the van when we had a rest stop. I don't know why they make up these lies about me!

LEN

Nothing aids bonding more than being in each other's company for 24 hours a day, being forced into confined spaces for hours on end and sharing each other's drunken thoughts, cold pizza and unpleasant smells.

STEFF

We eventually arrived at a motel in Białystok at about midday.

RAT

Every one of the band had 'stomach problems', and at one point all of us were sat in a row of cubicles passing the only roll of toilet paper to and fro under the partition, accompanied by Len's wry observation of how glamorous touring is.

LEN

I remember trying to wade through the crowd to the backstage area while NRM, a popular band from Belarus, was playing. I had to pass in front of the massively loud PA speakers and my ears were already ringing. I felt as nervous as hell and hadn't yet had a single drop to drink. Luckily, I had two small 250ml bottles of sweet herb vodka stashed in my bag backstage… one to drink before the first set and one before the second. That was my drinking blueprint for the tour and, more often than not, provided the ideal antidote to nerves.

JIM HOWE

This was a difficult one. A few elements conspired against us. The onstage monitors went down, I went deaf and we were all tired. But the crowd rallied us on and were supportive.

LEN

It got to the point where I couldn't hear my own voice or any drums or instruments, just a loud mush, so I chewed up some paper from a set list and pushed it into my left ear. That way at least I'd be able to hear a bit of my own voice reverberating in my own head. It's one of the rock 'n' roll tricks of the trade.

JIM HOWE
Mick crashed backwards into Steff and afterwards everyone except Paul and myself had a rock and roll shouting match in the dressing room. But everyone became friends again by the end of the night!

WOODY
After the gig, we were discussing the problems of too much booze before playing when the promoter turned up with four bottles of luxury Polish vodka. We were doomed… The whole gig wasn't bad, only the last third…

PAUL WEATHERHEAD
By the time we left, everyone was feeling happy and looking forward to Warsaw. We drank some vodka and Rat and Wlodek gave a moving rendition in the hotel room of Ewan MacColl's 'Dirty Old Town', as covered by The Pogues. The Ukrainians are a very noisy band, especially when they are asleep. Almost all of us snore, grind teeth or utter surrealistic but intriguing nonsense. It becomes part of everyday life with constant hours in the van or in shared hotel rooms.

 CDQ
17 OCTOBER 2004, WARSAW, POLAND

LEN
I woke up and noticed I was completely deaf in my left ear. I managed to pull out some chewed set list from the previous night, but it made no perceptible difference.

JIM HOWE
I felt like everyone was putting every last ounce of energy into this performance. The stage was boiling hot and sweat was dripping from my nose. The club seemed packed out and I got worried at a couple of points when members of the audience looked like they were getting crushed against the stage. I remember seeing a girl getting knocked off balance and

grabbing hold of a monitor speaker. I think she was still smiling though, and regained some space. Overall it was a hot, fun and fulfilling concert.

MICK WEST
I managed to break two strings on my guitar, as I did the last time we played there, and the audience's rabid baying for 'Cherez Richku, Cherez Hai' threatened to drown out the introductions to some of the quieter songs, but we were past caring by now, in a positive way. We played our arses off, no doubt much refreshed by a good night's sleep in a hotel.

PAUL WEATHERHEAD
On the way to the airport, Mirek and Barbara sang beautiful folk songs while Rat improvised his own Polish folk songs from the back. When we said goodbye, we gave Mirek some vodka as a gift and he gave us a present for the band and told us not to open it until we were in England.

MICK
Our equipment and baggage landed intact and complete, so after clearing customs we went for a medicinal pint in the airport's O'Neill's. Celebrity ex-wife Meg Matthews could be seen lurking in a corner and eyeing us with suspicion.

PAUL WEATHERHEAD
Me, Mick, Woody, Jim and Rat now had a seven-hour coach ride to Bradford. While we were waiting, we suddenly remembered Mirek's present. Now we were in England and could open it. We found it and it looked like a box of eight deodorant sprays. What was he telling us? When we opened the box, we discovered it was actually full of small bottles of his homemade vodka...

LEN
Three days after returning to England, I was still completely deaf in my left ear so I went to see the doctor, who sent me immediately to the Royal Berkshire Hospital. I had a minor operation to remove, er... the rest of the Białystok set list. The doctor said he reckoned I'd stuffed a complete Sunday newspaper in there, complete with colour supplements. Anyway, the good news is I got my hearing back.

THE UKRAINIANS
★★★★

A History Of Rock Music In Ukrainian
(ZIRKA) www.the-ukrainians.com

This is exactly what its title suggests, sixteen major rock songs delivered in Ukrainian. And while it's easy to mistake it for an elaborate joke or a mere gimmick, this album's a long way from either. For a start, it's immaculately produced with each song painstakingly reinterpreted, verbally and musically. The result is a beautifully crafted and remarkable oddity.

The Ukrainians were formed in 1990 by Peter Solowka (The Wedding Present) and Len Liggins (The Sinister Cleaners) to play Ukrainian music with a post-punk flavour. In many ways, then, this album is a summary of all they represent.

So buy it, sit back, and enjoy culturally crossed-over reworkings of 'Back In The USSR' (The Beatles), 'Ace Of Spades' (Mötörhead), 'Smells Like Teen Spirit' (Nirvana), 'The One I Love' (R.E.M.), 'Good Vibrations' (Beach Boys), 'Immigrant Song' (Led Zep), 'Children Of The Revolution' (T. Rex), 'Holidays In The Sun' (Sex Pistols), 'Hound Dog' (Big Mama Thornton), 'I Predict A Riot' (Kaiser Chiefs), 'California Dreaming' (The Mamas And The Papas), 'She's Lost Control' (Joy Division), 'Psycho Killer' (Talking Heads), 'The Queen Is Dead' (Smiths), 'The Model' (Kraftwerk), 'American Idiot' (Green Day) and 'Venus In Furs' (Velvet Underground).

A genuine classic wrought from sixteen classics.

Nick Toczek

NEW CDS

THE UKRAINIANS CELEBRATE 30TH ANNIVERSARY WITH 'SUMMER IN LVIV'

MAY 16, 2019   WORLD MUSIC CENTRAL NEWS DEPARTMENT   LEAVE A COMMENT

The Ukrainians

The Ukrainians' new album "Summer in Lviv" is based on guitarist Peter Solowka and vocalist/fiddle player Len Liggins's experiences in western Ukraine last summer, where they discovered the rejuvenated, modern city of Lviv, whose official motto is 'Live, work and enjoy yourself'.

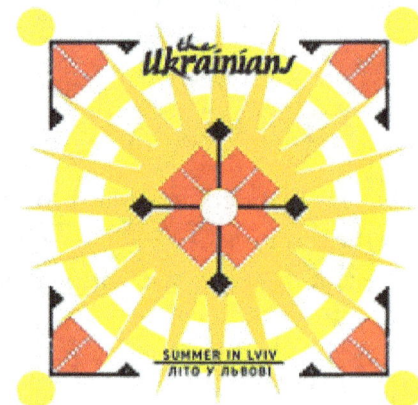

The Ukrainians – Summer in Lviv

Living in the west but with half the band having a background rooted in the cultures of Ukraine or eastern Europe, The Ukrainians have enjoyed success over the past three decades. Their music includes Ukrainian folk music and western rock music.

The Ukrainians
'Istoriya'
(Zirka Records)

The Ukrainians began as a side of 80s indie band The Wedding a joke session for John Peel, incl members of the band and Lege Len, a student of Slavonic langu who played traditional Eastern E fiddle. The response to the sessi so favourable that the band rapi became an entity in its own right bringing in new members and w their own compositions in Ukrain

'Istoriya' is a collection of the b from two albums and five EPs. N material in the mould of tradition music nestles alongside translate versions of oddities such as Joe 'Telstar' and songs by The Smith The Velvet Underground, and it's cover versions that stand out as material of this selection, especia of The Smiths. The Ukrainians' r highlight Eastern European facets phrasing of songs such as 'Batya ('Bigmouth Strikes Again'), which hitherto gone unnoticed.

Offer this weird collection of ro Eastern European folk anthems a in your heart and I guarantee tha won't regret having done so.

★★★★★

Mark Norton

My Life With T Thrill Kill Kult
Reissues
(Rykodisk/Vital)

The Chicago outfit have decided reissue their long-deleted first th albums to remind everyone who are. Their debut 'I See Good Spiri See Bad Spirits' (★★★★★) is reminiscent of Ministry's early Wa recordings (not surprising, conside was originally released on the sa label). It's a fusion of simplistic ke lines mixed in with raw film samp and demonic vocals that borrow

Assorted reviews

EGINNER'S GUIDE

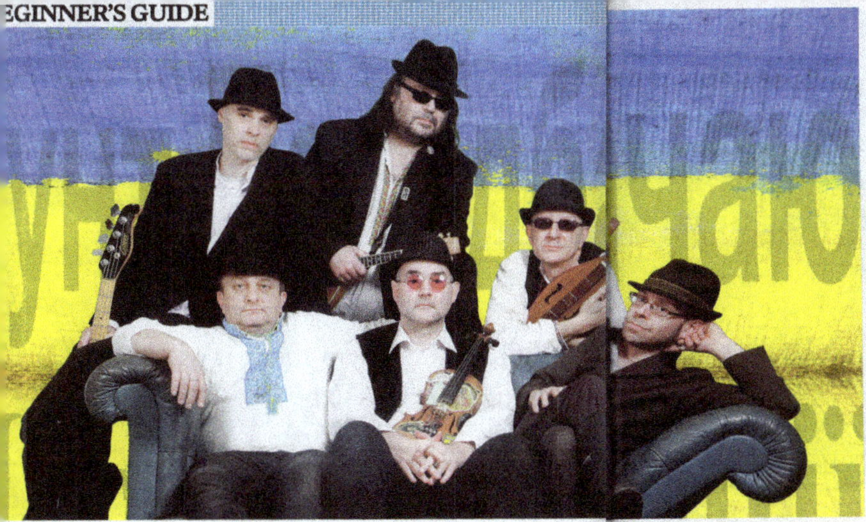

'he Ukrainians

rth Cartwright raises a glass to the British collective who have
.mpioned Ukrainian music in their unique way for the last 25 years

his year finds The Ukrainians celebrating a quarter century of music making, blending East European folk ıdie rock music. It certainly has been a :kable ride. That lesser American bands copied their sound and enjoyed much r success is, surely, annoying but the likely shrug and admit such events are ng new in showbiz. Let us then raise a o this English collective of largely unsung ers of what has been called everything Gypsy punk' to 'East Bloc rock'

Ukrainians grew out of The Wedding ıt, an indie band who, with their 1987 album *George Best*, won widespread ɔrt from the likes of *NME*, *Melody Maker* and John Peel on his Radio 1 show. Being feted on the then booming British rock circuit saw The Wedding Present sign a lucrative recording contract with RCA and gather a broad audience both in the UK and abroad. So far, so ordinary. Then, one day at a 1988 rehearsal, guitarist Peter Solowka began playing the Ukrainian folk song 'Hopak' – Solowka is of Ukrainian and Yugoslav descent and had learned Ukrainian music from his father – and his fellow Wedding Present members were intrigued. They decided to incorporate the song into the band's set and found it worked so well that, when invited to record a Peel session, they ended up recording four Ukrainian songs. Peel loved this diverse blend of East European folk and British indie rock and gave the songs plenty of airtime. He then invited them to return and record another session; again it was well received, so they decided to issue the recordings via RCA and the subsequent 1989 Wedding Present mini-album titled *Ukrainian John Peel Sessions* – title in English and Ukrainian (Українські Виступи в Івана Піла in Cyrillic lettering) – proved a surprise success, selling some 70,000 copies and reaching No 22 in the UK charts. Opening track 'Those Were the Days' is based on an old Russian folk melody – it had been a UK No 1 for Mary Hopkin in 1968 – and RCA begged the band to release it as a single but they refused, perhaps wary of being pigeonholed as Slav balladeers.

The success of the Ukrainian sessions overshadowed the group's original material albums and, in 1991, bandleader David Gedge fired Solowka, seemingly infuriated that a side project he had little control over had proved so successful. Solowka was hurt – he had been a Wedding Present member since the beginning – but countered by immediately forming The Ukrainians, turning what had been a casual dalliance into a full-time band.

He was accompanied by Roman Remeynes, Len Liggins and Stepan Pasicznyk – Liggins was a languages student who played violin while Pasicznyk was of Ukrainian-Irish heritage and played several instruments alongside being fluent enough to translate English songs into Ukrainian. They released their debut EP, *Oi Divchino* – filming the video in Kiev, so marking them as the first Western band to go there – and won Single of the Week in *NME*. Their eponymous debut followed in November 1991, coinciding with Ukraine's winning of independence from the Soviet Union.

While their debut did not enjoy the chart success of The Wedding Present's *Ukrainian Peel Sessions*, it did establish the band as witty purveyors of East European folk rock and won them an international audience.

> As communism crumbled, they helped provide the soundtrack

As communism crumbled across East Europe, The Ukrainians helped provide the soundtrack to the party. Solowka notes "the performance at London's Town and Country of 'Vesilini Podarunok'... That was such a special gig – to see Ukrainian dancers in national dress dancing to our supercharged versions of Ukrainian folk. When you come from a background where you're told 'you're from Ukraine, a wonderful country of hills and music but under a repressive regime,' when you have learned how to play music and speak the language but only a few hundred people in the UK really know what you're talking about... then to see those thousands of people accepting your heritage is a wonderful feeling." He continues, "it was really the start of quite a musical movement in Ukraine. Cassettes were passed around and duplicated. The sound was revolutionary, mixing tradition and Western in a way that had not been allowed. Many groups do that now – Ruslana won the European Song Contest doing a pop-folk mix. I like to think that she has got a 'Vesilini Podarunok' poster on her wall!"

Since then they have released several studio and live-in-concert albums as well as two acclaimed EPs – the first found them recording four Smiths songs in Ukrainian; the second doing the same for The Sex Pistols – that were received very enthusiastically across the former Soviet Bloc. How influential were The Ukrainians across this region? It's hard to judge from this distance but their ability to blend traditional folk songs and contemporary rock music, their wit and deft touch, their willingness to sing lyrics written by Morrissey and Johnny Rotten in Russian and Ukrainian, certainly inspired many Eastern Bloc youths who were tentatively embracing Western rock music. I can only speculate but I'm pretty certain that Gogol Bordello's Eugene Hütz studied The Ukrainians when he was growing up in Ukraine. These days The Ukrainians continue to record and perform, albeit after over 1,000 gigs they now operate at a much more part-time level: Solowka holds down a secondary school teaching position in Yorkshire, only strapping on his guitar when specific festival or cultural gigs are on offer. ◆

BEST ALBUMS

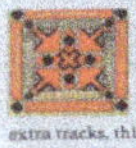

The Wedding Present
Ukrainian John Peel Sessions
(Fresh Ear Records, 2000)
Now reissued with several extra tracks, this compilation of Peel sessions and demos from the late 1980s was recorded before anyone realised that the Soviet Union would crumble and music from the Eastern Bloc would soon be embraced internationally. As far as lo-fi Eastern folk punk goes, it all starts here.

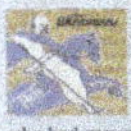

The Ukrainians
(Cooking Vinyl, 1991)
Here ten folk songs are reinterpreted by a bunch of hard-rocking Northerners who had grown up with their parents singing these songs at family gatherings.

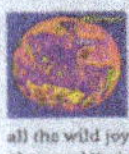

Drink to My Horse! Live
(Zirka, 2001)
Always a dynamic live band, this 20-track in-concert album from 1999 captures all the wild joy and hard drinking blend of Slavs and Yorkshiremen as they rock through their repertoire.

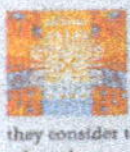

Diaspora
(Zirka, 2000)
This album finds The Ukrainians in a more mature, reflective mood as they consider the huge changes that have taken place across East Europe over the past two decades. Reviewed in #60.

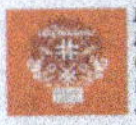

Evolutsiya! 40 Best and Rarest 1991-2016
(Zirka, 2016)
Released in August 2016 to celebrate the band's 25th anniversary, this double-CD compilation gathers both many of The Ukrainians' best-loved tracks alongside a slew of rare and odd tracks that will engage long-time fans. Reviewed in #122.

IF YOU LIKE THE UKRAINIANS, THEN TRY...

Kal

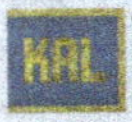

Kal
(Asphalt Tango, 2006)
The Belgrade-based Gypsy band mix traditional folk songs with rock dynamics on this, their debut album. Bandleader Dragan Ristić writes exciting songs that mesh contemporary sounds with Balkan Gypsy music. No other East European folk-rock album has yet bettered this wild, mercurial fusion. Reviewed in #37.

krainians – "Diaspora"

ı OMM-2045, 2009, CD)

ɔelieve it's been 18 years since this band's ase. While they've hardly been prolific — studio albums in that time, along with a f live releases and compilations — they've id legacy of great music to show for their ınd this new release doesn't let down their of greatness one bit. The basic modus features acoustic instruments (guitar, andolin, accordion, and so on) backed ic bass and drum kit; occasional electric ɔyboards, and brass add a little variety. The mostly original, though to naïve ears could rocked up version of Slavic folk songs. ɜ out they add an energetic arrangement of "Hungarian Dance No. 5," which of course rfectly. The lyrics are not in English, all ı, I think, and the brash male harmonies mind every clichéd Russian song ever to ı a movie, but the fact that they twist it up ınkish abandon lifts it to an entirely new de from that, it's just plain fun. Even if you lerstand a word, you find yourself wanting long or do a dance involving potentially ɹs squat-kicks. The performances are though not in a sterile or studious way. In s band belongs among the top proponents ɔck around the world today. – *Jon Davis*

krainians.com]

THE UKRAINIANS
20 Years
ZIRKA
★★★★

Anniversary Best Of from the Anglo-Ukes

Starting as an offshoot of The Wedding Present, The Ukrainians swiftly became more interesting than their progenitors. Led by guitarist Peter Solowka, the band have cut a unique path through the post-Soviet landscape, their East European folk-rock celebrating tradition while commenting archly on the present (*"the multinational corporation has come to visit"*). Their approach (often inebriated, always sincere) hasn't much altered – of the 20 tracks here, the early ones are fresher, the cuts from 2009's *Diaspora* more thoughtful. Like their droll versions of the Pistols, Smiths and Velvets they've become a surprising institution. Budmo!

Neil Spencer

BERLINER INDIE-CHARTS
BEST OF 1993
von Burghard Rausch

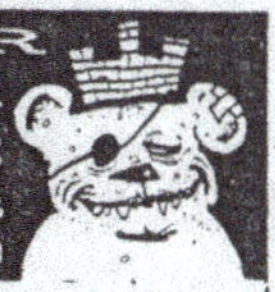

	Punkte	Interpret	Titel (Label)
1	(125)	The Ukrainians	Pisni Iz The Smiths (Cooking Vinyl)
2	(114)	Depeche Mode	Walking In My Shoes (Mute)
3	(109)	Slime & Heiter bis wolkig	10 kleine Nazi-Schweine (Weser-Label)
4	(107)	Depeche Mode	I Feel You (Mute)
5	(101)	Breeders	Cannonball (4 AD)
6	(99)	Einstürzende Neubauten	Interim (Our Choice/Mute)
	(99)	Chumbawamba & Credit To The Nation	Enough Is Enough (One Little Indian)
	(99)	Krupps	A Tribute To Metallica (Our Choice)
7	(95)	Advanced Chemistry	Welcher Pfad führt zur Geschichte (MZEE)
8	(87)	Front 242	Religion (Play It Again Sam)
9	(86)	And One	Life Isn't Easy In Germany (Machinery)
10	(84)	Frank Black	Hang On To Your Ego (4 AD)
	(84)	Depeche Mode	Condemnation (Mute)
11	(83)	Smashing Pumpkins	Cherub Rock (Hut)
12	(82)	Belly	Feed The Tree (4 AD)
13	(81)	The Jesus Lizard/Nirvana	Puss/Oh, The Guilt (Touch & Go)
14	(79)	Shamen	Phorever People (One Little Indian)
15	(78)	Nick Cave & Shane McGowan	What A Wonderful World (Mute)
	(78)	Hole	Beautiful Son (City Slang)
16	(76)	Revolting Cocks	Do Ya Think I'm Sexy (Devotion)
17	(75)	Smashing Pumpkins	Today (Hut)
18	(73)	Consolidated	You Suck/Crackhouse (Nettwerk)
19	(71)	Big Light	Let's Start Playing (SPV)
20	(70)	Suede	Animal Nitrate (Nude)
21	(69)	Levellers	Belaruse (China)
22	(67)	Islamic Force	The Whole World Is Your Home (Juicefull)
	(67)	The Fall	Kimble (Strange Fruit)
23	(66)	Advanced Chemistry	Fremd im eigenen Land (EfA)
	(66)	Das Auge Gottes	So isses Baby (D.D.R.)
24	(65)	Einstürzende Neubauten	Malediction (Our Choice/Mute)
25	(64)	Dub Syndicate	Feed The Tree (4 AD)
26	(63)	Run DMC	Down With The King (Profile)

THE UKRAINIANS
★★★★
***Evolutsiya! 40 Best And Rarest* 1991-2016**
(EASTBLOK MUSIC) www.the-ukrainians.com

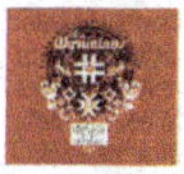

It must have been synchronicity. The day after the Euro referendum, this album dropped through the letterbox for review and it seemed that the death of British tolerance and cultural openness signalled by the referendum outcome might not have been as final as I feared. For twenty-five years The Ukrainians have melded the folk music of the Ukraine with the sounds of British alternative rock, into something rather more subtle than the 'Cossack punk' label may suggest.

These recordings are neatly sandwiched between the liberation of the Ukraine from Soviet rule in 1991 – and the creation of the band when, after playing with The Wedding Present, violinist and singer Len Liggins formed The Ukrainians with their guitarist Peter Solowka – and the Russian invasion of Ukraine and the success of the Brexit campaign to reinstate the U.K.'s borders. The Ukrainians, however, are a potent symbol that however well policed those borders, British culture will always welcome others.

The songs on *Evolutsiya* range from traditional Ukrainian folk songs sung with the passion of a people who spent many years under foreign domination, whether this be the Poles or the Russians, through their own Ukrainian language alternative rock anthems, to Ukraine language cover versions – from Sex Pistols to Kraftwerk.

Peter Tomkins

ssorted reviews & (bottom) top of the *Berliner* indie charts

FESTIWAL SPOTKANIE FOLKOWE
29 MAY 2005, CZEREMCHA, POLAND

LEN
In May 2005 we were back in Poland as we did a UK and Poland 'micro-tour'. It was 11am and already hot when we arrived in Warsaw. We got through customs to be met by Wlodek (our friend and Polish gig agency man).

PAUL WEATHERHEAD
It was a great day for the festival, hot and sunny and we sat around listening to the music for the afternoon. Mirek's band, Czeremszyna, were fantastic and it was nice to see him again.

STEFF
Mirek played a contra-bass that looks like something you'd use to stir in the hops and water in a brewery vat, a massive triangular wooden body with half a telegraph pole on one corner. I was awestruck in an absurdly hot and tired way. What a totally cool-looking and sounding bass guitar.

MICK WEST
We spent the rest of the pre-gig time drinking the odd pint and lazing about in, or rather out of, the sun.

LEN
I was walking round the site desperately trying not to drink any alcohol. I had no beer during the whole afternoon and therefore felt the full onslaught of extreme nervousness. Luckily, I had a 25cl bottle of my favourite amber-coloured sweet vodka secreted on my person, half of which was to pour down my throat ten minutes before our gig, and the other half for the interval. Tactics.

STEFF
The evening drew on and the heat died down a little. We were the final act on the last night of a week-long festival. Things were mostly going smoothly during soundcheck but my bass side was sounding distorted. We had next to no time between finishing soundcheck

and starting the gig, and by the time we realised that it was my pickup battery that needed replacing, it was too late. The cameras were rolling and the band wanted to start. I dashed to the dressing room to grab a new battery but there was no time to replace it.

MICK WEST

We played two sets, with the added bonus that the gig was being documented on 24-track audio and three-camera video for possible DVD release. What is more, the band members were surprisingly sober (with one possible exception, and that's not me, mate…).

LEN

Dunno who the culprit could have been, but suddenly I feel on the defensive…

PAUL WEATHERHEAD

Adrenalin overcame our exhaustion and despite everything the performance was great with maybe one or two slips. The audience was really into it and that helped us to relax. There was a spectacular stage dive when a bloke leapt head first off the stage and everyone in his trajectory pushed back and he belly-flopped heavily on the ground. For a moment, I thought this could be The Ukrainians' Altamont, but his mates dragged him to his feet and he seemed OK.

A mosquito the size of an albatross flew into my eye at the start of 'Teper My Hovorymo' and I had to stop and start again. In fact, I'd covered all exposed parts with mozzy repellant, but these could penetrate clothes. The next day my back was covered in welts.

RAT

I remember Peter's dancing on stage, Woody turning into a strobe light and me buying a glassware rat off some Ukrainian guys who were being really friendly and enthusiastic about the band. They insisted on giving me a sheaf of Bison Grass to spice up my vodka!

PAUL WEATHERHEAD

We stopped for a break between sets, but apparently the crew filming us thought we had finished for good and went home! The break was extended while we waited for them to come back.

LEN

Only two cameramen got their mobile phone messages and came back. The other two had disappeared off into the night with all their expensive equipment thinking the gig was over. I forgot the whole of the first verse of 'Tsilkom Vakantnyy' ('Pretty Vacant') but otherwise I think the gig was a pretty good one.

A CAFE
20 YEARS AGO, BRADFORD, UK

BA MITCHELS

I was doing research as a mature PhD student in the Peace Studies department at the University of Bradford, and living in a tiny farm cottage in Midgeley village, up on a hillside in the Calderdale Valley. One day, Paul Weatherhead was in a local cafe in Bradford, and somehow by chance we got talking about the band, mandolins and his love of Ukrainian music. Paul is a very kind man, and when I told him that I had a mandolin, was a novice player, and thought it would be great to learn some Ukrainian tunes, he said he would teach me. He trekked up the valley to Midgeley several times, bringing his mandolin and the band's recent CDs. He played some great tunes and was a good teacher. We started with 'Arkan', which I still play now, and I will never forget his generosity with his time and skill.

I am now in my seventies and still follow The Ukrainians. I have progressed to playing electric mandolin with a small band. We play tunes from around the world, including some by The Ukrainians. Thank you, Paul, for your generosity, and the inspiration and encouragement all those years ago!

ENDORSE-IT-IN-DORSET FESTIVAL
13 AUGUST 2005, SIXPENNY HANDLEY, UK

LAMMA MAUND

We first discovered The Ukrainians at *Glastonbury Festival* back in 1992 when they headlined in the acoustic tent on the Sunday night – and what a night it was! We had been burning the candle a lot over this weekend and we were camping behind the acoustic tent, so we were on our way back to camp and caught The Ukrainians by mistake. But, after a couple of tracks we were all hooked, and the gig ended up with all of us crowd surfing and enhancing the mosh pit. Well, I say 'enhancing'…! The show was so good, I went straight out and bought their back catalogue.

THE UKRAINIANS

Fast forward to 2005 and I am now part of a team that organises the *Endorset Festival* which takes place in the rolling hills of Dorset. The first three big acts that we booked as our headliners were Desmond Dekker, Zion Train and of course The Ukrainians. So, Desmond Dekker: this was also a fantastic show by him and his Aces. But the run up to this performance was, well shall we just say, challenging…? The man himself wasn't that bad. In fact, he was a very nice chap and was up for photos and autographs. It was his entourage that was giving us the run around! 'Can you get us this? Can you get us that? Desmond wants his steak rare, and he wants it now!' That sort of thing. But the thing that caused us all the biggest amount of stress was the bottle of brandy on his rider. He wanted a bottle of St Remy Napoleon and of course we had the wrong brand! I don't know what it was, just some cheaper alternative, but it was definitely the wrong type. Anyhow we soon heard this: 'Desmond is refusing to go onstage until he gets his St Remy Napoleon.'

So, Lisa from our team raced up to Tesco (which was about ten miles away) and found the correct bottle of brandy. Out of breath and feeling the pinch of the time restraint against her and massively relieved at her precious find, she approached the checkout with said bottle in hand. Fuck! She'd forgotten her purse and went into meltdown. Luckily, behind her in the queue was a guy from the festival who had nipped out for supplies and he purchased the item for her. She raced back to site; the show went ahead, and it was amazing.

Desmond and his Aces left promptly after their set and guess what they left behind? Yep! You've got it… the unopened bottle of St Remy Napoleon brandy. So The Ukrainians along with the Endorset team sat backstage in the ol' scout hut and drank it all with a large amount of pleasure and hilarity. One of the best and most memorable nights I have ever had. The Ukrainians are a top bunch indeed. And the best bit is Len still has the bottle.

Len, Peter, Steff, Woody, Paul, and Jim have been good friends ever since and The Ukrainians have become stalwarts of the *Endorset Festival* and our band Pronghorn has appeared on their latest *Together For Ukraine* album to raise money for the Disasters Emergency Committee (DEC) Ukraine Humanitarian Appeal.

REBECCA WALKLEY

Dekker behaved like a prima donna and insisted that he have a T-bone steak and a very particular bottle of Courvoisier brandy before he went on stage. The organisers were forced to ring around local restaurants in search of a perfectly cooked T-bone steak. They apparently brought back the 'wrong type' of steak, and the 'wrong type' of brandy. Dekker refused to play unless the correct brandy was found, so the 'wrong one' was dropped off at The Ukrainians' dressing room where it was gratefully received. Eventually Dekker grudgingly played his set. The next morning, allegedly, one of the festival staff hid a dead fish under the seat in Dekker's van before he left the site.

TRADES CLUB
26 JUNE 2006, HEBDEN BRIDGE, UK

DAVE BOARDMAN, FORMER BOOKINGS MANAGER, HEBDEN BRIDGE TRADES CLUB

As a manager of a small venue, you always love the bands that are guaranteed to fill your place. They love the venue, the audience loves them – and keep coming back. While I always really liked experiments in music, I loved it even more when bands you booked just clicked with your core audience. There were a few, and quite varied: Thomas Mapfumo, The Lion of Zimbabwe; The Baghdaddies from Newcastle; The Selecter; and The Ukrainians… Whenever they came, it sold out and the audiences had a great time, knowing some of the cover versions in English but attempting to sing along to the other songs in bits of Ukrainian.

In June 2006, the Trades Club managed to get a lottery grant to provide entertainment and information from the countries involved in the FIFA World Cup. The concert room was decorated in flags and football shirts, and there were promotional posters and information packs from various consulates and embassies. The games were shown on the big screen with entertainment before and after – and occasionally at half time. We had Caribbean drummers in the local High School to train kids in the kind of drumming that may go on at cricket and football matches. We filled the room with local school students performing Caribbean drumming all the way through Trinidad & Tobago vs England – England only managed a win through late goals by Crouch and Gerrard. I managed to find an Iranian folk singer, Javaad Alipoor, in Bradford and he was more entertaining than Iran vs Portugal. There were some great games in that tournament, but Switzerland vs Ukraine was not one of them.

Mick West was a local musician who was much more than a musician – he played anything and everything. He once did a show at *Hebden Bridge Arts Festival* in which he invited people to bring anything from their homes and he'd get a tune out of it. Bike pumps, kettles, plates, cutlery all arrived and he played a tune on every one, hitting things together, blowing into them, he was a genius.

Mick said he'd provide some 'Ukrainian music' after the Switzerland vs Ukraine match. It was not to be promoted as The Ukrainians as it was not an official gig, he didn't have the authority to use the name and they 'probably won't all be there.' Small venues often go along with such requests because we didn't want anyone getting any bother from managers or booking agents. When we had percentage deals, we always left it up to the musicians who turned up to inform their management how much they'd been paid. We were the musicians' friends.

Although Ukraine had a half decent team at the time, the match was among the most boring I've ever witnessed and I'm a massive football fan. People only stayed because word had gone around that Mick West of The Ukrainians was providing music. Mick was a local hero and was another who could always fill the Trades Club with any show he brought. The tedium of the game made the excitement of the music all the more playful and this band of Ukrainians got possibly the best reception of all the official gigs The Ukrainians played. There was a full range of instruments, including the famed theremin, but I promised Mick I would not name the band members who turned up. He has now sadly passed away and everyone knew it was him who organised it. But I promised Mick that the rest of the band would be known only by that old football name for when a non-registered player made an appearance… A N Other. A great night!

 A WEDDING
SUMMARY 2006, UK

MAREK WROBLEWSKI

My wife Kathryn and I are long time fans. My gateway drug to the band (as I imagine it was for many others) was the Wedding Present John Peel sessions, and in particular 'Katrusya', which I still find to be one of the most beautiful tracks I've ever heard. Still so ethereal and when the drums come in… wow! The first gig we saw was at Nottingham Ukrainian Club and we've seen them many times since, especially if they're playing near where we live in North Derbyshire.

I eventually got CD after CD, my favourite being the utterly brilliant *Vorony*. We got married in 2006 and the music for our registry office wedding music playing during the nuptials was… 'Vorony'. I thought it would be just right for the occasion, atmospheric in just the right wedding-y way and superior, superb music as well.

I'm Derby born with Polish/Irish parents (what a combination!) and folk at the wedding thought the music must be Polish. 'No,' I said, 'its style and lyrics are Ukrainian yet it's all written and performed by blokes from Leeds! Imagine that. And it's marvellous, isn't it?' 'But,' they opined, 'the singer doesn't sound like he comes from Leeds!'

 SPALDING FLOWER PARADE
5 MAY 2007, SPALDING, UK

REBECCA WALKLEY

I remember many of the places we stayed: a French farmhouse where they cooked home grown artichokes, a squat in Berlin where we had to break in every night to get to our rooms, and a French motel room made out of a single piece of moulded plastic, all curves (making it easier to clean, I guess). Of course, at Glastonbury it was just a tent! Elsewhere we were accommodated in everything from plush hotels (Sines in Portugal), to the world's worst bed (and breakfast). The latter was near Spalding, where karaoke blasted out from the bar below our room until 2am, where there was a sodden salmon pink carpet in our bathroom and where the bedroom was so icy cold that I had to sleep with all my clothes on, including my overcoat. If that wasn't bad enough, somebody was stabbed outside our window just after the thumping karaoke had stopped. We had to step over the blood the next day to get into the band's van.

The band were due to play at the local football ground in Spalding the following afternoon. However, the audience-to-be and the procession of tulip floats were still winding their way through the market town and hadn't reached the grounds by the time The Ukrainians were due on stage. The band had to play anyway as they needed to get back to Leeds that evening. Their only audience was a family of four and a couple of dozen pensioners who were sat in the stands. It didn't matter if the band was playing to one person (as at King Tut's Wah Wah Hut in Glasgow, when an anarchist and her dog were the only audience and the dog howled all the way through the set), or to tens of thousands of people at a festival (75,000 in Kyiv's Independence Square), they played with the same incredible energy and gusto. The music would usually inspire every last person in the place to get up and dance by the end of the set. The young family of four at Spalding did dance on the otherwise empty football pitch but the pensioners in the stands sat tight waiting for the band to finish. Len asked me at the end of the gig to try and sell some CDs. 'You're kidding,' I thought. I dutifully went over but I got laughed off the pitch by a gang of silver haired Lincolnshire ladies. Clearly, the music wasn't really their cup of tea. Spalding Flower Parade? Never again!

Len experienced a variety of hostelries. At the Bumbershoot festival in Seattle, the band stayed in a plush five star hotel which had a giant swimming pool on the fifth floor. Len remembers passing through the glass revolving door, him on one side and John Lee Hooker on the other. In Ukraine they drove for hours through flooded roads to reach the large gothic building, guarded by two impressive stone griffins. Another time they stayed at a castle in Przemyśl on the Polish / Ukrainian border. Their dressing room was a room at the top of one of the castle turrets. However, one of the band members couldn't find a bathroom so, desperate, he decided to relieve himself in the sink in the dressing room. The sink collapsed from under him, the room flooded, the landing flooded and the turret stairway became a waterfall. They weren't invited back.

Len once told me the worst night's sleep he had was in the band van in Canada's Rocky Mountains. Len drew the short straw one night and had to stay in the van (to protect the band's equipment) as opposed to by the camp fire with the others. But opening the van door at night and switching the light on was a lethal mistake as millions of bloodthirsty mosquitos flew into the vehicle. A video captured the band members the next morning as Len emerged looking like the Elephant Man with lumps and bites upon lumps on bites, his face swollen out of all recognition. When they drove off the following morning, the van's windscreen smeared crimson as the blades squashed the blood-quenched insects against the glass.

Having said that, the very worst place Len slept in was the night his fellow band mates threw him in a skip somewhere in Belgium after a drunken night out. He clambered out the next morning before the truck came to remove the skip with him in it. It's amusing but not amusing. He could have been crushed into a cube of waste material, in Belgium of all places.

LIVE IN CZEREMCHA
RELEASED 26 NOVEMBER 2007

LEN

Recorded at the *Spotkanie Folkowe Festival*, Czeremcha in Poland on 29th May 2005, *Live In Czeremcha* captures the band in raw, Punky, *Respublika* mode. Full-on zizzy guitars – courtesy of our fabulous now-departed Mick – are to the fore in many of the songs, yet I like to think there are a lot of tender, delicate moments here, too. The packaging is great as well: a gatefold, recycled card sleeve with a traditional-style embroidery glued onto the front. That idea came from artist and designer Piotr Pucyło who now runs the *Globaltica World Cultures Festival* in the northern polish city of Gdynia on the Baltic coast.

 DNI KULTURY UKRAINSKIEJ (DAYS OF UKRAINIAN CULTURE FESTIVAL)
31 MAY 2008, SZCZECIN, POLAND

WLODEK NAKONECZNY

We were crossing a two-lane road between gas stations near the hotel to buy alcohol after this concert when a group of youngsters followed us. Halfway there, they attacked us with their fists! I had a fee for the band and part of the costs in my pocket – a lot of cash. So when they hit me in the face and kicked me I instinctively, but bravely, like brave Sir Robin, gave up and bravely ran away, leaving my friends to the mercy of the bandits.

I ran into the station and gave the money to the girl behind the cash register, asking her to keep it safe and call the police. She was scared, but she took my wallet and grabbed her phone. After a while, the musicians began to enter the station, followed by the attackers, but when they saw the phones in action, they withdrew. I was slightly bruised, but they only tore my shirt. They robbed Len of everything he had with him, including his passport. Rat suffered the most. They beat him and broke his arm.

We spent the night with Rat in the emergency room, where they put him back together, and then a few hours with Len the next day at the police station. I sent Rat and the rest of the team to the airport as planned. Len's case was more complicated: he had to get to the British Embassy to obtain a document allowing him to return to the UK. It was Sunday, and the nearest embassy was in Berlin, closer to Szczecin than to Warsaw.

Poland had been in the Schengen area for a year, but as the charming young policewoman warned, German police patrols were randomly checking border roads. She knew what she was talking about, she lived on the German side – because it was cheaper – and she travelled these roads back and forth every day. If they caught Len without documents, he might not have got away with it; they might consider him an illegal immigrant from Ukraine.

And East Germany had a different mentality because of its communist tradition of Honecker, Stasi, etc. I was afraid for Len. The policewoman showed great empathy and she promised that when she came back from duty, she would find out where the polizei officers were patrolling and where it would be safest to smuggle Len through. I thought it was a joke, but she actually called and gave specific instructions on where to go! We did not hesitate to take advantage of her advice and Len arrived safely in Berlin and made it home. It was the first time in my life when I believed that the Polish police could help someone!

LEN

A very helpful guy called Ken at the British Embassy in Berlin helped me through all the paperwork, and arranged for me to get a temporary passport back to the UK. Meanwhile Rebecca was wiring me out money for the plane fare home. However, my trauma still wasn't completely over…

I had just enough change to get a ticket for the S-Bahn (rapid rail route) to take me from the embassy to the airport. It was rush hour and every seat on the carriage was taken except for one, which a middle-aged German lady was using to rest her handbag. I was feeling drained and exhausted, so I asked in my best German, 'Kann ich hier sitzen, bitte?' ('Can I sit here, please?') Maybe I scared her with my black eyes and puffed up face, because she stood up, picked up her handbag, and battered me round the head with it.

FESTIWAL 'WROCK FOR FREEDOM'
21 JUNE 2008, POLA MARSOWE, WROCŁAW, POLAND

JAREK KOZAK

This is a simple and prosaic story. It began in 1999 when I befriended the Polish Punk band Alians. I was preparing their first website for them. I received a lot of material from the band, including photos from various tours. Among them were photos from their joint concert tour in Poland with the band The Ukrainians, probably from 1996. In the meantime, I got my hands on a compilation album, which of course featured 'Cherez Richku, Cherez Hai', and so I heard The Ukrainians' music. After a while, it turned out that they were playing in my city, Wrocław.

Over the next decade, I attended four more concerts in Poland and, in 2018 and 2019, concerts in Leeds and London. In London, I was wearing a t-shirt I had bought a long time ago. Peter noticed me in the crowd, came up to me and asked: 'Hey, where did you buy it? It's a few years old.' I replied that I had bought it all those years before at that concert in Poland. (I'd also flown in from Dublin for the London gig!)

Thanks to The Ukrainians, I have become more interested in Ukrainian culture, and in Ukraine and its history.

SLAVSKE ROCK FESTIVAL
26 JULY 2008, SLAVSKE, UKRAINE

PAUL WEATHERHEAD

I got to visit Ukraine with the band in 2008. We flew to Poland and then drove across the border, heading for Ternopil for the first of two gigs. The weather was appalling. Torrential rain, thunder and lightning and no respite. The flooding was so bad that it was declared a state of emergency in Ukraine and some of its neighbouring countries. As we drove to the gig, there were frequent detours to avoid flooded areas and we passed house after house and village after village that had been flooded. When we reached the site for the second gig – *Slavske Rock Festival* in the Carpathian Mountains – the rain was still pouring and the festival site looked very grim indeed as we did the soundcheck on the afternoon of the show. One odd highlight, though, was the very strange hotel we stayed at while at the festival. It was made to look like a medieval fairy tale castle with towers, turrets, winding staircases, suits of armour and statues of dragons everywhere. Unlike anywhere I'd stayed before. It was in beautiful wooded valleys, but the constant downpours meant we couldn't really explore.

The festival was of course a washout. Many thousands had been expected, but the awful conditions meant that only a few hundred brave souls were still at the site. During the performances, a policeman would come on stage and give dire warnings between each song about the dangers of camping near the river, which was dangerously high. Everything and everyone was caked in mud, and it continued to lash it down.

I seem to remember that the previous band had overrun, meaning we had to cut our set short. This may have been for the best as it might have saved us from a Carpathian jail! I was playing the intro to 'Souveniry', a long tremolo-ed note waiting for Len to come in with the vocals. Instead I heard him shout, 'Leave him alone you militaristic bastard!' or words to that effect. A guy had run on stage only to be violently manhandled offstage by a policeman who Len had then pushed. It seems in the confusion that follows, the organisers had to persuade the cop not to arrest Len on the spot. Meanwhile, I didn't know what to do except carry on playing that long, high C note. I seemed to be playing for an eternity…

After the performance it seemed like a good idea to make ourselves scarce, so we headed out of the swampy festival site to the warm and dry venue for the festival after-party, which was a hoot with copious booze, a banquet and a Beatles cover band. We had an early flight the next day and no hotel that evening, so we had no choice but to party all night. As you can imagine, loading the van with the gear at 6am after a night of debauchery is no easy feat!

LEN

I was feeling quite down after our recent Poland and Ukraine experiences. It had all been very stressful and depressing and made me question whether I wanted to continue touring with the band. It was then I heard that our music had been played in space. I investigated and was so excited and reinvigorated by the news!

FROM KYIV TO THE KOSMOS

INTERNATIONAL SPACE STATION
ORBITING PLANET EARTH

HEIDEMARIE STEFANYSHYN-PIPER

I first heard about the band in the early 1990s. I had grown up in the Ukrainian community in St. Paul/Minneapolis, Minnesota and was used to hearing Ukrainian folk music and 'Zabava music'. After graduating from college and serving in the US Navy, I was never stationed near a large Ukrainian community, so not many opportunities to hear Ukrainian music. I did come across a catalogue from a Ukrainian store, Yevshan, (this was in the time before the internet, when the only 'remote shopping' was done through catalogues). The CD *The Ukrainians* was available and I decided to try it. I liked the CD and then purchased two more, *Vorony* and *Kultura*, which were also in the catalogue. I now have the CDs uploaded on my computer and the music available in my iTunes collection. Many of their songs are in my playlists, so I can listen to their music every day.

In 1996 I was selected into the Astronaut Corps by NASA and made two space shuttle flights: STS-115 in 2006 and STS-126 in 2008. Prior to the launch of a space shuttle, the family of each crew member is asked to submit a list of songs for 'Wake-up Music', which is played by MCC (Mission Control Center at the Johnson Space Center in Houston) to the crew to start each day (only about the first minute is played). My husband knew that I liked Ukrainian music, so together we selected a Ukrainian song for each of the flights. They both happen to be by The Ukrainians.

For my first flight, STS-115, we selected 'Slava Kobzarya'; the words of Ukrainian national poet Taras Shevchenko set to a nice melody. The song was played specifically for me on the morning of my first space walk. As I had spent the night on the International Space Station (ISS), the song was also sent over the common communication loop with the ISS so that I would be sure to hear it. It was a wonderful way to start that day. To hear the words 'Учітеся брати мої, Думайте, читайте…' ('Learn my brothers, think and read…') was very applicable to our mission of space exploration and learning onboard the International Space Station.

For my second flight, STS-126, we selected 'Rospryahaite', a very upbeat tune. It was played during the latter half of the mission, after all of the space walks were completed. It was a very lively and fun song to hear first thing in the morning.

Heidemarie Stefanyshyn-Piper listened to The Ukrainians in space, and on the morning of her first space walk on STS-115, she listened to 'Slava Kobzarya': 'Learn my brothers, think and read...' (all photos by kind permission of NASA)

DIASPORA

LEN

Ever since our Cooking Vinyl days we were always aware when recording tracks for an album that we would need to bring out a single or EP to 'announce' it. I think it was Peter who for the EP preceding the *Diaspora* album wanted to record Brahms' 'Hungarian Dance No 5'. One of the plusses of this was that everyone already knows the tune, including people who take little interest in classical music. So, we recorded two versions of it, one called 'Emigranty' or 'Emigrants', whose lyrics I made sure fitted in with the album's "diaspora" theme, and one just with 'dai, dai, dai' chants. We liked them both for different reasons so both went on the album.

HUNGARIAN DANCE EP
RELEASED 16 JANUARY 2009

LEN

The 'dai, dai, dai' no-lyrics chanty version was definitely 'radio-friendly' and perfect as the lead track on the EP. DJs get bamboozled and scared by foreign languages, and we didn't want our shiny new CD to get dropped into the radio station's 'I don't understand this so we're not going to play it' bin. For me the 'dai, dai, dai' version is part of a long tradition of rock bands covering classical works that goes back to B Bumble and The Stingers' Tchaikovsky-inspired 'Nut Rocker' and The Cougars' 'Saturday Nite At The Duck Pond', which is an early '60s beat version of the famous theme from 'Swan Lake'.

In one way it might seem a bit strange The Ukrainians recording a track called 'Hungarian Dance' by a German composer but we thought it would be interesting to cover a classical piece for a change instead of a British or American pop or rock song. We tried it out live and it went down really well, so we thought, 'Hmm, OK, why not release it?' Also, Brahms may have been a German composer, but his inspiration was his early musical collaborator, Ede Reményi. who grew up right in the heart of the Carpathian Mountains. Brahms repackaged folk music from eastern Europe for the classical theatres and opera houses of the late 19th century, in a similar way to what we did with Ukrainian folk themes and rock music in the 20th century.

DIASPORA
RELEASED 13 FEBRUARY 2009

PETER

The *Diaspora* album dealt with issues where you grow up in one country and your roots are in another. We tried to make those themes international and not just Ukrainian. We had to arrange the rehearsals months ahead because the band have all got other things going on in their lives. We'd put those weekends in the diary and say, 'These are the five songs we're working on. Have a think about it. Think about chords, think about keys, come up with ideas.' Then we'd have perhaps three days back-to-back and iron out the song in a rehearsal studio. You might spend a year or two years working on songs that you're going to do, and rehearse them every few months. You might then record them and think about the videos to go with them.

Diaspora sold enough copies around the world and brought in enough money to enable us to do another record.

LEN

I was noticing by this time that I was able to read Ukrainian newspapers and books quite well and wanted to write something a bit more challenging lyrics-wise. The most obvious subject to tackle seemed to be migration. Tens of thousands of young Ukrainians, Poles and other eastern Europeans had been travelling to the West in the hope of creating a new life with a higher standard of living, and they wanted to earn enough money to send some to their families back home. Historically there had already been a number of waves of Ukrainian immigration into the UK over the years, one of the biggest being in the 1940s, post-World War II. Many of the people we met in Ukrainian communities were the children or even grandchildren of these pioneers.

The word 'diaspora' comes from the Greek, meaning 'dissipation', suggesting that the culture and language of the diaspora will disappear as they assimilate into their newfound homeland. But I don't think that is always the case. Sometimes new arrivals will scatter like leaves in a field and sometimes they will disperse like seeds and grow. Whichever happens, it inevitably involves the heartbreak of leaving family and homeland coupled with the excitement of starting a new life. It's this I wanted to capture in some of the songs on *Diaspora*.

Some of our band members had Ukrainian parents or eastern European ancestry and most definitely continue to feel a connection to the lands of their ancestors. This is absolutely the case with Peter and Steff. My particular genetic connection to eastern Europe came as a surprise to me, but it has confirmed something I'd always thought and felt, that I had more than just an inexplicable interest in that part of the world. There had been a rumour in my family, which I remember being voiced by my dad's sister, my Auntie

Діаспора

Ми покажем: ми браття-козаки
Браття й сестри козацького роду
У серці живе Україна
В крові моїй - Україна

Покажем, що ми нові козаки
Іноземці козацького роду
Ми діти твої, Україно
Діти твої, Україно

Діаспора
Діаспора
Чи.. ми.. вірні козаки?
Діаспора

Вир емоцій, вир слова і пісні
А ми чужинці, в чужій країні

Diaspora

We will show you, we are Cossack brothers
Brothers and sisters of Cossack descent
Ukraine is alive in my heart
Ukraine is in my blood

We will show that we are new Cossacks
Strangers of Cossack descent
We are your children, Ukraine
Your children, Ukraine

Diaspora
Diaspora
Are... we... true Cossacks?
Diaspora

A whirl of emotion, a whirl of words and song
But we are foreigners in a foreign country

Звідки ви?

Імігранте, ви чужий!
Вам дорога, ой, □куди?

Імігранте, ненаський!
Іноземцю! Що коли
нам не подобаєтесь ви?

Імігранте! дивацький!
Вам дорога, ой, □куди?
Далеко від нас? Якби!

Гей! Ви їсте їжу!
Ой□, несмачну їжу!
У вас нема вареників!
Гей! Звідки ви?

Ви носите одяг!
Дивовижний одяг!
Ні кальсони, ні штани!
Гей! Звідки ви?

  Шукав я роботу
  Залишив свою сім҆ю
  А нічого не скажу

  Чесний я чоловік
  І порядний робітник
  Все ж ви кажете мені
  Гей! Звідки ви?

Говорите з акцентом
Із дивним акцентом
Я вас не розумію
Гей! Звідки ви?

У вас культура інша
У вас історія інша
Так, ми вас боїмося
Гей! Звідки ви?

  Шукав я роботу
  Залишив свою сім҆ю
  А нічого не скажу

  Я людина, як і ви
  У нас обох є сім҆ї
  Все ж ви кажете мені:
  Гей! Звідки ви?

Zvidky Vy? (Where Are You From?)

Immigrant, you're strange!
Where are you going?

Immigrant! Not like us!
Foreigner! What if
We don't like you?

Immigrant, you're outlandish!
Where are you going?
Far away from us? If only!

Hey, you eat food!
Unappetising food!
You don't have any varenyky*!
Where are you from?

You wear clothes!
Strange-looking clothes!
Neither pants, nor trousers!
Where are you from?

I looked for work
I left my family
But I say nothing

I'm an honest man
And a steady worker
And still you say to me
Where are you from?

You speak with an accent
With a strange accent
I don't understand you
Where are you from?

You have a different culture
You have a different history
Yes, we are afraid of you
Where are you from?

I looked for work
I left my family
But I say nothing

I'm a human being, just like you
We both have families
And still you say to me
Where are you from?

*A national dish made from parcels of fresh dough that can come with savoury or sweet fillings

Madge, that the Ligginses had come from Russia way back. So, for my 60th birthday my wife Rebecca bought me a DNA test. She herself was convinced that I was carrying genes from eastern Europe. When the results arrived, I was astonished. The DNA transmitted via the Liggins males had a rare subclade marker which originated in Bosnia-Herzegovina, and 14 per cent of Ukrainians also carried this marker. It was a revelation to me that I had eastern European roots. Sometimes in the early days I'd felt the odd pang of 'imposter syndrome' as a member of The Ukrainians but from here on I felt I really belonged.

It might sound over-romanticised, but now there's part of me that feels that the themes and melodies of the songs Peter and I have written together have mystically travelled down the generations by hitching a ride on our families' DNA until it reached us!

REBECCA WALKLEY

Len has always loved everything about eastern Europe, the languages, the traditional songs and folktales, the otherworldliness of parts of Europe that happily lacked some of the worst aspects of capitalist western values. He loved the vodka, the music, the soul of that part of the world. The DNA test results made perfect sense. Len told me Pete hugged him when the results came through, saying, 'You're one of us after all!'

LEN

As well as our own songs, we wanted to include a cover version on this album, so we chose T. Rex's 'Children of the Revolution', which somehow seemed appropriate title-wise. In another way though it was typically perverse of us to take a poppy glam-rock single from 1972 and completely re-interpret it. The mood of our version is definitely intense, and the message is political. We wanted to highlight the courage and defiance of the Ukrainian people at the time of the Orange Revolution.

I think with *Diaspora* we brought together a lot of very different strands and wove them into a surprisingly coherent-sounding album.

PETER

The title track from the album is a really significant song. I was driving to a rehearsal in

Hebden Bridge when the tune and chorus came into my head. These were the days before you could just get your phone out and sing into it so that you didn't forget a tune. As I was driving, I had to keep the tune in my head for nearly an hour. As soon as I got to the rehearsal, I had to play it to everyone, over and over so it wasn't forgotten. Mick added the wonderful middle eight riff and it was almost structured. Len got hold of it and perfectly crafted the words to express the feelings of the Ukrainian (or any) diaspora.

LEN

The song that took me the longest time to write a lyric for was 'Marusya Bohuslavka'. Based on a 17th century epic poem called 'Duma pro Marusya Bohuslavka', it was about a fictional priest's daughter who converted to Islam when she was taken as a slave by the Turks. When she saw the suffering of hundreds of Kozak prisoners she promised them she would get the keys to the prison and set them free. She has often popped up in Ukrainian novels and plays and is even the subject of a ballet.

My task was to tell the story while reducing a very long epic poem into a small number of song verses with very different line lengths and metre from the original, but to keep it in 17th century Ukrainian! I do like a challenge but that was a serious headfuck and it took eighteen months (on and off) before I was happy with it.

 FMM
18 JULY 2009, SINES, PORTUGAL

REBECCA WALKLEY

The deal with Cooking Vinyl came to an end around 1996. Life moved on for everyone. Len and I moved to Berkshire for my job. Band members, roadies, sound engineers peeled away to do more regular jobs or have children or both. Sadly, Roman died in 2014. But the band kept going thanks to Len and Pete. It was hard work for them both as Pete had a young family and Len was working and looking after his elderly father for many years, travelling constantly between Berkshire and Essex.

Without a record company or manager, they could choose the gigs and festivals they wanted to play and they released their live tracks and recordings on their own label, Zirka Records. They would play to world music audiences at European festivals, to Ukrainian audiences at Ukrainian social clubs, and also in rock clubs and arts centres back in Britain. Their fans were a broad church.

Len's knowledge of the Ukrainian language and devotion to all things Slavic pervaded the songs. The Ukrainian poet and novelist Oleksa Semenchenko praised his songwriting and grasp of the Ukrainian language. Len developed a love of Ukrainian poets and writers, sometimes referencing them in the songs. He had and still has a love of everything eastern European. For Pete it was in his DNA, his father was Ukrainian. Between them they had a passion which would continue to keep the project alive for several decades to come.

The heady days of long, manic tours around Europe were over but the band still played many memorable gigs. For me a world music festival in Sines, Portugal was a highlight. The venue was set on a beautiful cliff top overlooking the Atlantic Ocean. To keep the place mud-free, large palm tree fronds were laid over the bare ground of the festival site. The fronds filled the air with the palm's delicate scent which mixed with the smell of cannabis (possession for your own consumption is allowed in Portugal). The audience of around three thousand people didn't pogo or fist punch their way through The Ukrainians' set but gently swayed to the songs. It was hard to know if they were having a good time or just blissed out on the atmosphere.

 FOLKWOODS FESTIVAL
16 AUGUST 2009, EINDHOVEN, NETHERLANDS

REBECCA WALKLEY

This festival, set in a Dutch woodland, was in contrast to the modernness of nearby Eindhoven with its industrial landscape, its streamlined blocks of flats and conservative housing, where anything old or interesting-looking had been demolished. After The Ukrainians played, I remember selling a lot of CDs and albums to the well-heeled hippy festival goers. I also remember the long queue of young Dutch women waiting to have plaster casts made of their upper bodies. The sculptor hand-moulded the wet plaster over their bare breasts and then hung his finished products on a nearby tree to dry. It's as if the women wanted to capture a 3D memory of their youthful selves, something more than a photograph. I wasn't sure where I stood on this as a feminist. It was somewhere between appreciating the women's expression of body confidence and the disapproval of the actions of a man very happy in his chosen career. Anyway, I wasn't going to let him feel mine.

20 YEARS – THE BEST OF THE UKRAINIANS 1991-2011
RELEASED 11 MARCH 2011

LEN

It was now 20 years since we played our first tour in 1991, and it seemed like a tremendous feat. We had a good few gigs lined up, mostly in Ukrainian clubs in the UK, but our stock of CDs to sell at those gigs was getting low, so it made sense to put together a *Best Of*. As our publicity blurb said, the album was 'an intoxicating 20-track distillation of vodka-fuelled classics!'

UKRAINIAN CENTRE
30 APRIL 2011, LEICESTER, UK

IAN BRITTON

This was the kids' first proper concert. We had fun with an early sat nav so got there very early and it felt like an old music hall joke. ('What time does it start?' 'What time can you get here?') We were first in and for some reason we were given a table and chairs midway up the hall. Off to the bar I went to be told, 'No glasses, it's a band.' Fine, but they wouldn't serve Guinness in plastic, the kids' J2Os were glass bottles and the other half wanted a vodka so that had to be served in a glass! It was one of the best concerts I've ever been to, and the only one that was paused briefly so that the hall manager could come on to say that hot dogs were on sale! The end felt like the end of the best wedding you'd snuck into, with Cossack dancing (led by the Kinks' covers support band) and everyone with their new best friends.

I saw them at the Brudenell Social Club promoting *A Short History*... Child number one wondered why I'd left her and turned to see me talking to a bloke in a Leeds United shirt who she assumed was an old mate. I was asking Mr S (Peter) how the school he taught me in was now a Co-Op (don't ask). They opened with a version of 'Ace of Spades'. It took the older part of the audience a while to get up to speed, but it finished in the usual happy fury.

When I'm out on my bike thinking, 'I'll take it easy up this hill' and 'Verkhovyno' randomly comes on in the mix and I think, 'Oh, I can keep up...' I then realise that 'er, no, you can't...'. It should be a standard fitness test tune!

PETER

All the way through our career as The Ukrainians, we've always known that female voices make a big difference to the emotion attached to our music and we've always tried to incorporate them wherever possible. We did a little bit of recording with Irena and Julia Kuszta for the *Kultura* album in 1994. We then brought two Ukrainian backing vocalists, Irena and Marika, on tour with us to support the *Kultura* tour later that year. It made a great difference to the live sound.

On 28th October 2011 we played a gig at the Ukrainian club in Edinburgh and the artist supporting us was a vocalist from Poland called Monika. She sang in Polish, Ukrainian, Russian and Georgian. She and two or three of her friends specialised in singing a capella folk music. They were really good at the emotional sounding music. We asked her if she'd come and do some rehearsals with us and she came all the way down from Edinburgh for a couple of weekends to work on songs. It made a real difference to some of the songs we were working on for our next album. We recorded around five songs and some of those

(clockwise from top left) Peter at London's 100 Club, October 2009 (Steff Tymruk); Len & Mick at London's 100 Club, October 2009 (Steff Tymruk); The Ukrainians in action at Rock Na Bagnie, Goniadz, Poland, 2023 (Pawel Krupek Krupka) (four photos)

(clockwise from top left) The Ukrainians in action at Rock Na Bagnie, Goniądz, Poland, 2023 (Pawel Krupek Krupka)

tracks made it onto the album *Summer in Lviv*. There's a track called 'Oy Dunayu Dunayu' on YouTube where the voices work particularly well. I love the way her voice works with Len's. We worked with her for about two years.

We played a festival in Poland with her. We flew out on a Friday or Saturday with a whole day to lounge around and relax, because we were just playing the festival in the afternoon. After the show, we were in this little guest house with four or five double rooms. We may even have booked the whole place out. It was late and a really warm night, so we sat in the garden talking, with beers and vodkas, and with candles on a table that created a really low light. The whole place was in the middle of nowhere. It was surrounded by a sea of sunflowers, as high as they could be and going on and on out into the distance as far as you could see. There were some gentle rolling hills and there was just one light in the distance from a farm a few miles away. The only sound was the sound of crickets and the occasional dog barking.

At one point, Monika and Wlodek started singing old Ukrainian songs. It was just the two voices and it was such an emotional experience for me. Everybody else was sat around the table, having a bit of chat and a few more beers and listening to the songs. I must have been 30 or 40 metres away, not even looking towards them, but just looking out over these really dark, barely visible moonlit sunflower fields, and listening to the music. The melodies and the two voice harmonies in a field full of nothing but sunflowers on a warm evening was the closest I've ever felt to the music, close to the roots of where it should be sung, and sung in the way it should be sung. And I thought, 'This is probably the closest I'll get to sharing musical experiences with my dad because he'll have grown up in environments like that.'

We were staying in Poland right next to the Ukrainian border. The next day we walked up the road to a really old Ukrainian church, with circular stone walls, a roof made of wood and thatch and with the altar in the middle. It's a museum rather than a church now, because there are no people of Ukrainian background there anymore.

We walked in and looked around and it was absolutely quiet and still. Monika just said, 'Give me a drone now' and so I went 'mmmmm' and kept doing that while she sang an old Ukrainian prayer. I felt a really deep connection that I've never felt anywhere else. It came from the combination of place and history and sounds and voices, this really deep thing. I'm sure people who are Christians feel it when they're singing hymns and things that go back through the past, like Welsh people do when they hear songs being sung in their native tongue in the valleys.

There's a richness on the recordings she's on which I wish we could have all the time. But Monika found it difficult working in a laddish environment. She could hold her own but I don't think she found it as relaxing as she would have liked. Normally she works with her friends, who are all women, just singing quiet songs and she was playing rocky things with us.

THE UKRAINIANS

I think we were just too loud and she was more into the spiritual side of things. We tried to do other songs and creations that didn't quite mix but I loved the sound and feel of the songs that we did create together. We did a video for 'Chy Znayesh Ty', which is basically a song about relatives that have been lost in wars and conflicts and struggles. It's a beautiful song in the way that Len and Monika's voices work together. It's one of the most significant periods of the band for me.

PISNI IZ THE SMITHS (TWELVE-INCH VINYL EP)
RELEASED 19 APRIL 2013

LEN

Out of the blue I got an email from a guy in Germany called Jochen Kozel. He ran a record label called Estate 11, based in Aachen and asked why we hadn't re-released our *Pisni Iz The Smiths* EP. It hadn't been commercially available for many years; we didn't have the financial backing of a major label to ensure that all of our back catalogue was available all of the time.

'I'd like to release it on vinyl,' he said. I contacted Cooking Vinyl Records for the artwork files so that they could be modified for the new release. Unfortunately, they'd had a clear out a few years before and those files no longer existed. If we had tried to copy the design from an original Cooking Vinyl CD the quality would have suffered too much, so my friend Rob Bowker created some new artwork. It was colourful and abstract but with a hint of the original design. Perfect!

As for procuring the audio tape masters, that could have been a big problem had it not been for my foresight, or should I say paranoia. Cooking Vinyl had also consigned these to landfill when they had their big clear out. We could have used the mastered-for-CD files from the original 1992 CD release but when doing re-releases or compilations it's always best to work from the original unprocessed files. And, as fate would have it, I had requested a copy set of the unprocessed DAT (digital audio tape) masters in 1992 for the band archive I keep at home.

Jochen wanted to make a limited edition in two colours, black and orange. The orange ones were individually numbered 1 to 500. I was so excited when I got my copies in the post! Thanks are due to Jochen not only for releasing the EP in the first place but also for donating a few dozen copies years later to help our fundraising for Ukrainian refugees following the full-on invasion of Ukraine by Vladimir Putin's Russian forces in February 2022.

Чи Знаєш Ти?

Чи знаєш ти, де моя родина?
Я приїхав тут з далекого краю
Щоб побачити село моє
Щоб побачити мою Вкраїну!

Півстоліття тому село винищили
І в Сибір всіх селян вивозили
Де село було тепер є дорога
І коло неї там стоїть могила

Покажи мені, де є ця могила?
Бо я хочу коло неї помолитись
За мою родину, за село
І за нещасливу Україну

Візьму від неї, візьму я чорну землю
Землю рідну, чорноземлю з
України

Вже знаю я, чому ви не писали
Я вже знаю, хоч хотіли, щоб не знав я
Бо мені буде це пригадувати
Як я сиротою залишився

Chy Znayesh Ty? (Do You Know?)

Do you know where my family is?
I came here from a distant land
To see my village
To see my Ukraine

Half a century ago the village was destroyed
and the villagers were all taken to Siberia
In the village there was a road
and by it stood a grave

Can you show me where the grave is?
I want to pray by it
for my family, for the village
and for misfortunate Ukraine

From there I will take some black earth
native earth, black earth from Ukraine

I know now why they didn't write
I know now why they didn't want me to know
because it would make me feel
left behind, like an orphan

Надія Пішла

Надія пішла
але далеко не зайшла

Раз зимою
Надія захворіла
я там був
вона не затужила

Надія пішла

теплим літом вона видужувала
«Краще буде», ти мені сказала

Nadiya*Pishla (Hope Went Away)

Hope went away
But not far away

Once in the wintertime
Nadiya* fell ill
I was there
She never lost heart

Hope went away

She recovered during the warm summer
And you told me: "everything will get better"

*Nadiya is the Ukrainian word for 'hope' and is also a popular name amongst women and girls

JUMBO RECORDS
20 APRIL 2013, LEEDS, UK

STUART HANCOCKS

Back in 2013, Record Store Day was more of a celebratory event rather than the blatant profit-making commercial event it has mutated into. That particular year, Jumbo Records in Leeds had a full line-up of artists playing live in store to celebrate the day. Headlining were The Ukrainians. Well, when I say 'in store' I mean more like 'just outside the store', on the balcony in the shopping centre where Jumbo Records was situated at the time. It was quite a squeeze to shoehorn all six band members and their instruments into the limited space allocated. Then there was the audience, who sat on fold-away chairs or stood around the perimeter of the venue.

Despite the limitations afforded by the location, The Ukrainians played a lively and well received half hour set comprising eight songs, mainly to promote the first vinyl release of their *Pisni Iz The Smiths* EP, a collection of Smiths cover versions that had been unavailable for many years.

There's a video clip of the band playing 'Koroleva Ne Pomerla' ('The Queen Is Dead')' on YouTube. At the end of the video, the camera pans around the audience and takes in the scene of The Ukrainians playing a shopping centre on a balcony overlooking the Card Factory shop, with bemused Saturday afternoon shoppers travelling up and down the shopping centre's escalators and obviously wondering what on earth was going on!

At the end of their set, I managed to have a chat with a most friendly Peter Solowka who was more than happy to not only sign the CD I had with me, but also kindly got all the other band members to sign it for me too.

As it turns out, the rather bizarre location did not put the band off in any way, because twelve months later they returned to Jumbo Records to perform on Record Store Day once again. This time, however, Jumbo had managed to acquire a much more suitable setting for the bands to perform, including a purpose-built stage away from the quizzical gazes of casual Saturday afternoon shoppers.

Incidentally, the balcony area where The Ukrainians played on that April 2013 afternoon now serves as a nail bar!

NATIONAL UKRAINIAN FESTIVAL (CNUF)
4 AUGUST 2013, DAUPHIN, MANITOBA, CANADA

REBECCA WALKLEY

In 2013 The Ukrainians were invited to play at the *Canadian National Ukrainian Festival* (CNUF) in Canada, where there is a large Ukrainian diaspora population. They drove for hours and hours over roads through wheat fields which joined the sky at every point on the horizon, until in the middle of the wheat wilderness they reached the town of Dauphin. The band were paraded around the streets on the back of a trailer. Len says he recalls the band was playing 'Anarchy In The UK' as the trailer slowly drove past the old people's home, which somehow didn't seem appropriate.

 CIESZANÓW FESTIWAL
24 SEPTEMBER 2013, CIESZANÓW, POLAND

PAWEL KORDACZKA

 Me and my Punk rock friends have been listening to The Ukrainians since 1987. We are from Ustrzyki Dolne, a town in the eastern Carpathian Bieszczady mountains, 74 kilometers from Przemyśl, near the Polish/Ukrainian border. I saw The Ukrainians at the Cieszanów Festiwal in 2013, and in London – where I now live – in October 2014.

WIKTOR MARSZALEK

My first encounter with The Ukrainians was hearing their music on cassettes released by Koka Records around 1993, and then seeing concerts in Poland, especially the one at the Centrum Kultury Zamek in Poznań with Pidżama Porno in June 1997. Songs by The Ukrainians accompanied me all the time, both their own work and their brilliant covers, especially of The Smiths and The Velvet Underground. I had the opportunity to support the band at the *Cieszanów Rock Festival*. It was a kind of journey back to high school. It seemed that I was going to get involved with their music by listening to records and going to concerts, but it turned out differently.

For the last one-and-a-half years my wife and I have been helping our Ukrainian friends in Poland and Ukraine. Nothing breaks the ice with people from across our eastern border who are fleeing war like knowing and trying to sing 'Cherez Richku, Cherez Hai'. Their music has become a bridge between ordinary people, but also between nations whose history has not always been easy.

PETER

On 4th March 2014 Roman Revkniv (aka Remeynes) died of bowel cancer at the age of 52. In some ways he epitomised what it was like to be part of that hardcore Ukrainian community that I was never part of, and he brought a bit of that into the band. In some ways, I was a little bit too divorced from some of the essences that are important to being Ukrainian – but without that distance, we could never have felt free enough to Westernise the sound.

JOHN HUNTER (AKA MACHEATH), VOCALS, HANG THE DANCE (1984-1988)

Roman Revkniv joined Leeds Post-Punk band Hang The Dance in 1985 and stayed until their demise in 1988, touring much of the UK and Germany in that time. As the self-styled Roman Remeynes, he contributed keyboards, bass and mandolin to one album and two singles which graced the alternative Punk charts in a creative three-year period. Roman was a special person. In fact, he was multiple people. Fiercely intelligent, musically talented and articulate, juxtaposed with a sometimes provocative, opinionated and occasionally abrasive persona. You never knew who you were getting other than, on stage, an excellent musician.

In 1988 he went to see The Wedding Present play live and, in an assertive conversation afterwards, stated that unless our band changed to follow a similar musical direction, he would have to consider his options. Shortly thereafter he left our band to contribute to the early chapters of The Ukrainians' story.

I lost touch with Roman until an unexpected email in 2014 from him telling me he was unwell. Through mutual friends, our last contact was in a Leeds hospice in March of that year when he, sadly, passed. He is fondly remembered as a great talent who will forever be missed for his contribution to the local music scene and beyond.

NEVER MIND THE COSSACKS
RELEASED 19 APRIL 2014

LEN

A number of factors converged to make this release inevitable. It was the 25th anniversary of The Sex Pistols' 'Anarchy In The UK' single, we'd run out of our *Anarchy In The UK* CDs, Record Store Day was beginning to become a thing… and I loved vinyl records. It was a no-brainer! I had a look through my archive boxes at home and found our original 2002 masters, including a previously unreleased version of 'Holidays In The Sun' I'd forgotten about. I also found a live version of 'Anarchy In The UK' recorded at a festival in Poland in 2005 and one of 'God Save The Queen' from a show we did at the London Ukrainian Club in 2011. To make the number up to eight tracks, four a side, we quickly recorded a version of 'Problems', one of the songs on the original Pistols' *Never Mind The Bollocks* album. Yayyy, we were ready to go!

Our mandolin player Paul came up with the title, and our graphics guy Rob Bowker created the artwork, a fine tribute to Jamie Reid, the designer of the original *Never Mind The Bollocks* sleeve. Time-wise, the album sides were quite short, so we chose to make it run at 45rpm instead of 33rpm to give it a better quality sound. Finally, to make it nice and collectable for Record Store Day, we pressed it on yellow vinyl and limited it to 500 individually numbered copies. It sold out within three weeks.

REVOLUTSIYA EP
RELEASED 30 JUNE 2014

LEN

The first track on this EP, 'Zrada', which means 'betrayal', questions who betrayed who when former prime minister Yulia Tymoshenko was imprisoned for abuse of power and embezzlement. Was she a criminal who betrayed her people or was she the victim of a conspiracy, betrayed by her political enemies? It came from a session of four recordings we did with our friend Monika Niemczynowicz, who we'd met at a gig we did in Edinburgh. She had her own vocal group who sang that night, and when we heard her we thought, 'We must try to record a few tracks with her, she has a great voice!'

The second track, 'Skil'ky Revolutsiy?' ('How Many Revolutions?') was originally released on our *Diaspora* album and asks how much more upheaval is yet to be inflicted on the Ukrainian people. Ukraine was victim of the absorption into the Soviet Union in 1922 following the 1917 revolution, which held back the country's development and suppressed its culture and language for much of the 20th century. Also, it had only been ten years since the Orange Revolution of 2004 that Yulia Tymoshenko had led. Tracks 3 and 4, which translate as 'Evolution' and 'Europe's Newest Child', were previously unavailable tracks from our mysterious never-to-be-released dance album. We decided to include them on the EP because these songs complemented the other two tracks subject matter-wise.

PETER

In 2014 came the big set of demonstrations known as the Maidan Revolution. It came to a head politically when one of Ukraine's leaders went back on an electoral pledge to move Ukraine closer to the European Union, and instead signed the deal which brought Ukraine economically closer to its Russian neighbour. This provoked enormous and very intense demonstrations in Kyiv where the city centre – the Maidan (Independence Square) – was taken over for months by people who set up a 'protest city'. They had food kitchens, entertainment and education centres and medical facilities, which were constantly staffed

(clockwise from top left) Jumbo Records, Leeds, 2014: Steff, Len, Len, Peter & Jim; Jim, Paul (Danny Barbour)

(clockwise from top left) Jumbo Records, Leeds, 2014: Len & Paul; Paul; Steff; Pete, Jim, Woody & Len; Pete & Jim; Woody (Danny Barbour)

by thousands of people. Despite violence and despite many attempts by police and security forces to remove them, the demonstrators stayed put.

I could really feel the struggle. I could watch live streams of the demonstrations in Independence Square – the same place where we had played to thousands just 21 years before. It felt so odd to think that 21 years earlier, most people thought it strange to link Ukrainian culture with Western culture, but that now people were physically struggling and risking death to try to make that cultural link a reality. I was emotional, I was distraught, I certainly wasn't sleeping well, but overall I felt a sense of helplessness. I felt that a lot was at stake here, and that if the principle that Ukraine should be closer to Europe than Russia could be upheld, then the dream that Ukraine would be fully independent would likely happen.

Part of the struggle in the Maidan involved musicians. Almost every day there were bands playing for the thousands of people that were protesting in the square. There was an enormous stage with a light and sound system and all the large bands from Ukraine, all the musicians that you'd ever heard of, would play there. They were showing the crowds that Ukrainian artists were with the people.

At that time we received an approach from the organiser of a music venue who apologised for the fact that his Ukrainian wasn't good as his native language was Russian. He said that the demonstrations that were happening around the country were increasing tensions between Ukrainian speakers and Russian speakers in Odesa. He thought this was wrong because Ukrainians and Russians should be able to work together. He said that if we could come and play, and just entertain with music that everyone could dance to, it would help people get through these more difficult times. I really felt for him because this is how I feel about music and how it should be used by people. It should be that everyone can feel the joy in each other's culture, and not fear it. But it was just impossible to do. There was no way that we could travel to Odesa in any way that was secure. It just felt so bad to say 'no' to him. It also feels bad now, to know that I have tried to contact him a few times since and I've had no reply. I sometimes wonder if he safely got through the revolution of 2014.

'ZRADA' JOHN KNOWLES, WRITER/DIRECTOR

I'd been a big fan of The Ukrainians for years though sadly never managed to see a live gig. I'm a playwright and had for some time been trying to put my thoughts together on how I felt about war and the absurdity of it all from a human perspective. This eventually led me to write my stage play *Hitleria Pizzeria*, an absurdist comedy drama set in Ukraine. The play sees three regular café attendees arrive at their usual café one morning only to discover that barman Emile is now sporting a Hitler moustache and haircut. These three taciturn men, who usually keep their own company, are thrown into confusion and unable to confront Emile (after all it is one of the few cafés still open in the midst of the war all around them). Emile's new look, which let's face it comes with some baggage, acts as a catalyst for the three men and the young revolutionary soldier who enters later, stirring up past lives and hidden betrayals. I wrote to Len Liggins asking for permission to use The Ukrainians' music within the play, and shortly after sent him the script. To my delight, Len gave us a 'yes' to use the songs in the theatre show. Thanks to Len and the band, the music was perfect and remains a favourite of all of us who worked on the show, especially the song 'Zrada' which appears on the *Revolutsiya* EP.

FROM KYIV TO THE KOSMOS

A HISTORY OF ROCK MUSIC

A SHORT HISTORY OF ROCK MUSIC IN UKRAINIAN EP
RELEASED 18 APRIL 2015

LEN
The *Never Mind The Cossacks* LP was so successful that we decided to release another vinyl record for Record Store Day 2015. We put together a collection of cover versions of western pop and rock songs, this time a limited issue of 750 copies, again all individually numbered. We already had a version of The Velvet Underground's 'Venus In Furs' from our *Vorony* album, an unreleased cover of Plastic Bertrand's 'Ça Plane Pour Moi' from the same sessions, 'Children Of The Revolution' from *Diaspora* and 'Telstar' from *Istoriya*. We also rehearsed and recorded a clutch of new cover versions. There was a certain amount of bickering about which songs to work on but that was inevitable and 'all part of the fun', as they say. The Beatles, The Beach Boys, Talking Heads, fellow Leeds band The Kaiser Chiefs, Kraftwerk, The Mamas and The Papas and Joy Division all made it to the final track list! It was a big challenge for me because I was translating all the lyrics, and I wanted them not only to sound good, but also to rhyme, and to keep the metre of the originals as well as being faithful translations.

ANDREW 'WHITEY' WHITE, KAISER CHIEFS
I first got into The Ukrainians through their excellent cover of 'Bigmouth Strikes Again'. I never thought back then that one day they'd be covering one of my songs. I love the fact that 'I Predict A Riot' has been 'Ukrainianed'!

 FIBBERS
26 MAY 2015, YORK, UK

MIKE FORBESTER
Many years ago, I had a singing gig (a wedding, I think) in Leeds Cathedral. In between the rehearsal and the actual service, we had some free time so I went off into the city centre to browse through some shops. While in the then Leeds HMV store, I was casually going through some CDs and found one by a band I'd never heard of before but with a catchy name. Having Ukrainian friends (mainly based in Oldham, but one or two now in Ukraine itself) I was intrigued as to what this might be all about, so, on the basis of nothing

ventured, nothing gained, etc., I decided to buy it. That disc was *Vorony*, and many discs and live gigs later, I remain a huge fan.

One gig that stands out was at Fibbers in York. It was a huge disappointment (not the band's fault) due to the lack of support from the locals. I remember Peter telling me some time afterwards that it was just like a studio session. At least it didn't deter the band from coming back, and I'm pleased that there's been much more support since when they've come back to York to play at The Crescent.

I keep telling friends that they haven't lived until they've heard 'Anarchy In The UK' sung in Ukrainian!

 RAINBOW
29 MAY 2015, YORK, UK

DAVID GARSTON

I've seen The Ukrainians around ten times, right from the start up to their March 2022 benefit gig in King's Heath. I was a Wedding Present fan pre-Ukrainians, and saw The Wedding Present at the Town & Country Club (never 'The Forum') in Kentish Town in '89. They were doing Ukrainian songs in full dress with dancers, etc., and with TWP supporting themselves in acoustic mode.

I saw The Ukrainians in Barnet in April 2002. It was only round the corner from where I lived at the time, and I remember they had to leave promptly at the end to get the last train back north. Funny that the ticket price in 2002 was £10, and in 2009 it was only £7! I also saw them at some sort of outdoor festival in North West London, playing on a Saturday lunchtime, and having a chat with Pete afterwards. And the gig in Digbeth a few years ago supporting the *History of Rock Music In Ukrainian* release. With no discernible promotion there were only about 20 other people there. But that's not the smallest audience I've ever been a part of. That honour goes to a band called Section 25, in Derby somewhere in the early 2000s. There were 12 people there, and that includes the support act!

A HISTORY OF ROCK MUSIC IN UKRAINIAN
RELEASED 15 JUNE 2015

LEN

A month after the vinyl *A Short History…* LP came out, we released *A History Of Rock Music In Ukrainian* on CD. (Note that there's no 'short' in the title of this one! This has really confused people who have tried to put together our discography online.) While we'd been waiting for  the manufacturers in the Czech Republic to press the vinyl record, we'd finished off some more cover versions and so the CD had 16 tracks, whereas the vinyl had only ten. We left 'Ça Plane Pour Moi' and 'Telstar' off and added eight new recordings that included cover versions of songs by Nirvana, REM, Led Zeppelin, Big Mama Thornton, Green Day and Motörhead.

This was a very satisfying album to put out and it got some really good reviews. It also appealed to a lot of people outside our usual range of fans because they just thought the cover versions were really interesting. One thing we like to do is to make them very different from the originals. I don't understand what pleasure a musician can get from just copying a song. The worst example of this I've ever heard is The Stereophonics' take on 'Handbags and Gladrags', which is an almost direct copy of Rod Stewart's recording. Why? What's the point?

'RADIOACTIVITY'
RELEASED 26 FEBRUARY 2016

LEN

Released to mark the 30th anniversary of the Chornobyl nuclear disaster of 1986, this seven-inch single came into being thanks to our friend and superfan Vlad Lee's contact with the Aby Sho Mzk label in Kyiv. Both sides of the single were Kraftwerk songs. 'Radioactivity' was taken from our *Radioactivity* CD EP that had come out 20 years before and 'The Model' was from the previous year's *A History Of Rock Music in Ukrainian* album. Wearing my record collector's hat, this is probably one of our most collectable releases. It's certainly the rarest. Only 250 copies were pressed, 50 on black vinyl, 100 on red and 100 on white/grey. I've seen them online selling for as much as £100 each.

VLAD JONATHAN LEE

I have a long-time connection to Ukraine; I grew up in Lviv and Ismail, Ukraine. I first heard The Ukrainians in 1993; it was their *Vorony* album and I was amazed by the music and the melodic arrangements. They hit my heart hard and since then I am following The Ukrainians as much as I can. I was living in Russia and didn't have access to all that Europe had to offer, so had to make do with this poorly-taped recording as there was no way to find CDs or vinyl.

In 1995 I moved to Israel. I immediately acquired all the possible releases on CD. I was a constant client of the Cooking Vinyl airmail shop, where I bought all the singles and other items I was missing from my collection. One of the CD singles I bought was 'Radioactivity'. I am a huge Kraftwerk fan and a Chornobyl catastrophe survivor, and this cover version was so amazingly done. The music and rhythm pierced my heart and soul.

As the years have gone by, I've completely changed my views on Ukraine and the post-Soviet period. I understand many things and the more time passed the more I got emotionally tightened to the band's message to the world, its message for Ukraine and its people. I still have shivers while listening most of the songs and verses, it hits me and pains in me for Ukraine's sake. The Ukrainians help me to struggle along with people of Ukraine, from far but right to the target.

April 2016 and the thirtieth anniversary of the Chornobyl disaster was approaching. I wanted to commemorate this date and have something special on that day, maybe a special seven-inch of my favourite band with 'Radioactivity' on it? Andrij Smirnov, manager of AbyShoMzk, a record company in Kyiv, is a dear friend and I pitched to him an idea which we then approached Len about, releasing 'Radioactivity' on seven-inch vinyl. Len was delighted with the idea, and we did a short run of 250 copies of 'Radioactivity' seven-inch singles in four different colours: black, red and grey/white. (You can still find some copies on Discogs if you search.)

Two years later, I took part in the band's crowdfunding campaign for *Summer In Lviv*. I fell in love with this masterpiece even before I had heard it, because Lviv is the place of my childhood, kindergarten, my first love, school. I felt like the album was made for me. I'm very proud of my fully-signed double LP.

I continue to collect all the Ukrainians' releases. I hope to see them perform one day. Thanks a lot to my beloved Ukrainians for giving me my life, my spirit, my emotions. I love you all.

EVOLUTSIYA - 40 BEST & RAREST 1991 – 2016
RELEASED 24 AUGUST 2016

LEN
We put *Evolutsiya* together as a double CD compilation for Germany to celebrate the 25th anniversary of Ukraine's independence. It was released on Berlin's Eastblok label, which specialises in eastern European music. We worked out the track list with label boss Armin Siebert, having decided that there should be one 'Best Of' CD and one with 'Rarities'. The first collected together the most popular recordings from our six studio albums to date, and the second featured what we considered to be the best tracks from deleted singles, EPs and live albums, plus previously unreleased live and studio tracks. It's one of my favourites, with nice artwork from Piotr Pucyło.

SHCHEDRYK (CAROL OF THE BELLS) EP
RELEASED 4 DECEMBER 2017

LEN
'Shchedryk' is a winter well-wishing song based on a chant that goes back to pre-Christian times. Of all Ukrainian melodies this is probably the most well-known globally although when we hear it in the West it's often as 'Carol Of The Bells' which unfortunately isn't a translation of the traditional Ukrainian lyric. The original speaks about a swallow that flies into a household in the spring and tells the owner that he has newly-born lambs outside and that his farm animals are healthy. He has a beautiful wife and all is well. It was great fun condensing all this into our one minute 23 second version! I think this is one of my favourite Ukrainians recordings, short and Punky.

PETER
Most people in the northern hemisphere have heard this song. It is known as 'Carol of the Bells', but its origin is Ukrainian. Leontovich was a Ukrainian composer in the 1920s who wrote a piece based on Ukrainian new year songs – shchedryvki (yes, there are a separate group of songs just for new year celebrations). The song was re-arranged and given 'English' lyrics. I always thought that it was very twee and sanitised. The original Ukrainian has no Christian references. It's about wishing people happiness and good

fortune in the new year. So we thought we'd go back to the original and give it some of its pagan energy. It ended up as a one-and-a-half minute Punk song. The video, shot by Alex Ochman, completed the pagan theme. It's really high up in my list of favourite tracks, and the video is certainly the best we've done.

ROB BOWKER
At the risk of stoking controversy, on my desert island I get to take two favourite CD/LP covers out of the six or seven I've done: *A Short History Of Rock Music In Ukrainian* (ZRKLP9 – so pleased the magenta got the thumbs up), and *Shchedryk* (ZRKCDS11) because we didn't have to dig too deep to find the gold.

 A WEDDING
SUMMER 2018, UK

OLEG & ELENA MUCHA

Back in 2018 we were truly lucky to have the band perform at our wedding. It was The Wedding Present, you could say… Being Ukrainian myself, it was an absolute pleasure to share our special day with The Ukrainians. We always have fond memories of the best day and the best gig of our lives!

 CHEMIEFABRIK
15 MARCH 2019, DRESDEN, GERMANY

STEFAN HERRMANN, DIE UKRAINIENS

In 2002 I came back to Germany from Odesa in Ukraine, where I had been working in a guitar workshop and as a janitor in a school. I had spent many evenings there with friends and acquaintances, singing, eating and drinking. That summer, my father got married and for the occasion I founded a band which played Ukrainian songs and songs from the Soviet Union. After several performances we got the name 'Die Ukrainiens'.

None of us knew that a band with a confusingly similar name already existed in England. Only years later did some concert-goers tell us that they had come along to see us expecting another band to play. They said that we were still quite young and that it couldn't be us. From that moment we started to be interested in the band 'The Ukrainians'.

A few years later we received emails which were not addressed to us but to this mysterious band called 'The Ukrainians'. On a warm summer evening, after a good Slavutych / Славутич (Ukrainian beer), I decided to contact the band 'The Ukrainians' by email and ask if they wanted to play some concerts together with us.

The answer was quick and clear: 'Yes!'

I brought the unique Leipzig event promoter of Slavic Night on board and that's how we ended up playing two great and beautiful concerts together, in Dresden and Leipzig, in March 2019.

Four years later, we repeated these events. It was more than just a concert, with Ukrainian food, a Ukrainian choir and a Polish house band… It was just great! We are waiting for a repeat. Побачимося!

 ABSTURZ
16 MARCH 2019, LEIPZIG, GERMANY

HENRIETTA MEYER, ORGANISER OF THE SLAVIC NIGHTS

My story begins in a small alleyway in Budapest on a September night in 1997. After a successful journey from Leipzig via Prague and Bratislava to Budapest, me and my friends were eager to toast with a traditional Hungarian Palinka. It was late at night but we found a small, mysterious and colourful shop, where there were not only beverages but also a small department where I came across a diverse jumble of music cassettes by the likes of the Rolling Stones, Piotr Leshchenko, Smetana, ABBA, Johann Strauss and... The Ukrainians.

Being a fan of eastern European music since my early childhood and studying Slavic languages at the time, I had to choose between Leshchenko, whose songs I was very familiar with, and The Ukrainians, whom I had never heard of before this very moment. After much deliberation, I left the shop with a bottle of Palinka and a music cassette by The Ukrainians. Both proved to be a phenomenal choice – I had one of the happiest nights of my life as the music introduced me to the mystical and passionate world of Ukrainian music and language.

The cassette accompanied me to all my parties and lengthy car rides and a lot of people had to listen to my favourite songs 'Cherez Richku, Cherez Hai' and 'Oi Divchino' – whether they liked it or not! I spent many wonderful hours with the music of The Ukrainians, which managed to touch my heart.

As we had no internet back in those days, I did not know much about the musicians behind The Ukrainians, so they were just 'the mysterious Ukrainian band from England'. Eleven years later – during which time I had become a Polish translator, had four children and found my soulmate from Poland – we founded a cultural association with our friends from Poland and Ukraine and organised the first Slavic Night, a music festival for Slavic and eastern European music and culture in Leipzig.

So many guests came to the first Slavic Night on a cold evening n November 2008 – with musicians, bands and choirs from Poland, Slovakia, Russia and Ukraine – that our pub in the infamous east of Leipzig became overcrowded and people celebrated and sang out on the street. Jokingly, I said, 'All right, someday we'll have to invite Haydamaky from Kyiv and The Ukrainians from Great Britain to the Slavic Night. Na zdrowie!' At that time, we could not have guessed that one day this would come true.

Our music festival became more and more successful, and I was regularly looking for new interesting bands. One day in 2015 I saw a poster advertising Die Ukrainiens. Could this be a mistranslation really referring to The Ukrainians? Or a band that covered the songs of The Ukrainians? I searched the internet for Die Ukrainiens and was surprised to find that this band had been performing for several years in Dresden, only a 100-kilometer drive from Leipzig. I sent them an email to invite them to our next Slavic Night where they delivered a fantastic performance, so beginning a beautiful, long-lasting collaboration.

In December 2018, my phone rang. It was Stefan from Die Ukrainiens asking me if we would like to organise a Slavic Night with a double concert of both Die Ukrainiens *and* The Ukrainians, who had already promised to come to Dresden the following March. This was quite short notice for us and I was sceptical as to whether we could get this to work out as typically you have to plan the dates a year in advance.

But it all worked out, and the two bands travelled to Leipzig after their concerts in Dresden. I was thrilled to finally meet The Ukrainians personally and listen to a live concert by them. It was a such wonderful night with The Ukrainians, Die Ukrainiens, the Slavia choir and the Kapela Polska in the club Absturz. So nice, in fact, that we decided to repeat it in 2023.

On 2 June 2023, The Ukrainians once again travelled to Leipzig for the Slavic Night. The wonderful performances of The Ukrainians, Die Ukrainiens, the Slavia Choir and the Kapela Polska, who sang together with the entirety of the audience, will remain in our memories for a long time. The next day we went directly to Dresden after a breakfast in the sculpture garden of our association. This was something very special in the history of the Slavic Nights, being the very first Slavic Night in Dresden. Together with The Ukrainians, Die Ukrainiens and Kapela Polska and many, many guests, we experienced a unique Slavic Night in Dresden, a beautiful eastern European gathering. I can only hope that one day we can repeat it all once more.

THE COMPLETE UKRAINIAN JOHN PEEL SESSIONS BY 'THE WEDDING PRESENT'
RELEASED 2 APRIL 2019

LEN

The Complete Ukrainian John Peel Sessions was a lavish package that included all three John Peel sessions re-mastered for the first time. Released on Hatch Records, it came with a booklet and new sleeve artwork designed by the artist Jonathan Hitchen who had been responsible for the original *Ukrainski Vistupi V Johna Peela* artwork. There were two formats of this new release, CD and vinyl LP, both of which include a bonus DVD.

I love the DVD. It includes two live songs from a sold-out Leeds Polytechnic gig in 1989. These were taken from a VHS cassette which I had squirreled away in a cobweb-covered box in the attic. There was also a fantastic rare TV performance of us from 1988 playing 'Verkhovyno' on a BBC 2 programme called On A Personal Note, which either me or David contributed, again from an old VHS cassette. Included as well was a Ukrainians performance of 'Davni Chasy' ('Those Were The Days') at David's 'At The Edge Of The Sea' festival in 2010.

Not only that, there was a brand new video of Gedgey, Pete and me being interviewed at the Brudenell Social Club in Leeds by Ken Garner, author of the definitive BBC John Peel sessions book, *In Session Tonight*. I had to get a train from Reading to Leeds and it was massively delayed. I ended up running to the Brudenell in order to get there on time for the interview and arrived about two minutes before the cameras rolled, sweaty and flustered!

It's a great package though, and personally I prefer the vinyl version to the CD version because the accompanying booklet is bigger and has more things in it.

'DAVNI CHASY' / 'KATRUSYA' BY THE WEDDING PRESENT
RELEASED 13 APRIL 2019

LEN
30 years after being set as The Wedding Present's first release on RCA in 1988 but pulled because the band felt that the song was not appropriate for their first single on a major label, and even though test pressings had already been pressed, 'Davni Chasy' and 'Katrusya' at last saw the light of day for Record Store Day 2019. Billed as 'The Single That Never Was' on the publicity blurb, the tracks were re-mastered for 21st century ears and the artwork for the sleeve done by Jonathan Hitchen.

JOHN PEEL CENTRE FOR THE CREATIVE ARTS
4 MAY 2019, STOWMARKET, UK

DARREN HAYWARD
I am lucky enough to live in Stowmarket, home of the John Peel Centre. Having seen The Wedding Present and numerous others at this venue, it was a no-brainer to attend this event. At just £11 it was a riot of fun. With some local Ukrainian lads performing some Cossack-style dancing at the front, it was an eventful evening that was topped off by getting a signed setlist.

THE UKRAINIANS

SUMMER IN LVIV

SUMMER IN LVIV
RELEASED 21 JUNE 2019

LEN

Many of the songs on *Summer in Lviv* came about through mine and Pete's experiences in western Ukraine the previous summer, when we re-discovered the changed city of Lviv. Since our last visit it had become a rejuvenated, modern, vibrant and forward-looking place whose official motto is 'Live, work and enjoy yourself', which we incorporated into the lyric of the title track.

Inspired by those experiences, and conversations with people in the city, the album dealt with themes that reflected pre-invasion Ukraine: populations on the move, emigration and a struggle for identity. The album considered the benefits and pitfalls of freedom, and the delicate balance between asserting a national or ethnic identity and denying it to others. If this balance is achieved, it can result in a diversity and acceptance that was very apparent amongst the young in Lviv at that time; but if not, it can lead to conflict – as it did in Ukraine's Donbas region. Of course, at that time we were unable to foresee the horrific events that began with Putin's invasion in February 2022.

This is the serious side, of course, but *Summer in Lviv* also celebrates the Ukrainian nation's natural exuberance and love of life, and the respect and high place that Folk song and dance hold in their culture. Lyrically, I was definitely being influenced more by my experiences and perceptions of modern day western Ukraine and less by traditional Folk styles. In many ways I think this album is probably the best we made.

PETER

We went to Ukraine as tourists just for a few days to see how the country had changed since I'd been before in 1990, 1993 and 1996. I hadn't been for 20 years and it was just like any Western country that you can imagine. Western Ukraine was no different from Poland or the Czech Republic or Hungary. You've got western brands on the high street, you've got café culture, and you've got bars and restaurants selling all sorts of stuff. The city has still got its own architecture, history and identity alongside that, but it's got everything you'd expect of the West. The aspirations of people in that part of the world, particularly Lviv, were that they should be part of Europe. It was such a nice thing to see, and to feel that I'd been a small part of it. It felt to me like a journey had been completed.

Літо у Львові

Тут у місті Лева ти можеш знайти
музику та літні фестивалі
старовинні площі
та кольоритні вулиці

Живи! Працюй! Насолоджуйся!

Тут у Львові можеш себе знайти
В місті культури, історії
архітектури вишуканої

Давай, давай, сподіватися…

Що літо у Львові буде назавжди
Що літо у Львові буде назавжди

тут живуть поети, музиканти
історики, студенти, художники
кожен хоче жити, працювати
всі чекають кращого майбутнього
світлого майбутнього

Літо у Львові буде назавжди
Літо у Львові буде назавжди

Lito u L'vovi (Summer In Lviv)

Here in the city of the lion you can find
Music and summer festivals
Ancient squares
And picturesque streets

Live! Work! Enjoy yourself!

Here in Lviv you can find yourself
In a city of culture, history
And exquisite architecture

Let us, let us hope…

That summer in Lviv will be forever
That summer in Lviv will be forever

Here live poets, musicians
Historians, students and artists
Each one wants to live and work
Everyone is waiting for a better future
For a bright future

Summer in Lviv will be forever
Summer in Lviv will be forever

Photo: Terry Jones

Коли Я Танцюю

Коли я танцюю, коли я танцюю
У танці я існую
І я все розумію
Коли я танцюю, коли я танцюю
Це сильне відчуття
Є лиш танець і я

Коли я працюю, в середині танцюю
Я весело співаю
І про все забуваю
В душі я танцюю, в душі я танцюю
Це сильне відчуття
Є лиш танець і я

Коли я танцюю, коли я танцюю
Це як… вічна весна
Для мене це життя
Коли я танцюю, коли я танцюю
Це сильне відчуття
Є лиш танець і я

Koly Ya Tantsyuyu (When I Dance)

When I dance, when I dance
I exist in the dance
And I understand everything
When I dance, when I dance
It's a powerful feeling
Just the dance and me

When I'm not working, I'm dancing inside
I cheerfully sing
And forget about everything
In my soul I dance, in the shower I dance
It's a powerful feeling
Just the dance and me

When I dance, when I dance
it is like eternal springtime
for me it is life
When I dance, when I dance
It's a powerful feeling
Just the dance and me

Photo: Paul Jackson

We'd gone out for Len's birthday. His partner had arranged for some musicians to play and they actually played some of our songs while we were sat on the rooftop terrace of this café, having a meal overlooking Lviv as the sun was going down. You couldn't imagine a more complete musical feeling.

LEN

Lviv was now like a modern Western European city. It used to be in Poland and the feel of the whole place is Austro-Hungarian. When I went there for my 60th birthday, young people seemed to be going out having fun, going to clubs and enjoying themselves, having money and buying clothes. I'd never ever seen that in Ukraine before. It had become a lot more westernised. I can't imagine what the atmosphere's like now, having experienced Putin's air strikes.

JIM HOWE

My favourite of our newer songs is 'Koly Ya Tantsyuyu', or in English, 'When I Dance'. I love the raw energy and heavy Punky fuzz effect on the bass and how the mandolins weave around.

LEN

The lyrics for 'Dva Vinochky' ('Two Garlands') were inspired by the words of 19th century Ukrainian writer Yakiv Holovatskyy. I wanted one song on the album to have a literary reference and a more folky subject matter – and this was it! The lyric re-tells Holovatskyy's story of a young woman who makes two garlands, one for her Kozak who had to go off to war, and one for herself. She takes them to the edge of a stream and lets them float away. What she doesn't realise is that her Kozak is buried under a cranberry bush in a faraway land after dying in battle.

One of my favourite songs on this album though is 'Zvidky Vy?', which addresses the idea of prejudice and racism. You wander round city streets sometimes and you can feel the tension in the air when there are immigrants walking around. It's really uncomfortable, as well as terribly sad. Unfortunately it exists everywhere, not just in Britain. I've felt it in so  many countries, including Ukraine. The lyric puts the listener into the mind of the immigrant, who just wants to keep their head down and have a peaceful life; mostly they have a healthy work ethic and just want their family to survive – and they just can't understand the hostility. Maybe one day we'll grow up as a species and realise that we're all citizens of the world.

THE UKRAINIANS

PETER

The song 'Chy Znayesh Ty?' first appeared on the *Vorony* album. It's quite unusual because it's a song that I had very little input into. Stepan Pasicznyk wrote most of the lyrics, and Len the tune. Although I liked it a lot it was never anything that we could play live because it was purely vocal with very eastern European time signatures. I forgot about it until we played in Poland in the early 2000s. At one gig, a whole group of people were singing this song at the top of their voices. Clearly this song meant something to them. When I spoke to people after the show, I learned that many people of Ukrainian background in Poland were from families who had been forcibly removed from their villages at the end of the Second World War.

When we started working on the album *Summer in Lviv*, we decided to re-work the track so that it could be played live. The tempo changed, as did the time signature, and of course we added all our instruments.

On our next Polish tour we played it live, and I remember the response of the crowd was even more intense with them singing along and I got all emotional. I remember playing the track, hardly being able to see my guitar because of the tears running down my face. Later, we recorded the track with Monika sharing vocals with Len, which gave an extra emotional angle to it. The video was filmed mainly in my back garden in Leeds and featured a Carpathian blanket which I bought from Lviv in 1996.

LEN

Another song we re-recorded for the album was 'Cherez Richku, Cherez Hai'. It's a firm fan favourite and always goes down well live. But I always thought that there were elements of the original recording that could have been done better, and after years of playing it live it had morphed into something different from the 1991 version. We decided to re-record it

and this time make a video for it as well. For the video we used the event space next to Eiger Studios in Leeds, where we recorded the album. Local photographer Lucy Cartwright, who made our 'Ace Of Spades' video the previous year, came to shoot it. Pete had arranged for Manchester's 'Volya' Ukrainian Choir to sing on the choruses and they did a fabulous job!

GABRIELLE LEWKOWICZ

There is a special place in my heart for The Ukrainians which goes beyond my Polish-Ukrainian roots. Quite simply, I first heard what would evolve into The Ukrainians on John Peel's nightly radio show back in the late '80s. My Polish-born, classical music enthusiast father disapproved mightily of my wild, teenage rebellious adulation for alternative music

(clockwise from top left) Meet the band: Stepan 'Ludwig' Pasicznyk, Kherson, Ukraine, 1993; Allan Martin, Steff Tymruk & Mick West, Poland, 1997; Gordon Clark, roadie & driver; Peter Solowka & Len Liggins; Luddy; Roman Revkniv; Steve 'Steff' Tymruk, Turin, 2008; the seven-piece line-up, April 2007 - Len, Mick, Woody, Paul, Jim, Peter & Steff

(clockwise from top left) Len, Peter, Steff & Paul live in London, 2014 (Pawel Kordaczka); Steff at Leeds Brudenell Social Club, 2022 (Iam Burn); group shot with Monika Niemczynowicz, Leeds, 2014; Steff, Rock na Bagnie, 2023 (Pawel Krupek Krupka); band shot April 2007 (Steff Tymruk); Pete, Woody, Steff & Len live in London, 2014 (Pawel Kordaczka)

and, worst of all, Punk. I was sitting in my bedroom, doing my homework, listening to Peelie and The Wedding Present were doing their Ukrainian session, playing 'Cherez Richku, Cherez Hai', when my dad walked in with a confused, quirky look on his face. He stood and listened for a second. That song had awakened a distant memory for him. I'd never seen that look on his normally stern, darkly pensive face. He even smiled. He told me he knew that song from his youth.

My father passed away when I was 20. He never managed to speak to me of his painful and traumatic youth. His parents had lived in Ukraine and escaped to Poland. He himself grew up under Nazi occupation, near Auschwitz, and then the Russians came. This moment of precious, fleeting connection with him stays in my heart. He's been gone now more than 30 years but when I hear 'Cherez Richku, Cherez Hai', or for that matter anything played by The Ukrainians, I'm back in my bedroom and my dad is smiling. As much as I love all my other music, The Ukrainians is the music I treasure most.

(In Memory of Dr Alexander Lewkowicz.)

DANIEL BAGAN-JONES

My dad, Mykola Bagan, was born in in 1920 in the Western Ukrainian village of Hrushivka. He came to England in 1948 and, after several moves around the country, eventually settled in Waltham Cross, Hertfordshire, and married my mum, Raffaela, who came from Italy. I was born in 1968, and we lived in a shared house with another Ukrainian/Italian family in Enfield, North London.

Growing up, I fondly remember going on coach trips to many Ukrainian events around the country, especially Cheshunt, Guildford, Nottingham, Leicester and Derby, and it was at these that I first experienced and fell in love with traditional Ukrainian music and dance. I remember my dad singing some of the songs to me as a kid, so imagine my surprise when I discovered The Ukrainians, and that they were singing some of these songs on the radio! During that time, I was deeply into the Indie scene, so I was pleasantly surprised with the link with The Wedding Present too! Then, even better, I discovered there were Smiths, Sex Pistols, Kraftwerk and Joy Division, etc. covers. Just brilliant!

Sadly, my dad passed away in 2002, a day before my birthday. As you can imagine, this time of year has become very emotional for me, but I celebrate his life both on that day, and on his birthday in August, by listening to the music that brings back all my childhood memories. I don't know what the neighbours think, but on those days I play songs like 'Verkhovyno', 'Oi Divchino' and 'Cherez Richku Cherez Hai' at full blast!

I hope one day to be able to visit my dad's homeland, hopefully including Hrushivka, but like everyone, I am waiting for a more peaceful and settled time. Many thanks to The Ukrainians, and good luck with all that you do. Slava Ukraini!

THE UKRAINIANS

AT THE EDGE OF THE SEA, CONCORD 2
10 AUGUST 2019, BRIGHTON, UK

DAVID GEDGE

About 15 years ago, Shaun Charman and I went to see The Ukrainians in London and we really enjoyed it. They're brilliant live. Even if you know nothing about them – and they're not even singing in English – it still works because it's such a great sound. It's exciting and people love it.

They've performed at my *At The Edge Of The Sea* festival here in Brighton twice. We had them quite early on, actually – it was only the second festival, in 2010 – because they were a band I wanted to have play as soon as possible. And then, in 2019, they did a tour for the 30th anniversary of the release of *Ukrainski Vistupi V Johna Peela*. I don't usually have bands playing the festival more than once but I just felt that *that* had *At The Edge Of The Sea* written all over it! It was The Ukrainians playing all the tracks from that Wedding Present mini-album and it was actually quite emotional for me to watch. Shaun and I even joined them up on stage for a couple of songs. I love doing things like that at the festival.

SHAUN CHARMAN

Peter was always proud of his Ukrainian-Austrian heritage. Through his dad, his family were involved in the Ukrainian cultural scene in Middleton in Manchester and he'd go to events when he was home. It was interesting visiting his house with the band. His parents were very friendly but didn't speak English that well, so Peter would be talking slowly. It was just part of his background until The Wedding Present had been going for a year or so, but Peter had picked up some of the traditional Ukrainian folk songs, and started to doodle with them at practices.

One particular song was called 'Hopak', and the rest of us would join in. It was one guitar phrase and gradually sped up, so it was fun to play. We had been lucky enough to start recording Peel sessions, and at the third one Peter started playing it as he often did. We all joined in and recorded a minute or so, and left it in the session as a fifth track. John Peel always liked things that were a bit different, and made some kind of approving noise when he played it.

Back in the pub, the idea formed that for our fourth session we could do something really different, rather than another straight session. We knew Len Liggins, who could speak Russian. Peter started to get the songs together and the whole thing took shape. Peel loved it of course, and it was a lot of fun – standing by the mic shouting, 'Hey hey hey'. We were still basically The Wedding Present though, so had more than a touch of us about it, especially the heavy bass.

Over the years, lots of people have asked me why we did it, to which the obvious answer is, 'Why not?'. We always liked to have fun, back to ripping through 'Felicity' and other early cover versions. We used to go to the pub after (and sometimes during) practices and didn't take things too seriously once we'd found our sound. We also appreciated the wide range of musical styles John Peel used to play – it wasn't all post-Punk – and didn't feel like we had to be constricted by anything. We thought Peel would like it too and he did.

I lost contact with Peter for a while after leaving the band, but had been back in contact with David down in Brighton where we both now live. David and I once went up to London to see The Ukrainians at an eastern European centre – watching the crowd go completely nuts. We met more properly with the release of The Wedding Present film, *Something Left Behind*, at the Hyde Park Picture House in Leeds. We bumped into each other in the Brudenell Social Club, talked about football as usual and took part in the Q&A for the film.

It was great being back in touch, but still a surprise when Peter asked if I would join The Ukrainians on stage again. They were playing the original Peel sessions album for the *At The Edge Of The Sea* festival. The idea was for me to play drums on the original session tracks I'd played on first time round. I play the guitar these days with Jetstream Pony, so was really out of practice, and the style was always very different for me. I had a scary practice in Leeds (not fast enough – really?!), but it came together – they are a friendly bunch. We played a warm up gig at the 100 Club in London in May, and then it was on to Brighton.

David also joined us on stage for two songs – the first time three original members of The Wedding Present had been on stage together for more than 30 years and it was for The Ukrainians! David said he looked over at one point, but I was just lost in concentration. It's been great watching the band develop over the years, even before recent events made them so relevant. Peter the mild-mannered teacher by day, mandolin maestro at festivals across eastern Europe in the holidays. Who knew where those original doodles of 'Kossachok' would end?

KAI MAGILL

I was first introduced to The Ukrainians music about 12 years ago when I was a teenager. My dad got me to listen to a record he had, The John Peel Ukrainian Sessions. I hadn't very much interest in music at the time but I had started taking an interest in cossacks and their history and I got hooked on that record. I was very happy to learn that it hadn't just ended with the Peel Sessions, and I have since gone on to collect every other record The Ukrainians have released. During that time I also acquired my own hi-fi system and I have branched out into collecting records of various genres from all over the world. In a way I feel like I have The Ukrainians to thank for sparking that interest, so I'd like to take this opportunity to finally be able to express my gratitude.

The music of The Ukrainians has been a really key part of the soundtrack to my life and has also been well known and admired by my friends because it is so often playing in my car. It would be hard for me to just pick one favourite track but I'd probably have to say 'Cherez Richku, Cherez Hai' if I had to choose. I would also have to give 'Tebe Zhdu' an honourable mention as it's the track I would listen to most when I am feeling down. I'm not really sure why, I don't speak Ukrainian so I have no idea what it's about. I was also really happy to support the crowdfunding campaign for the *Summer in Lviv* album, of which my signed copy is one of the most prized records in my collection.

I was fortunate enough to get to see The Ukrainians live twice, first in 2015 in Newcastle and then again in 2019 in Brighton. Both concerts were awesome experiences that I will never forget.

STOGFEST, FACE BAR
13 NOVEMBER 2021, READING, UK

STEPHEN CHOMIAK

Everyone remembers where they were at the height of the Covid lockdown. At home of course! It gave me an opportunity to plan my 60th birthday celebration, something I wanted to be different from the norm as well as extra self-indulgent. Originally planned for 19 June 2021, lockdown restrictions forced a couple of reschedules and finally it became possible that November. I wanted to host something in the form of a mini-festival including the music most dear to me. A couple of other bands were at the party, and the support included Stranglers tribute band Straighten Out, but what better headliner than The Ukrainians? They were a band I had fallen in love with from their very first release, and which I still proudly own in cassette format.

My origins are Ukrainian and I'm first generation here in the UK. My father was born in the region of Lviv, which I visited for the first time in 2019, inspired by the release of *Summer in Lviv* by The Ukrainians. What a joy it was to hear 'O Ukraino' blasting out in the Prava Beer Theatre! My father held the position of Chairman of the UK Ukrainian Federation back in the 1960s. Sadly, he passed away in 1984 aged 59, so my memories are built on childhood visits to the Ukrainian clubs of Holland Park, London and Nottingham as well as time spent at a Ukrainian boys' camp in West Linton, Scotland. My Ukrainian language skills however are limited to 'dva pyva' (two beers).

I have enjoyed every single album and gig, none more so than their performance at my 60th. Our children's first ever gig was The Ukrainians at the Holland Park Ukie Club, so we hope the love of their music will continue with yet another generation. A big thanks go to Len, Peter and the boys for being such an important and integral part of my life.

FESTYVAL DVD
RELEASED 26 NOVEMBER 2021

LEN

We couldn't play gigs or get together to write or rehearse during the Covid 19 lockdown, so we set about making a few videos by recording and filming a few songs in the cosy isolation of our own homes. Each of us made a recording of our own instrument or voice, simultaneously filming ourselves doing it, then sent the results to Jim and Paul who edited the videos together. That way we had something to put up on YouTube to let people know we were still alive. Once we'd done this, I began to think about all the footage that we'd amassed over the years in the band archive, and the idea for a DVD was born. It was our 30-year anniversary, so I thought it would be nice to have 30 videos together on a disc. What I underestimated was the amount of work that was going to be involved.

I contacted Andrew Lurcuck from Leeds-based True North Productions, who worked for BBC TV. He had already compiled videos for The Wedding Present, so I gave him a ring. It turned out he was a Ukrainians as well as a Wedding Present fan. As I'd recently moved house, all the band archive boxes were still piled up in my living room, so I started to have a mooch to see what we had, and I was pleasantly surprised. I found old VHS tapes and big broadcast quality Beta video cassettes as well as DVD-R disks. They all contained forgotten videos, short films, rare live performances and even a couple of animated films. There were also four videos edited by our old drummer Dave Lee that featured some really atmospheric footage taken of us in Ukraine in the early 1990s by film maker Mark Keane.

As luck would have it, we'd recently done an interview for Kyiv-based TV channel Ukrainer that August, so we got permission from them to reproduce the 14-minute documentary they'd made called 'Who Are The Ukrainians?'. That bonus feature was the icing on the cake.

With all this material collected together, the first job was to get everything digitised and into one format. Andrew kindly did that and then I set about sifting through the lot and picking the 30 most interesting and varied bits, before Pete and I put together a running order. I researched the info for the accompanying 12-page booklet… Who made the videos and when? Where was the footage taken, and what did band members past and present remember about the filming, if anything? Our graphics guru Rob Bowker did some great artwork based on the text and stills I sent him and to cut a very long and incredibly laborious story short, we 'suddenly' found ourselves with a fabulous career-spanning DVD to release!

After all the slog, it was extremely satisfying when world music magazine *Songlines* reviewed the DVD in their May 2022 issue, saying, 'For fans of The Ukrainians this is a true feast, and the most fascinating footage comes from the band's initial visits to the newly independent Ukraine (still looking very Soviet). Some of this is taken from old video tapes, adding a fascinating sense of 'a lost time' to the proceedings.'

MERRY CHRISTMAS EVERYBODY EP
RELEASED 21 DECEMBER 2021

LEN

For a number of years running, Gideon Coe used to play our 'Shchedryk' single on BBC 6 Music in the run-up to Christmas, so this year we thought we'd record something different for him to play. We ventured into the studio to record a fun, Punked-up version of Slade's 'Merry Christmas Everybody'. Sod's law – he didn't play it, but a lot of fans liked it. At the same session we laid down a version of 'V Halitskiy Zemli', which translates as 'In The Galician Land', a kolyadka or Christmas season song that Pete is very fond of. It has a beautiful melody. You can imagine groups of carolers in Ukrainian villages singing it as they walk through snow from house to house to wish their neighbours peace and prosperity. Also on this CD EP is one of our first self-written songs, 'Kolyadka', only previously available on our 1991 'Oi Divchino' twelve-inch vinyl EP.

BRUDENELL SOCIAL CLUB
6 MARCH 2022, LEEDS, UK

IAM BURN

My first engagement was the release of the ten-inch album from The Wedding Present, *Ukrainski Vistupi V Johna Peela*, back in 1989. A friend had already loaned me his copy of *George Best* by The Wedding Present and I really enjoyed it. He told me a few months later that a new album was due to be released and it was a take on Ukrainian music. I had no real idea what this would sound like, but figured it would certainly be intriguing.

   On the day of release, I trundled down to Our Price in South Shields and bought a copy of the new album. I was immediately impressed by the album cover design and the booklet contained within it. I got home and placed it on to my turntable, a little wary of what I was about to hear. A Ukrainian version of the Mary Hopkin classic, 'Those Were The Days', blasted out at me. I thought it was a belter! Surely, the rest can't be as good as this, I thought. I was right, they were even better! I played this album over and over for days, completely hooked but not having a clue of what the lyrics were... I'm not very educated

(clockwise from top left) Brudenell fundraiser for Ukrainian refugees, Brudenell Social Club, Leeds, March 2022: Jim, Peter, Len & Paul; Jim; Len; Peter, Len, Steff & Paul; Peter, Jim & Len; Paul (Iam Burn)

(clockwise from top left) Brudenell fundraiser for Ukrainian refugees, Brudenell Social Club, Leeds, March 2022: Peter; Len & Paul; Paul; Peter; Steff; the crowd (Iam Burn)

(clockwise from top left) Brudenell fundraiser for Ukrainian refugees, Brudenell Social Club, Leeds, March 2022: Woody; Peter & Jim; Peter; Peter & Jim; Peter; Peter, Len & Paul (Iam Burn)

(clockwise from top left) Brudenell fundraiser for Ukrainian refugees, Brudenell Social Club, Leeds, March 2022: Peter; Paul; Len; Peter, Jim, Len, Woody & Paul; Steff; Peter & Len (Iam Burn)

in the Ukrainian language. When The Ukrainians first eponymously-titled album landed a couple of years later, I bought my copy and raced home. Again, I played it to death. I couldn't get enough of it! This has continued until today.

In 2022, Russia invaded Ukraine. I, like the rest of the world, looked on in disbelief. The look of fear and confusion in the faces of the country's populace broadcast into my home via various news outlets was shocking and heartbreaking. Through this band, I felt a connection to the Ukrainian people that would not have existed without their music. The band announced a charity fundraiser at the Brudenell Social Club in Leeds in March. Whilst I wanted to attend the event, I wanted to try and do more. I contacted Peter Solowka via social media and offered my services as a photographer. I volunteered to photograph the event and send the images out to various news outlets in the hope they may be picked up. I also wanted to do something that documented the coming together of people from all walks of life, and from across the UK, to stand together in a vitally important common cause. The images captured also went to MP Alex Sobel and to Tracy Brabin, Mayor of West Yorkshire, who both spoke at the event, so they could demonstrate the positivity and togetherness on display through their channels. And all this because of a band of musicians who like to play their variant of Ukrainian music.

I didn't think I could love the band more than I did. But the gathering at the Brudenell Social Club elevated them to a whole new level. I only wish we had more bands like them!

PETER

Crimea is annexed and there's a low-level continuous war going on in the east. And then the big war comes. The shock of February the 24th 2022 was really immense. It was a feeling like all the progress of Ukrainian independence in the last 30 years – all these dreams that people had, all these stories my father told me about the inevitability of a free Ukraine, were about to come to an end. Those old stories of people trying for independence and failing horribly were about to be re-lived.

I spent the first few days in shock. Looking back on it, I don't think I ate or drank very much. I spent a long time just watching television and looking at news on the internet and feeling helpless. It seems a bit strange now, but it took quite a while to actually think of something that we could do to help. It was the streams of refugees that really got me. Both my parents were refugees from war and to see the helplessness of the Ukrainian people – children and old people just leaving their homes carrying bags filled with their possessions – was too much. These refugees needed support – they lacked basic things like food, medication and shelter. This was beyond the politics of who is right and wrong. Helping the needy was something we could do.

So The Ukrainians would play benefit gigs, with all funds going to support refugees.

THE UKRAINIANS

And we were lucky. Most venues are booked up months in advance, so I was thinking we would be doing benefit gigs which might be in May or June or July, well after the actual invasion. But I checked on the website of the Brudenell Social Club in Leeds and luckily a band had just cancelled a Sunday night show. It was only a week away. I contacted Nathan (the promoter at the Brudenell Social Club) and asked if we could have that date for a Ukrainian benefit and he said 'sure you can'. This left us just seven days to organise as big an event as we possibly could.

I contacted as many artists as I knew with an eastern European connection in Leeds and the surrounding area and asked them if they would want to be involved in a benefit concert for Ukrainian refugees. As you can guess, the response was amazing. Everyone wanted to help as much as they possibly could, so it didn't take long to get a line-up with about six bands who were willing to play from around four in the afternoon until our headline slot around 9pm on the Sunday.

It was a really multi-cultural response. We had groups with so many different European backgrounds: Polish, Spanish, Celtic, Ukrainian, Balkan, even Russian. (This war wasn't caused by Russian jazz musicians living in Leeds!) It was a great feeling to be able to do something to help. It felt completely opposite to the helplessness at the start of the invasion.

And then it just snowballed. The Hebden Trades Club, a venue we had often played, contacted us and asked if we would play a Ukrainian Refugee benefit at their venue too. The problem with that was we couldn't really do midweek shows, and like most venues, their weekend slots were full. We were about to give up on the idea when I said, 'Just a minute, we're playing Leeds on Sunday night, so why don't we do a Sunday lunchtime benefit concert?' Weird as it was, Mal Campbell at the Hebden Trades Club said 'yeah'. So we were set up to play two benefit gigs in one day!

The atmosphere at both gigs was amazing. Both were sold out and everyone was so generous. All the bands played for free, the venues did not charge anything, nor did the sound engineers – even the security guys at the Brudenell donated their wage for that day. The Brudenell bar gave a hefty donation, and we got hundreds more pounds by passing around a bucket! All of our merchandise sales went directly to the charity (not just the profits), and we covered all our food and travel expenses from money the band had saved. In one amazing day, we managed to raise nearly £12,000 for refugees.

Those events started the ball rolling. Word got around and it wasn't too long before we were contacted by local radio and local press asking us to tell the story of the gigs. They were interested in the history of our group and our desire to help the refugees, plus a little bit of the story of the Ukrainian struggle for independence. I was more than happy to help. Pretty soon we had loads of offers to do benefit shows, so many that we had to choose carefully which ones to do. Within a week we had another six shows booked almost every weekend until the middle of April.

We started to think about other ways to raise money for refugees. The first thing we did was start up a 'Just Giving' web page and pointed people to it from our website and Facebook page. It didn't take long before it had over £3,000 on it. Then we thought about merchandise. T-shirts have always sold quite well on our website, so we designed one which was specifically a fundraiser. We translated the Ukrainian national anthem into English and printed it onto the front of a t-shirt (complete with the original Ukrainian script) in the colours of the Ukrainian flag. We sold over 200 of them. We also made some button badges – hundreds were sold. Then I was asked to appear on a TV show where the difficulties of getting Ukrainian refugees into Britain was discussed. All of this helped us to raise awareness of the plight of refugees, and to encourage music fans to donate.

We gave the money to a whole variety of organisations. Our first lot of money went to the AUGB (the Association of Ukrainians in Great Britain). We thought they were best placed to know exactly how Ukrainians would need the money initially. Then we gave substantial amounts to the DEC (Disasters Emergency Committee) Ukraine Humanitarian Appeal. But you could still see there were hundreds of thousands of people pouring across the Polish-Ukrainian border and that not enough aid was getting there. Clearly the organised charities had not got their act together yet.

Then somebody from Leeds approached us needing diesel and ferry tickets for their minibuses. Since the war started, people had been dropping clothes, food and basic supplies at the Leeds Ukrainian Club. They had rooms full of useful stuff, but no way to get it to Poland. Phil Knowles from Octopus Building Services offered to drive to Poland in his two minibuses. So the club volunteers sorted the donations, Phil loaded and drove the vans, and we paid for the diesel and ferries. In all we covered two trips by Phil. We planned a third but by then the focus was supporting the refugees in their new country.

Other groups were doing what they could to raise funds and awareness of the plight of refugees. My favorite of these is a version of our song 'Dity Plachut' sung in English and Ukrainian by Canada's Verkhovyna Choir.

LEN

We gave some of the money to Ukrainians in Leeds. Hundreds of refugees had come to the city and the Leeds Ukrainian Community Centre was their first port of call. Saturdays were the busiest days, when they organised a food kitchen. The last of the funds we raised went there to help provide hot meals for refugee women and children. It was around this time that we got involved with Jah Wobble.

THE UKRAINIANS

'UKRAINIAN NATIONAL ANTHEM IN DUB' (DIGITAL SINGLE) JAH WOBBLE AND THE UKRAINIANS FEATURING JON KLEIN
RELEASED 25 APRIL 2022

LEN

This started with a meeting set up by Mark Hubbard, who used to run the Old Chapel rehearsal studio we often frequented in Leeds 11's Czar Street. The plan was for me to hook up with John Wardle, aka Jah Wobble, who Mark now worked for as part of his road crew. I was totally up for this as John had been the original bass player and co-founder of PIL (Public Image Limited) with ex-Sex Pistol John Lydon. I hopped on a Tube and met up with the legendary Jah, as arranged, at the exclusive Chelsea Arts Club, a private members club in the heart of London for artists, sculptors, writers, film makers and musicians. The idea was for us to discuss a musical collaboration to raise money for the DEC.

John was playing a gig at the club with his band, The Invaders Of The Heart. He signed me in, did a great gig and then we got to chat afterwards. We went through a few options and settled on the idea of a dub version of the Ukrainian National Anthem. The next day I sent John an English translation of the words and waited for him to come back with ideas for a rhythm track. Meanwhile The Ukrainians recorded a choral version of the track and shot some footage of me, Pete, Paul and Steff singing it outside Salisbury Cathedral on the day we were due to play a gig nearby.

John also drafted in his mate Jon Klein, who used to be in Siouxsie and the Banshees and who is also known for his work with Talvin Singh and Sinéad O'Connor. Jon was to play guitar and mix the track, and once the mix was done, I went over to Merton Arts Space in Wimbledon Library, where John does musical jam sessions for local musicians with loneliness issues. It was there that the remaining footage was shot for the video, which involved me, John and Jon Klein playing along to the final track. We also had a jam after, which was nice.

Oh yes, and one little detail I forgot… just before we shot the video footage in the library John said, 'Well, I'm wearing a blue jacket, but it's a shame I haven't got anything yellow, because then I'd be wearing the colours of the Ukrainian flag as a symbol of my support.' I whipped the yellow duster out of my fiddle case and we wrapped it round his neck. Job done!

JOHN WARDLE (AKA JAH WOBBLE)

I was introduced to Len from The Ukrainians by Mark Hubbard, my bass tech. I was very keen to help in any way that I could, so I enlisted the help of Jon Klein and Anthony

Hopkins, who I run 'Tuned in' with. It's a community music project based in the London Borough of Merton. We have built a recording studio there. Anthony is presently involved in the process of the settlement of Ukrainian refugees coming into the borough. It was a lot of fun putting the track together. And well done to Len and the rest of the band for initiating this.

PETER

The first six months of 2022 were certainly a busy and very positive time for us. In all we managed to raise over £26,000 for refugee charities, a figure I am really proud of. It seems small compared to the millions that mega big corporate fundraising machines can do, but it came from the fans and followers we've built over the years. This book is another place where I can say thank you on behalf of those whose suffering we managed to reduce, at least a little bit.

THE UKRAINIANS

TOGETHER FOR UKRAINE

TOGETHER FOR UKRAINE
RELEASED 24 AUGUST 2023

LEN

I wanted to put a record together to raise more funds for the Ukraine Humanitarian Appeal, but we didn't have any new, unreleased recordings. What we *did* have in our archive were three or four cover versions of our songs that we'd been sent over the years, including 'Oi Divchino' by a 'no-wave queercore' band from New York City called God Is My Co-Pilot. I contacted all the artists to find out if they'd be happy for their recordings to go on a fundraising EP, and they were. Great! Then I thought, why don't I contact other musicians I know to find out whether they'd be up for recording one of our songs as well? Maybe we could get an album together? I sent out dozens of emails and Facebook messages, waited… and was overwhelmed by the reaction. Even though they'd have to pay their own recording costs, a lot of people really wanted to be part of the project.

Over the next few months tracks started arriving: David and The Wedding Present came up trumps with a surf-style version of our 'Teper My Hovorymo' instrumental featuring our Peter on guitar; TV Smith, who I'd recently met at a festival, did a stripped-down vocal and acoustic guitar version of 'Polityka'; Attraktor from Kyiv, featuring our first drummer Dave Lee and bass player and singer Sasha Pipa, who had been in the massively successful Ukrainian band VV, turned out a full-on manic version of 'Cherez Richku, Cherez Hai'… and they kept on coming! We got tracks from the fabulous Warsaw Village Band and Czeremszyna in Poland, then three more popped into my inbox from the Canadian Ukrainian bands Tyt i Tam, Zapovid and Vostok. Eventually we got 18 tracks. I was so excited!

PETER

Over the years we've come across many bands that have been influenced by us or who we like, and so to raise further money for Ukrainian refugees, we released an album of cover versions but with a twist, i.e. we've asked *other* people to cover *our* songs. We put one of our own songs on as well, at the end. It's atypical because it's a capella with three voices. It sounds like a prayer. Roman took a lead in writing it and sings on it. It's called 'Dity Plachut' and means 'The Children are Crying'. He wrote it before there was an independent Ukraine. It's as relevant now as when we wrote it. It was on the very first album and appeared on one of our Peel sessions. It's almost full circle, from Roman's nightmare vision of what Ukraine could be, because its coming true now in many parts of Ukraine.

LEN

What I really like about this album when I listen to it now is that it's a journey of a listen. There are bands from the UK, Germany, Poland, Ukraine, the USA and Canada, and the styles of music they each play vary so much. It took a lot of trial and error and discussion for Pete and myself to find a track order that we thought worked, but as always we eventually got there.

TV SMITH

I first came across The Ukrainians in the early '90s when I signed to the same label as them. I'd heard some of their songs on John Peel already, and had wondered why a band would choose to sing in Ukrainian. It seemed a bit of a gimmick but it worked – folky and exotic at the same time – and now I got the chance to take their CD home with me, one of the advantages of them being label mates. I liked it and played it quite a bit.

  We played a few gigs together too, and then dropped out of touch for 30 years or so, until we both ended up on the bill at a small festival in a cowshed in Dorset in 2022. Len from the band introduced himself to me again, we did a bit of reminiscing, and then he told me about a project he was planning to raise money for Ukrainian refugees, a selection of bands and artists covering songs by The Ukrainians, either sung in the original language or translated into English. He asked me if I would help out.

  Of course, it would have been too simple to try the English option. Always up for a challenge, I said I'd have a go at singing in Ukrainian and recorded an acoustic version of one of the songs in my home studio. I was pretty pleased with my attempt at phonetically copying Len's vocal, and sent it off to him. There then followed weeks of email exchanges with Len correcting every wrong syllable, of which – so it turned out – there were many, followed by me heading back into my studio to re-record single words and phrases. Eventually we settled on a final version that Len seemed happy with, and by now the lyrics were so embedded in my head that I went out and performed the song at a few gigs, singing in Ukrainian – much to the confusion of the audience. But I also flogged a few copies of the finished CD at the merch stand, and raised a bit of money for the cause. All in all, it was a project well worth being involved with, and I can only salute The Ukrainians for, far from using Ukraine as a gimmick, showing their complete commitment to the country and people they love.

DAVID GEDGE

I've recently been working with Peter again for the first time since 1991, because The Ukrainians decided to release a benefit album for refugees from the Russian invasion of Ukraine. Len contacted me and explained that the idea was that different bands would cover a Ukrainians track. I spoke to the rest of the current members of The Wedding Present and they were up for it, but Jon (Stewart, Wedding Present guitarist) was busy doing stuff for Sleeper, his other group. However, the suggested recording date coincided with Peter being in the south, for the Womad festival, so I said, 'Why don't you come to Brighton while you're down and we can go into the studio here?' It's the same studio that we recorded our *24 Songs* seven-inch singles series in. We recorded a track called 'Teper My Hovorymo' with Peter playing his part on electric guitar. We did it in 'classic' Wedding Present style, so, in a strange way, it'd now come full circle. By that, I mean, here we were, in a studio recording Ukrainian music, but in the same way that we started out doing, with 'Cossachok' in 1986, on electric guitars, bass and drums.

When I was compiling tracks for The Wedding Present's *24 Songs* compilation album, I had six sides of vinyl to fill and so I decided to put all the extra tracks on it that I could find. I asked Len if he minded me using 'Teper My Hovorymo' and he said 'It's your recording, you can do what you want with it,' so it's the final track on the new Wedding Present album!

And, when we toured in 2023, Jon had the idea that The Wedding Present should walk out on stage as it played over the PA. It worked very well. It's a very evocative piece of music, as is all of the music of The Ukrainians.

CHEMIEFABRIK
3 JUNE 2023, DRESDEN, GERMANY

OKSANA HENDYS

Amazing individuals and timeless values make up the world, staying with us forever. A Ukrainian girl was introduced to unforgettable vibes in 2003 in Kraków. She was in love with life and a very special man. 'Oi Divchino', 'Oy Dunayu Dunayu' and 'Vorony' were there in sorrow and joy. Time flies by… a day of peace was marred by war. The girl abandoned her home. 'Hopak', 'Chy Znayesh Ty?' and 'Koroleva Ne Pomerla' accompanied her. It took just 20 years to see The Ukrainians again in Dresden in 2023. The musicians radiated so much warmth and energy, as if we were back in those old good moments of joy and happiness. Magic tunes healed her weary soul, and made her believe that light will overcome the darkness.

OLEKSANDR PROKOPCHUK
(translated from Ukrainian by Christian Weißenborn)

From Kyiv to Dresden…
It was a time when everything seemed possible, when Ukraine became free, but the cultural space was littered with Russian music, books and films. When Ukrainian rock music was making its first tentative steps. When we didn't really understand where we were going, but it seemed that we had wings. And at that moment a concert took place in Kyiv in the 'Podil' district, and only many years later we understood the importance of this concert, played by The Ukrainians. It was an explosion! It was full of "western drive". Rock, post-Punk, new fresh wave, but in our native Ukrainian language. Of course, we knew about the existence of Ukrainian culture in the diaspora, and even listened to some bands, but it was something distant and forbidden. And then the legends were there on the Kyiv stage. And we were young, drunk and happy. After the concert, we bought cassettes and t-shirts of the band, which made us even happier. We put on these shirts and sang 'Oi Divchino' and 'Cherez Richku, Cherez Hai' in the streets of Kyiv.

But now it's 2023 and the world has changed completely. It has become crazy and unpredictable. Fate has taken me to other worlds and countries. I've been living in Germany for many years now. And one day I luckily could live another concert of The Ukrainians. I felt young and happy again when I saw The Ukrainians again, this time on the stage of a small club in Dresden. For me, they were like old best friends. It was an evening full of drive, nostalgic memories, joy and tears. I remembered the past peaceful times in Ukraine. I remembered about my friends with whom we were in Kyiv 30 years ago for a concert. Some of them are no longer with us, some of them are now defending with weapons in their hands the freedom of Ukraine, we are now at war with our eternal enemy Russia.

Thank you, my favourite group, thanks to The Ukrainians. Your music is always full of freedom and faith in our victory. Long live The Ukrainians! You are what rock'n'roll should always be! Glory to Ukraine and its heroes!

 ROCK NA BAGNIE FESTIVAL
1 JULY 2023, BIELSK PODLASKI, POLAND

RAFAL KASPRZAK, ALIANS
We toured with The Ukrainians many years ago and performed with them again at the *Rock Na Bagnie Festival* in Poland. We work with so many Ukrainian citizens in our everyday life, because of the war started by Putin.

THE UKRAINIANS

ALEXANDER OCHMAN

Being a Mancunian with eastern European roots meant the music of The Ukrainians resonated with me instantly. Having a Polish heritage meant I grew up surrounded by folk tales, dancing and music at the Polish Saturday School in Moss Side. A lot of these songs and tales involved a shared history with neighbouring Ukraine, which ignited a fascination with Ukrainian culture and its similarities. Some years later, I befriended a number of Ukrainians and started travelling there frequently, all over, and even documenting and interviewing soldiers in the Donbas. I got more and more engrossed in Ukrainian folk music and one day I came across the track 'Davni Chasy' from The Wedding Present *John Peel Sessions*. I loved it and started finding more and more tracks of The Ukrainians that were fusing Slavic folk tunes with Western Punk and rock. This fusion was electric for me as it combined the two sides of my identity: British innovation with a Slavic soul.

When I was in my last year of studying filmmaking at the Northern Film School in Leeds, I saw a leaflet advertising a concert of The Ukrainians at the Brudenell Social Club. I couldn't believe it. A band I'd known for a few years was performing down the road from me in Hyde Park, Leeds. I put on my Dr Marten's and a vyshyvanka (an embroidered Ukrainian shirt) that I had bought on a market in Lviv and got lost in musical ecstasy. The next day, I popped the band a message saying that I was a film director and that I wanted to make them a music video. Pete Solowka met me for a pint later that week and we talked about the band, the music and its message. I presented some of my ideas and I got working on a script for the band's rendition of 'Shchedryk', or 'Carol of the Bells'.

This was one of the most magical music videos I've directed, because it was a truly community experience. The Ukrainian community in Huddersfield allowed us to use their grounds for the setting of our video that would tell the tale of the last night of the pagan gods and the rise of Christianity.

We had spectacular costumes thanks to Manchester's Ukrainian community and Linda Szlachetko helped massively with choreography. The Podilya Dance Ensemble put on a fantastic show, one that we'd rehearsed in Manchester's Ukrainian Cultural Centre, 'Dnipro'. I'm forever grateful that we could get such a large turnout of young and old British Ukrainians who appeared and danced in the video. Len Liggins played the leader of a pagan tribe and the rest of the band members played Orthodox priests who would later topple a totem and crash the party. Len was a born actor and fitted the role perfectly. After the filming, we continued partying into the night enjoying good vodka and jumping over the bonfire like true Slavs. Our cameraman Dennis Galenkov even walked across the embers barefooted.

The band loved the video and we got a lot of positive feedback from fans so the same year we ended up doing more music videos. One was called 'Shche Sto Hram' ('One More Drink'), where we played around with themes of communist repression and satirised it.

Afterwards, we made another music video called 'Sterezhitsya Kozakiv' (which roughly translates as 'Beware of the Kozaks'). This song is one of my favourites because I loved the lyrics and it really fuelled my writing when completing the script of the video. It was politically relevant, as it reflected how many oppressive regimes have tried to subjugate the Ukrainian people but they would always get toppled. We recreated the Kyiv Maidan protests and created a neon paint folk-patterned wall that was the backdrop of our video. Additionally, we created a calendar with months in which different tyrants ended up torn and scattered on the floor. Community togetherness once again made the video possible, with Leeds Ukrainian Club providing the venue and catering. My Dad, Jan Ochman, also helped us massively, creating the masks and totem for the video. Later we donated the totem to the club in Leeds for future kids to enjoy.

Since these amazing times creating for the band, I continue to follow them and filming their gigs whether in the UK or abroad. The last gig in Poland was called *Rock Na Bagnie* ('Rock on the Swamps'). The journey there was mental as I drove from Warsaw to a remote town in eastern Poland seeing elk, deer and wolves along the way. Luckily, a CD with tracks of the Ukrainians kept the animals at bay and nothing flew through the windshield.

THE PIER
14 OCTOBER 2023, BRIGHTON, UK

CHRIS GLEED-OWEN

Len and I met briefly at the Brighton Pier gig and I was saying about how me and my mates used to listen to The Ukrainians' *Pisni Iz The Smiths* EP (especially 'Batyar') before going out on a Friday night, when we were students in Coventry. We used to get totally razzed up on a couple of cans of Helden Bräu Super before going out and The Ukrainians provided the soundtrack!

I was a Weddoes fan originally, and had the Peel sessions album, which I loved. When The Ukrainians formed, I used to go to a few of their gigs around the Midlands in the early days, c1993-1994. I'm pretty sure I went to at least one in a Ukrainian club. Maybe Derby. I'm from Notts originally, so there were always Polish and Ukrainian clubs around. I have a red t-shirt with a blue logo somewhere still from the early days. I reckon me and my mates were always on the folky side of Indie/Rock, so their music was right up our straße.

A memorable gig was the *Endorse It In Dorset* festival in 2005. Then I saw them in London about 2010, and again for the Wedding Present Peel album show at David Gedge's *At The Edge of the Sea* in Brighton in 2019. I couldn't make it to any of the more recent benefit concerts but I was glad to catch them at Brighton Pier. It was a great gig, albeit a bit er... seated!

HAIRY DOG
13 JANUARY 2024, DERBY, UK

SEURAS OG

I hadn't ever really thought myself a massive Ukrainians fan; after all, in music junkie parlance, I only have about four of their albums. But it was as I was relenting to my wife's entreaties to cull my t-shirt pile that I realised I must be, in that I had two of theirs. No single other band has ever achieved that pinnacle of acceptance!

Dial back rather too many years, and I was a somewhat impoverished CD buyer, reduced to scouring the local library for anything and everything I could copy. Yup, I was killing music with my C90s, and the record library at Solihull was pretty impressive back in the '80s and '90s; much better than Birmingham, tickets held with both. Amongst the array of Punky new wave, heritage rock dinosaurs, folk and country, they also had a 'world' section. It may have been called international then, for all I know, but, in the early to mid-90s, the cover of *Vorony* looked out at me appealingly, all exotic and exciting. The label gave few clues, but I had a dim recollection of reading, a year or so before, about an experimental side project of The Wedding Present, Indie faves of John Peel that I had never quite latched onto. Nonetheless, worth a punt, I thought, imagining something pastoral and plunky, maybe a bit like Planxty.

I was wrong, it proving a brutal and profoundly uplifting shock. The mix of stentorian vocals, clattering mandolins, soaring accordion and the full-on assault of the rhythm section was nothing like anything I had even ever imagined. Rhythm section is a quaint way to describe the steamroll of industrial-grade bass and drums, pounding and pulverising the background, with electric guitar scything rhythmically through the gaps. I won't deny it, it wasn't instantaneous; it took at least a minute or so to completely find myself immersed in this magnificent, thorny-barbed hedge of sound.

Everyone I knew had to listen. Not all shared my enthusiasm, it's true, it becoming one of my many yardsticks to determine the savvy of my friends and family. They loved it? Wise and sensible people. They didn't? Fools and civilians.

Over the years I picked up both the debut and the fabled John Peel sessions. And later stuff too, although *Vorony* remained my first love. Or maybe *Respublika*. Anyhow, the century changed and circumstances changed with it. I still hadn't seen them, something I was eager to amend. It was 2015 before I did, at the now burnt down Rainbow in Digbeth, Birmingham. They weren't even in the main room, but down in a concrete dungeon, window-free and stark. It was to promote *A History of Rock Music in Ukrainian*. I had seen the video for their take on 'Ace of Spades' and was excited, all the more so as I spied the band in the nearby Old Swan, Brum's oldest pub, where they had had some pre-gig tea. I suspect I gushed some nonsense about what I was hoping for.

Given that I was just picking up the rudimentaries of writing reviews, my then platform was a blog/blorum/bulletin board, *The Afterword*, the post mortem online community bequeathed by *Word* magazine. (Look it up, it's still going!) In the way they still do now, the band were manning their own merch, and I recall asking Mr Liggins' permission to use the YouTube clip in my review, feeling very chuffed that he was all for my so doing. It's possible he'll remember the gig, as his voice was near shot that night and he was taking slugs alternately from a noxious linctus and from a bottle of vodka circulating the tiny audience. It was fab. My review? It was never written, another poster having caught them in York the night before.

As the years passed, I always seemed to miss their somewhat rare outings down my way. But I kept an eye out. The horrors of the further Russian incursions of 2022 gave them some unexpected publicity, though the opportunities were taken to raise funds for the victims of that aggression. It shouldn't have taken a war to bring about a tribute album to the band either. If you've bought this book and haven't yet bought this album, do so immediately! It's very good as well as being for an acutely vital cause.

Full circle; I have just seen the band play live once more, this time in Derby in 2024 and this time I did get to write my review. To spare you reading it, it were bloody great. The band, obviously. But you knew that, they always bloody are. And then that nice Mr Liggins asked me to pen this piece.

Why are The Ukrainians not huge? They should be, but shhhh! Maybe it's better they're not. Our secret. Not a recipe for world domination, that's true, but as long as they ply their idiosyncratic muse, please, please, make it at least worth their while. They are worth mine.

 GREEN TOWERS
23 MARCH 2024, HINCKLEY, UK

MARK GRIFFIN

In 1991 I bought a Cooking Vinyl compilation CD which included a Ukrainians track and I was blown away by their music. The following year we went to *Glastonbury Festival*. We knew the Ukrainians were playing so we made our way to the Acoustic Tent to see them live for the first time. They were even better than we could have imagined and the music just lured you in, the tent was packed and the crowd were bouncing. I knew then we would be seeing these guys again. Over the years we have watched them many times all over the country, and recently, 32 years after we first watched them at Glastonbury, we were over the moon to have them play our little festival in Hinckley, Leicestershire. It was a surreal moment for us and one we will always cherish.

THE UKRAINIANS

PAUL BRIGGS

Being in the band was all fairly bizarre and memorable, but it's funny how the thing I used to really detest is now my fondest memory, and that is being in the back of a crappy old transit van on the M62 or somewhere with the rest of the band. We were a strange, weird bunch to be put together and the stories and the banter would just be hilarious. The band and the crew were mostly northerners and just really decent people and the funniest people you could imagine. If you were on your way somewhere, and you need a bit of cheering up, there were things you could do. I used to ask Luddy to do his impression of the pervy priest. It was hilarious.

GORDON CLARK

We got on pretty well most of the time. Everybody gets niggles about other people's smelly feet from their socks or whatever. As the driver, you want to stay awake when you're driving the van so you're playing music but other people want to sleep so they want you to turn the music down and they want you to close your window, even though you need the fresh air to keep you awake. Of course, it was vice-versa when we changed drivers and I was the one trying to sleep.

We had some great gigs in Lucerne in Lake Geneva. We supported The Prodigy at one of them. When we arrived at the big open area that was serving as our dressing room, we proceeded to demolish the rider, drinking all the beer and vodka and eating all the food. Later, someone came along and told us that the rider wasn't just for us but was for the other headline bands as well, including The Prodigy. I don't think they were very happy with us.

One night, Roman decided to empty the contents of my bum bag on stage and show everyone what I had in it while I was changing the strings on his mandolin. It was quite funny, but I guess you had to be there...

LEN

The thing I have the greatest regret about not remembering is something Gordon casually mentioned many years after it happened. He turned up to a gig we were playing and afterwards we all had a beer together and reminisced about our years 'on the road' in the early '90s. Then, across the table, through the chatter, I overheard heard Gordon's words '…It's like that time Len met John Lydon and Paul Weller.'

Uh?

'Gordon, what was that?'

'You know, Len, after that festival wherever it was and you were pissed and holding your own with John Lydon and Paul Weller.'

'Yeah, right. You're pulling my plonker.'

'No! You did!'

GORDON CLARK

Touring with The Ukrainians changed my life. I was exposed to so many brilliant world music bands when we toured around Europe. It opened my eyes and ears to all different sorts of music. When I finished touring, I did an access course so I could go back to university and I ended up studying and getting a BA Honours degree in world music. So The Ukrainians did change my life and I think their music changed a lot of people's perceptions as to what Indie music can be. It introduced the folk elements of Ukrainian music and listening to music in a different language as well. A lot of people would probably think they couldn't do that but the music spoke for itself, so you didn't really need to understand what the words were. It was just the energy and the fun. They were a really fun band to watch, and standing at the side of the stage in the evenings I really, really enjoyed myself. I sang along to the songs, joined in with the late night drinking sessions afterwards and sang along because I knew quite a few of the songs. I didn't have a clue what the words are – but I can still sing them!

We had some really, really dedicated fans who followed us round all over Europe. They'd look after us, show us around towns and the local haunts and they'd make our lives more bearable while we were on the road. It's a shame we don't meet up with them. I really do miss some of those guys.

One word to sum up being with The Ukrainians? An education. I saw parts of the world that I would never have seen otherwise, met some wonderful people and made friends for life. It had a very profound impact on my life.

PAUL BRIGGS

The trip to Ukraine completely changed me. I came back a very different person, but being a young musician from the UK back then, there were certain things that you know you wanted to accomplish and achieve. You wanted to play on a proper tour and you want to be in a proper studio. We were at Monnow Valley studios on the Rockfield complex – a studio people have actually heard of – things like that. You want to record albums and have a proper tour bus and stuff like that. You want to do a John Peel session, which we were incredibly privileged to do in Maida Vale. That was amazing, just to be in there and witness the history. I went over to the guy who was the engineer on that day and I said, 'Is this the actual room that David Bowie was in? And Marc Bolan?' He said, 'Yeah, yeah, this is the one, the exact one.' You see it in the background on old BBC footage. Not only that, but he was the actual engineer on those sessions and the stories he had were absolutely incredible. The Ukrainians fulfilled all those ambitions for me. I became a fan rather than a participant after that, which was much more fulfilling for me. So I'm very grateful for the opportunity and the chance I got.

The Ukrainians work extremely hard at being different. They took their sort of underreported culture and made something new and unique. Nobody else can do what The Ukrainians do. You get bands come out every now and then – Oasis are a good example, fantastic as they are, and there's 200 other bands all trying to be Oasis. There's very little that's unique or different. But The Ukrainians are absolutely wonderful, and if you were to write the concept of the Ukrainians on a piece of paper, it wouldn't make any sense whatsoever. But go to a gig and try and stand still. It's impossible. You can't do it.

If I had to use one word to describe being in The Ukrainians, it would be 'permanently knackered'. Okay, that's two words. It was a privilege. It was an absolute privilege to be accepted into the band and for me to then have all those experiences with them.

ALARIC NEVILLE

Like anyone who has toured with bands, I hold to the convention of omertà even if decades have passed since the escapade. What goes on on the road stays on the road. Many of my memories of live performances by The Ukies stay in my mind as fabulous nights when the alchemy between band, audience and venue all combined to make magical musical moments. The songs live on in studio recordings and thankfully some live albums too. Fans in the audience will have their own memories of special nights but the band and road crew see the whole picture of what is, after all, a job. As the legendary Charlie Watts of the Rolling Stones put it, being in a band for 25 years, you work for five but spend 20 years hanging around, so my insider stories come from the hanging around part the punters rarely see. Thankfully, The Ukrainians are still touring and still recording, so the story isn't finished yet.

WOODY

I have plenty of memories from going to gigs; Mick using an ironing board as a keyboard stand; Mick spilling a whole bottle of beautiful Polish vodka driving back to Germany in a van after a Polish gig and me wanting to kill the fecker; Mick being driven around the airport in a wheelchair, getting priority boarding when he had sciatica (he looked like a lucky tramp); buying beautiful hashish in Holland at a festival and the mission (should we accept it) of trying to smoke it all before flying home (we were so pied); many shocking and terrible, long drunken drives over rough Polish roads in various minibuses; seeing a wolf (or coyote) and two bears in the Rockies; being eaten by giant mosquitoes; being given a famous reggae star's posh brandy at a festival in the UK because it wasn't the right brand.

I like playing 'Zavtra'. It's one of my consistently favourite Ukies songs – short, dynamic and folksy with a full-on Punk rock ending. It's got all the best tricks that the band use. And I thought the Sex Pistols EP had pretty good hybrid arrangements of Punk songs on it.

Mick was a great Punky guitarist and those recordings blew some life into the band.

I do like the traditional music but I'm generally not into nationalism too much. I remember driving back from Knockengorroch, a fab festival in the hills of Dumfries and Galloway, and listening to *Diaspora* on the stereo and hearing the word 'Ukraino' way too much. It made me a bit worried. It would be like being in a traditional Scots band and singing the word 'Scotland' all the time. Although, I get that in the current situation pride in Ukraine is to be celebrated.

JIM HOWE

One of the main things I like about being in The Ukrainians is the range of audience members that attend our shows. We seem to bring together people of all ages from various ethnicities and cultures. As a band we are comprised of individuals from different backgrounds and geographical locations. We may have arguments at times but I think we get on well with each other on the whole, and we love each other really.

LEN

Although we had our occasional differences, instinctively both myself and Pete knew what we wanted The Ukrainians to be. It has been a very creative partnership and I'm very proud of what we've achieved together.

REBECCA WALKLEY

After *Summer In Lviv* was released in 2019, I assumed the gigs would thin out and that Len would spend more time on other recording projects and less time playing with The Ukrainians. I retired, Covid temporarily stopped play and we decided to move to East Anglia. Then in February 2022 Russia stepped up its hostilities towards Ukraine and everything changed. The band went on the road, eventually raising on the way to £30,000 from merchandise and gig ticket sales for the DEC Ukraine Humanitarian Appeal. I helped by selling merchandise and people gave generously.

Little did my 14-year-old dancing cossack self know that I would be dancing to Ukrainian tunes for most of the rest of my life. It's been a rollercoaster of a ride. When you marry someone, you marry their family. When you marry a musician, you marry the band. Holidays and high days are often when the band needs to rehearse and play, so you have to learn to share. But my life would not have been so rich without The Ukrainians being a part of it, and I count myself lucky that Len chose me and didn't settle for one of the contestants on the cruise ship!

WLODEK NAKONECZNY

Enthusiasm and energy are always constants with The Ukrainians. I realised this after the concerts on the first tour in 1996 and at every concert thereafter. I always got a boost of energy that carried me for a long time and motivated me to work. A certain ritual was repeated; after the concert, with each beer I drank the stress melted away, the language loosened and the layers of English hidden in my subconscious were activated, which I awkwardly wanted to share. With each of their arrivals, I had more to share because I was working on it.

As befits English gentlemen, they always complimented my 'better and better' knowledge of Shakespeare's language. They spoke with accents, which made it impossible for me to understand them. The exception was Rat, with whom I had normal contact from the beginning. Why? Maybe because he was speaking slowly and clearly. I not only had a good conversation with him, but also sang with him. One evening we murdered The Pogues' 'Dirty Old Town' together, although other voices were also involved in the crime.

I suffered in that my level of English prevented them from discovering the depth and sensitivity of my personality – and they could possibly suffer from a similar dilemma, so it's a draw on that point. Not to mention the mutually enriching philosophical debates and multi-level discussions on historical and contemporary issues that we have not had. But I liked them very much, individually and collectively, and I simply loved being with them. Unlike me, they were a very modest, unproblematic, sociable team who enjoyed worldly pleasures (we happened to converge on this last point). And they had a great sense of humour, so English.

Without a doubt, The Ukrainians are a very important band. Their concept was ahead of its time. No one before had translated Ukrainian folklore into the universal rock 'n' roll language in such a natural, unobtrusive way, with such casual, unobtrusive virtuosity and with such knowledge of the matter – traditional Ukrainian music – whilst creating a completely original, interesting creation.

There are many things I don't know – what Peter's idea was, how he managed to convince other musicians to follow it and why they consistently followed this path. Back then, I thought that such an attempt to exist and stay in the Western music world with a non-English-language programme (quite exotic, because who knew what Ukraine was at that time?) was an act of courage; today I would say it was a backbreaking task. And they did it, they did it very professionally. The addressee of this music was probably not the Western diaspora, raised on polka-folk hybrids or wistful adaptations of traditional songs, and therefore resistant to this type of expression.

Poland, where the mental revolution after August 1980 also affected the Ukrainian minority, was slightly different in this case. In the 1980s, the foundations of alternative culture were already established. The audience was sophisticated enough to appreciate this offer. For Ukrainians in Poland, The Ukrainians became a cult band. And – let it not sound trivial or pathetic – naturally, because they came from the UK, they positioned Ukrainian culture within the framework of Western culture. This was already the building block for the creation or self-assertion of a Ukrainian identity – oriented towards the West and breaking with colonial subordination to Moscow. This was nothing new; this trend had been defined in the 1920s, but it had been drowned in blood during the Stalinist era. After 1980, the continuation of this process began in Poland slightly earlier than in Ukraine, which had been pacified for centuries and was stuck in a cultural divide. (Today's war in Ukraine is another bloody attempt to reverse this trend.)

The Ukrainians were an important band also for many Poles. Because there was sentiment in Poland for Ukrainian folklore, a legacy of centuries of coexistence of both cultures within one country. And there was a sentiment for Punk-rock that made it easier to survive the dark times in the 1980s. All this had a significance greater than aesthetic experiences. It helped build bridges, integrate different environments and generations, and open the minds and hearts of many people. And it also had a real impact on the development of the Polish folk and world music scene, which was just emerging in the 1990s. The music of The Ukrainians is perceived as one of the most important inspirations for many bands from this community in the search for their own path.

It was similar with Belarusians. The Ukrainians' creation greatly influenced them (and they were always present at concerts, especially in Białystok) and their identity choices, including the choice of the Belarusian language or the ethno-rock convention of their own artistic expression. Many musicians and artists I met emphasised this fact whenever we talked.

It seemed to me that The Ukrainians were destined to be massive in Ukraine, but nothing like that – to the extent I expected – happened. This was for a few reasons. There was never much interest in rock there. The USSR was isolated from society, so it was difficult to find a listener with a developed taste and awareness of the product he was dealing with. Interest in this genre of music was limited to strictly niche circles, equally undereducated in the history of the genre and its evolution. There was no place for such music at all in the media. And there was especially no room for more ambitious Ukrainian-language music. Apart from a short-term revival during subsequent revolutions, this has always been pushed to the margins. It was dominated by a bizarre – from a Western perspective – 'entertaining music' product, based on post-Soviet sentiments, mass-produced and created according to Moscow patterns. And it was this product that achieved mass triumph. It was intended for the entire post-Soviet market, so there was huge money behind it and it was also one of the post-colonial chains serving to control Ukraine in the sphere of pop culture. This situation began to change only after Maidan 2014.

I wouldn't dare to estimate how much influence The Ukrainians have had on the development of rock, ethno-rock, folk-Punk, etc. in Ukraine. I have been following this music from the very beginning. The band appeared at the beginning of Ukrainian rock music, and their attempts to combine ethnic inspiration with different styles were often very successful. However, I would say that it became the most interesting when it comes to quality and style in the 2000s – all a decade after the band's debut. This proves something… pioneers in any field never have it easy. In the case of Ukraine, the process of learning and assimilating Ukrainian cultural heritage is still ongoing and evolving. When I presented Oseledec recordings there in the 1980s, they were not impressed at all. Today, Ukrainian teenagers cover their songs! I know that for many contemporary teenagers, the music of The Ukrainians remains important – they listen to it and discover it. And I'm sure this won't be the last generation that does.

REBECCA WALKLEY

Like most people I found it unbelievable what was happening in Ukraine. I had visited Lviv, twice, with Len in 1993 and again in 2017. In 1993 the country had only just gained its independence from the Soviet Union and the place looked drained after years of Soviet rule. Returning in 2017, Lviv had grown into a bright vibrant modern day European city. There was a throng of bars, restaurants and clubs filled with youngsters embracing western values. Putin invaded in 2022 on the cusp of the country joining the EU. The invasion aimed to pull the country back into line, to close the gate on the West, which was a crazy notion as the horse had already bolted.

The Ukrainians' path has strangely mirrored Ukraine's history for the last 30 years. The band started to form in the late '80s, releasing its first recordings in 1991. Protests in Ukraine gained ground in the late 1980s leading to the country proclaiming its independence in 1991. By 1996 the band broke away from its contract with Cooking vinyl, going it alone. In 1994 Ukraine signed the Budapest Memorandum, separating it from the Soviet Union and giving it full sovereignty. In 2019, the band's most recent album was recorded and it was uncertain whether the band would continue. Not long after in 2022 Ukraine was invaded by Russia.

In the early heady days, The Ukrainians inspired many young people in eastern Europe to form bands that played music based on their own culture rather than copying American bands. Since then, some of the band's songs have become adopted and thought of as traditional in Ukraine.

The Ukrainians' albums have been licensed to record companies in Britain, France, Germany, Poland, Ukraine, Greece, Japan, Australia and the USA and Canada, selling well over 250,000 copies worldwide. The band receives orders for Ukrainians albums from all corners of the Earth: from Jerusalem to Japan, Amsterdam to Alaska. They even had a fan based in a research station at the South Pole! The Ukrainians have played to hundreds

Собаче Життя

Ігор – фашист-міліціонер
Віра – католицький місіонер
Тато - екс-солдат СРСР
А я соціал-революціонер!

Це наша сім›я!
Це життя-буття!

Над нами старшує старшина
Не гризе його хробак сумління!
Він автократ, він «діяч культури»
Він психопат і не йде між люди

Це наше життя!
Це життя-буття!
Це наше життя!
Ну, так ще не біда!

То є слова слова, що що бабця моя казала:
«Наше життя! Це собаче життя!»
«О, Боже мій! Голову мені розриває!»
«О, Боже мій! Ціна життя падає!»

Скажіть чому старі сумують?
Предківські кістки на смітник викидають

То є слова слова, що що бабця моя казала:
«Наше життя! Це собаче життя!»

Ра-ра-ра-раоо!

Це наше життя!
Це життя-буття!
Це наше життя!
Ну, так ще не біда!

Sobache Zhyttya

Ihor is a fascist military man
Vera is a catholic missionary
Father is an ex-Soviet soldier
And I'm a social revolutionary!

This is our family!
This is our life, our existence!

An old man, an official rules over us
He is not eaten away by the worm of conscience!
He is an autocrat, a 'purveyor of culture'
He's a psychopath and he doesn't go amongst the people

This is our life
This is existence
This is our life
But it could be worse

These are the words my old grandma used to say:
"This existence – it's a dog's life!"
"Oh, my God, there's a shooting pain in my head!"
"Oh, my God, the value of life is falling!"

Will you tell me why are the old people are sad?
Because the bones of our ancestors are being thrown into the rubbish

These are the words my old grandma used to say:
"This existence – it's a dog's life!"

Ra-ra-ra-raoo!

This is our life
This is existence
This is our life
But it could be worse

Сувеніри

Чи у вас є самогон?
Чи у вас є горілка?
Чи у вас – горілка з перцем?
Бо у нас нема

Чи у вас є голубці?
Чи у вас – копчене сало?
Чи у вас – домашня ковбаса?
Бо у нас нема

Чи у вас є вишивка?
Чи у вас є писанка?
Чи у вас є Українські сувеніри?
Бо у нас нема

Чи у вас є самогон?
Чи у вас є горілка?
Чи у вас – Кримське вино?
Бо у нас нема

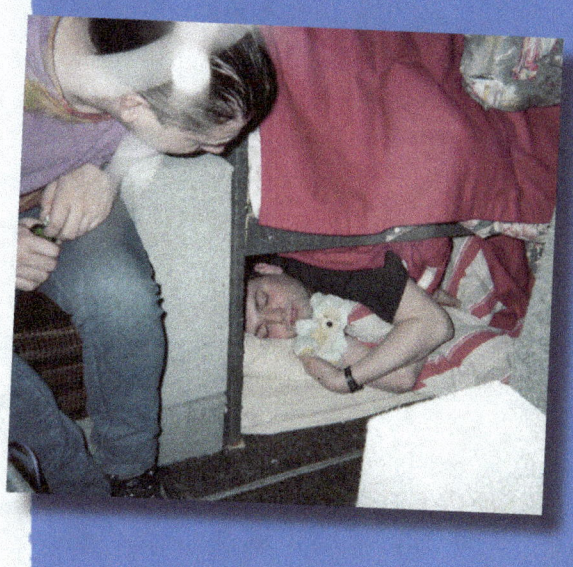

Souvenirs

Do you have home-made spirits?
Do you have horilka*?
Do you have horilka with pepper?
Because we don't have any

Do you have stuffed cabbage leaves?
Do you have smoked pork fat?
Do you have home-made sausage?
Because we don't have any

Do you have a piece of embroidery?
Do you have a painted Easter Egg?
Do you have Ukrainian souvenirs?
Because we don't have any

Do you have home-made spirits?
Do you have horilka?
Do you have Crimean wine?
Because we don't have any

*Horilka is Ukrainian alcoholic spirit usually distilled from wheat or rye

of thousands of people across the world. Their songs are uplifting, moving and joyous. I know for Len that this is his passion as a musician. He loves to entertain people, make them happy, make them dance.

Whatever happens in Ukraine, I believe its culture will always prevail, and helped to survive in a small part by The Ukrainians. Their music has spread an awareness of Ukraine and a knowledge of Ukrainian songs, language and culture around the world during the past 30 years. And Ukrainians won't let their culture or their country die. If the Russians reach for their guns wherever they find Ukrainian culture, they will be fighting a very long war.

JAKE THRUSH

I had started a job in Oxford in early 1992 and was feeling pretty lonely and low, moving to a new town where I didn't really know anyone. I read that this amazing band, The Ukrainians, had released a new album. I hurried into town and rushed back with my new LP. I played it and was just bowled over...

Ever since then I have loved the music of The Ukrainians. Seeing the band live over the years and getting each new CD has been magic, just magic. There is an overwhelming sense of joy to many of the songs and a sort of mad, Slavic craziness – it is incredibly uplifting and brings a huge smile to my face. As well as this, there seems to be an all-pervading feeling, an overarching message, that no matter how bad it gets, keep going. This seems to be a trait of the Ukrainian people, all so tragically being put to the test at the moment in the war with Russia.

ALEX JAKOB-WHITWORTH

I started going out with Roman Reykniv around the time that The Ukrainians formed. He had taught himself Ukrainian using some pretty huge dusty old books. He spent many hours poring over them. His parents spoke Ukrainian at home and Roman went to Saturday school to be taught Ukrainian as a child.

He was hugely committed to the Ukrainian project - it meant the world to him. From his point of view, the sound had to have integrity to the Ukrainian language, culture and the people, aligned with a contemporary twist.

He was passionate about the music and the language, and would spend hours and hours writing and practising songs, instrumental parts of songs; especially on the mandolin. He was quite a brilliant and unique player on that instrument.

When writing his parts for the mandolin, they were formed in his head and through the process of playing. There was no annotated music.

He was however deeply troubled by family and personal problems, not least his own mental health - which led to a couple of hospital admissions.

He once stayed behind in Ukraine after a tour visit by the band on his own, to learn more about the music and 'his' culture, but I believe he experienced the equivalent of such a culture shock that he had a breakdown. The fall out from that had a huge and damaging impact on many parts of his life - not least his relationship with the band.

His health problems led to issues with tours and his involvement with the band - including leading him to no longer being part of it during his most unwell time.

Even though his time with the band was relatively short, Roman was a seriously talented musician and an incredibly strong performer - he was electric (a 'Tigger') on stage, immersing himself completely and utterly in the music - how he jumped and pinged around the stage whilst his hands were moving so fast on the mandolin that they were actually blur, I'll never know.

I believe Roman brought the authenticity, energy and magic to The Ukrainians.

CHRIS POINTON

I'd been a fan of The Wedding Present since I heard their cover of Orange Juice's 'Felicity' on the John Peel show in 1986. I was in a sixth-form post-punk band who did a similarly energetic rendition of the same song. It was exciting to hear our sort of sound on the radio. I went to a few Weddoes gigs over the next few years, and when I heard they were touring a new album of Ukrainian music, I thought I'd go along to the London gig at the Town and Country Club with some friends and see what's up.

As we waited for the support act, the crowd around us was much more – well – Ukrainian than I expected. Apparently quite a lot of Weddoes fans had stayed at home. Which was a mistake as the support act was The Wedding Present themselves, cranking out a cracking short set. I'm not sure what the surrounding Ukrainian audience made of the Weddoes set, but when The Ukrainians came on stage they erupted. The excitement was infectious and we were soon barrelling around the floor along with the rest of the crowd, sweating and panting between each number. It was an utterly joyful evening – one of those occasions where everyone's on the same wavelength and completely enveloped by the music. I went home wearing the t-shirt and clutching a copy of the CD.

I wore the t-shirt until it disintegrated. My girlfriend Linda and I saw The Ukrainians in the summer of 1992 at Glastonbury. By this time, they'd got quite famous and we didn't manage to get near the front. We just danced like lunatics out in the field outside the marquee.

Linda and I got married in 1993, and long after the demise of the t-shirt, I still played the Peel Session album regularly. When our boys were little, we'd have silly dances in the living room to it, tiptoeing to the quiet bit of 'Yikhav Kozak Za Dunai' and then chasing each other round in circles to the chorus, hooting with laughter. I bought a mandolin and often twanged along to 'Hude Dnipro', trying to keep up as the pace got more and more frantic. The Peel Sessions were such a constant accompaniment to our lives that we sort of thought everybody knew about them, and that the band was famous. So when we went to see them at the 100 Club in London in 2019 we were quite surprised the venue wasn't packed. It turns out we are members of a quite exclusive club.

My 50th birthday present, that same year, was a replica t-shirt that Linda had made from a scan of the original CD cover. I wore it at my birthday party. Like the first t-shirt, I intend to wear it until it disintegrates. Hopefully it'll see many more sweaty Ukrainians gigs before then!

AFTERWORD

LEN

By the time this book is out, I'll be 67 years old, and Pete isn't that far behind me. We're getting older and less able to tour like we used to. Being in The Ukrainians has been an incredible journey, and massively enlightening. Thirty-seven years after Pete and myself held our first tentative rehearsal in his bedsit, it has been an education all over again remembering what we did during all those years, and researching what we'd forgotten!

Thanks to everyone who has contributed to this book. It has been amazing to track down old contacts and rekindle old friendships, and to capture so many memories while most of us are still enjoying the oxygen of life on this planet. Unfortunately, we were too late to capture the thoughts of Roman and Mick though. Bless them both.

Thanks also to everyone who helped us along our way: members of the Ukrainian community, managers, booking agents, promotors, record labels, journalists – you know who you are – and of course all our faithful fans who have stayed by us for decades and often travelled crazy distances to see us.

One thing I hope you take away with you after reading this book is the idea that different cultures really do enrich our human experience and need to be preserved and defended. Everyone should have the right to enjoy their own – and other people's – cultures, and to thereby pass on their collective knowledge, history and wisdom to those who come after them.

And those cultures deserve to continue to survive even when borders change, or countries disappear, and that culture's very existence is threatened. Domination is what empires do when their leaders become intoxicated with their own power. We've seen it so many times throughout history.

From watching the news and the cynical machinations of politics, the message we get loud and clear is that leaders tend to make it to the top because they're ruthless. Many politicians will walk over others to get to where they want to be. They are too often self-serving and lose a sense of responsibility for the wellbeing and happiness of the people they were elected to serve. And tragically, wars are much more likely to happen when we have leaders who appear to have absolutely no empathy.

It might be a romantic and sentimentalised view, naive even, but in spite of this there are real, caring and inspiring people everywhere – of course there are – from the city of London to the most remote of Ukrainian villages. I hope as a species we never lose track of that thought, no matter what the future brings.

PETER

Writing the end part of a book is much more difficult than putting the book together. Trying to find something that summarises a lifetime of fantastic interesting activities isn't that easy. So I'm not really going to try.

All that needs to be said is that I've been tremendously fortunate to have followed this path in life. Initially, by being born into a Ukrainian culture, and having kept (at least) some of it, to my adulthood; in meeting my old school friend David Gedge, and having success with him in The Wedding Present; in meeting Len and finding someone else with the same musical weirdness as me; in getting our music championed by John Peel; in getting our music promoted by Red Rhino Records, then RCA; and then, of course, in having tens of thousands of people who value what we do.

But the biggest bit of fortune is to be able to make others happy. Every time I get on the stage to see people smiling and dancing, I smile too. Sharing culture, enriching lives – it can all sound a bit theoretical, but when you are at the gigs, those cultures really do mix and those people really do feel enriched.

We've helped to bring Ukrainian culture to the West and Western culture to Ukraine. As the cultures get closer, the ties between people get stronger, and strong ties make people safer. Safety, peace and the sharing of cultures – quite a dream, but it's one I share with Len and I know, with most of this planet too. We'll keep promoting that ideal, playing where we can, collaborating when we can, and creating new music while we can.

ПОДІЛІТЬСЯ КУЛЬТУРОЮ, ЖИВІТЬ У МИРІ!

Yes, I will laugh despite my tears,
I'll sing out songs amidst my misfortunes;
I'll have hope despite all odds,
I will live! Away, you sorrowful thoughts!

Lesya Ukrainka (1871-1913)
Ukrainian playwright & poet

THE UKRAINIANS GIGOGRAPHY
(all UK except where stated)

1989

Concerts by 'the Ukrainian line-up' of The Wedding Present:
April 16, Queen's Hall, Edinburgh; 17, Riverside, Newcastle; 18, Irish Centre, Birmingham; 19, Bierkeller, Bristol; 20, Town & Country Club, London; 28, Leeds Polytechnic; 29, University of East Anglia, Norwich; 30, Civic Hall, Middleton, Manchester

1991

Concerts by The Ukrainians:
September 03, Adelphi, Hull; 04, Underworld, London; October 02, Bangor University; 03, Reading University; 04, Leeds University; 10, Princess Charlotte, Leicester; 11, Wherehouse, Derby; 22, HdjT (Haus der jungen Talente), Berlin, Germany; 25, Mean Fiddler, London; 26, The Venue, New Cross, London; 31, Duchess of York, Leeds; November 08, York University; 09, Adelphi, Hull; December 11, Queen's Hall, Bradford; 12, Hull University; 13, Sheffield University; 15, Fleece & Firkin, Bristol; 16, Kingston Polytechnic, London; 17, Square Club, Cardiff; 18, Riverside, Newcastle; 19, King Tut's Wah Wah Hut, Glasgow; 20, Marquee, London; 23, Perry's, Darlington; 31, Markthalle, Hamburg, Germany

1992

January 02, Ecstacy, Berlin, Germany; 03, Kulturfabrik, Krefeld, Germany; 04, Forum, Enger, Germany; 05, Lagerhaus, Bremen, Germany; 06, Line Club, Braunschweig, Germany; 07, Spot, Kassel, Germany; 08, Borse, Wuppertal, Germany; 09, Sonneck, Kempten, Germany; 10, Crash, Freiberg, Germany; 11, Alegria, Tarrenz, Austria; 12, Arena, Vienna, Austria; 14, Sheune, Dresden, Germany; 15, Schwimmbad, Heidelberg, Germany; 17, Patronaat, Haarlem, Netherlands; March 20, Sheffield Polytechnic; 21, Riverside, Newcastle; 24, Wherehouse, Derby; 25, Lampeter University; 27, The Roadmender, Northampton; 28, Middlesex Polytechnic, London; 29, Mean Fiddler, London; 30, Wheatsheaf, Stoke. April 30, Festival du Printemps, Bourges, France; May 02, De Media, Eeklo, Belgium; 03, Mean Fiddler, London; 08, Aston University, Birmingham; 21, Thames Polytechnic; 22, Hackney Empire, London; 29, *WOMAD* Festival, Morecambe; 30, *WOMAD* Festival, Morecambe; June 07, Mean Fiddler, London; 16, St. John's College May Ball, Cambridge University; 21, Ludlow Festival; 28, Glastonbury Festival; July 03,

Sheffield University; 09, Modernes, Bremen, Germany; 10, Zeche Carl, Essen, Germany; 12, Blumenwiese, Stuttgart, Germany; 13, Rockfabrik, Übach-Palenberg, Germany; 14, Musiktheater Bad, Hannover, Germany; 15, Line Club, Braunschweig, Germany; 16, Huxleys, Berlin, Germany; 17, Forum, Enger, Germany; 18, KFZ, Marburg, Germany; 19, Kreuzsaal, Fulda, Germany; 21, Negativ, Frankfurt, Germany; 22, Schwimmbad, Heidelberg, Germany; 23, Schreinerei, Schweinfurt, Germany; 24, Circus, Gammelsdorf, Germany; 26, Arena, Vienna, Austria; August 21, Underworld, London; 22, Coverbridge Festival, Yorkshire; September 04, Rogue Folk Club, Vancouver, Canada; 05, Bumbershoot Festival, Seattle, USA; 26, University of Greenwich, London; October 04, Mean Fiddler, London; 14, Arts Centre, Aberystwyth; 15, Buttermarket, Shrewsbury; 17, The Venue, Oxford; 19, Witchwood, Ashton-under-Lyne; November 28, Le Volcan, Le Havre, France; 29, Markthalle, Hamburg, Germany; 30, Knaack Club, Berlin; December 01, Romer, Bremen, Germany

1993

January 31, Mean Fiddler, London; February 10, La Salamande, Strasbourg, France; 11, Theatre Maxim Gorky, Petit-Quevilly, France; 12, Virgin Megastore, Paris, France; 12, Passage du Nord Ouest, Paris, France; March - 03, University of London Union (ULU), London; 04, Wedgewood Rooms, Portsmouth; 05, General Wolfe, Coventry; 11, Perry's, Darlington; 13, The Venue, Oxford; 14, Duchess of York, Leeds; 18, Joiner's Arms, Southampton; 19, Adelphi, Hull; 20, St. Paul's Centre, Bristol; 25, University of Greenwich, London; 26, College of Higher Education, Bath; 27, Arts Centre, Colchester; 28, Powerhaus, London; 29, Boat Race, Cambridge. April 02, The Venue, New Cross, London; 08, WOM, Bremen, Germany; 08, Schlachthof, Bremen, Germany; 10, WOM, Hamburg, Germany; 10, Markthalle, Hamburg, Germany; 11, Scheune, Dresden, Germany; 12, Loft, Berlin, Germany; 13, Easy Schorre, Halle, Germany; 14, Blumenwiese, Stuttgart, Germany; 15, Schwimmbad, Heidelberg, Germany; 16, Circus, Gammelsdorf, Germany; 17, Forum, Enger, Germany; 19, Live Music Hall, Köln, Germany; 20, Zeche Carl, Essen, Germany; 21, WOM, Frankfurt, Germany; 21, Nachtleben, Frankfurt, Germany; 22, Bad, Hannover, Germany; 23, WOM, Nürnberg, Germany; 23, E-Werk, Erlangen, Germany; 24, Café Daneben, Jena, Germany; 25, Hyde Park, Osnabrück, Germany; 28, Melkweg, Amsterdam, Netherlands; 29, Effenaar, Eindhoven, Netherlands; 30, Zanetti, Breda, Netherlands; May 01, Night Town, Rotterdam, Netherlands; 05, Bevrijdings Festival, Leuwarden, Netherlands; 07, La Telecoresca Festival, Barcelona, Spain; 08, La Fundación, León,, Spain; 15, Hayes Island Band Stand, Cardiff; 18, Passage Du Nord Ouest, Paris, France; 19, FNAC, Paris, France; 20, Festival des Nuisances, Lausanne, Switzerland; 21, Bikini Test, La Chaux-de-Fonds, Switzerland; 22, Rock am

See Festival, Konstanz, Germany; 22, Spielboden, Dornbirn, Austria; 23, Utopia, Wourgle (??); 24, Arena, Wien, Austria; 27, Albani, Winterthur, Switzerland; 28, Jugendcentrum, Zug, Switzerland; June 12, Rock sur la Blanche, Brest, France; 13, Festival Mundial, Tilburg, Netherlands; 23, Wool Exchange, Bradford; 25, Glastonbury Festival; 27, YMCA, Gdynia, Poland; July 02, Tanz und Folkfest, Rudolstadt, Germany; 04, Tanz und Folkfest, Rudolstadt, Germany; 11, Leadmill, Sheffield; August 01, City Park, Gloucester; 07, Rock Gegen Rechts Festival, Speller, Germany; 14, Open Air Festival, Jagdburg, Switzerland; 17, BK 'Slavutych', Kyiv, Ukraine; 18, Palace of Culture (DK Svyazy), Kharkhiv, Ukraine; 20, Lesya Ukrainka Cruise Ship, River Dnipro, Ukraine; 21, International Festival 'Tavriys'ki Ihri', Kakhovka, Ukraine; 23, ????, Lviv, Ukraine; 24, Independence Square, Kyiv, Ukraine; September 03, Uferloss Festival, Rorschach, Germany; 04, Potsdamer Abkommen '93, Potsdam, Germany; 10, ARP Plan Rock Festival, Castres, France; 11, Winterthurer Musikfest, Winterthur, Switzerland; 15, La Salamande, Strasbourg, France; 17, Le Bacardi, Callac, France; 18, Run Ar Puns, Châteaulin, France; 23, Festival San Mateo '93, Valladolid, Spain; 30, Les Casemates, Mons, France. October 02, Rock Spectakel Festival '93, Hamburg, Germany; 03, Spot Club, Kassel, Germany; 08, Borderline, London; 09, La Sainte College Students Union, Southampton; 10, General Wolfe, Coventry; 12, Keele University; 13, Joiners Arms, Southampton; 14, Hub Club, Bath; 15, Boat Race, Cambridge; 16, 'Tarasivka' Ukrainian Festival, Weston-on-Trent; 19, Salle Georges Daël, Tourcoing, France; 20, Le Rockstore, Montpellier, France; 22, Foyer du Théâtre, Romans, France; 23, Rock à L'Ouest - MJC, Oullins, France; December 17, Borderline, London

1994

February 01, Corn Exchange, Cambridge; 12, University Union, Bangor; April 15, Lampeter, University; 17, Loft, Berlin, Germany; 18, Markthalle, Hamburg, Germany; 19, Nachtleben, Frankfurt, Germany; 20, Albani, Winterthur, Switzerland; 21, Altes Schützenhaus, Stuttgart, Germany; 22, Forum, Enger, Germany. 23, Kulturfabrik, Krefeld, Germany; June 25, Arts Centre, Norwich; July 02, Festival Rock du Gibloux, Freibourg; 09, Left at the Pier Festival, Brighton; 10, Roundhay Park Heineken Festival, Leeds; 30, Rock am Schloss Festival, Osnabrück, Germany; August 12, Band Stand, Cardiff; 23, Ukrainian Social Club, Holland Park, London; September 19, *In The City* Festival, Manchester; October 01, Ukrainian Club, Bradford; 12, Blue Lamp, Hull; 14, General Wolfe, Coventry; 15, Duchess of York, Leeds; 20, Joiners Arms, Southampton; 21, Mean Fiddler, London; 22, Esquire's Club, Bedford; 23, Boardwalk, Manchester; 25, JB's, Dudley; 27, Old Trout, Windsor; 28, Guild Hall Arts Centre, Gloucester; 29, Boat Race, Cambridge; November 03, Kultuurkaffee, Brussels, Belgium; 04, Dour Festival, Rockamadour, France; 05, Le Centre, Verviers, Belgium; 06, La Gare, Lauwe, Belgium; 15, Grosse Freiheit, Hamburg,

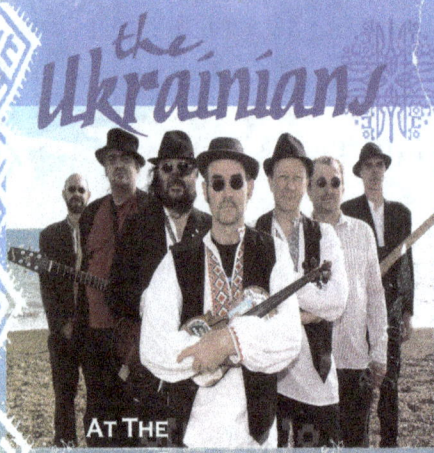

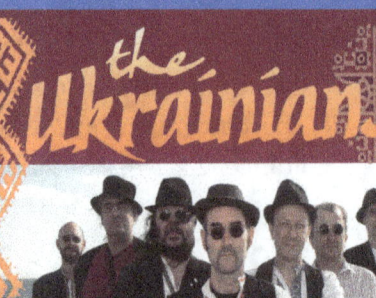

Assorted gig posters

Assorted gig posters & flyer for the *Shchedryk* EP

Germany; 16, Loft Im Metropol, Berlin, Germany; 17, PC69, Bielefeld, Germany; 18, Vier Linden, Hildesheim, Germany; 19, Löwensaal, Nürnberg, Germany; 21, Batschkapp, Frankfurt, Germany; 22, Backstage, München, Germany; 23, La Laiterie, Strasbourg, France; 28, Zeche Carl, Essen, Germany; 29, Luxor, Köln, Germany; 30, Spot Club, Kassel; Germany; December 01, Altes Schützenhaus, Stuttgart, Germany; 02, Szene Wien, Wien, Austria; 03, Avalon, Alte Kino, Allensteig, Austria; 04, Utopia, Innsbruck, Austria; 14, The Junction, Cambridge; 16, Underworld, London

1995

March 11, Arrasate Folk '95 Festival, Mondragón, Spain; 26, Trades Club, Hebden Bridge; 29, Blue Lamp, Hull; 30, Duchess of York, Leeds; 31, Flapper and Firkin, Birmingham; April 01, Mean Fiddler, London; 03, Concorde, Brighton; 04, Joiners Arms, Southampton; 15, Doctor Brown's, Huddersfield; 27, Festival Rock 'n' Solex, Rennes, France; 28, Gibus, Paris, France; 29, La Cave à Musique, Mâcon, France; June 22, SO 36, Berlin, Germany; 23, Mau, Rostock, Germany; July 07, La Voulte-sur-Rhône Festival, France; 08, Le Grand Duc, Apremont, France; 09, Festival du Grand Bourreau, MJC, Joué-lès-Tours, France; 12, La Locomotive, Millau, France; 13, Wave Rider, Frontignan, France; 15, Festival au Châteux de Couzan, Sail Sous Couzan, France ; August 12, Wolvestock Festival, Hickman Park, Wolverhampton; September 17, Festival 'Alternativa', Spartak, Lviv, Ukraine; October 26, Festival Regard Rock, Crest, France; 27, Festival Rock Nevers à Vif, Nevers, France; December 16, Windsor Baths, Bradford; 20, Telford's Warehouse, Chester; 21, Duchess of York, Leeds; 22, Mean Fiddler, London

1996

January 31, Narodniy Dim 'Kosciuks', Przemyśl, Poland; February 01, Kinoteatr Tęcza, Warszawa, Poland; 02, Kino Fama, Białystok, Poland; 03, Ack 'Esculap', Poznań, Poland; 04, Kwadratowa, Gdańsk, Poland; 05, Sala PKP, Wrocław, Poland; 06, Cafe Teatralna, Piła, Poland; April 12, Virgin Megastore, Leeds; 13, Sound City Virgin Megastore Stage, Leeds; 26, Bad, Hannover, Germany; 27, Knust, Hamburg, Germany; 28, Huxley's JR, Berlin, Germany; 29, Stollwerk, Köln, Germany; 30, Odeon, Münster, Germany; May 01 (or 02?), Zeche Carl, Essen, Germany; 03, Jazzhaus, Freiburg, Germany; 04, Backstage, München, Germany; 05, Altes Schützenhaus, Stuttgart, Germany; 06, MTW, Offenbach, Germany; 07, Moments, Bremen, Germany; 08, Hechelei, Bielefeld, Germany; 09, Easy Schorre, Halle, Germany; 10, Kulturladen, Konstanz, Germany; June 21, Festival De St Jean, Loudeac, France; 28, Gratwanderung Festival, Zell am See, Austria; 29, Międzynarodowy Festiwal Muzyki Folk, Pińczów, Poland; July 10 (or 17?), Level 3, Swindon; 27, Calgary

Folk Festival, Calgary, Canada; 28, Folk Festival, Calgary, Canada; 31, Sidetrack Cafe, Edmonton, Canada; August 01, Amigos, Saskatoon, Canada; 02, Lydia's, Saskatoon, Canada; 03, Lydia's, Saskatoon, Canada; 04, Ukrainian Youth Unity Centre, Edmonton, Canada; 07, Bamboo, Toronto, Canada; 09, Ukrainian Caravan Restaurant, Toronto, Canada; 11, Museum of Civilization, Hull (now called Gatineau), Quebec, Canada

1997

June 23, Klub Gwint, Białystok, Poland; 24, Klub Graffiti, Lublin, Poland; 25, Centrum/Palac Kultury Zamek, Poznań, Poland; 27, Festiwal Muzyki Andyjskiej i Folkowej, Ząbkowice Śląskie, Poland; 28, Stadion, Przemyśl, Poland; 29, Proxima, Warszawa, Poland; July 07, Duchess of York, Leeds; August 16 Festiwal 'Tam Gdzie Biją Źródła', Ustroń, Poland

2001

April 15 Trades Club, Hebden Bridge; 16, New Roscoe, Leeds; May 19, Primrose, Leeds; 25, Klub Graffiti, Lublin, Poland; 26, Teatr Animacji, Poznań, Poland; 27, Proxima, Warsaw, Poland; June 09, Festival 2001, North Harrow; August 18, Malborough Festival, Devon

2002

April 28, Bull Arts Centre, Barnet; May 02, Mayfest Festival, Brent Pelham, Herts; June 01, 'Never Mind the Jubilee' Festival, Hebden Bridge; July 06, *Art in the Park* Festival, Blackburn; 19, Norwich Arts Centre, Norwich; October 24, Fiddlers, Bristol; 25, Borderline, London

2003

February 28, Klub Re, Kraków, Poland; March 01, Festiwal Szanty, Wrocław; 02, CDQ, Warsaw; August, 29, Chapel Allerton Festival, Leeds; September 27, 491 Gallery, Leytonstone, London

2004

April 16, Marshall's Bar, Hebden Bridge; 17, 'Karpaty' Ukrainian Social Club, Holland Park, London; May 29, South Street Arts Centre, Reading; July 22, The Boardwalk, Sheffield; 23, Compass Club, Resolution Hotel, Whitby; 24, The Studio, Hartlepool; 25, New Roscoe, Leeds; 29, Grimaldi Forum, Monte Carlo, Monaco; October 09, Borderline, London; 10, Trades Club, Hebden Bridge; 12, Klub Ucho, Gdynia, Poland; 13, Blue Note,

Poznań, Poland; 14, Centrum Kultury, Lubin. Poland; 15, Ływend, Wrocław, Poland; 16, Gwint, Białystok, Poland; 17, CDQ, Warszawa, Poland

2005

May 21, Ashton Ukrainian Centre, Ashton-under-Lyne; 27, Marshall's Bar, Hebden Bridge; 28, 'Karpaty' Ukrainian Social Club, Holland Park, London; 29, Festiwal Spotkanie Folkowe, Czeremcha, Poland; August 13, *Endorse It in Dorset* Festival, Oakleigh Farm, Sixpenny Handley; September 03, Harbourfront Festival, Toronto, Canada

2006

July 09, July, Polesden Lacey Festival, Dorking; August 12, *Endorset It in Dorset* Festival, Sixpenny Handley; September 23, Nottingham Ukrainian Club; December 02, Ashton Ukrainian Centre, Ashton-under-Lyne

2007

January 19, *Celtic Connections* Festival, The Classic Grand, Glasgow; May 05, Spalding Flower Parade, Lincolnshire; 19, Town Hall Arts Centre, Selby; July 21, *The World On Your Doorstep* Festival, Hebden Bridge; August - 12, *Endorse It in Dorset* Festival, Sixpenny Handley, Dorset; 14, New Roscoe, Leeds; September 02, *To Freedom* Festival, Centrum Kultury 'Muza', Lublin, Poland

2008

May 31, Dni Kultury Ukrainskiej (Days of Ukrainian Culture Festival), Szczecin, Poland; June 21, Festiwal 'wROCK for Freedom', Pola Marsowe, Wrocław, Poland; July 24, Ternopil Rock Festival, Ternopil, Ukraine; 26, Slavske Rock Festival, Ukraine; October 11, Ecomuseo dell'argilla (The Ecomuseum of the Brick), Cambiano, Italy

2009

February 14, Ukrainian Social Club, Nottingham; 15, New Roscoe, Leeds; 21, Ukrainian Social Club, Ashton-under-Lyne; 22, Trades Club, Hebden Bridge; April 03, The Shire Hall, Howden, Goole; May 19, The Approach, Nottingham; 28, Ływend, Wrocław, Poland; 29, CDQ, Warszawa, Poland; June 27, Cargo, Shoreditch, London; July 18, Festival Músicas do Mundo (FMM), Sines, Portugal; August 16, Folkwoods Festival, Eindhoven,

Netherlands; October 23, Musicport Festival, Bridlington Spa Theatre; Bridlington; 24, Sumo Club, Leicester; 25, 100 Club, Soho, London

2010

May 27, 100 Club, Soho, London; 28, *Off The Tracks* Festival, Castle Donington; 29, Knockengorroch Festival, Kirkcudbrightshire; August 07, Tarptantinis Muzikos Festivalis LABADABA, Latvia; 28, At the Edge of the Sea Festival, Concorde 2, Brighton; 29, Fruit, Hull

2011

April 29, Ukrainian Centre, Gloucester; 30, Ukrainian Centre, Leicester; May 01, Ukrainian Social Club, Leeds; 07, 'Karpaty' Ukrainian Social Club, Holland Park, London; June 17, South Street Arts Centre, Reading; 18, Half Moon, Putney, London; October 28, Ukrainian Social Club, Edinburgh; 29, Ukrainian Social Club, Bradford; November 11, Bull & Gate, Kentish Town, London; 12, Man on the Moon, Cambridge

2012

September 29, Festiwal *Inny Wymiar* (Other Dimension Festival), Fama, Białystok, Poland; November 02, Bull & Gate, Kentish Town, London

2013

April 20, Jumbo Records, Leeds (Record Store Day in-store appearance); July 05, Brudenell Social Centre, Leeds; 06, Love Music, Glasgow (in-store gig); 06, Nice N Sleazy, Glasgow; 31, Trades Club, Hebden Bridge; August 04, Canadian National Ukrainian Festival (CNUF), Dauphin, Canada; September 24, Cieszanów Rock Festival, Poland; November 15, CDQ, Warszawa, Poland; 16, 37th Ukraiński Jarmark Młodzieżowy, Gdańsk, Poland

2014

April 19, Jumbo Records, Leeds; 20, 'Dnipro' Ukrainian Centre, Manchester; July 19, Visegrad Wave Festival, Czeremcha, Poland; October 17, Doncaster Ukrainian Club; 18, 'Karpaty' Ukrainian Social Club, London; November 05, 'Eastern Partnership Days', Le Bouche-à-Oreille, Rue Félix Hap, France; 11, 1040 Brussels, Belgium

2015

May 21, New Adelphi, Hull; 22, Hoxton Square Bar and Kitchen, Shoreditch, London; 24, County Fair Festival, Bransgore, Dorset; 25, Junction 2, Cambridge; 26, Fibbers, York; 27, Ruby Lounge, Manchester; 28, Trades Club, Hebden Bridge; 29, Rainbow, Birmingham; 30, South Street Arts Centre, Reading; June 26, Cluny, Newcastle; 27, Brudenell Social Club, Leeds

2016

February 18, Arts Centre, Norwich; 19, Esquire's, Bedford; 20, 'Karpaty' Ukrainian Social Club, Holland Park, London; June 04, Beeston Festival, Leeds; August 06, Green Gathering, Chepstow; October 21, Cluny 2, Newcastle; 22, Kultura Ukrainian Festival, 'Dnipro' Ukrainian Centre, Manchester

2017

May 28, Brudenell Social Club, Leeds; August 18, Northern Green Gathering, Ashbourne

2018

January 12, Esquire's, Bedford; 13, Borderline, London; May 04, *Musicport on the Moors* Festival, Goathland, North Yorkshire; 12, Paradise, Kensal Green, London; June 15, Trades Club, Hebden Bridge; 16, *Muzikantes* Festival, The Wardrobe, Leeds; 29, Roots Music Club, Doncaster; 30, *Proud to BD* Festival, Bradford

2019

February 23, 'Karpaty' Ukrainian Social Club, Holland Park, London; March 15, Chemiefabrik, Dresden, Germany; 16, Absturz, Leipzig, Germany; April 03, Trades Club, Hebden Bridge; 20, Brudenell Social Club, Leeds; May 03, 100 Club, London; 04, John Peel Centre for the Creative Arts, Stowmarket; June 01, Junction (J2), Cambridge; 15, Muzikantes Festival, The Wardrobe, Leeds; July 06, Tannerfest, Kettering; August 09, At the Edge of the Sea Festival, Brighton

2021

September 18, Provenance Kitchen, Cambridge; October 29, Prince Albert, Brighton; 30, 'Karpaty' Ukrainian Social Club, Holland Park, London; November 13, Stogfest, Face Bar, Reading; 19, Trades Club, Hebden Bridge

2022

March 06 (afternoon) Trades Club, Hebden Bridge; 06 (evening) Brudenell Social Club, Leeds; April 09, The Crescent, York; 13, Hare & Hounds, Birmingham; 23, Arts Centre, Salisbury; May 06, Victoria Theatre, Halifax; 07, Junction (J2), Cambridge; July 09 (or 08?), Endorset in Dorset Festival, Cerne Abbas Brewery, Dorset; August 22, Northern Green Gathering, Scholey Park, Coningsby, Lincoln; October 21, Whitby Pavilion, Whitby, North Yorkshire

2023

January 13, Trades Club, Hebden Bridge; 14 (afternoon), Ukrainian Community Centre, Leeds; 14 (evening) The Crescent, York. April 29, St Thomas Aquinas School, Milton Keynes; June 02, MoritzBastei, Leipzig, Germany; 03, Chemiefabrik, Dresden, Germany; July 01, Rock na Bagnie Festival, Bielsk Podlaski, Poland; 22, Endorset in Dorset Festival, Cerne Abbas Brewery, Dorset; October 14, The Pier, Brighton; November 11, Ukrainian Club, Leeds

2024

January 12, Trades Club, Hebden Bridge; 13, Hairy Dog, Derby; April 27, Old Woollen, Leeds; 28 Deaf Institute, Manchester

(clockwise from left) The Ukrainians playing at Oleg & Elena Mucha's wedding; Mike Robinson, who discovered The Ukrainians in HMV, with wife Anthea; Dr Alexander Lewkowicz disapproved of daughter Gabrielle's musical tastes but his face lit up when he heard 'Cherez Richku, Cherez Hai'; John Boocock frightened a chicken with a Ukrainians tape; Harriet Simms did press for Cooking Vinyl; Eugene Czauderna taped that legendary first Ukrainian Peel session featuring The Wedding Present; Seuras Og not wearing one of his enormous collection of Ukrainians t-shirts (he has two); Slavko Mykosowski with Roman Revkniv (left) & Luddy (right) in Ukraine, 1993

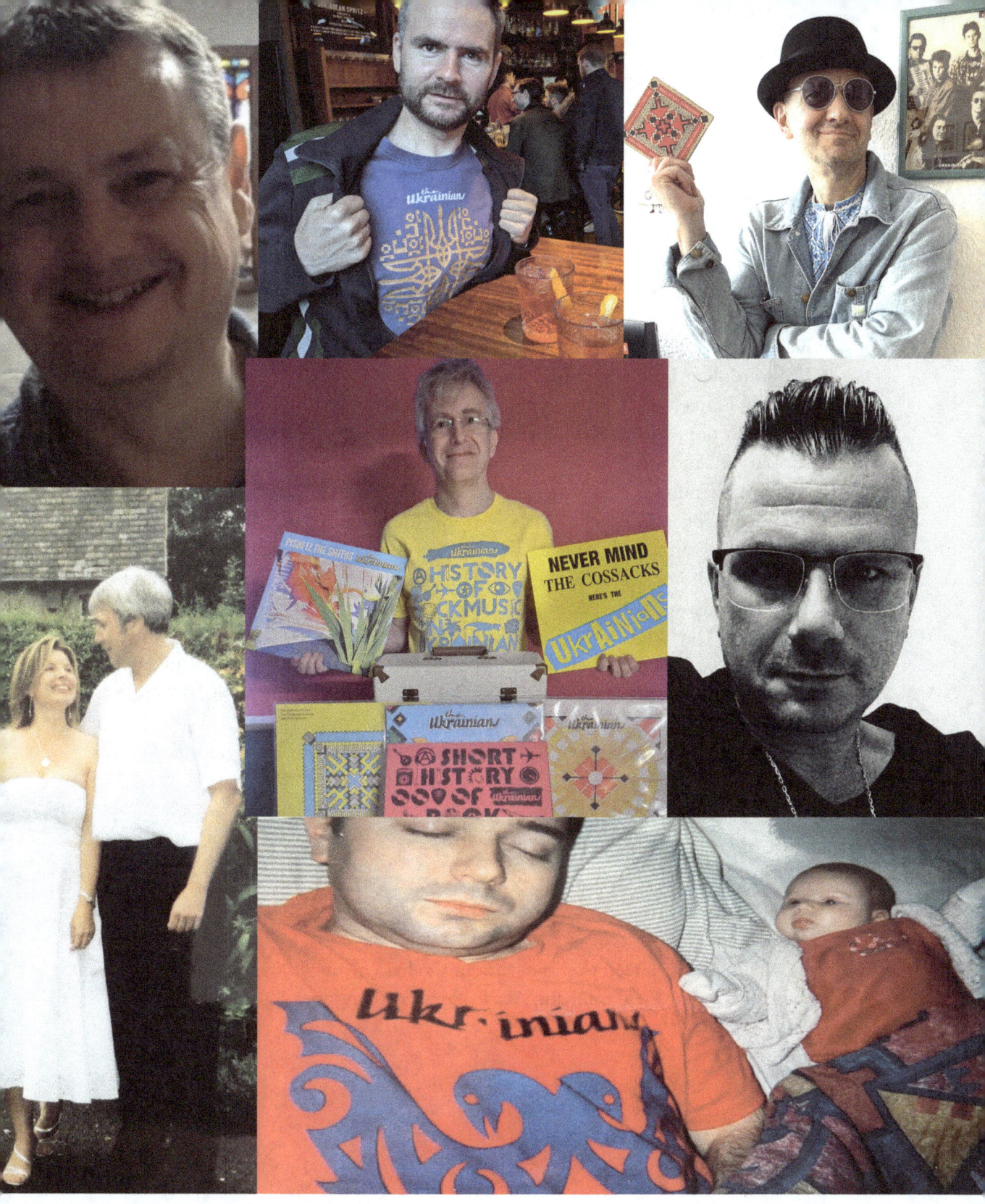

(clockwise from top left) Jake Thrush's mood was lifted by listening to The Ukrainians; listening to their music has given Jarek Kozak a greater interest in Ukrainian culture; Oleksandr Prokopchuk has gone from Kyiv to Dresden; after moving to Israel from Ukraine, Vlad Jonathan Lee was a good customer of Cooking Vinyl's overseas mailings; Helen McIntyre's husband wearing one of her Ukrainian t-shirts and pretending to be asleep, in 1998 with their first child; Marek & Kathryn Wroblewski got married in 2006 & had 'Vorony' playing during the service; Tim Bourne is a bit of a Ukies fan

SPECIAL THANKS

Special thanks to the following for ordering this book in advance and choosing to be named as a sponsor:

Ian Corless; Christian Pletz; Lew Wolczko; John Danaher; Danny Barbour; Lapis; Richard Poppleton; Matthes Kersting; Stylophonix; Matthew Rayner; Alan Thomas; David Jordan; Karey Parsons; Helen McIntyre; Dr Claire Mitchell; Ian Rowley; Mike Forbester; Darren Hayward; Jens Lameyer; Stuart Hancocks; Mark Armitage; Brian Wilson; Yuriy Kis (Для Агати Ванкевич); Bill Bailey; Oleg Mucha; Elena Izmaylova Mucha; Simon Scholes; Anna Mironiuk; John Flexman; Maurice Bann; Nigel McAllen; Invisible Tom; Michael Robinson; Andrew Mason; Guy Clifton; John Boocock; Tim Bourne; Matthew Rhodie; Rebecca Urquhart; Graeme Kirkwood; Adrian Spink; Hava & Vlad Jonathan Lee; Daniel Bagan-Jones; Gabrielle Lewkowicz (for my father, Dr AK Lewkowicz); Jake Thrush; Britton-Duigan family; Rebecca Walkley; Peter & Julie Mastenko; Lamma Maund; Danylo Centore; Dan Whaley; John Knowles, Fetch Theatre; Sabine Knipp; Paul Oakley; Dean Fawcett; Benjamin Goldhagen; David Garston; Howard Dickins; Iam Burn; John Uttley; David Hirons; Peter Fuller; the entire extended Czauderna family; Lisa Martin; Tony Ereira; Lonny Chu; Kjell Gunnar Barstad; Kenneth Odland; Tony Higgins; Joe Fedynyshyn; Ann Birrell; Tony Pidkalenko; John Fedynsky; Alan Dawson; Adam Miljenovic; Brian Wheatcroft; Vitaliy Ishchuk; Stefan Lesnianski; Chris Gleed-Owen, Mike Hobby & Simon Hemingway; Alexander Fitch; Roger Tooth & Raymonde Watkins; Roman Suchyj & Helen Jubb; Steve Thomas; Vance Whelpy.

ACKNOWLEDGEMENTS

This book would not have been possible without the help of the following: Ian Gittins; Karl Kathuria; David Gedge; Kate Sullivan, Alaric Neville, Allan Jones.

www.ingramcontent.com/pod-product-compliance
Lightning Source LLC
Chambersburg PA
CBHW081707100526
44590CB00022B/3686